Andrea Vicari
European Company Law
De Gruyter Studium

I0033318

Andrea Vicari

European Company Law

—

DE GRUYTER

Andrea Vicari
Full Professor of Company Law at the University of Milan Law School

ISBN 978-3-11-072246-8
e-ISBN (PDF) 978-3-11-072502-5
e-ISBN (EPUB) 978-3-11-072513-1

Library of Congress Control Number: 2021930367

Bibliographic information published by the Deutsche Nationalbibliothek
The Deutsche Nationalbibliothek lists this publication in the Deutsche Nationalbibliografie;
detailed bibliographic data are available on the Internet at http://dnb.dnb.de.

© 2021 Walter de Gruyter GmbH, Berlin/Boston
Printing and binding: CPI books GmbH, Leck

www.degruyter.com

Preface

This is a book written primarily for law students taking basic courses in company law or in European company law.

European company law lives as a part of a multi-level legal system; it is positive – and not comparative – law. It comes into force whenever EU directives and regulations address current domestic company laws. It will exist as long as directives and regulations cover new company law rules.

Should the harmonization process be weakened due to increased competition between different national laws, European company law would remain steady in order to fulfil (even the only) principles of free movement of persons and capital.

As the jurisprudence of the Court of Justice of the European Union has once again recently shown, the mere presence of these principles prohibits certain domestic laws from adopting rules that may result in the deterrence of companies and investors from making cross-border transactions and thus hampering these freedoms, which have to be considered irreversible as long as EU treaties are in force.

Beside harmonization, it is therefore probable that we will see further revolutionary changes in EU company law in the near future due to the Court of Justice case law.

Regarding the approach, this book considers that the issue regarding the desirability of more or less harmonization in company law is often considered in the absence of a real understanding of the individual domestic company laws; one should probably first get acquainted with the national laws and then take a position on one side or the other at a more generic level. Therefore, while this work does not purport to be a compilation of Member States' company laws, at least it strongly supports the idea of increasing the circulation of knowledge about these national company acts. Many books and articles (especially in the reviews on European company law) have already taken this route and are currently of great support. Outstanding scholars are engaged with this task (as also demonstrated by the major "European Model Company Act" project).

As far as the themes are concerned, this book aims to highlight the core concepts of the directives and (possibly) the main similarities and differences among Member States' laws in approaching the great themes of company law (the financial structure of the company, the role of directors, shareholders, supervisors in the corporate governance, the groups, the right to exit, the way in which extraordinary transactions are carried out, etc.). The explanation of the similarities

https://doi.org/10.1515/9783110725025-001

and differences between the domestic models may help in the overall comprehension of the main legislative trends, with a view from above.

This description may also be useful, without prejudice to the characteristics of the book, for lawyers and judges interested in these developments. Of course, legal advice and court decisions require precise knowledge of the details of the national local laws, but the bigger picture is important too.

Finally, given the chosen setting, not all topics could be dealt with. Some of them were considered to be less important or were omitted as a matter of judgment or taste. In any case, I hope that the book will reward the reader.

Milan, October 2020

Contents

Special notice —— XIII

1   What is European Union company law? —— 1
   1.   The concept of "public" and "private" companies in Europe —— 1
   2.   "EU company law" in the broader context of EU
        lawmaking bodies —— 4
   3.   EU legislative acts and the jurisprudence of the Court of Justice
        of the EU —— 6
   4.   The competence of the Union in the area of company law: the EU
        may only "harmonize", through directives and regulations, national
        company laws and does not have exclusive power —— 8
   5.   The main directives adopted in the area of company law (and the
        ones that remained at the draft stage) —— 13
   6.   The theoretical debate on EU "harmonization" versus "regulatory
        competition" among national State legislations —— 17
   7.   The "rush to incorporate" in different States and the jurisprudence of
        the CJEU: the Daily Mail, Centros, Überseering, Inspire Art (and
        Cartesio, Sevic, Vale, Polbud) cases —— 21
   8.   Towards "soft" harmonization? Recommendations, "Action Plans"
        and the "European Model Company Act" —— 27
   9.   The foreseeable expansion of the jurisprudence of the CJEU: the
        "horizontal direct effect" of the principles of free establishment and
        free movement of capital (*Volkswagen* and *Vivendi*
        as flagship cases) —— 31
   10. "Transnational" corporate types (with different fates): the "Societas
        Europea", the "Societas Privata Europea" and the "Societas
        Unius Personae" —— 35

2   Formation and share capital —— 37
   1.   The reasons for relatively uniform national laws. The main
        fundamental arguments not addressed by the directives (and the
        question of contractual freedom: "mandatory" and
        "default" rules) —— 37
   2.   Formation of the company: instrument of incorporation
        and statutes —— 42
   3.   Nullity of the company —— 44
   4.   Single-member company —— 46

5. Share capital. From "minimum" to "adequate" capital? —— **47**
6. The assessment of capital in kind: the evaluation by experts —— **51**
7. Rules on capital protection. (a) Distributions —— **53**
8. (b) Share buy-backs —— **56**
9. (c) Financial assistance —— **57**
10. (d) Cross-shareholdings —— **60**
11. (e) Relevant losses and compulsory recapitalization (or liquidation) —— **62**
12. The reduction of capital in excess —— **66**

3 Management of the company and controls —— 69
1. The different governance systems and the failed proposal of the Fifth Directive —— **69**
2. The "menu" legislative approach adopted in most Member States —— **71**
3. Main features of the different governance systems: monistic (one-tier), traditional and dualistic (two-tier) —— **76**
4. A controversial issue: the balance of powers between shareholders and directors —— **84**
5. "Internal" controls on management: audit committees, statutory auditors, supervisory boards —— **92**
6. "External" controls on management: audit firms and special examiners —— **96**
7. Management board and supervisory board meetings and resolutions —— **98**
8. Shareholders' agreements —— **100**

4 Shares —— 105
1. Characteristics of the shares (bearer, name, paper, dematerialized, par and no-par) —— **105**
2. Basic and secondary rights of shares —— **109**
3. Classes of shares: special financial, voting and administrative rights —— **111**
4. "Golden shares" and the jurisprudence of the CJEU (cases *Elf-Aquitaine, BBA, Volkswagen* and others) —— **120**
5. Transferability of the shares (clauses of consent, first refusal, tag along, drag along, change of control). The jurisprudence of the CJEU on national laws preventing investors to pursue cross-border transactions (cases *Tipou, Vivendi* and others) —— **126**

5   Financing —— 133
    1.   Capital increases —— 133
    2.   Equity linked instruments (convertible bonds,
         warrants, options) —— 136
    3.   Hybrid instruments —— 138
    4.   Bonds —— 141
    5.   Shareholders' loans (and reserve contributions) —— 143

6   Protection of minorities (right to vote and right to exit) —— 147
    1.   Shareholders' voice and exit (and directors' liability). Different
         approaches of national laws —— 147
    2.   Right to vote in general meetings and to challenge
         shareholders' resolutions —— 149
    3.   Right to information —— 155
    4.   Right to withdrawal —— 158
    5.   Right to sell out (and to winding up) —— 161
    6.   Shareholders' litigation and jurisdiction: the jurisprudence of the
         CJEU (case *E-ON Czech Holding*) —— 163

7   Groups —— 165
    1.   A brief history of company groups in Europe and
         their regulation —— 165
    2.   The legal definition of group: "control" and
         "unitary direction" —— 169
    3.   Main issues addressed by Member States' laws: (a.1) unitary
         direction, binding instructions, group interest and parent company's
         liability: the German model (followed by other Member States) of
         "contractual groups" and "de facto groups" —— 171
    4.   (a.2) Unitary direction, binding instructions, group interest and
         parent company's liability in other Member States. The position of
         the EMCA —— 175
    5.   (b) The disclosure of the existence of the group and the results of
         the unitary direction —— 182
    6.   (c) Rights of the minority shareholders of subsidiaries (to special
         investigation, to withdrawal) —— 184
    7.   (d) Rights of the minority shareholders of the parent company (to
         information, to withdrawal, to vote) —— 187
    8.   (e) Cross-shareholdings, intercompany loans and
         group financing —— 188

9. Cross-border groups and applicable law: the CJEU judgment on the *Impacto Azul* case —— **191**

8 Accounting and financial statements —— **195**
1. An overview on EU companies' financial reporting —— **195**
2. Layouts and principles of financial statements —— **198**
3. Consolidated financial statements —— **205**
4. Audit of the financial statements —— **205**
5. Approval and publication of the financial statements —— **207**
6. Financial statements in listed and other companies using the "International Accounting Standards" and "International Financial Reporting Standards" ("IAS/IFRS") —— **208**
7. Profit and dividends (and the "right to dividend" acknowledged by some legislations) —— **210**

9 Duties and liabilities of directors and supervisors —— **213**
1. Directors' duties —— **213**
2. Supervisory board members' and statutory auditors' duties —— **223**
3. Auditors' duties —— **225**
4. Liabilities and proceedings —— **227**
5. Liability rules between "company" and "insolvency" law: the CJEU judgment on the *Kornhaas* case —— **230**
6. Shareholders' liability —— **232**

10 Extraordinary transactions —— **235**
1. Basic principles on extraordinary transactions —— **235**
2. Mergers —— **237**
3. Divisions, spin-offs and carve-outs —— **248**
4. Leveraged buyouts —— **253**
5. Sales of company's assets —— **258**
6. Shares purchases —— **260**
7. Squeeze-outs and freeze-outs —— **260**
8. Conversions —— **263**
9. Cross-border transactions —— **266**

11 Dissolution and liquidation —— **271**
1. Causes for dissolution and directors' duties —— **271**
2. Liquidators' powers and duties —— **274**
3. The liquidation proceedings and the cancellation of the company —— **275**

12 Listed companies —— 277
1. The "three legs" of the EU listed companies' legislation —— **277**
2. Enhanced rights of shareholders in listed companies —— **279**
3. Rules on takeovers —— **281**
4. Rules on audit committees —— **288**

13 Private companies —— 291
1. Harmonization of the national laws on private companies? A "disproportionate" effort, according to the EU. Despite this, the attempt by the EMCA —— **291**
2. The "private company" in the Member States and the EMCA: (a) formation and legal capital —— **293**
3. (b) Management and control —— **297**
4. (c) Shares —— **300**
5. (d) Financing —— **302**
6. (e) Protection of minorities —— **304**
7. (f) Directors and shareholders' liabilities —— **306**

14 Societas Europea and other forms —— 309
1. The regulation on the "European Company" ("Societas Europea", "SE") —— **309**
2. The establishment of the SE —— **311**
3. The corporate governance of the SE —— **313**
4. Accounts and dissolution of the SE —— **314**
5. The (aborted) projects on the "Societas Privata Europea" ("SPE") and the "Societas Unius Personae" ("SUP") —— **315**
6. Branches of foreign companies —— **318**

Table of cases —— 321

Index —— 324

Special notice

Since the directives and regulations are aimed at basically governing the "public" company model, this book mainly deals with public companies (both with shares listed on the market and not). However, some sections address "private" companies (see Chapter 13) or both public and private companies (see i.e. Chapter 8 on accounts, Chapter 10 on extraordinary transactions and Chapter 14 on supranational models).

The directives and regulations can easily be found at the EU website (https://eur-lex.europa.eu).

The company laws of the Member States are laid down in either civil or commercial codes or specific company acts; the laws on listed companies are often set forth in separate acts. Other bodies of law contain further specific rules or govern sector-specific aspects.

Since reference is repeatedly made in the book to the laws of the Member States, the main acts (as also later amended) and their abbreviations are listed below.

The first letter refers to the Member State. The law refers to both public and private companies unless stated otherwise.

– Austria	A-PuCA	law on public companies, act no. 98 of 31 March 1965
	A-PrCA	law on private companies, act no. 58 of 6 March 1906
– Belgium	B-CA	code of companies and associations, act of 28 February 2019
– Bulgaria	Bu-CA	commercial law, act of 18 June 1991
– Cyprus	Ci-CA	chapter 113 of companies law, act of 16 February 1951
– Croatia	Cr-CA	companies act, act of 23 November 1993
– Czech Republic	Cz-CA	business corporation act, act no. 90, of 25 January 2012
– Denmark	Da-CA	companies act, act no. 470 of 12 June 2009
– Estonia	E-CA	commercial code, act of 15 February 1995
– Finland	Fi-CA	limited liability companies act, act no. 624 of 21 July 2006
– France	Fr-CC	commercial code, act of 13 September 1807
– Germany	Ge-PuCA	law on public companies, act of 6 September 1965
	Ge-PrCA	law on private companies, act of 20 April 1892
	Ge-InsA	law on insolvency, act of 5 October 1994
	Ge-TA	transformation act, act of 28 October 1994
– Greece	Gr-PuCA	law on public companies, act no. 4548 of 4 July 2018
	Gr-PrCA	law on private companies, act no. 3190 of 16 April 1955
– Hungary	H-CC	civil code, act no. 5 of 26 February 2013
– Ireland	Ir-CA	companies act, act no. 38 of 23 December 2014
– Italy	It-CC	civil code, royal decree n. 262 of 16 March 1942
– Latvia	La-CA	commercial law, act of 13 April 2000

https://doi.org/10.1515/9783110725025-002

– Lithuania	Li-CA	law on companies, act no. VIII-1835 of 13 July 2000
– Luxembourg	Lu-CA	law relating commercial companies, act of 10 August 1915
– Malta	M-CA	chapter 386 of companies act, act of 1 January 1996
– Poland	Pol-CC	commercial companies code, act of 15 September 2000
– Portugal	Por-CC	code of commercial companies, law decree no. 262, of 2 September 1986
– Romania	R-CA	law on trading companies, act no. 31 of 16 November 1990
– Slovenia	Slove-CA	companies act, act no. 42 of 19 April 2006
– Slovak Republic	Slova-CC	commercial code, act no. 513 of 5 November 1991
– Spain	Sp-CA	law of limited liability companies, royal legislative decree no. 1 of 2 July 2010
	Sp-LSC	law on structural changes, act no. 3 of 13 April 2009
	Sp-InsA	insolvency act, act no. 1 of 5 May 2020
– Sweden	Sw-CA	companies act, act no. 551 of 16 June 2005
– the Netherlands	Du-CC	civil code, act of 1 October 1838

The European Model Company Act ("*EMCA*") is available at https://papers.ssrn.com/sol3/papers.cfm?abstract_id=2929348

The main reviews on European company law and other laws are quoted as follows:

– Common Market Law Review	CMLR
– European Business Law Review	EBLR
– European Business Organization Law Review	EBOR
– European Company Law Journal	ECL
– European Company and Financial Law Review	ECFR
– European Law Journal	ELJ
– European Law Review	ELR
– German Law Journal	GLJ

The essays contained in the book Vicari/Schall (eds.), *Company laws of the European Union*, Beck, 2020 – to which reference is largely made to – are quoted as follows: [name of the Author], in *Company laws*, [page].

Any comments and suggestions are welcome (andrea.vicari@unimi.it).

1 What is European Union company law?

Summary:
1. The concept of "public" and "private" companies in Europe
2. "EU company law" in the broader context of EU legislative bodies and law-making
3. EU legislative acts and the jurisprudence of the Court of Justice of the EU
4. The competence of the Union in the area of company law: the EU may only "harmonize", through directives and regulations, national company laws and does not have exclusive power
5. The main directives adopted in the area of company law (and the ones that remained at draft stage)
6. The theoretical debate on EU "harmonization" versus "regulatory competition" among national State legislations
7. The "rush to incorporate" in different States and the jurisprudence of the CJEU: the *Daily Mail*, *Centros*, *Überseering*, *Inspire Art* (and *Cartesio*, *Sevic*, *Vale*, *Polbud*) cases
8. Towards "soft" harmonization? Recommendations, "Action Plans" and the "European Model Company Act"
9. The foreseeable expansion of the jurisprudence of the CJEU: the "horizontal direct effect" of the principles of free establishment and free movement of capital (*Volkswagen* and *Vivendi* as flagship cases)
10. Transnational corporate types (with different fates): the "Societas Europea", the "Societas Privata Europea" and the "Societas Unius Personae"

1. The concept of "public" and "private" companies in Europe

The first issue that has to be addressed in order to answer the question "What is European Union company law?" is what a "company" actually is in Europe.

For the purpose of this book we are not interested in companies without limited liability (i. e. partnerships); we shall only consider companies with limited liability, i. e. companies which allow their shareholders, at least as a general rule, to remain insulated from the obligations arising from the activity of the company.

The question also remains open with this limitation.

Even though there are only two main categories of limited liability companies in most European countries – the "public" limited liability company and the "private" limited liability company – there are some other partially different

https://doi.org/10.1515/9783110725025-003

types besides these that are only in some Member States and remain specific to them (for instance the "GmbH & Co. KG" in Germany or the "SAS" in France[1]).

For the sake of simplicity, this book will thus focus only on companies which have similar basic features in all Member States: "public" and "private" limited liability companies.

Public companies are basically meant to have access to the capital markets in order to raise funding, both in terms of equity capital from shareholders and loan capital from bondholders (and, more generally, lenders). They therefore aim to reach a larger audience of equity or debt providers.

The second element of distinction has to do with the legal structure of the company, which is more flexible for private entities and is basically rigid for public ones. Shareholders enjoy more contractual freedom and can bargain around corporate charters to a far greater extent in private companies.

A public company is here deemed "public" due to its choice of company form and should not be confused with companies that have securities admitted to trading on a regulated market. The latter are referred to in this book as "listed" companies.

The difference between public and private companies cannot be found in the size of the company. The two legal models are indeed often employed by the various Member States for enterprises of very dissimilar sizes (in the EU, there are around 15 million companies with both public and private limited liability; 2 million have at least 10 employees).

The public company is used for bigger enterprises in some States (Germany, the Netherlands) and also for smaller firms in other States (France, Italy). Otherwise, in some countries a private company may sometimes run giant enterprises

---

[1] The "Gesellschaft mit beschränkter Haftung & Compagnie Kommanditgesellschaft" is a hybrid form where a private company serves as the only fully liable partner, thus providing the limited liability shield to the natural persons involved only. A similar model (under the form of public company) is present in other Member States (moreover, for instance, the company is a limited liability company pursuant to German law, while it is a type of partnership according to Austrian legislation). The "société par actions simplifiée" is a limited liability public company introduced firstly in 1994 (and extended in 1999 to other companies), normally used for small and medium-sized enterprises. No minimum capital is required. The company structure may be freely determined by the articles of association; the company is managed by a chairperson (or a board of directors) and most of the important decisions are taken by the shareholders. For an overview of the various types of business organization which exist in (selected) Member States see Andenas/Wooldridge, *European comparative company law*, Cambridge UP, 2009, 99.

(for instance in Germany), while it represents the model only for the smallest companies in others[2].

Therefore, there is no uniformity in how public companies are employed in the different Member States.

For example, in the Netherlands there are about 1.100 public companies compared to about 370.000 private companies, with a ratio of 1/336; in Germany there are 16.000 public companies compared to 1.200.000 private companies, with a ratio of 1/75; in Poland the ratio is 1/41 (12.000 out of 500.000), while in Italy it falls to 1/5 (200.000 public companies and around 1 million private companies).

Only a small percentage of public companies are listed on the stock markets. For instance, the domestic companies traded on the German Bourse amount to around 500. The listed company in Germany is thus the example for the public company. On the other hand, the Spanish Stock Exchange has around 3.000 listed firms, but Spain has more than 80.000 public companies.

The issue is relevant since most European legislative acts regard only public companies (and not private ones) and therefore the EU legislator sets forth rules that apply to companies that have very heterogeneous characteristics in the various Member States[3]. Should UE legislation be tailored to the model of large enterprises, this could leave many small enterprises uncovered, and vice versa.

---

2 For instance, Robert Bosch GmbH (or Bosch) is a German multinational engineering and technology enterprise structured as a private company, ranked the 6th biggest corporation for turnover in Germany (around 90 billion Euro) and 77th in the list of 500 most important companies worldwide; it has more than 400,000 employees (source Fortune.com; 2019 data).

3 Nordic countries are an exception since in their company laws the categorization is far less rooted ("the distinction between public/private as a matter of company form is basically an alien one introduced upon accession to the EEC/EU": see Hansen, *The Report of the Reflection Group on the future of EU company law – as seen from a Nordic perspective*, 2011, at *ssrn.com*, 8). In Dutch law, private companies were only regulated in 1971 (see De Jong, *The distinction between public and private companies and its relevance for company law: observations from the United Kingdom and the Netherlands*, in *EBLR*, 2016, 1). As noted by Stöber, in Vicari/Schall (eds.), *Company laws of the European Union*, CH Beck, 2020 (quoted as "*Company laws*": see above the "special notice"), 324: "the legal form of the [private company] is an invention of the German legislator, created without any prior historical model. In contrast, the legal form of the [public company], the roots of which go back to the 16th century, already existed in Germany by the end of the 19th century. However, due to the complexity of the legal provisions applicable to it, the [public company] was rather suitable for larger companies than smaller ones. By establishing the GmbH [the German private company], the German legislator wanted to make companies with limited – or, more precisely, excluded – liability of the shareholders available to small and medium-sized enterprises as well. Following Germany's example, numerous other

This situation has to be taken into account when we compare provisions on public companies belonging to different Member States, but also if we think about the future development of company law in the EU[4].

On a different level, we have to consider the introduction in 2001 of the European Public Company model (the "Societas Europea" or "SE"), which is a brand new supranational type of company actually "invented" by EU legislation, flanking domestic corporate forms.

An SE may relocate to any other Member State governed by the same rules and only secondarily by the laws of the State of incorporation (which operate as gap-fillers), thereby overcoming the legal and psychological obstacles that often hinder entrepreneurs from pursuing cross-border transactions.

There are currently around 3.300 SEs, mostly big companies and mainly established in Germany, the Czech Republic, Slovakia and France, but also in other Member States[5].

2. "EU company law" in the broader context of EU lawmaking bodies

We are all well aware that different national company laws are in force in the Member States. These laws have various cultural backgrounds: some belong to the Scandinavian law tradition (Denmark, Sweden, Finland), other to the common law (Ireland, Malta, Cyprus), with most following the civil law tradition (ba-

---

countries introduced the legal form of a limited liability company in the subsequent years after 1892 so that this legal innovation spread worldwide".

4 This view is shared, for example, by Gorriz, *EU company law: past, present and ... future?*, in *Global jurist*, March, 2018, 11: for the "assessment of EU company law [of the] near future [...] it is important to know what kind of enterprises can be found in the EU and what the importance of each type is". EU actions seems to be more concerned with the "size" of the enterprise than with the "legal model": see for example the Recommendation of 6 May 2003 regarding the definition of micro, small and medium-sized enterprises [C(2003) 1422]; the category of "SMEs" "is made up of enterprises which employ fewer than 250 persons and which have an annual turnover not exceeding € 50 million, and/or an annual balance sheet total not exceeding € 43 million. Within the SME category, a small enterprise is defined as an enterprise which employs fewer than 50 persons and whose annual turnover and/or annual balance sheet total does not exceed € 10 million. Within the SME category, a microenterprise is defined as an enterprise which employs fewer than 10 persons and whose annual turnover and/or annual balance sheet total does not exceed € 2 million".

5 Another important factor that could be considered has to do with the economic sectors in which the companies operate. European enterprises are more active in the "services" area. On average, only 9.6 % of active enterprises in the EU are found in industry.

sically the remaining States). That is why they are sometimes very dissimilar and inspired by different underpinning principles.

Is there, however, also an "EU company law", i.e. released from Brussels? Which form does this law take? In a multi-level legal system, at what level does it stand? How are domestic companies impacted by EU law?

The answer to these questions requires a certain order. That brings us back to the main treaties establishing the UE, the legislative powers of EU bodies, the form of the legislative acts, etc., which we should clearly bear in mind if we want to properly understand the EU's position in shaping the company law rules.

While the following notions may be well known, we will summarize them briefly[6].

The first treaty to remember is the "Treaty on the establishment of the European Community" (the "Rome Treaty") of 25 March 1957. Its purpose was the establishment of the European Community.

The second is the "Treaty on the European Union", the "Maastricht Treaty" of 7 February 1992 (the "TEU"). It aimed to prepare for the European Monetary Union and introduced some elements of a political union. The main changes from the Treaty of Rome included the establishment of the European Union (previously "European Community") and the empowerment of EU bodies with more say in decision-making in areas of common interest. New forms of cooperation between EU governments – for example on defense, justice and home affairs – were also implemented.

Finally, the "Treaty on the functioning of the European Union", the "Lisbon Treaty" of 13 December 2007 (the "TFEU") was signed, in order, *inter alia*, to clarify which powers belong to the EU, the EU Member States, or were shared.

The functioning of the EU bodies is also of interest.

The European Council (governed by Arts. 13, 15 TEU) is formed by the heads of state (or government) of the EU countries: it defines the general political direction and priorities of the European Union (meets every three months in Brussels).

The Council of the European Union (the "Council of Ministers"), also based in Brussels, assembles government ministers from all the EU countries in accordance with the policy area to be discussed. It adopts EU laws and coordinates EU policies (pursuant to Arts. 13, 16 TEU). Each EU Member State holds the presidency on a six-month rotating basis.

---

6 As reference textbooks you may use, among others, at a general level, Chalmers/Davies/Monti, *European Union law*, 4th ed., Cambridge UP, 2019, and, with a more specific focus on company law, Gerner-Beuerle/Schillig, *Comparative company law*, Cambridge UP, 2019.

The legislative process of the Council is rather peculiar: normally it first promotes the drafting of "green papers" which stimulate discussion on given topics; those papers invite the relevant parties (bodies or individuals) to participate in a consultation process. This stage is followed by the "white paper" stage, containing the initial proposals for EU action in that specific area. Finally actual legislative "proposals" are implemented, leading to EU laws.

The European Parliament (governed by Arts. 13 and 14 TEU) comprises – after Brexit – 705 members, directly elected by EU voters every five years. It adopts EU laws along with the European Council. It is located in Strasbourg (France), Brussels (Belgium) and Luxembourg.

The executive branch of the EU, the European Commission, proposes and enforces legislation, implements policies and controls the EU budget (see Arts. 13, 17 TEU). Its members comprise a college of commissioners, one from each EU Member State (currently 27). It also meets in Brussels.

Finally, the Court of Justice of the European Union ("CJEU") ensures that EU law is interpreted and applied in the same way in every EU Member State (as per Arts. 13, 19 TEU). It can also be used, under certain circumstances, by individuals or companies to take action against EU institutions if they feel their rights have been infringed.

The CJEU is divided into two courts, both located in Luxembourg. The "Court of Justice", which deals with requests for ruling from national courts, certain actions for annulment and appeals. It comprises one judge from each EU Member State (thus 27), and 11 advocates general (each appointed for a renewable six-year term). The "General Court" rules on actions for annulment brought by individuals, companies and, in some cases, EU governments. It is currently made up of 54 judges.

3. EU legislative acts and the jurisprudence of the Court of Justice of the EU

Lastly, we have to consider the legislative acts of the EU. Pursuant to Art. 288 TFEU, they include the regulations, directives, decisions and the recommendations.

A "regulation" is a binding legislative act. It must be applied in its entirety across the EU. For example, when the EU wanted to make sure that there were common safeguards on goods imported from outside the EU, the Council adopted a regulation.

A "directive" is a legislative act that sets out a goal that all EU countries must achieve. However, it is up to the individual Member States to produce their own laws on how to reach these goals. One sample is the EU consumer rights directive which strengthens rights for consumers across the EU, namely by eliminating hidden charges and costs and extending the period under which consumers can withdraw from a sales contract.

A "decision" has direct effect, but is limited in scope. It is binding on those to whom it is addressed (e.g. an EU country or an individual company) and is directly applicable.

A "recommendation" is not binding; it allows institutions to make their views known and suggest a line of action without imposing any legal obligation on those to whom it is addressed.

As far as the CJEU, the main tasks of the Court are the following.

1) Interpreting the law (presenting "preliminary rulings"). National courts of EU Member States are required to ensure EU law is properly applied, but they might interpret it differently. If a national court is in doubt about the interpretation or validity of an EU law, it can ask the Court for clarification.

2) Enforcing the law (managing infringement proceedings). These types of cases are taken against national governments for failing to comply with EU law. They can be started by the Commission or another EU country. If the State is found to be at fault, it must put things right at once or risk a second case being brought, which may result in a fine[7].

3) Annulling EU legal acts (taking actions for annulment). If an EU act is believed to violate EU Treaties or fundamental rights, the Court can be asked to annul it – by an EU government, the Council, the Commission or (in some cases) the Parliament. Private individuals can also ask the Court to annul an EU act that directly concerns them.

4) Ensuring the EU takes action (beginning actions for failure to act). The EU Parliament, EU Council and EU Commission must make certain decisions under certain circumstances. If they do not, EU governments, other EU institutions or – under certain conditions – individuals or companies can complain to the Court.

5) Sanctioning EU institutions (taking actions for damages). Any person or company who has had their interests harmed as a result of the action or inaction of the EU or its staff can take action against them through the Court.

---

7 The specific problem of enforcement of the directives in the specific field of company law has been addressed i.e. by Sørensen, *Enforcing EU company law: requirements and limitations in implementing penalties for infringements of EU company law*, in *EBOR*, 2017, 701.

To date, the Court has made most of its rulings in the exercise of its competence to decide matters referred to it by national courts so that it can interpret EU rules.

4. The competence of the Union in the area of company law: the EU may only "harmonize", through directives and regulations, national company laws and does not have exclusive power

We can now get back to our original question: what is EU company law?

The TFEU stipulates (see Art. 2.1, "Exclusive legislative competence of the Union") that "when the Treaties confer on the Union exclusive competence in a specific area, only the Union may legislate and adopt legally binding acts [...]". Art. 3 TFEU defines the areas in which the EU has this "exclusive" competence and national law-making bodies have to surrender to the EU's legislative power: "the Union shall have exclusive competence in the following areas: (a) customs union; (b) functioning of the internal market; (c) monetary policy [...]; (d) the conservation of marine biological resources under the common fisheries policy; (e) common commercial policy".

It is clear that company law is not listed among the sectors in which the EU has exclusive competence.

Art. 2.1 TFEU governs the "shared competence between Union and States". It reads as follows: "when the Treaties confer on the Union a competence shared with the Member States in a specific area, the Union and the Member States may legislate and adopt legally binding acts in that area". The EU can always advocate the competence. Art. 4.2 lists the shared competences between the Union and the Member States, which concern these areas: "(a) internal market; (b) social policy [...]; (c) economic, social and territorial cohesion; (d) agriculture and fisheries [...]; (e) environment; (f) consumer protection; (g) transport; (h) trans-European networks; (i) energy; (j) area of freedom, security and justice; (k) common safety concerns in public health matters [...]".

Once again, company law is not encompassed within the sectors where competence is shared between the EU and the single States' legislators.

Finally – and most importantly – Art. 2.5 TFEU ("competence of the States and coordination of the Union") affirms that "in certain areas [...] the Union shall have competence to carry out actions to support, coordinate or supplement the actions of the Member States, without thereby superseding their competence in these areas". Art. 6 adds that "the Union shall have competence to carry out actions to support, coordinate or supplement the actions of the Member States.

The areas of such action shall, at European level, be: (a) protection and improvement of human health; (b) industry; (c) culture; (d) tourism; (e) education, voca-
tional training, youth and sport; (f) civil protection; (g) administrative cooperation".

"Industry" – and therefore including companies that operate in industry and
more generally in entrepreneurial activities – belong to the field in which the EU
has specific competence, which is however limited to initiatives of "coordination" of the actions of the single Member States.

As a consequence, the EU may not directly legislate in the area of company
law, but it can operate to coordinate – "harmonize" – the legislative actions of
the national legislators.

As we have previously seen, the legislative act that the EU may adopt to obtain this harmonization is typically the "directive": a directive is binding, as to
the result to be achieved, upon each Member State to which it is addressed,
but leaves the national authorities in charge of the choice of form and methods
(see again Art. 288 TFEU).

In some occasions, however, harmonization may also be pursued by using
the more stringent "regulation" instrument (especially in the areas of major interest for the "internal market", where the competence of the EU is exclusive).

As it has been noted, this system of directives (and, to a minor extent, regulations) "has many advantages: in a multicultural, multilingual economic area
it makes it possible to reach agreement on common principles without having to
agree about the precise wording in the actually applicable provision. It allows
the bridging of the considerable differences in the legislative traditions of the
Member States. It further allows each State to use its own wording and language,
as the directive only binds as to its result, not as to its forms and methods"[8].

On the other hand, the drawback in mainly using directives is that non strictly uniform laws result: "looking at the national company law statutes, one will
find numerous and sometimes considerable differences in the respective Member
States. It is up to the CJEU to check whether the Member States have adequately
implemented the directive and whether the goal put forward has been achieved"[9].

Moreover, harmonization has to be pursued in connection with the principle
of "subsidiarity", as defined in Article 5 TFEU. This principle aims to ensure that
decisions are taken as closely as possible to the citizen and that constant checks
are made to verify that action at EU level is justified in light of the possibilities

---

8 See Wymeersch, *Company law in Europe and European company law*, 2001, at *ssrn.com*, 7.
9 See Wymeersch, *Company*, 7.

available at national, regional or local level. Specifically, according to this principle the EU must not take action (except in the areas that fall within its "exclusive" competence) unless it is more effective than action taken at national, regional or local level[10].

The principle is closely bound up with the other principle of "proportionality", which requires that any action by the EU should not go beyond what is necessary to achieve the objectives of the Treaties.

One last remark on the EU legal framework is necessary at this point.

Although the process is essentially one of harmonization and the principles of subsidiarity and proportionality are firmly in place, it must be clear that Union law takes precedence over Member States' laws. Conflicting national laws cannot be applied and the primacy of EU law is not up for discussion[11].

Moreover, since Member States have agreed to surrender to this primacy, they must implement laws decided at EU level (and apply it directly if involving regulations), they must contribute towards a common EU budget[12], etc., they

---

10 See Chalmers/Davies/Monti, *European*, 383: "its ethos is that local decisions are, in principle, better than more central ones. This ethos is not fully followed through as the article does not express a preference for local or regional laws over national laws. However, the preference for national law over EU law seems to be for two reasons. The first reason is ownership over the laws. As Member States are smaller than the Union, there is a sense of individual citizen having the possibility of proportionately more voice and these laws being more proximate to them. The second reason is a cultural one. National laws express traditions and beliefs which are seen as valuable insofar as they give meaning to citizens' lives, symbolize belonging and allow these citizens to orient themselves in the world. The [Irish] decision to drive on the left-hand side of the road is thus idiosyncratic but is valued because it is seen as an expression of distinctiveness and, for [Irish] people, a reminder of home".

11 See the "17. Declaration concerning primacy", annexed to the final act of the conference which adopted the Treaty of Lisbon: "The Conference recalls that, in accordance with well settled case law of the Court of Justice of the European Union, the Treaties and the law adopted by the Union on the basis of the Treaties have primacy over the law of Member States, under the conditions laid down by the said case law". In the landmark case "Costa vs. Enel" (C-6/64), the ECJ ruled that "the law stemming from the Treaty, an independent source of law, could not, because of its special and original nature, be overridden by domestic legal provisions, however framed, without being deprived of its character as community law and without the legal basis of the community itself being called into question". As noted by Andenas/Wooldridge, *European*, 36, the principles of subsidiarity and proportionality "may have some inhibiting effect on further harmonization of company law, although the existence of these concepts does not seem to have had an inhibiting effect in the field of consumer and environmental law".

12 Pursuant to Art. 311 TFUE and other connected laws, EU sources of funding include contributions from member countries, import duties on products from outside the EU and fines applied to companies that do not comply with EU regulations. EU countries agree several years in advance on the size of the budget and how to finance it.

should also be well aware that other Member States' laws must comply with EU law (and this is obvious), and be concerned about how this compliance takes place, i. e. they should be interested in other States' domestic rules (and this is much less acknowledged).

From this standpoint, any Member State's national company law becomes relevant for the national company law of the other Member States: the compliance, say, of Dutch company law with EU rules is a matter of direct interest also to German companies, and vice versa. This may be a concept that we are not accustomed, but we should get used to considering it.

Finally, what about the role on the CJEU in this process of harmonization?

It mainly relates, as anticipated, to its power to interpret the directives and set forth general principles which are binding on national judges.

An example of a recent case of company law addressed by the CJEU (in January, 2020) may explain how the Court works in the field of company law[13].

In October 2018, the Court of Appeal of Naples (Italy) asked the CJEU to give a preliminary ruling in order to clarify the extension of a national rule on corporate divisions (de-mergers) compared to a rule contained in a directive. The case concerned a division that had been carried out by a company, whereby some assets had been transferred to a newly established one, allegedly defrauding creditors. The creditors tried to invalidate the transaction so that they could attack the assets of the original – now divided – company.

In court, however, the company objected that the Italian legislation contain a rule which prevents it from invalidating a deed of division once it has been entered onto the companies register. More specifically, Art. 2504-*quater* It-CC (entitled "Invalidity of the merger", applicable also to divisions) states that: "Once the deed of merger [or division] has been registered in [the companies register], said deed may not be ruled invalid. This does not affect the right to compensation for damages that may be caused to shareholders or third parties harmed by the merger [or division]".

Notwithstanding that rule, the Italian court of first instance declared the division to be invalid by applying the Italian clawback rule which allows actions that defraud and harm creditors to be deemed invalid (Art. 2901 It-CC, which governs the "actio pauliana")[14].

---

13 Case C-394/18 ("IGI"); the case is commented by De Luca, *Actio pauliana and divisions (IGI v Cicenia, C-394/18): not everything that is done, is well done*, in *ECL*, 2020, 97.

14 Under that rule, "a creditor may request that a transfer of assets whereby a debtor harmed its interests to be declared invalid vis-à-vis that creditor, where the following conditions are met: (1) the debtor is aware of the harm that the act has caused to the interests of the creditor [...];

The company appealed, claiming that this type of invalidation is not permitted by Art. 2504-*quater* It-CC and, more generally, by the EU rule that the Italian provision has implemented: Art. 108 Directive 2017/1132/EU, reproducing Art. 19 of the Directive on divisions (1982/891/EEC, called also the "Sixth Directive"). This latter rule states that the laws of Member States may lay down "nullity rules for [divisions] in accordance with the following conditions only: (a) nullity must be ordered in a court judgment; (b) [....]; (c) nullification proceedings may not be initiated more than six months after the date on which the [division] becomes effective".

The Court of Appeals of Naples devolved the interpretation of the Italian rules to the CJEU to clarify whether the articles (domestic and contained in the Directive) on the invalidity of divisions should apply also to clawback remedies like the "actio pauliana" which are aimed at invalidating actions that are fraudulent and harmful to creditors.

The CJEU ruled that: "As regards the objectives pursued by the Sixth Directive, it is apparent [...] that the EU legislature considered it necessary to limit the cases in which nullity can arise [...]. However [...] while nullification [pursuant to Art. 19 and 2504-*quater*] seeks to penalize failure to comply with the requirements for [division proceedings], an 'actio pauliana' [...] has the sole aim of protecting creditors to whose rights the division has caused harm [...] Therefore, that action is not covered by the concept of 'nullity' referred to in Art. 19 Sixth Directive".

This case (on which we shall return at a later stage: see Chapter 10, § 3) illustrates how the Court works: the national court had a doubt about the interpretation of an EU law (i. e. Art. 19 Sixth Directive and 108 Directive 1132, as reflected in the national provision, Art. 2504-*quater* It-CC); it asked the CJEU for clarification; the CJEU set forth the interpretation, which is now a binding precedent for all the national judges of the Member States.

Courts of Member States are under an obligation to interpret national law, as far as possible, in accordance with EU laws that apply to the same subject matter[15].

---

(2) furthermore, in relation to an act for consideration, the third party was aware of the harm [...]".

15 See especially the "Von Colson" and "Marleasing" cases, decided in 1984 and 1990 (cases C-14/83 and C-106/89). The same is also true for recommendations: although they "cannot be regarded as having no legal effect at all, the national courts are bound to take them into consideration in order to decide disputes submitted to them, in particular where they cast light on the interpretation of national measures adopted in order to implement them or where they are designed to supplement binding Community provisions" (ruling "Grimaldi", C-322/88).

5. The main directives adopted in the area of company law (and the ones that remained at the draft stage)

In order to fulfil the task set forth by the Treaties, over the years, EU legislative bodies have adopted a certain number of directives in the field of company law[16].

The first Directive, adopted by the Council, dates back to 1968; it is the Directive no. 1968/151/EEC (also called the "First Directive").

Its objective was to coordinate regulations concerning public compulsory disclosure, the power of representation of company bodies and the nullity of companies with limited liability.

Disclosure has been made mandatory as far as the act of incorporation of the company is concerned. The same applies to the appointment and termination of office of the persons who are authorized to represent the company, and persons who take part in the supervisory processes.

Moreover, as a general rule, it has been set forth that actions by officers of a company may be relied upon by third parties. An action carried out outside the statutory objects of the company pursuant to its articles of association may also be relied on by a third party unless national laws allow the company to prove that said third party knew or could not have been unaware of the fact.

The Directive also contained a set of rules on the "nullity" of the company. Nullity may not be automatic and a court judgment is required. A list was given of the circumstances in which nullity may be ordered (for example, the statutory object of the company is unlawful or contrary to public policy, or the rules concerning the minimum amount of capital to be paid up are not complied with).

The Directive was later amended by Directive 2003/58/EC following an initiative of simplification of the formalities imposed on companies. This Directive has enabled the benefits of modern technology to be exploited, and companies may now file the compulsory documents by paper as well as electronic means. In addition, companies will continue to publish their documents and details in the language or in one of the languages of their Member States, but will also be able to publish them voluntarily in other EU languages to facilitate cross-border access to company information.

The First Directive was substantially amended on a number of occasions and, in the interests of clarity and rationality, has been re-codified in Directive 2017/1132/EU (also to further limit the cases in which nullity can arise and the retroactive effect of a declaration of nullity).

---

16 For a useful description of the legislative developments, see Gorriz, *EU*, 1.

A second Council directive was enacted in 1977: Directive 1977/91/EC (the so called "Second Directive"). It has been particularly important since it regulated the formation of public companies and, above all, the maintenance and alteration of their capital.

The Directive coordinated the national provisions on the formation of public companies, minimum share capital requirements, acceptable considerations, distributions to shareholders and increases and reductions in capital. The Directive also stated principles and exemptions on the subscription and purchase by a company of its own shares, and loans made and security provided by a company for the acquisition of its shares by a shareholder or a third party.

This Directive has also been substantially revised several times (for instance, by Directive 2006/68/EC) and it has been finally recast into Directive 2017/1132/EU.

Turning to the "Third Directive", it was adopted in 1978 and laid down the rules concerning mergers between limited liability companies – public and private – from the same Member State (Directive 1978/855/EEC).

The Directive regulated the drawing-up of merger documents (merger proposal, merger financial statements, report of the directors, etc.) and their content. The Directive concerned also the approval of the merger proposal by the general meeting of shareholders, the disclosure of that resolution in the companies register and the final merger deed. Rules governing the nullity of mergers were also laid down in the Directive in order to protect members and third parties: the cases of nullity were limited to serious illegalities and the protection of harmed parties (shareholders, creditors) was shifted towards forms of liability of the company, directors and supervisors.

The Third Directive was substantially amended several times and has been finally re-codified in Directive 2017/1132/EU.

The Fourth Directive (1978/60/EEC) coordinated Member States' provisions concerning the presentation and content of annual accounts and annual reports, the valuation methods used and their publication in respect of all companies with limited liability.

The Directive moved from the perceived need that annual accounts must give a true and fair view of a company's assets and liabilities, financial position and profit (or loss). To this end a mandatory layout and shared principles were prescribed in order to ensure that annual accounts (of companies from different Member States) disclose comparable and equivalent information.

Some years later, in 1982, a further directive concerning divisions (de-mergers) took effect (Directive 1982/891/EEC): the Directive – the "Sixth", as we have already seen – established minimal rules concerning the splitting of limited liability companies from the same Member State (it is similar to the Third Directive).

Strict safeguards ensured the protection of shareholders and, in particular, creditors. As regards the latter, the main defense entailed the joint and several liability of the recipient companies. The Sixth Directive was later amended and finally recast as Directive 2017/1132/EU.

The "Seventh Directive" (1983/349/EEC) and the "Eighth Directive" (1984/253/EEC) completed the directives concerning company accounts: the former coordinated national laws on consolidated – i.e. group – accounts; the latter defined the qualifications of persons responsible for carrying out the statutory audits of the accounting documents required by the Fourth and Seventh Directives.

Afterwards, two very specific Directives followed.

On the one hand, Directive 1989/666/EEC providing for the rules concerning the disclosure requirements imposed in a Member State for branches of companies governed by the law of another State in order to deliver an equivalent level of protection for shareholders and third parties (the "Eleventh Directive"); on the other hand, Directive 1989/667/EEC, creating the possibility of the limitation of liability for individual entrepreneurs and allowing single-member private companies to be established (the "Twelfth Directive").

The next directive to be adopted came into force fifteen years later.

It was the "Thirteenth Directive" of 2004 (2004/25/EC) on takeover bids, regulating the proceedings and main terms of mandatory bids for listed companies, aimed at protecting the interests of minority shareholders and other interested parties. The Directive imposed the requirement on Member States to ensure protection by obliging the person who has acquired – or intends to acquire – control of a company to make an offer to all the holders of that company's shares for all of their holdings at a fair price.

One year later Directive 2005/56/EC (the "Tenth") was enacted, relating to cross-border mergers; it was motivated by the recognition that companies from different Member States encounter many legislative and administrative difficulties in the process of consolidation. It was considered necessary, with a view to the completion and functioning of the single market, to lay down provisions to facilitate the carrying-out of cross-border mergers between various types of limited liability companies governed by the laws of different Member States.

In 2007, there was the Directive on the exercise of shareholders' voting rights (Directive 2007/36/EC, or the "First Shareholder Rights Directive", or "SRD"; for the first time, this Directive was not given a progressive number in relation to the others). Its scope was to define minimum rights for shareholders in listed companies across the EU. It laid down a number of specific provisions including the right of shareholders to obtain all information relevant to general meetings, the exercise of voting rights by correspondence and by proxy and the right to ask questions at the general meeting.

Therefore, in the 40 years between 1968 and 2007 there have been fourteen main directives adopted, basically on the topics of publicity (of company's activity, accounts, etc.), on capital, and on extraordinary transactions (mergers, divisions, takeovers).

Two very important directives were proposed but have not been approved and have remained at the stage of "draft directive" in two crucial fields of company law: corporate governance and groups of companies[17].

The Draft "Fifth Directive" (1972–1991) was primarily aimed at regulating the balance of powers between shareholders and the board of directors and the external controls on the latter. However, since the Directive also tried to implement, *inter alia*, a right by employees to vote for the boards of directors in large companies, it generated great debate and no agreements by the Member States was ever reached.

The Directive went through three major revisions, but always stayed at the proposal stage.

The other Directive which remained a project is the draft "Ninth Directive" on company groups, which also never overcame the unofficial scheme stage (in 1974/75 and 1984). In that case the proposal touched very sensitive issues like the formation of groups and the protection to be accorded to shareholders and creditors of interrelated companies; it encountered fierce opposition from many Member States and was finally rejected.

From 2007 on, the other approved directives were mainly to consolidate, clarify, re-codify previous ones.

As already mentioned, the First, Second, Third and Sixth Directives were amended by Directives 2003/58/EC, 2006/68/EC and 2009/109/EC. Later on, the first three Directives were recast: the First turned into Directive 2009/101/EC34; the Second became Directive 2012/30/UE; and the Third Directive 2011/35/EU. The First, Second, Third and Tenth were re-codified into Directive 2017/1132/EU. In 2019, Directive 2121 amended the section of Directive 2017 on cross-border mergers, also governing cross-border conversions and divisions (also called the "Mobility Directive")[18].

---

17 Another relatively important directive that has not been implemented is for instance the one on liquidation and dissolution of the company: see the draft Proposal DOC XV/43/87–EN.

18 This Directive, together with the one on the use of digital tools and processes in company law referred to below in the text, were part of the *"Company Law Package"* approved by the Commission in April 2018, aimed at establishing "simpler and less burdensome rules for companies" regarding incorporation and cross-border transactions; see Teichmann, *The Company Law Package – Content and state of play*, in *ECFR*, 2019, 4.

The "Accounting Directive" (2013/34/EU), later amended by Directive 2014/95/EU, replaced the Fourth and the Seventh Directives to adapt them to the international accounting standards.

Directive 2007/36/EC (the First SRD) was also recast – with some relevant extensions – into Directive 2018/828/EU, the "Second SRD" (especially with regard to rules regarding transactions with related parties which have to be publicly announced and approved by the general meeting or by the administrative or supervisory body).

No other major directive was therefore actually put in force by the EU after 2007 in the field of company law. The very last directives have been devoted to single specific aspects. For instance, Directive 2019/1151/EU (also called "Digitalization Directive") contains provisions on the use of digital tools and processes in company law, etc.

The only significant exception towards more uniform legislation of the EU has been the approval in 2001 – as already stated (above, § 1) – of the statute for the Societas Europea (SE), a supranational corporate type. In that year two fundamental acts were passed regarding the European Company: Regulation 2001/2157/EU on the statute and Directive 2001/86/EC supplementing the statute with regard to the involvement of employees.

Finally, one should consider that other Directives may have an impact on company law, although not directly focused on it: in this regard Directive 2019/1023/EU is particularly important – concerning restructuring and insolvency proceedings (the "Restructuring Directive") – which explicitly sets forth that "Member States should be able to derogate from the requirements laid down in Directive 2017/1132/EU" and permit the waiver to some rules on the maintenance of legal capital in case of pre-insolvency with the aim of facilitating the reorganization of the company.

6. The theoretical debate on EU "harmonization" versus "regulatory competition" among national State legislations

The way chosen by the EU to foster common "European company law" by means of directives has led to probe the opportunity to carry out this type of harmonization over the years.

A theoretical debate has begun, focusing on a very significant question, that had never been raised in the pro-European climate of the first decades: is it better for company law to be shaped through EU harmonization or by single States laws, with the States competing against each other to win shareholders' preferences and trying to attract them to incorporate their companies (or relocate them) under their foreign national laws?[19].

The main argument in favor of a process of strong harmonization holds that this type of coordination, by making the laws of the various States uniform, would help companies to expand their activities in other countries: entrepreneurs may rely on the fact that foreign laws are similar to the ones in their States. Harmonization would then support the process of consolidating companies on a continental scale.

The second line of reasoning often employed in favor of harmonization focuses on the risk that single Member States, if totally permitted to set forth their own rules, would implement looser laws to attract companies to incorporate in their countries, and that would lead to less efficient laws (i.e.: less protective for creditors, minority shareholders, etc.). This claim of a possible worsening of the level of Member States' legislation is called the "race to the bottom" argument.

---

19 See in particular Deakin, *Regulatory competition versus harmonisation in European company law*, 2000, at *cbr.cam.ac.uk*; Enriques, *EC company law and the fears of a European Delaware*, in *EBLR*, 2004, 1259; Id., *Company law harmonization reconsidered: what role for the EC?*, 2005, at *ssrn.com*; Id., *EC company law directives and regulations: how trivial are they?*, 2005, at *ssrn.com*; Kieninger, *The legal framework of regulatory competition based on company mobility: EU and US compared*, in *GLJ*, 2005, 741; Tröger, *Choice of jurisdiction in European corporate law – perspectives of European corporate governance*, in *EBOR*, 2005, 3; Gelter, *The structure of regulatory competition in European corporate law*, in *J. corp l. stud.*, 2005, 247; Id., *Centros and defensive regulatory competition: some thoughts and a glimpse at the data*, 2019, at *ssrn.com*; Armour, *Who should make corporate law? EC legislation versus regulatory competition*, at ecgi.org, 2005; McCahery/Vermeulen, *Does the European company prevent the 'Delaware effect'*, 2005, at *ssrn.com*; Krieger, *The legal framework of regulatory competition based on company mobility: EU and US compared*, 2005, in *GLJ*, 2005, 740; Zumbansen, *Spaces and places: a systems theory approach to regulatory competition in European company law*, in *ELJ*, 2006, 534; Enriques/Gelter, *Regulatory competition in European company law and creditor protection*, in *EBOR*, 2006, 417; Kroeze/Vletter/Van Dort, *History and future of uniform company law in Europe*, in *ECL*, 2008, 114; Braun/Eidenmüller/Enhert/Hornhuf, *Does charter competition foster entrepreneurship*, 2011, at *ecgi.org*; Ringe, *Corporate mobility in the European Union – a flash in the pan? An empirical study on the success of lawmaking and regulatory competition*, in *ECFR*, 2013, 230; Hornuf/Linder, *End of regulatory competition in European company law?*, 2014, at *ssrn.com*; Zorzi, *A European Nevada? Bad enforcement as an edge in state competition for incorporations*, in *EBOR*, 2017, 251; Gelter, *EU company law harmonization between convergence and varieties of capitalism*, 2017, at *ssrn.com*; Ghetti, *Unification, harmonization and competition in European company forms*, in *EBLR*, 2018, 813.

On the other hand, supporters of regulatory competition try to show the superiority of single "national" company laws over harmonization and illustrate the limits of a possible common company law.

They believe that companies, if let free to incorporate in the State they want, would naturally choose the legislation that is more appealing for all stakeholders (shareholders, creditors, employees, etc.) and would shift towards countries with more efficient laws. Member States will thus be encouraged to enact rules perceived as attractive by companies and consequently experiment and shape "better" laws: a "race to the top" will begin.

Moreover, the "market" for superior regulations would enhance legislative innovation, which is a good result per se.

That kind of debate actually reproduces the one already started years ago in the United States, where each constituent State has its own company laws, in spite of the country's integrated national economy, without any national harmonization effort as such.

US scholars have discussed at length the superiority of one model over the other (federalism vs. nationalism). In any case, American corporations do actually gain from regulatory competition[20].

The absence of federal company law has also led – as a kind of corrective – to the drafting of the "Model Business Corporation Act" (MBCA) in America which is a company law model prepared (originally in 1950) by the American Bar Association – i.e. the association of American lawyers – and revised every year.

The MBCA is not mandatory and States can choose to incorporate all its clauses into law or only some or none. The model has currently been transposed into law by 24 American states out of 50. As a consequence, in the US there are currently states that have similar or even identical legislation, based on the MBCA, and states that have taken their own path and do not follow the MBCA at all.

---

20 For a summary of the debate see Gelter, *Centros*, 3, who notes that in the US corporations often tend to avoid States with laws containing mechanisms to protect minority shareholders (like the application of heightened fiduciary duties towards shareholders stuck with an investment for which there is no market) or laws particularly severe towards directors and creating liability risk matters. Nevada, for instance, is a state perceived as friendly for founders (of the so called "Wild West" corporations), considering, *inter alia*, the guarantees accorded by making it difficult to pierce the corporate veil, by acknowledging bearer shares, etc. (the state is sometimes named as a "liability-free" jurisdiction).

The fact that in the US the states are split (half rely on a common model, the other half does not) probably demonstrates that the arguments in favor of federalism or nationalism are not easily predominant in one sense or the other.

It is true, on the other hand, that some of the states that have chosen to refuse harmonization and have created their own company law have had a tremendous impact. The most notorious example is Delaware (a small state, but home of the most important American corporations), that has produced laws that are unanimously considered valid, innovative and often groundbreaking[21].

Coming back to this side of the Atlantic, it is not clear where the process of evolution of European company law is heading to: towards more harmonization or more competition. The vision is not clear-cut and we shall have to wait and see what happens in the years to come.

The comparison between the US and EU legal systems should not, however, be overestimated. As it has been observed, "there are roughly two reasons for the fact that what does not work in the EU does work in the US. The first reason is the American Constitution and US conflict law. These constitutional and conflict rules guarantee much better and more absolutely that there is freedom of establishment within the US than the EC Treaty and the different national conflict rules up to now do for the European territory. The second reason is that different company law systems in the US have more in common with one another on a basic level than the different company law systems in Europe. Company law in the fifty American States and the District of Columbia may well be different, but the similarities between the different systems are striking. In the course of a century and a half, the systems have grown together to such an extent that they are founded on the same starting points and are largely interchangeable"[22].

Common language, easily accessible national legislations, interrelated case laws, etc. have made the rest. On the other hand, distances (cultural, linguistic, etc.) in that regard are still significant in Europe (for example it is not easy to find an official English text of each of the 27 Member States company laws).

---

21 Delaware has, at the same time, created both laws that are considered liberal and a class of judges with great expertise in corporate law, which makes their case law reliable and well-accepted. As of January 2020, over 1 million business entities have made Delaware their legal home, including over two-thirds of the "Fortune 500" companies; Delaware is also the jurisdiction of incorporation for 80% of all firms that "go public", i.e. list their shares on the market (see Bruner, *Leveraging corporate law: a broader account of Delaware's competition*, 2020, at *ssrn.com*, 3). Nevertheless, most of the advice on listed firms incorporated in Delaware is not provided by lawyers practicing in Delaware, but in large cities, like New York.
22 See Kroeze/Vletter/van Dort, *History*, 114. See also Andenas/Wooldridge, *European*, 34.

7. The "rush to incorporate" in different States and the jurisprudence of the CJEU: the Daily Mail, Centros, Überseering, Inspire Art (and Cartesio, Sevic, Vale, Polbud) cases

(A) The EU Court of Justice cannot obviously take a stand on the debate set out above (harmonization vs. competition). The judges cannot adopt views, above all on discussions that, at the end of the day, are strictly theoretical, if not political.

Nevertheless, the Court has de facto favored the process of competition among different legislations by letting the companies freely choose the State where to incorporate and run their business.

The legal basis which brought this result was the principle on the freedom of establishment, as provided for firstly by Art. 44(2)(g) TEU.

This rule – contained in the chapter devoted to the right of establishment – compels European institutions to attain freedom of establishment "by coordinating to the necessary extent the safeguards [...] of companies or firms [...], with a view to making such safeguards equivalent throughout the Community".

Later on, Art. 49 TFEU was introduced (superseding Art. 44 TEU): it stipulates that "restrictions on the freedom of establishment of nationals of a Member State in the territory of another Member State shall be prohibited. Such prohibition shall also apply to restrictions on the setting-up of agencies, branches or subsidiaries by nationals of any Member State established in the territory of any Member State. Freedom of establishment shall include the right to take up and pursue activities as self-employed persons and to set up and manage undertakings, in particular companies or firms".

Art. 50 TFEU sets forth that "the European Parliament, the Council and the Commission shall carry out the duties devolving upon them under the preceding provisions, in particular: [...] (g) by coordinating to the necessary extent the safeguards which, for the protection of the interests of members and others, are required by Member States of companies or firms [...] with a view to making such safeguards equivalent throughout the Union".

The Court has been therefore involved over the years in several cases, concerning entrepreneurs aiming to set up (or relocate) their companies to other EU States, and invoking their right to move to those countries and "choose" the other legislation.

The practice of companies incorporating in a different Member State only for "legislative" reasons – taking advantage of laws deemed to be more favorable – is noteworthy. Often companies only have their "legal" seats in the Netherlands or in Luxembourg for example (or even only a "post office box" necessary for the legal seat: they are known as "letterbox companies"), while continuing to operate mainly in a different country where they keep their "real seats".

This "forum shopping" (which in its more extreme and abusive forms should be contested, as we shall see) is well-established; it actually began soon after the founding of the EU, in the 1980s.

The legal issue has always been basically the same: is it legal for citizens/companies of a Member State (for instance Germany) – living/operating in that country – to set up/move to another State (for instance the Netherlands) in order to take advantage of the local legislation and then continue to operate – through a branch – in another state (for instance, again in Germany)?

On this matter the jurisprudence of the CJEU has changed dramatically over the years, with a series of famous rulings.

The first decision was taken in the "Daily Mail" case of 1988 (case C-81/87).

Daily Mail PLC was an UK company, based in England, and wanted to move its "legal" seat to the Netherlands because of the more favorable Dutch tax regime; at the same time it planned to remain a company operating in the UK through a branch (and keep therefore its "real" headquarters in England).

The UK Treasury Department – which, at the time, had to be asked by the company for authorization – refused permission for the transfer of the legal seat. The company thus referred the question to the CJEU, asking whether the rules of the EC Treaty (on the "freedom of movement of goods, persons, services and capitals") precluded the transfer of the legal seat from a Member State to another.

The CJEU rejected the case, declaring that the issue fell outside the scope of the Treaty provisions on the freedom of establishment. The Court stated that the rules "on the abolition of restrictions on movement and residence within the Community for nationals of Member States refer solely to the movement and residence of natural persons, and the provisions of the directive cannot, by their nature, be applied by analogy to legal persons. Therefore [EU laws], properly construed, confers no right on a company to transfer its central management and control to another Member State".

The argument was actually formalistic and was soon to be overruled. The occasion came in 1999 when the Court was asked to take a position on the "Centros" case (C-208/00).

In 1999 two Danes, living in Denmark, established Centros Ltd. in England, under UK company law. The company intended to operate however only in Denmark through a branch. Moreover, the two shareholders openly stated that they had established the entity under UK company law solely to avoid the minimum capitalization requirements for Danish limited liability companies (which were more stringent). The Danish Commercial Registry considered this to be an unlawful circumvention of the Danish minimum capitalization rules and refused to register the company's branch office in Denmark.

The CJEU took the opposite position. It ruled that where a company exercises its freedom of establishment under the EC Treaty, Member States are prohibited from discriminating against this company on the grounds that it was established in accordance with the law of another State in which it has its registered office but does not carry on any business. Secondly, a State is not authorized to restrict freedom of establishment on the grounds of protecting creditors or preventing fraud if there are other ways of countering fraud or protecting creditors (i.e. criminal law or others). Freedom of establishment always has to prevail[23].

Along the same lines was the decision of the CJEU in the Überseering case of 2002 (C-212/97).

All the directors of Überseering BV, a limited liability company organized under Dutch law, were resident in Germany. The German courts decided that German corporate laws should apply to the company, since the "real seat" of the company was located in Germany.

The CJEU ruled – on the contrary – that where a company incorporated in another Member State (in that case: the Netherlands) exercises its freedom of establishment in another State (Germany), that other State (Germany) is required to recognize the company's legal capacity as set forth by the other member state (the Netherland).

The fourth paradigmatic case was "Inspire Art" in 2003 (C-167/01).

A Dutchman set up the company Inspire Art Ltd. under the laws of the UK and requested the registration of the company's Dutch branch office in the Netherlands. The Dutch Registry took the position that specific Dutch rules for foreign entities registered in the Netherlands were to apply to the company. As a conse-

---

23 This decision was particularly important, since it impacted (as with the ones that followed) also on the Member States' domestic rules of international private law. European national laws have traditionally followed two different approaches regarding conflict of laws for companies, which consider opposite "connecting factors" to determine the applicable law. Some states – like the Netherlands – embrace the so-called "incorporation theory", which regards the company's "seat of incorporation" as the sole connecting factor for determining the applicable law (this means that if a company moves its main business abroad without changing its place of incorporation, its connecting factor with the State of origin remains in force, and the company continues to be governed by the same law of the State in which it was originally registered). Other states – like Germany – adopt the so-called "real seat theory", which considers the place where the company's real business activity is performed as the connecting factor between companies and a country's legislation (if a company is incorporated in a Member State, but its most relevant commercial activity is carried out in a different country, the applicable law is not the one of the State of registration, but the one of its main operative office).

quence, Inspire Art would have been required, *inter alia,* to use a company name indicating its foreign origin (UK) and comply with the minimum capitalization rules for Dutch limited liability companies.

The CJEU refused again to follow the reasoning of the Dutch authority and continued its tendency to decide in favor of freedom of establishment, by holding that a foreign company is subject to the company law of its state of incorporation even if it operates in another country. Any "adjustment" to the company law of the home state is, hence, not compatible with European law.

Those principles were confirmed in other four cases of 2006 ("Cartesio" and "Sevic"), 2010 ("Vale") and 2017 ("Polbud"), all regarding cross-border transactions[24]. In those rulings, the Court held that the refusal of an administration or a

---

[24] Cartesio Oktató és Szolgáltató b.t. was a Hungarian private company intending to transfer its legal seat to Italy, while continuing to operate under Hungarian company law. The Hungarian companies register refused and the question was thus referred to the CJEU. The Court (case C-210/06) reaffirmed its Daily Mail stance and stated that "Articles 43 EC and 48 EC are to be interpreted as not precluding legislation of a Member State under which a company incorporated under the law of that Member State may not transfer its seat to another Member State whilst retaining its status as a company governed by the law of the Member State of incorporation".

Sevic Systems AG was a German company intending to merge with a Luxembourg one. The Neuwied Administrative Court denied the registration of the merger arguing that German law only referred to national mergers. The CJEU (case C-411/03) ruled in favor of Sevic holding that international mergers were covered by the freedom of establishment, because "the right of establishment covers all measures which permit or even merely facilitate access to another Member State and the pursuit of an economic activity in that State by allowing the persons concerned to participate in the economic life of the country effectively and under the same conditions as national operators".

In Vale, the case (C-378/10) concerned a cross-border conversion of a company established under Italian law, Vale Construzioni s.r.l., into a company incorporated under Hungarian law, Vale Építési k.f.t.. Pursuant to Italian law it is possible for a company to convert into a company established under foreign law. According to Hungarian law, only companies incorporated under the law of Hungary were allowed to convert. The Court stated that the State of origin cannot prevent a company from converting into a company governed by the law of the other Member State, to the extent that it is permitted under that law to do so.

The Polbud decision (C-106/16) regarded a Polish private company aiming to convert to a Luxembourg one and the conclusion of the CJEU was basically the same.

Cases are analyzed for instance (as far as Centros, Überseering and Inspire Art are concerned) by Hansen, *A new look at Centros – from a Danish point of view,* in *EBLR,* 2002, 85; Id., *The Vale decision and the Court's case law on the nationality of companies,* in *ECFR,* 2013, 1; Siems, *Convergence, competition, Centros and conflicts of law: European company law in the twenty-first century,* in *ELR,* 2002, 47; Bälz/Baldwin, *The end of the real seat theory (Sitztheorie): the European Court of Justice decision in Ueberseering of 5 November 2002 and its impact on German and European company law,* in *GLJ,* 2002; Kersting/Schindler, *The ECJ's Inspire Art decision of 30 September and its effects on practice,* in *GLJ,* 2003, 1277; Lombardo, *Conflict of law rules in*

national court to register a cross-border transaction (merger, conversion), also on the basis of national regulations treating national and international operations differently, violates the basic principles on freedom of establishment laid down by Art. 49 TFEU.

As a consequence, after these cases, the CJEU allows companies to move their registered offices provided that they comply with the conditions for incorporation in the state of destination. In other words, it allows companies to change their place of incorporation, and all this while these firms keep their real seat (i.e. operating branch) in another country.

Of course fully "artificial" schemes should be forbidden. This has, however, more to do with tax law issues (since the applicable taxation – pursuant to EU tax law – is the one of the country where the company actually operates, it is

---

company law after Überseering: *An economic and comparative analysis of the allocation of policy competence in the European Union*, in EBOR, 2003, 301; Wymeersch, *The transfer of the company seat in European company law*, in CMLR, 2003, 661; De Kluiver, *Inspiring a new European company law*, in ECFR, 2004, 121; Ebke, *The European conflict-of-corporate-laws revolutions: Überseering, Inspire Art and beyond*, in EBLR, 2005, 9; Klinke, *European company law and the ECJ: the Court's judgments in the years 2001 to 2004*, in ECFR, 2005, 270; Kirchner/Painter/Kaal, *Regulatory competition in EU corporate law after Inspire Art: unbundling Delaware's product for Europe*, in ECFR, 2005, 159; Schön, *The mobility of compromise in Europe and the organizational freedom of company founders*, in ECFR, 2006, 122 ; Becht/Enriques/Korom, *Centros and the cost of branching*, in J. corp. l. stud., 2009, 171; (mainly with regard to the others) by Schlindler, *Cross-border mergers in Europe. Company law is catching up! – Commentary on the ECJ's decision in Sevic Systems AG*, in ECFR, 2006, 109; Vossestein, *Companies' freedom of establishment after Sevic*, in ECL, 2007, 177; Id., *Cross border transfer of seat and conversion of companies under the EC Treaty provisions on freedom of establishment. Some considerations on the Court of Justice's Cartesio judgment*, in ECL, 2009, 115; Siems, *Sevic: beyond cross border mergers*, in EBOR 2007, 307; Becht/Mayer/Wagner, *Where do firms incorporate? Deregulation and the cost of entry*, 2007, at ssrn.com; Lombardo, *Regulatory competition in company law in the European Union after Cartesio, 2009*, in EBOR, 627; Id., *Regulatory competition in European Company Law. Where do we stand twenty years after Centros?* 2019, at ecgi.com; Biermeyer, *Shaping the space of cross-border conversions in the EU. Between right and autonomy: VALE Építési Kft*, in CMLR, 2013, 571; Van Eck/Roelofs, *Vale: increasing corporate mobility from outbound to inbound crossborder conversion?*, in ECL, 2012, 319; Szydło, *Cross-border conversion of companies under freedom of establishment: Polbud and beyond*, in CMLR, 2018, 1549; Soegaard, *Cross-border transfer and change of lex societatis after Polbud, C-106/16: old companies do not die … they simply fade away to another country*, in ECL, 2018, 21; Fabris, *European companies' 'mutilated freedom'. From the freedom of establishment to the right of cross-border conversion*, in ECL, 2019, 106; Gerner-Beuerle/Mucciarelli/Schuster/Siems, *The illusion of motion: corporate (im)mobility and the failed promise of Centros*, in EBOR, 2019, 425; Sibony, *Centros and the internal market*, 2020, at ecgi.org; Fillers, *Free movement of companies after the Polbud case*, in EBOR, 2020, 571.

often the branch that is set up as a fake entity in order to pay lower taxes in the state of the location of the operative office). The Court – in the leading case "Cadbury-Schweppes" of 2006 (C-196/04) – therefore established that, while it is perfectly legitimate for a company to include tax considerations in the choice of domicile for its branch, there should be limitations on "wholly artificial arrangements". The presence of the branch must therefore be genuine (with staff, facilities and other substance[25]).

This jurisprudence is however less interesting for company law, since "forum shopping" for company law purposes usually regards the choice of the seat of the company (which brings the application of a one national law instead of another) and not the choice of the seat of the branch.

From this point of view – as it has been observed – company law (and the interpretation of the CJEU) accepts companies entirely on a pro forma basis where the choice of the nation domicile is motivated entirely by differences in national company laws (like minimum capital requirements), while tax law accepts the choice of registered offices on the basis of tax law but it does not accept companies purely on a pro forma basis[26].

In any case, the rush to incorporate or relocate to other jurisdictions has slowed down over the years, and that is for a series of reasons.

Since 2004 the number of "foreign" companies incorporated in the UK (the most coveted jurisdiction at the time) grew from 4.400 to 28.000 per year. Despite this – as it has been noted – the latter "has been a passing fad; the costs and bureaucratic burdens drew attention to this practice. Language's barriers, the translation and certification costs, the expenses of legal advice and the duplication of accounting obligations were disincentives in some countries". Although around 48.000 companies with German management were incorporated in England between 2004 and 2011, more than 70% had been dissolved or gone into bankruptcy by 2012[27]. The registered number of private companies with a branch in Germany (one of the countries with the higher number of "expat

---

25 See Werklauff, *Pro forma registration of companies: why a brass plate in the host country is enough in some respects, but not in others*, in *ECL*, 2010, 25; see also Gelter/Vicente, *Abuse of companies through choice of incorporation*, 2019, at *ecgi.org*; and Andenas/Wooldridge, *European*, 95, with particular reference to the Dutch legislation.
26 See Werklauff, *Pro forma*, 29.
27 Numbers and text are taken from Gorriz, *EU*, 5.

firms", also given its restrictive companies act) decreased to less than 8.000 in 2017[28].

In addition, a series of legal reforms in the Member States rapidly took place, seeking – for the purpose of "defensive regulatory competition" – to make legislative environments more attractive and discourage the flow to other States perceived as more beneficial (consider, for instance, the reduction of the minimum legal capital required to set up a company to just 1 euro for some types of private firms in many States, as we shall see later on).

New waves of incorporation (driven by regulatory competition) cannot however be excluded and are even expected (the Netherlands, for instance, seems to be currently perceived as a particularly market friendly jurisdiction; it has also been on top of the list for the so called "Brexit companies", which relocated from the UK after the 2016 referendum voted to leave the EU[29]).

8. Towards "soft" harmonization? Recommendations, "Action Plans" and the "European Model Company Act"

In 2003, the Commission – at a stage, as we have seen, when the process of strong harmonization was slowing down – adopted a first "Action Plan" on company law. The scope for the proposal was to foster further "substantive" harmonization for the upcoming years[30].

---

28 See Mucha, *The spectre of letterbox companies: an empirical analysis of the bankruptcy ratio of private limited companies operating in Germany in years 2004 – 2017*, in *ECL*, 2019, 59; Gelter, *Centros*, 18 ff.

29 According to statistics, together with Germany: see Tidey, *Brexit: Number of companies relocating to the Netherlands "is accelerating"*, in *euronews.com*, 19 February, 2020, and Biermeyer/Meyer, *The use of corporate mobility instruments and Brexit: an empirical analysis*, in *ECL*, 2020, 15.

30 See COM(2003) 284 final. The plan is entitled *"Modernising company law and enhancing corporate governance in the European Union – A plan to move forward"* and dated 21 May, 2003. Basically the aim of the plan was to reduce the bureaucratic burdens for the companies and simplify the content of the laws. The Commission deemed it essential to encourage the use of telematic technologies. An enhanced protection of shareholders and creditors was also suggested, by providing more transparency and better information on the companies' activities. Finally cross border mobility and the promotion of intra-European international operations within the Union was considered essential. The gradual slowdown of the harmonization process is well described i. e. by Wouters, *European company law. Quo vadis?*, in *CMLR*, 2000, 257; Baums, *European company law beyond the 2003 Action Plan*, in *EBOR*, 2007, 143; Armour/Ringe, *European corporate law 1999 – 2010: reinaissance and crisis*, in *CMLR*, 2011, 125.

Apart from the content (to which we will return), it is important to note the main guidelines set forth: the concept of "substantive" harmonization (or "convergence"), which can be reached by introducing "soft principles" and not necessary by adopting directives with a strict aim to be reached (or even more rigid regulations).

That concept was confirmed in a subsequent "Action Plan" of 2012[31].

The draft action plans had been preceded by expert working groups recruited by the Commission to prepare reports and provide suggestions in the field of company law (and also by publication of a Commission's "green paper" in 2011 on the EU corporate governance framework[32]).

Other legislative techniques have been introduced by the EU, like the "weak" harmonization instrument. Directives have begun to offer Member States the option to opt out of some provisions or core provisions have started to become vaguer and require definition by national regulators so that Member States can retain the right to legislate around the harmonized framework (this can be seen at length in the "Takeover Directive")[33].

As it has been noted, very important is also the evocation of the principle of subsidiarity laid down in Art 5 TEU and the "closely related view that flexibility is necessary because there is no one size that may fit all, that is, harmonization should not be total, but only undertaken where necessary due to a proven inca-

---

31 See COM(2012) 740 final. The plan is called *"European company law and corporate governance – a modern legal framework for more engaged shareholders and sustainable companies"* and focused mainly on transparency and the initiatives to be taken in order to increase the engagement of shareholders and the control on management. See in particular the collection of essays edited by Geens/Hopt, *The European company law Action Plan 2003 revisited. Reassessment of the 2003 priorities of the European Commission*, Leuven University Press, 2009; Roth/Kindler, *The spirit of corporate law. Core principles of corporate law in continental Europe*, CH Beck, 2013, 22.
32 In 1996 the Commission appointed a working group to write a report on the *"Simpler legislation for the Internal Market initiative (SLIM)"*; on that report see for instance Wymeersch, *Company*, 7 f.; in 2010 the Commission established – as we have already seen – a *Reflection group on the future of EU company law* to provide it with a report that could guide it on future initiatives; the *Report* was delivered in 2011; on it see extensively Hansen, *The Report*; in 2016, another group of experts presented *A proposal for reforming group law in the European Union – Comparative observations on the way forward* (available on *ssrn.com*). The "green paper" of 2011 [COM(2011) 164 final] is commented by Van der Elst/Vermeulen, *Corporate governance 2.0: Assessing the corporate Governance Green Paper of the European Commission*, in ECL, 2011, 165.
33 See in particular Hertig/McCahery, *Optional rather than mandatory EU company law: framework and specific proposals*, in ECFR, 2006, 341; Bartman, *The impact of EU law making on national company law*, in ECL, 2008, 271; Humphery/Jenner, *The desirability of 'weak' form legal harmonization: perspectives from statutory interpretation and legal coherence*, in GLJ, 2012, 808.

pacity among Member States to respond adequately to serious problems of a Union dimension and only upon prior consultation with Member States' authorities and the public. What is recommended is focused harmonization and not harmonization for its own sake"[34].

The change of direction of EU company law is also highlighted by the use of the "recommendation" instrument. In 2004 the Commission published the Recommendation 2004/913/EC on the payment of directors of listed companies (added to by Recommendation 2009/385/EC)[35]; in 2005 it issued the Recommendation 2005/162/EC on the role of independent directors again in listed companies[36]; in 2014 it enacted a Recommendation on the quality of governance reporting[37].

EU company law appears thus shifting from a regime of "directives" to a – more flexible – regime of principles. This leaves any single State free to choose its own rules, according to the principles set forth by the Commission.

So, what is EU company law at present?

We may say – with some degree of approximation – that EU company law at present is a set of (i) rules contained in the directives, that have to be implemented in the single Member States, or in more limited cases in specific regulations; (ii) proposals of principles from EU soft legislation (recommendations, action

---

34 See Hensen, *The Report*, 5, and Grundmann, *The structure of European company law from crisis to boom*, in *EBOR*, 2004, 601.

35 Shareholders should be provided with a clear and comprehensive overview of the company's remuneration policy. This disclosure would enable shareholders to assess a company's approach to remuneration and strengthen a company's accountability to shareholders in order to increase accountability, the remuneration policy should be submitted to the annual general meeting for a vote. The vote at that meeting could be advisory, so that the rights of the relevant bodies responsible for directors' remuneration would not be altered.

36 The Recommendation notes that the presence of independent representatives on the board, that can challenge management decisions, is widely considered as a means of protecting the interests of shareholders and other stakeholders. In order to ensure that management is subject to effective and sufficiently independent supervision, the board should comprise a sufficient number of committed non-executive or supervisory directors, who play no role in the management of the company or its group and who are independent in that they are free from any material conflicts of interest. The supervisory role is commonly perceived as crucial in three areas, where the potential for conflict of interest of management is particularly high: nomination of directors, remuneration of directors, and auditing.

37 The Recommendation advises listed companies on the writing and disclosure of corporate governance reporting. They must provide detailed and specific explanations, in an easily understandable way (especially when the company is making an exception to a code). National authorities should monitor compliance with reporting' duties.

plans, others); (iii) trends in CJEU jurisprudence; (iv) interpretative principles from scholars and groups of interest.

From the latter standpoint two important facts have to be underlined. On the one hand, legal doctrine in the field of EU company law – and comparative law – is significantly growing in importance. Scholars set out their positions in books and law reviews intended for a supranational audience on a more frequent basis (like the "European Company Law Journal", the "European Company and Financial Law Review", etc.).

On the other hand, interest groups have begun to advance proposals or even "models". The most important example of a private – i.e. not from EU political bodies – proposal is the "European Model Company Act" ("EMCA") published in 2017[38]. The EMCA is a "model" for possible legislation which could be put into force by the single Member States, referring both to public and private companies.

It recalls the model elaborated in the US (the Model Business Corporation Act or MBCA) that we discussed above. As we have seen, in the US company law is "state law", but each single State can take inspiration from the MBCA.

The idea of the EMCA is similar: the Model is designed as a free-standing general company statute that can be enacted by Member States either substantially in its entirety or by the adoption of selected provisions.

The implementation of the EMCA project is coordinated by the "EMCA Group", which was officially formed at a meeting at Aarhus University, in Denmark, in 2007, at the initiative of some Scandinavian universities: Aarhus University, Stockholm University, University of Copenhagen, University of Oslo, etc.

Currently the EMCA Group has a member for each of the 27 EU States. We shall come back to the EMCA in more detail below, given its great importance.

---

38 See for a general illustration Perakis, *The EMCA: general principles and main content*, in *ECFR*, 2016, 200; see also Baums/Krüger Andersen, *The European Model Company Act project*, in Tison et al. (eds.), *Perspectives in company law and financial regulation. Essays in honour of Eddy Wymeersch*, Cambridge UP, 2009, 5.

9. The foreseeable expansion of the jurisprudence of the CJEU: the "horizontal direct effect" of the principles of free establishment and free movement of capital (*Volkswagen* and *Vivendi* as flagship cases)

Finally, one has to consider the fundamental impact that the CJEU's jurisprudence may progressively have on Member States' company laws.

The Court has already intervened over time in sanctioning domestic provisions not aligned with the principles of the Treaties, and in particular the laws which granted special powers in public companies to the national States or to local governments (by means of the set of judgments on the so called "golden shares": see among others the "Volkswagen" cases of 2007 and 2012: C-112/05 and 95/12) or which prevented foreign firms from acquiring stakes in other companies (see *inter alia* the recent decision on the case "Vivendi" of 2020, C-719/18).

The legal background is provided both by Art. 49 TFEU (on the freedom of establishment, see above § 7) and especially by Art. 56 TFEU, which stipulates that "restrictions on freedom to provide services within the Union shall be prohibited in respect of nationals of Member States who are established in a Member State other than that of the person for whom the services are intended" (that is to say, citizens should be free to offer and provide their services in other Member States also on a temporary basis while remaining in their country of origin, and the same is valid for the solicitation of investment in equity by companies, which should not be impeded to provide easy access to their capital to foreign investors; Art. 56 thus covers also measures that may impede "capital" movements; see also Art. 63).

We shall come back on the Courts' jurisprudence below in Chapter 4, § 4 and 5 (speaking more extensively of "golden shares" and the limits to the free circulation of shares)[39].

Especially from the latter point of view (overruling by the Court of national provisions which did not attribute golden powers but nevertheless prevented shareholders from acquiring stakes in foreign companies), the question is cur-

---

39 The Volkswagen case regarded a German law which attributed certain special rights for the Federal State and for the Land of Lower Saxony, among which a provision capping the voting rights of every shareholder at 20%, a provision implementing an 80% majority requirement for important company decisions and the right of the State and of the Land to appoint two members of the company's supervisory board. According to the Court, the combination of these provisions violate the principles of free movement of capital and of free establishment, since they make it substantially less attractive for other EU investors to acquire shares of the company with a view to effectively participating in management decisions or controlling the company.

rently very sensitive and has the potential of becoming one the main topic of EU case law in the next years.

The Court has developed its jurisprudence especially in the cases "Commission v. Italy [pharmacies]" (C-531/06, decided in 2009), "Commission v. France [bio-medical laboratories]" (C-89/09, decided in 2010), "Tipou v. Tipou" (81/09, decided in 2010) and – more recently – "Vivendi v. AGCM" (C-719/18, quoted above). In each of them, single Member States' laws de facto limited the possibility for investors (national and foreign) to acquire shares into domestic companies.

In the first case, companies distributing medical products were not permitted by Italian law to acquire shares in companies operating pharmacies. In the second case, biologists were not allowed by French law to acquire shares in companies operating biomedical analysis laboratories. In the third case, investors willing to acquire more than a certain shareholding in private and television companies were exposed by Greek legislation to the risk of receiving fines jointly and severally with the company. In the last case, companies with a significant turnover in the telecommunication and television sectors were not permitted by Italian legislation to acquire more than 10% of the share capital in television companies[40].

In all four cases the Court judged the domestic laws to be illegitimate, having the effect of preventing or deterring investors from making cross-border investments in companies and restricting the freedom of establishment and the free movement of capital[41].

The Court actually extended the reasoning already followed in other cases regarding golden shares. In these new cases, however, the overruled national provisions did not favor the position of a Member State in the relevant companies (by giving to that State extra – golden – powers), but created legal mechanisms in sector-specific legislation in order to regulate definite markets, with the effect of advantaging some companies and disfavoring others and, more generally, perspective investors.

Golden shares case are simpler to handle: they confer to States or public authorities special rights, which – according to the Court's jurisprudence – are deemed legitimate only as long as they strictly regard companies operating in

---

40 The first three cases are commented on by i.e. Van Bekkum, *Cross border investments in undertakings and the future of EU company law*, in *EBLR*, 2014, 811.

41 The statement according to which the acquisition of stakes in a company by an EU investor is a form of capital movement is contained, e.g. in the EU *Commission's Communication on certain legal aspects concerning intra-EU investment*, 1997 O.J. (C 220), 15.

the area of "public" or "strategic" national services and are proportionate to the effect (see below Chapter 4, § 4).

On the opposite, national "sector specific" provisions are addressed to private companies and have the practical effect of disfavoring some of them. The possibility of attacking these provisions depends thus also on the right of private parties to take "directly" advantage from rules contained in the Treaties, like the principle of the free movement of capital (so called "horizontal effect" of EU laws).

The "Vivendi" case is a good example.

In 2016, the French company Vivendi s.a. – at the top of a group operating in the media sector and in the creation and distribution of audio-visual content – initiated a hostile campaign to acquire shares in Mediaset Italia s.p.a. – an Italian company operating in the same sector, belonging to the Fininvest Group – by acquiring 28,8% of the share capital, equal to 29,94% of voting rights.

Mediaset then reported Vivendi to the Italian Communications Authority ("AGCom"), accusing it of having violated Italian law which prohibits a company from making, either directly or indirectly, more than 20% of the total revenues of the "integrated communications" sector in order to safeguard the pluralism of information. This percentage is reduced to 10% if the company simultaneously makes more than 40% of the total revenues of the electronic communications sector in Italy. This happened in the case of Vivendi, which already occupied an important position in the Italian electronic communications sector, by virtue of its control over the telephone company Telecom Italia s.p.a.

In 2017, AGCom ascertained that Vivendi, having acquired the above mentioned shareholding in Mediaset, had violated Italian law and ordered it to cease such violation. While complying with the AGCom's order, by transferring ownership of its share in Mediaset of 19,19%, Vivendi challenged AGCom's decision before the CJEU.

The Court held that the various provisions of Italian law limiting the option for companies from other Member States to enter the Italian media sector affected the freedoms of establishment and movement. The protection of pluralism of information constitutes an overriding reason of general interest, whose protection may justify, in the abstract, the adoption of national measures restricting freedom of establishment. However, in addition to being capable of achieving it, this national legislation must be "proportionate" to the objective of protecting pluralism of information, that is to say it must not go beyond what is necessary to reach it. In the actual case, the Court found Italian law disproportionate and needlessly disfavoring a foreign investor and ruled in favor of Vivendi.

Among scholars, these Court's rulings have been greeted with great interest, above all for their potential expansion to other areas of domestic company laws.

This jurisprudence directly tackles national legislations and has its foundation mainly on the principles of free movement of services and capitals (Arts. 56, 63 TFEU), which are considered to be capable of direct effect not only where one of the parties is the state ("vertical direct effect") but also where there are only private parties involved ("horizontal direct effect")[42]. According to the Court, national provisions which may have the effect of preventing or deterring investors from making cross-border investments in companies can be judged "restrictive" of the free movement of services and capitals and considered against the Treaties.

As a consequence, the question of "which" national company law provisions may have that "restrictive" effect acquires great importance (and becomes very sensitive to deal with). The academic debate has begun, showing more or less inclination by scholars towards the extension of the CJEU's standards (applied in "golden shares" and "sector specific" cases) more generally to national company law provisions (like the ones, for instance, on non-proportional voting powers or "special classes" shareholders' rights)[43].

Where this process will lead is uncertain. As it has been observed, "national company laws and practice will be subject to gradual review through the case law, and the ECJ' jurisprudence on the free movement of capital will give new impetus to the harmonization effort in EU legislation. The basic foundation is now laid in the cases discussed above, but the actual impact and speed of this process is another matter"[44].

---

[42] The doctrine of the "horizontal direct effect" has been developed by the CJEU and affirms that individuals can rely on the direct effect of provisions in the treaties, which confer individual rights, in order to make claims against other private individuals before national courts or the CJEU (see in particular the case "Defrenna", C-43/75). More recently, see above all the case "Viking" (C-438/05); on the horizontal effect of Art. 56 TFEU see *inter alia* Chalmers/Davies/Monti, *European*, 747

[43] Cf. especially Van Bekkum, *Golden shares and European company law: the implications of Volkswagen*, in *ECL*, 2008, 6; Ringe, *Domestic company law and free movement of capital: nothing escapes the European Court?*, at ssrn.com, 2008; Artés, *Advancing harmonization: should the ECJ apply golden shares' standards to national company law?*, in *EBLR*, 2009, 457; for more prudent views see e. g. Gerner-Beuerle, *Shareholders between the market and the state. The VW law and other interventions in the market economy*, in *CMLR*, 2012, 97; Szabados, *Recent golden share cases in the jurisprudence of the court of justice of the European Union*, in *GLJ*, 2015, 1099; also Andenas/Gütt/Pannier, *Free movement of capital and national company law*, in *EBLR*, 2005, 759. For further analysis and references to literature see below Chapter 4, § 4.

[44] Cf. Andenas/Wooldridge, *European*, 20.

10. "Transnational" corporate types (with different fates): the "Societas Europea", the "Societas Privata Europea" and the "Societas Unius Personae"

As debate continued over the years on the superiority of competition over harmonization, the European Council passed Regulation 2001/2157 and Directive 2001/86/EC on the statute of the Societas Europea (SE).

This model, as a supranational corporate type, goes beyond (at least to a certain extent) the debate on federalism versus nationalism. The law on the SE is the same in all countries since it was enacted as a regulation.

The practical advantage of the SE is that if a company intends to relocate to another EU country, it will be governed by rules that are the same in all Member States. It is also easier to merge two companies if both have the same SE structure.

Moreover, if the SE operates in a business that require public monitoring (like banking or insurance), the company is only answerable to one supervisory authority (in the Member State where it is registered) rather than several (in the different Member States where the company has subsidiaries), thus assuring considerable annual savings.

However, despite Regulation 2157/2001, the law applicable to an SE is not completely identical in all countries. Since the regulation leaves some gaps in many areas, they have to be filled by the single national company laws.

The SE has had relative success. As of Autumn 2020, more than 3.300 registrations were reported, including nine members (18%) of the "Euro Stoxx 50 stock" market index of leading Eurozone companies[45]. We shall come back to the regulation on the SE at a later stage (see Chapter 14).

On the other hand, the "European Private Company" ("Societas Privata Europea" or "SPE"), whose aim was to replicate the success of the SE for private companies, has not fared so well. A draft of the Regulation was presented in 2008, but it was finally withdrawn in 2014 for reasons that we shall see later on (see Chapter 14).

The same fate was suffered by the directive proposal on single-member private limited liability companies (2014/0120(COD)). It should have amended the Twelfth Directive by providing a more simplified company template, the "Societas Unius Personae" or "SUP". The European Commission published its legislative draft on SUPs in 2014. Some of the rules were however considered problem-

---

45 They are Airbus, Allianz, BASF, E.ON, Fresenius, LVMH Moët Hennessy Louis Vuitton, SAP, Schneider Electric and Unibail-Rodamco.

atic and that proposal was also withdrawn in 2018. For further details see again below Chapter 14.

2 Formation and share capital

Summary:
1. The reasons for relatively uniform national laws. The main fundamental arguments not addressed by the directives (and the question of contractual freedom: "mandatory" and "default" rules)
2. Formation of the company: instrument of incorporation and statutes
3. Nullity of the company
4. Single-member company
5. Share capital. From "minimum" to "adequate" capital?
6. The assessment of capital in kind: evaluation by experts
7. Rules on capital protection. (a) Distributions
8. (b) Share buy-backs
9. (c) Financial assistance
10. (d) Cross-shareholdings
11. (e) Relevant losses and compulsory recapitalization (or liquidation)
12. The reduction of capital in excess

1. The reasons for relatively uniform national laws. The main fundamental arguments not addressed by the directives (and the question of contractual freedom: "mandatory" and "default" rules)

(I) A solid result of harmonization has been reached over time on the rules governing the first phase of life of public companies: the establishment and provision of share capital.

This relatively consistent level of convergence is due to a series of interrelated reasons. The directives were adopted at a stage (the end of the 1960s) where European sentiment was strong. Moreover, the need for harmonization in the field embraced by the directives was particularly felt. Finally, the aspects regulated did not touch sensitive nerves at a political level, nor did they face insurmountable habits rooted in the different legal traditions[1].

Let us take the example of the public disclosure of the incorporation of a company. It is difficult to imagine dissenting opinions on this type of matter these days: public disclosures were organized at local commercial registries, in

---

1 Wymeersch, *Company*, 28.

https://doi.org/10.1515/9783110725025-004

some countries the information was centralized, filing procedures were different, in some jurisdiction almost no supervision was exercised, while in others a court had to authenticate the documents, etc.[2].

So, as a matter of fact, the First and Second Directives were easily adopted and similarly implemented in the various Member States.

(II) Before examining the most important features of these directives (and their application in the domestic legislations), we should note that a fundamental aspect of company law has never been addressed by the directives: the concept of the "interest" of the company (i.e.: in whose interests the company is run).

The directives consider the other topic of the corporate "objects" (see Art. 11 First Directive and Art. 2 Second Directive); the two concepts stand however obviously on very different levels. The "objects" of the company means the activity (i.e. business sector) in which the company is involved, while the "interest" of the company identifies the interests that directors have to consider while managing the corporate assets: of sole shareholders, of shareholders and creditors, of shareholders, creditors, employees, future investors, etc.[3].

Most Member States do not specify in their laws the concept of the interest of the company, and thus give the option of interpreting it as the interest of the shareholders for maximum profit, as reflected by maximizing the value of their shares, as long as specific laws do not constrain it to consider the interests of other stakeholders, like creditors or employees.

This is the "shareholders' primacy" model (or "shareholders' wealth maximization" model") and it is actually the simplest one, basically aligned with the liberal economic theory (which considers that companies should focus on shareholders' interests only and not consider any social goals unless otherwise set forth by the law: according to the statement of a famous economist, "there is

---

2 Wymeersch, *Company*, 28.
3 This and related themes have been analyzed especially by Keay, *Shareholder primacy in corporate law: can it survive? Should it survive?* in *ECFR*, 2010, 369 and Skog, *The importance of profit in company law – a comment from a Swedish perspective*, in *ECFR*, 2015, 563 (further references in both essays). Usually the shareholders' primacy is said to be the consequence of the fact that the firm should be run for the benefit of its residual claimants, the shareholders (at least as long as the firm is solvent); since the shareholders have the greatest stake in the outcome of the company (if it is well managed, they receive dividends and increased share values), they have also the highest incentive to control managers. Moreover, directors will have a clearer objective in their management of the company – and will be more accountable – if they are asked to focus only on the interest of the shareholders instead of the interests of a multitude of different stakeholders. The shareholders' primacy models is often therefore considered to bring optimal results in terms of overall efficiency.

one and only one social responsibility of the company: to use its resources and engage in activities designed to increase its profits so long as it stays within the rules of the game").

Some domestic laws take the opposite view and require directors to ponder also other stakeholders' interests: they require managers, for instance, to act "in the interest of the company, taking into account the long-term interests of shareholders and concerning the interests of other stakeholders relevant to the sustainability of the company, such as their employees, clients and creditors" (this model is called "stakeholderism")[4].

The differences are thus very relevant, between Member States that either require (or permit) directors to consider the interests of other stakeholders besides the shareholders and States that simply do not provide for that possibility.

We shall come back on these themes in Chapter 9, § 1 (discussing the topic of directors' duties).

(III) Another question left open by the directives is whether the company may introduce provisions that leave out the "profit" purpose in its instrument of incorporation. Even if it seems quite natural that companies must operate to make a profit, this goal is not actually mandatory in all Member States.

Most national laws do not allow companies to be run wholly or partly for another purpose besides profit (unless they incorporate as other types of companies such as "cooperative" companies). Some, however, either introduce special forms of limited liability companies that can constrain their purpose to make profits (or limit the distribution of profits, known as "benefit companies") or simply allow any company to run its business wholly or partly for another purpose, only requiring the specification of how any profits will be used in the articles of association[5].

In any case, these models should be regarded as exceptions: the standard – also according to EU directives and Member States' laws – is that companies are managed essentially for profit.

(IV) Another issue is not considered by the EU legislation, but plays an important role at a general level. It concerns the "space of freedom" – more or less restricted – that shareholders enjoy when they want to introduce rules into the

---

4 See Art. 64 Por-CC (from which the quote is taken). See also, e. g., Sect. 70 A-PuCA, which stipulates that the board of directors is responsible for managing the company in the way required by the well-being of the firm, taking into account the interests of shareholders and employees, as well as the public interest.

5 This is respectively the case in Italy, which has introduced in 2016 § 376 – 384 of law 208/2015 ("benefit companies" maintain the profit purpose, but they add a further one, that is to pursue social objectives) and Sweden: see Chap. 3, Sect. 3, Sw-CA.

company charter that deviate from the provisions of their domestic company law (this has also to do with harmonization, since States allowing a great possibility of deviation may provide shareholders with the faculty of introducing rules which risk being incoherent with the principles of the directives).

In this respect, academics usually draw a line between "mandatory rules" (which cannot be changed by shareholders) and "default rules" (that, on the contrary, can be negotiated and that are to be considered as standard clauses, to be amended in order to meet specific needs)[6].

However, also if a default rule regime is deemed to have been put in place, to which extent can these rules be modified?

Some companies acts, like the German one, have expressly adopted a provision stating that "the articles of association can deviate from the provisions of the law only if it is expressly permitted" (Sect. 23 Ge-PuCA). That means that deviations must result from the wording of the law, by means of a clear statement (of course interpretation plays an important role). Contractual freedom is thus rather constrained[7].

On the contrary, other Member States have chosen to follow a path of basic "deregulation". A typical example is the one of Finland, perhaps the most "Americanized" – according to itself – of the EU Member States[8]. With the new companies act of 2006 – as noted by scholars – "on one hand, the number of mandatory rules and formalities was decreased, and, on the other, the general principles of company law were given more weight. In practice, this meant that the flexibility (i.e., freedom of contract) of the law was increased to promote efficiency"[9].

---

6 Mandatory rules striving to "protect" people outside – or inside – the contract are normally driven by externality concerns, i.e. the need to avoid indirect costs to individuals (in company law, other than majority shareholders): see for all Wymeersch, *Comparative study of the company types in selected EU States*, in *ECFR*, 2009, 71.

7 Also Art. 2.25 Du-CC reads as follows: "it is only possible to derogate from the statutory provisions of the present Book (Book 2) as far as the law allows a derogation"; notwithstanding, "analysing the substantive provisions relating to the [public] and the [private company], many of these allow the promoter to derogate"; "in general Dutch law contains a considerable number of default provisions" (so Wymeersch, *Comparative*, 92).

8 The debate on contractual freedom in corporate law has been particularly vivid in the US literature over the years, with reference to opting out of the rules both at the initial stage of the establishment of the company and by later charter amendment. The approach of the American academics is basically liberal.

9 See Pönkä, *The convergence of law: the Finnish Limited Liability Companies Act as an example of the so-called "Americanisation" of European company law*, 2016, at *https://helda.helsinki.fi*; on the Finnish model, see also Airaiksinen, *The Delaware of Europe? – financial instruments in the new Finnish Companies Act*, in Krüger/Sörensen (eds.), *Company law and finance*, Karnov

Usually the deregulation of company law is supported by a belief in the sustainability of informal institutions in society; if – as it has been observed – "these institutions are strong and reliable, laws (i.e. formal institutions) do not have to be as defensive (casuistic and mandatory) as in societies where informal institutions are weak and unreliable"[10] (this is actually true up to a certain point, as is demonstrated by the same German example, since the institutions of this State have a reputation for being reliable).

The question of which rules are mandatory remains open to debate to a great extent, also in more permissive States. It is actually a rather theoretical (and fascinating) one and the answer ultimately depends on the identification of the basic principles of each company law regime: it generally has to be decided on a case-by-case basis[11].

It is however obviously different to move from a legislation that expressly states that all rules all mandatory, unless otherwise stated to one that recognizes on the contrary that freedom of contract should be at the core of company law. In any case, the fundamental principles set forth by the directives remain in the background, also in view of the "horizontal" effect of the latter (see Chapter 1, § 9)

Group, 2008, 311; Airaiksinen/Berglund, *Corporate governance in Finland*, in Lekvall (ed.), *The Nordic corporate governance model*, 2014, at *https://scholarship.law.columbia.edu/faculty scholarship*, 168.

10 See Pönkä, *The convergence*, 7. Spanish law has also traditionally approached the issue with a rather permissive attitude: pursuant to Art. 28 Sp-CA (entitled "contractual freedom"), "the instrument of incorporation and the articles of association may include all the agreements and conditions that the founding shareholders deem appropriate to establish, provided that they do not oppose the laws or contradict the principles of the chosen company type". Another example of a domestic law explicitly addressing the issue is Art. 3.4 H-CA, according to which "the members and the founders of a legal person shall not derogate from the provisions of this Act if the derogation a) is prohibited by this Act; or b) manifestly violates the rights of the creditors, employees or a minority of members of the legal person, or prevents the effective supervision of the lawful operation of legal persons" (see Veress, *Report from Hungary: is it possible to issue bearer shares in Hungary? Remarks on mandatory and default rules in Hungarian company law*, in *ECL*, 2019, 97, who reports that, notwithstanding such a rule, "determining the set of mandatory company law rules based on section 3:4 of the C[A] constitutes a serious professional challenge"); for Slovak law, see Patakyová/Grambličková, *Mandatory and default regulation in Slovak commercial law*, 2020, at *https://blr.flaw.uniba.sk*.

11 See Wymeersch, *Comparative*, 88, noting that one has to infer the mandatory character mostly from the formulation or the nature of the provision itself (or, more generally, from general principles or company-type principles).

2. Formation of the company: instrument of incorporation and statutes

The basic rules set forth in the First and Second Directive require the company's statutes to be drafted, shares to be paid up, the company to be registered and the cases of nullity of the company to be strictly curbed.

(I) Beginning with the shareholders, the Directives contain no limitations[12], even if some domestic laws impose a minimum number of members. That prerequisite reflects historical traditions, with seven being a frequent number, at least in the past (this figure originated from the UK 1846 Companies Act)[13]. The trend in Europe is however clearly oriented towards the elimination of any minimum number of shareholders. The EMCA Group also considers that there is no convincing reason to restrict the number of shareholders (see the comment to Sect. 2.02).

If the company is formed by a sole shareholder, specific rules apply (so called "single-member company": see below § 4).

(II) The First Directive requires the company to be set up by means of an "instrument of incorporation" (see Art. 4 Directive 2017/1132/EU; it is also called the "memorandum of association" or the "company charter"). The instrument of incorporation has to be notarized (pursuant to the legislation of many countries); however that feature is not mandatory according to the Directive.

Some jurisdictions provide the option of a set up by means of an initial public offering or an establishment in subsequent phases (instead of a document signed at the same time by all the constituent members).

The minimum terms that have to be indicated in the instrument are: type, name, objects of the company; amount of subscribed legal capital (which cannot be less than € 25.000), appointment of the management and the supervisory bodies and allocation of their powers; duration, except where this is indefinite (see Art. 3, 45 Directive 2017/1132/EU; see also Sect. 2.03 EMCA).

The fact that the amount of the legal capital has to be indicated in the instrument has an important consequence in terms of the distribution of powers between shareholders and managers and the actual functioning of the company.

---

12 Some Member States have however set forth some restrictions: pursuant to Art. 301 Pol-CC a private company cannot be the sole shareholder of a public company (at the stage of its incorporation).

13 For example under Portuguese law five persons are required; the French civil code followed the UK model but reduced the minimum number of shareholders for public companies from seven to two in 2015 (see Art. 7 Por-CC; Art. 220-1 Fr-CC); in Belgium the requirement of a minimum of two shareholders was only eliminated recently by the new B-CA in 2019.

Since the amount of the legal capital is fixed in the company's charter, the shareholders have the right to change it (on the contrary, in the US, the board of directors is normally in charge of deciding on capital increases and this makes it much easier to raise money from existing and new shareholders).

The power to issue new shares – and thus modify the share capital – may however be delegated to a certain extent by the shareholders to the directors, rendering the transaction more flexible (see below Chapter 5, § 1).

Other elements – if not indicated in the instrument of incorporation – have to be inserted in a separate document, called the "statutes" (or "articles of association" or "by-laws"), including: the nominal value of subscribed shares (or the number of subscribed shares without stating the nominal value, where said shares may be issued under the national law); the special conditions limiting the transfer of shares; whether there are several classes of shares and the rights attached; the rules on the functioning of the company bodies, etc. (see Art. 4 Directive 2017/1132/EU).

Both documents (instrument of incorporation and statutes) have to be published in the companies register, as key information for shareholders and third parties (they must be made publicly available also electronically)[14]. Matters which are not included in the published documents cannot be enforced against the company or its shareholders. At the same time, these documents may be relied on by the company against third parties after they have been disclosed (before disclosure has taken place, the company may however prove that the third parties had knowledge thereof).

(III) The disclosure is made at the companies register of the place where the company has its registered office. If the company has established branches in other Member States, the information, translated, has to be filed at the register of those States as well.

As far as information that is compulsory to disclose, that entails, among others, the following documents and details: the instrument of incorporation and the articles of association; any subsequent amendments to those documents; the appointment, termination of office and personal details of the directors and members of the supervisory body; the persons who are authorized to represent the company in dealings with third parties and in legal proceedings; the financial statements for each financial year; any change of the registered office;

---

14 The Directive has also launched the creation of a sort of European common companies register, the "Business Register Interconnection System" (or "BRIS"), originally established by Directive 2012/17/EU. Not all of the Member States are currently connected, and the BRIS is still under construction, but the target is clear.

the winding-up of the company; the appointment of liquidators and their respective powers (Art. 16 Directive 2017/1132/EU).

Companies' letterheads, order forms and websites have to report the information necessary in order to identify the companies register where the company has been filed.

(IV) Shares are to be paid up. At the time the company is incorporated, at not less than 25% of their nominal value[15].

The timing for payment of the balance is different from State to State (the Directive is silent on this point): it must be paid up within some months from the company's registration under some laws, while the decision to call up the balance is left to the directors' discretion in others[16].

If the consideration is "non cash" (contributions "in kind"), the Directive states that the consideration shall be transferred in full within five years (Art. 48). This provision has also been implemented in different ways[17].

The company acquires legal personality (i.e. comes into existence) with registration. Third parties contracting with the company at its formation stage are protected by the provision that persons who acted before the company was registered are jointly and severally liable (Art. 7 Directive 2017/1132/EU).

3. Nullity of the company

One important principle laid down in the First Directive – that was to be further developed by subsequent directives, as we shall see later on – is that the protection of third parties (and shareholders) should be ensured by provisions which restrict to the greatest possible extent the grounds on which obligations entered into in the name of the company are invalid.

The corporate contract and the activity of the company involve several parties. Both the charter and the activity may be affected by irregularities. In such a case, the simple termination of the contract or of its effects – often after a signif-

---

15 The minimum cash consideration has been raised, for instance, to 30% in Romania, 50% in France (see Art. 9 R-CA and Art. 225-3 Fr-CC).

16 Twelve months i.e. pursuant to Sect. 344 Cz-CA and Art. 8 Li-CA. For companies acts that leave the decision up to the directors see i.e. Art. 225-3 Fr-CC, Sect. 77 Ir-CA and Art. 2342 It-CC. Normally simplified procedures aimed at collecting credit from shareholders are laid down by domestic laws.

17 For instance under Art. 21 R-CA half of the contribution has to be provided at the time of the capital subscription and the rest within two years; pursuant to Art. 2342 It-CC contributions in kind have to be totally transferred to the company at the time of the capital subscription.

icant lapse of time – could produce more harm than advantages for the parties affected.

As a consequence, the general rules on the invalidity and ability to terminate contracts – which normally result in the elimination of the effects produced once invalidity has been ordered by the court (both in civil and common law) – are considered inadequate in the field of corporate law.

The First Directive (and lately Directive 2017/1132/EU) stipulate that the invalidity of the contract setting up the company can be ordered only in – very limited – cases of significant irregularities and that that a court always has to rule on the invalidity.

Originally the cases leading to nullification of the company were numerous (see Art. 11 First Directive). Directive 2017/1132/EU has reduced them to six. Nullity may only be ordered on the grounds: (i) that no instrument of incorporation was executed; (ii) that the objects of the company are unlawful or contrary to public policy; (iii) that the instrument of incorporation or the articles of association do not set forth the name of the company, the amount of the individual subscriptions of capital, the total amount of the capital subscribed or the objects of the company; (iv) of failure to comply with provisions of national law concerning the minimum amount of capital to be paid up; (v) of the incapacity of all the founder members; (vi) that the number of founder members is less than two (unless the national law governing the company permits the setup of a sole shareholder public company).

Two other important rules were introduced by the First Directive: on the one hand, the effect of a decision of nullity will be to wind up the company, taking effect from the date of the court's ruling (and not the elimination of the company contract from the beginning); on the other, nullity as such does not affect the validity of any commitments entered into by or with the company, without prejudice to the consequences of the company's being wound up[18].

Of course, the cases of "nullification" of a company that have been decided by a court are rare in the practice. This rule has however been fundamental in both shaping the concept and establishing the model for other provisions, introduced by subsequent directives, which currently limit the option to invalidate company resolutions and acts, above all with reference to important company transactions like mergers, divisions, capital increases, etc. For these operations the principle of stability is crucial and the extensive deviations laid down by

---

18 Moreover, holders of shares in the capital shall remain obliged to pay up the capital that they agreed to subscribe to, but is still unpaid, to the extent that commitments entered into with creditors so require (Art. 12).

these directives – and subsequently by national laws – from the general principles stipulated for the invalidity of "ordinary" contracts has daily impacts in the praxis.

4. Single-member company

The Twelfth Directive (later re-codified by Directive 2009/102/EC) introduced the possibility of setting up a "private" company with a sole member.

That Directive does not consider the "public" company with a sole member, but stipulates that its rules may be applied where Member States allow public companies to be a one-man company[19].

The main features of the single member company – as outlined by the Directive – are the following: the company can be established by a unilateral act; only the company with its assets is liable for the corporate obligations; the fact of the sole ownership (together with the identity of the sole member) must be entered in the companies register; contracts between the sole member and the company as represented by the former must be recorded in minutes or drawn up in writing.

Member States may set forth "penalties" for the failure to disclose or record the necessary information. Moreover, they "are free to lay down rules to cover the risks that single-member companies may present as a consequence of having single members, particularly in order to ensure that the subscribed capital is paid" (Recital 5).

The issue of the risks raised by the presence of a sole shareholder has, however, gradually lost its importance for most national legislations and has been mainly reduced to the requirement of having the agreements between the sole shareholder and the company duly registered.

The relatively indulgent approach taken by the EMCA is significant. On the one hand, the Model sets forth a rule (along the lines of Art. 5 Directive 2009/102/EEC) regarding the agreements of the company with the sole shareholder: pursuant to Sect. 8.26, "save for agreements made on usual terms in the ordinary course of business, agreements entered into between a sole shareholder and a limited liability company are valid only if drafted in a manner that can subse-

---

19 That is also the reason why – as we have seen (above § 2) – some Member States do not permit the establishment of single member public companies. The case of France is significant where it is possible for a single-member to incorporate a non-listed public company, but only if that is a "société par actions simplifies". An ordinary "société anonyme" cannot be set up by a single member (Art. 225-1 Fr-CC provides that the company "is founded by two members or more").

quently be verified" (agreements "on usual terms" mean contracts on arm's length terms).

On the other hand, the EMCA acknowledges that the other rules on formalities – like the ones on the necessity to hold a general meeting with the presence of the sole shareholder – should not apply to companies with only one member (see Sect. 11.03). The underlying idea is that limited liability companies have a robust corporate structure and are subject to forms of external and internal control. The need to sanction the sole shareholder (if he does not respect the rules on the general meeting, give adequate disclosure to the sole ownership, record minutes, etc.) becomes less stringent.

5. Share capital. From "minimum" to "adequate" capital?

(I) Legal capital is the amount necessary to provide the minimal resources to start up the company's activity.

As already seen, the mandatory minimum capital is set by the Directive as € 25.000; however, many laws have set a higher threshold[20]; moreover, shareholders are always free to establish a superior amount in the articles of association.

After a long debate on the function of legal capital in corporate law (fuelled also by the fact that in the US a minimum share capital is not required in most States), the main opinion currently considers that sum of money as the amount deemed compulsory for the company in order "to commence business" (as expressly stated in Art. 45 of the Directive). Therefore the "initial capital" is not actually intended to protect creditors or others, but only to properly start the activity of the company[21].

This sum of money has however to remain at the disposal of the company during its lifetime. If the net assets go significantly below the amount of the share capital fixed in the instrument of incorporation, the directors will have

---

20 37.000 in France, 45.000 in the Netherlands, 50.000 in Germany, Italy and Portugal, 60.000 in Spain, 61.500 in Belgium, etc.

21 See, among others, the overview of Eidenmüller/Grunewald/Noack, *Minimum capital in the system of legal capital*, in Lutter (ed.), *Legal capital in Europe*, De Gruyter, 2006, 17. See also Roth/Kindler, *The spirit*, 36: "the inadequacies of fixed capital in general, and minimum capitalization in particular, are long-known. Thus, this principle is today maintained and justified primarily as an indication or threshold of seriousness and respectability. What is meant is that the founders and the owners of an enterprises share in the entrepreneurial risk by making a significant equity contribution, namely in the amount of the statutory minimum or a greater amount chosen voluntarily, which prevents all too reckless entrepreneurial risks at the costs of the public and which signals to the public trust and responsibility on the part of the founders".

to intervene and basically ask – as we shall see below in § 11 – the shareholders to provide extra-capital in order to cover losses.

Moreover, some corporate transactions – which are considered risky and potentially harmful for the company (i. e. share buy-backs and financial assistance to third parties for the acquisition of company's shares) – may only be executed with the amounts that the company has in excess of the legal capital. The amount of that capital therefore provides a benchmark below which corporate money cannot be used in order to pursue such transactions (see §§ 8, 9).

Profits can also be distributed by the company to shareholders only as long as the legal capital remains intact (see § 7).

Therefore the amount of capital established in the instrument of incorporation is especially meaningful "during" the life of the company, in order to govern a series of transactions which are considered worthy of attention since they could put the sum originally provided for by the shareholders at risk and which the company is expected to release at its termination. Rules on legal capital have thus been put in place with reference both to its "formation" and to its "maintenance".

On the other hand, there is no minimum capital requirement for private companies, which were not considered by the Second Directive (and with regard to that section, by Directive 2017/1132/EU). Many Member States therefore allow private companies to be set up with capital equal to zero (or 1 euro). We shall return to this topic at a later stage when we address the issue of private companies (see Chapter 13, § 2). In this chapter we shall only consider the rules regarding legal capital in public companies.

(II) Above the threshold of € 25.000, public companies are basically free – as noted above – to choose the amount of share capital deemed necessary to commence and continue business and they are thus not required to provide a sum connected to the kind of activity actually performed by the company (which can be risky to a greater or lesser extent).

Therefore, it has been noted – among others, by the EMCA Group – that "minimum capital requirements are arbitrary [since they] do not take into account the riskiness of the business" (see comment on Sect. 2.07).

The concept of a mandatory "minimum" capital is therefore losing importance and new rules tend to consider to be more significant that the company has – instead of "minimal" resources – "adequate" means to run its activity (and a right balance at the level of its debt/equity ratio)[22]. Moreover, the idea

---

[22] There have also been proposals for the implementation of alternative systems, more focused on a strengthened regime of directors' liability and the development of the agreements between

of an "enterprise-specific" minimum capitalization is also taking ground: the amount of capital needed should also consider the business sector in which the company operates.

These new rules on "adequate" capital, however, are not provided for by EU directives (which remain linked to the traditional idea of a "fixed" capital) and have only been introduced on a national basis and to a limited extent, by means of specific provisions often aimed at tackling other particular problems (and not "capital adequacy" as such).

Namely, the idea of adequate capital originated from the need to fight an abusive phenomenon. Often shareholders prefer to provide loans to the company (i.e. "financing") instead of capital (i.e. "equity"), because if the company goes bankrupt they may claim to be treated as creditors and get at least a partial re-payment of the financing provided (all unsecured creditors are paid "pari passu" in the event of bankruptcy). This leads to the "thin capitalization" problem: the share capital of the companies remains low because shareholders provide fi-nancing rather than equity (and ask to sit unfairly "at the same table" as the creditors). As a consequence, in many countries (Austria, Bulgaria, Germany, and others) rules have been conceived aimed at increasing the companies' cap-italization[23].

These provisions stipulate that the loans provided by the shareholders have to be requalified by courts from "debt" into "equity" if the company goes bank-rupt. More precisely, the loans are "postergated" – i.e. legally subordinated –

---

the company and its creditors. On this debate, and the reform initiatives that have been under-taken at the Europen level, see especially Rickford (ed.), *Reforming capital: Report of the inter-disciplinary group on capital maintenance*, in *EBOR*, 2004, 919; Merkt, *Creditor protection and capital maintenance from a German perspective*, in *EBLR*, 2004, 1045; Miola, *Legal capital limited liability companies: the European perspective*, in *ECFR*, 2006, 413; Haaker, *The future of European creditor protection and capital maintenance from a German perspective*, in *GLJ*, 2013, 637; and the various essays contained in Lutter (ed.), *Legal*.

23 The aim of having the capitalization aligned to the real risks borne by the enterprise remains, on the contrary, mostly untreated at normative level. See however (even if with reference to private companies) Art. 5.3 B-CA "the founders shall ensure that the private company, when it is formed, has equity capital which, taking into account other sources of financing, is sufficient in the light of the planned activity"; pursuant to Art. 5.16 B-CA shareholders are liable, in the event of bankrupt-cy pronounced within three years of the company' incorporation, if the initial equity was manifest-ly insufficient to ensure the normal exercise of the planned activity for a period of at least two years. For public companies, Art. 7.3 B-CA requires however that the founders at the stage of in-corporation draft a financial plan (with a minimal time horizon of two years); the document, kept by the notary, must include, among others, an overview of the sources of financing, a project of profits and losses after twelve and twenty-four months, a budget of projected income and expen-diture for a period of at least two years from the date of incorporation, etc.

and paid only after all other creditors' loans have been reimbursed (this is the "postergation of shareholders' loans" rule[24]). Often this rule is followed by a second one which stipulates that any loans reimbursed by the company to the shareholders within a certain time frame before the insolvency declaration have to be returned to the company upon the request of the insolvency receiver (so called "restriction on repayment of shareholders' loans" rule[25]).

In Germany these provisions were originally restricted to loans granted at a crisis stage (excessive debts, illiquidity), but were later amended to embrace any shareholders' loan, regardless of when it had been conceded (the fact that the company is in crisis is thus no longer relevant). Other laws still limit their application to financing in cases of crisis.

We shall return to these national provisions at a later stage (see Chapter 5, § 5, and Chapter 13, § 5). They represent in any case a strong disincentive for shareholders to grant loans and encourage them to provide equity, also taking into consideration the specific activity of the company: in other words, they "stimulate" shareholders to provide "adequate capital" and consequently combat the thin capitalization phenomenon.

(III) Beside the rules on capital "formation", the above-mentioned acknowledgement of a reduction of the importance of legal capital is however strongly disputed by a large part of European scholars for the rules on capital "maintenance", i.e. the laws regulating profit distributions, share buy-backs, financial assistance, etc., during the company lifecycle (we shall examine these provisions below in § 7 ff.).

According to a widespread view, a change in the current rules (at least on capital maintenance) – as laid down by the directives – should not be encouraged since the alternative solutions (like strengthening the directors' liability regime) are perceived to be less efficient or, in the best case, equivalent.

Moreover, it has been predicted – also in a scenario of the gradual weakening of the legal capital system – that the concept will not be easily abandoned: rather "the issue will melt into a different form of deregulation and lead to solutions trying to combine legal capital with other forms of creditor protection"[26].

---

24 See paradigmatically Sect. 39 Ge-InsA.
25 See Sect. 135 Ge-InsA. On these (and other) provisions see Huber/Habersack, *Special rules for shareholders' loans: which consequences would arise for shareholders' loans if the system of capital should be abolished?*, in Lutter (ed.), *Legal*, 308; Verse, *Shareholder loans in corporate insolvency – A new approach to an old problem*, in *GLJ*, 2008, 1109; Schall/ Machunsky, in *Company laws*, 222.
26 See Miola, *Legal*, 486.

6. The assessment of capital in kind: the evaluation by experts

Getting back to the Directives, as said a "minimum" amount of capital has to be provided by the shareholders and that capital has to be "effectively" assessed.

(I) Of course, the best and easiest way to provide "effective" capital is to contribute cash ("cash is king", as the saying goes). Other assets – other than cash – may, however, be contributed.

Those assets must be "capable of economic assessment" (see Art. 46 Directive 2017/1132/EU). The meaning is that these assets should be of actual value for the operations of the company. Therefore, real estate assets, credits, trademarks, etc. are allowed; on the contrary, the undertaking to perform work or supply services is forbidden (which is deemed to be too risky in the medium-long term to be considered effective).

The concept of "assets capable of economic assessment" is rather general and is thus interpreted in slightly different ways in the Member States: the prevailing view holds that contributions in kind must consist of assets that are "accountable in the balance sheet" (their evaluation has to follow the strict principles laid down for the preparation of the financial statements); this opinion is shared also by the jurisprudence, even though opinions sometimes diverge. Contracts, for instance, are normally considered in the category of eligible assets; however, in some jurisdictions it is unclear whether rent and lease agreements can be qualified as valid contributions in kind[27].

(II) Another fundamental rule contained in the directives aims to avoid noncash contributions from being overvalued and requires an independent evaluation to be made by professionals appointed by the court or an administrative body who must write up an "experts' report".

---

27 See on this, i.e. for the German and Polish perspectives, respectively, Schall/Machunsky, in *Company laws*, 227 (noting that it is "enough that the contributed asset bears economic value. It is not necessary either that those assets can be transferred or seized"); and Sójka, *ibidem*, 678 [holding that "the possibility to pay for the shares by contributing prior tenancy or lease agreements by way of transferring them to the company along with the duty to pay rent should be considered doubtful. It seems unlikely that rights under property lease involving the duty to pay rent at market value could be contributed as contributions in kind if the value of the contribution would be determined solely based on the attractiveness of the asset or thing to the company (e. g. the right to lease commercial premises in a very attractive location). The economic value of such a right would not stand to test of the verifiable criterion, as it would be based, in fact, on the subjective opinion of the company. What is more, if the location of the leased property is highly attractive indeed, the attractiveness is typically reflected in the rates of the rent"].

Art. 49 Directive 2017/1132/EU clearly states that "a report on any consideration other than in cash shall be drawn up before the company is incorporated or is authorized to commence business, by one or more independent experts appointed or approved by an administrative or judicial authority"[28]. The experts' report must contain at least "a description of each of the assets comprising the consideration as well as of the methods of valuation".

However, this type of evaluation becomes both complex and costly. That is why – from Directive 2006/68/EC on – EU rules have provided for the possibility of derogation from the requirement of the experts' report (see currently Art. 50 Directive 2017/1132/EU).

This is the case if: (i) the consideration has already been subject to a fair value opinion by an independent expert (at a date not more than six months before the date of the contribution); (ii) the consideration consists of securities or money-market instruments, the value of which is derived from another company's financial statements (of the previous financial year), provided that these financial statements have been subject to an audit by an audit firm; (iii) the consideration consists of securities or money-market instruments traded on a regulated market.

The aim of these rules is well expressed in the Recitals of Directive 2006/68/ EC (see especially no. 3), which set forth that "Member States should be able to permit public limited liability companies to allot shares for consideration other than in cash without requiring them to obtain a special expert valuation in cases in which there is a clear point of reference for the valuation of such consideration"[29].

In any case, the directors must still verify whether the expert's assessment is fair and make a revaluation whenever deemed necessary (this is clearly stated in Art. 50 also for the case of derogation from the report, since the external "point of reference" taken at the basis of the evaluation may have been subject to exceptional circumstances: for instance, the market for the securities contributed may have become illiquid and their value therefore changed).

---

28 Art. 225-8 Fr-CC however stipulates that the experts may also be appointed unanimously by the shareholders (or failing this, by court order at the request of one or more of the shareholders). The initial general meeting has to decide on the valuation of the contributions in kind. If the general meeting refuses to accept the evaluation, the company can come into existence only if the capital is reduced accordingly (that requires again a unanimous decision of all the subscribers).
29 See in particular Van der Elst, *New capital preservation law, Belgian style*, in *ECL*, 2009, 110 and Notari, *The appraisal regime of contributions in kind in the light of amendments to the second EEC directive*, in *ECFR*, 2010, 63.

If an asset that is contributed does not correspond to its fair value, the shareholder who has made that contribution is liable for the difference[30]; if the sum needed is not promptly paid up, the company must reduce its capital.

(III) Finally, in order to avoid shareholders and directors evading the law once the capital has been correctly established (for instance, by having the company buy assets from a shareholder that are overvalued), Art. 52 Directive 2017/1132/EU establishes a further safeguarding mechanism.

Before the expiry of a time limit (which has to be fixed by national law, but cannot be less than two years from the date of the company incorporation), if the company acquires any asset belonging to a shareholder for consideration of not less than 1/10 of the subscribed capital, the acquisition must be subject to an independent experts' assessment and – moreover – to the approval of the general meeting (the rule does not apply to acquisitions made in the normal course of the company's business, or at the instance or under the supervision of an administrative or judicial authority, or to stock exchange transactions). This type of rule has been implemented similarly by almost all Member States[31].

7. Rules on capital protection. (a) Distributions

As we have seen in the previous paragraphs, even if mandatory legal capital is losing importance with regard to some aspects, it remains at the core of the EU legislation, as the yardstick that has to be taken into account for a series of corporate transactions which are considered lawful only if the company has an amount of assets corresponding to the sum of capital fixed in the instrument of incorporation: distributions of dividends, acquisition of own shares, financial assistance. Therefore, rules on capital "maintenance" are still at the centre of EU laws on public companies.

Starting from distributions, dividend payments to shareholders are admissible only if the legal capital remains intact after the distribution.

Art. 56 Directive 2017/1132/EU is clear in this regard: "no distribution to shareholders may be made when on the closing date of the last financial year the net assets as set out in the company's annual accounts are or, following such a distribution, would become, lower than the amount of the subscribed

---

30 If substantial: for instance, pursuant to some laws the difference becomes material only if it is higher than 20% of the fair value of the contribution: see Art. 2343 It-CC.

31 Some Member States do not always require a shareholders' vote, which becomes mandatory only if a certain number of investors so require (5% of the share capital, for instance, according to Art. 5.7 B-CA).

capital plus those reserves which may not be distributed under the law or the statutes of the company".

The provision also adds that "the amount of a distribution to shareholders may not exceed the amount of the profits at the end of the last financial year plus any profits brought forward and sums drawn from reserves available for this purpose, less any losses brought forward and sums placed to reserve in accordance with the law or the statutes".

Therefore, the proposed distribution requires the directors to run a preliminary test based on the profits and losses that emerge from the financial statements, which has the capital as the main benchmark: a so called "balance sheet test". For instance, if the company has assets of 100, profits of 100, debts of 100 and share capital of 100, it cannot distribute profits; share capital stands on the "liabilities" column of the balance sheet, together with debts as an amount that has to be repaid to shareholders; dividends could be distributed if the company, for instance, had profits or assets of 110 or 120, and in that case only in the amount of 10 or 20 respectively.

These rules have been studied at length in comparison with the ones set out in the US. As is well known, profits can be distributed without limits in many North American States as long as the distribution does not render the company insolvent (see i.e. § 6.40 MBCA). The "balance sheet test" is replaced by a much more flexible standard which only requires directors to perform a forecast-orientated ("ability-to-pay") "solvency test" before the distribution takes place (if the company has assets of 100, profits of 100, debts of 100 and equity contributions of 100, it may still distribute profits, on condition that the transaction does not impact on the business continuity: it may even distribute profits taken out from the loans provided by third parties)[32].

Under EU legislation, therefore, the concept of legal capital introduces more stringent limits on distributions: requiring a certain capital buffer to always be present, aiming to reduce the risk that the directors bring the company to the brink of insolvency[33].

---

[32] On these alternative rules see *inter alia* Veil, *Capital maintenance. The regime of the Capital Directive versus alternative systems*, in Lutter (ed.), *Legal*, 79 ff. For a critical viewpoint, see for instance Haaker, *The future*, 649 s. ("the solvency test remains a vague concept, the precise details of which remain wholly unclear"; "it is hard to understand how a form of deobjectivisation [...] should be acceptable for dividend payout purposes").

[33] Moreover, although EU public companies are not subject to a liquidity test as such, the board of directors is nevertheless required to consider – as part of its general duty of care – the company's viability and refrain from any distributions that might endanger it. Under some laws, a liquidity test is mandatory: see e.g. Ch. 18, Sect. 4, Sw-CA. Also the regime of the reserves

At the same time, however, this framework significantly constrains the ability to make payments to shareholders, even when the company is financially fit, leaving them often unsatisfied and consequently less disposed to invest further.

The interpretation of the provisions of the directives on legal capital has been particularly "orthodox" in some member States, to the point of extending the concept of "distributions" to other corporate transactions ("hidden distributions"). For example, for a certain period German courts forbade companies from providing loans to shareholders since these loans may create a lack of liquidity: company loans to shareholders have therefore been treated like "dividends" (such interpretation was based on Sect. 57 Ge-PuCA).

Later on, the law was changed to override that strict jurisprudence and these types of loans are currently allowed. Nevertheless, directors may be eventually responsible for any financing to shareholders which results in a lack of liquidity (specific rules have been dedicated to this issue; to a certain extent, they are still the result of the traditional approach: see Sect. 92 Ge-PuCA[34]).

A provision similar to the original German one is currently in force, for instance, in the Polish companies act with regard to contracts signed between the company and shareholders, which in some cases may be considered to be "hidden distributions" (see Art. 355 Pol-CC)[35]. Also, the EMCA affirms that "under certain conditions a loan to a shareholder may constitute a disguised distribution of profit" (see comment on Ch. 7).

Dividends received in good faith by shareholders are safe. Pursuant to Art. 57 Directive 2017/1132/EU, any distribution made contrary to Art. 56 shall be returned by shareholders who have received it, if the company proves that those shareholders knew of the irregularity of the distributions made to them, or could not in view of the circumstances have been unaware of it.

(made up of undistributed profits and/or shareholders' contributions to reserves) is regulated differently in Member States (see on that also below Chapter 5, § 5).

34 If a company is unable to pay its debts as they fall due, or it is clear it has too many debts, the management board shall be prohibited from making any payments. See on the changes of the law especially Cahn, *Intra-group loans under German law*, in *ECL*, 2010, 44.

35 This provision prohibits the establishment of remuneration for services and other kinds of performance provided to the company by shareholders (and affiliated persons) at an amount higher than the remuneration applicable in "usual business transactions"; see Opalski/Moskala, in *Company laws*, 845.

8. (b) Share buy-backs

Another rule originally laid down in the Second Directive, which aims to protect stakeholders from the risk that the company loses its share capital, is the one limiting share buy-backs[36].

The safeguards introduced by the directives in this regard are both procedural (in particular, the transaction has to be approved by the shareholders) and quantitative (the purchase is legitimate only if it leaves intact an amount of assets corresponding to the legal capital and the reserves).

The transaction is therefore considered – per se – risky and unworthy to be left totally to the discretion of the directors (once again, US laws are normally different, giving liberty to management on decisions to purchase company shares, as long as the buyback does not render the company insolvent).

The Directive 2017/1132/EU provides the Member State with an alternative option: either to prohibit the opportunity for such a purchase or to limit it. Art. 60 states that "Member States may permit a company to acquire its own shares. To the extent that the acquisitions are permitted, Member States shall make such acquisitions subject to the [...] conditions" set out in the same Article.

Some national companies acts basically refuse to allow companies to purchase their own shares: in particular Germany has established the ban in Sect. 71 Ge-PuCA (even if the rules provide for many exceptions: the purchase is permitted for buying out minority shareholders as a result of certain company transactions or in order to prevent "serious and imminent harm" to the company, etc.)[37].

Others domestic laws have taken a more permissive approach and have adopted rules implementing Art. 60 Directive 2017/1132/EU (see, *inter alia*, Belgium, Cyprus, the Czech Republic, Italy, Poland, Portugal, Romania[38]).

---

36 As far as subscribing to own shares is concerned Art. 59 Directive 2017/1132/EU is particularly clear in simply forbidding the possibility: the shares of a company may not be subscribed to by the company itself. If the shares of a company have been subscribed to by a person acting in his or her own name, but on behalf of the company, the subscriber shall be deemed to have subscribed to them for his or her own account.

37 A similar system has been adopted e.g. by Arts. 208 f. Fr-CC. In both jurisdictions, moreover, the general meeting of the shareholders may authorize the company for a period of no more than five years to acquire its own shares of up to 10 % of its legal capital, out of distributable profits (cf. also i.e. Art. 2.98 Du-CC).

38 Many of these laws for example give further possibilities (including the acquisition of own shares aimed at preventing "substantial damage directly threatening the company"); Sect. 302 Cz-CA stipulates also that "a company, acting by itself or through another person acting in his or her own name for the account of the company, may not acquire its own shares if such

The conditions under which the purchase – either directly or indirectly – is allowed are the following: 1) the transaction must be authorized by the shareholders' general meeting (which shall determine the terms and conditions of such acquisitions: the maximum number of shares to be acquired, the duration of the period for which the authorization is given, without exceeding five years, and the maximum and minimum price)[39]; 2) the purchase cannot have the effect of reducing the net assets (legal capital plus reserves) below the minimum amount of the company subscribed capital; (3) only fully paid-up shares can be acquired; furthermore, Member States may subject acquisitions to further conditions (among which) (4) the nominal value of the shares does not exceed a limit to be determined by Member States, not lower than 10 % of the subscribed capital; (5) an amount equal to the nominal value of the shares purchased must be included in a reserve which cannot be distributed to the shareholders (these shares are thus not treated as an ordinary assets and they must be neutralized on the company's balance sheet).

Member States may also decide not to apply the limits contained in Art. 60 to shares acquired – among others – as a result of a universal transfer of assets or from a shareholder in the event of failure to pay up, or as a consequence of a merger, etc. (see Art. 61).

Shares acquired in contravention of the provisions of the Directive must be disposed of within one year of their acquisition (three years in the exceptional cases described above). If they are not disposed of within that period, they must be cancelled (Art. 62).

During the period that the shares are held by the company, the right to vote attaching to the shares must be suspended (in order to avoid any abuse by the directors).

9. (c) Financial assistance

Company loans to third parties and to shareholders are not regulated by EU directives. This kind of legislation is left to the individual Member States.

---

an acquisition would result in the company's bankruptcy pursuant to another legal regulation"; Sect. 57 A Ci-CA allows the board to purchase the shares without the shareholders' approval if it "becomes urgently necessary" (the meeting must be convened within two months afterwards). **39** The quorum requirement to pass the resolution is left to national laws: it is particularly high for instance in Belgium (the same as required for the modification of the articles of association: Art. 7.215 B-CA).

A specific kind of financing transaction has however been considered by the directives on an exceptional basis since the 1970s: the company providing loans or securities to third parties or shareholders for acquisition of the company's own shares.

The Second Directive was particularly restrictive in this regard and simply banned the possibility. The main reasons for the ban had to do with the risk of abuse by directors (who could finance related persons in order to have them buy shares, support their activity and re-appoint them) and the need for capital protection (if the company finances a party to acquire its own shares and later gets into difficulties and needs to recall the loan, it will meet a debtor into a dire situation: if the debtor wants to sell the shares on the market to repay the company, the shares will have lost their value; the more the company gets into trouble, the more difficult it will be to achieve repayment of the loan, a kind of downward spiral).

The Second Directive was however somewhat liberalized by means of the amendments of Directive 68/2006/EU; Directive 2017/1132/EU now also allows for financial assistance[40]. More precisely the Directive gives Member States an alternative: either to prohibit companies from providing financial assistance or to limit it. Art. 64 Directive 2017/1132/EU stipulates that Member States "may permit a company to advance funds or make loans or provide security with a view to the acquisition of its shares by a third party, they shall make such transaction subject to the conditions set out" in the same article.

Some companies acts have taken a rigid approach: Austria, France, Germany, Lithuania, Portugal, Romania, Spain (and others) have maintained an absolute prohibition of financial assistance[41]; the Nordic countries also basically forbid such loans and securities, with a few exceptions[42].

---

40 See *inter alia* Hooft, *The financial assistance prohibition: origins, evolution, and future*, in *ECL*, 2011, 157; Strampelli, *Rendering (once more) the financial assistance regime more flexible*, in *ECFR*, 2012, 530.

41 However in Germany the significance of the ban is highly debated. For instance, a very sensitive issue is whether the financing granted by subsidiaries to the holding company pursuant to a central cash pooling agreement (stipulated to make financial management more efficient) violates the Directive since it does not serve a real "financing" function. According to the jurisprudence "all this is highly controversial and can only be decided authoritatively by the CJEU. Therefore, learned authors advise to abstain from payments back and forth in the public company": see Schall/Machunsky, in *Company laws*, 237.

42 This prohibition actually follows a more generalized ban for loans to shareholders (see Sect. 210 Da-CA and Ch. 21, Sect. 1, Sw-CA). As an exception Sect. 211 Da-CA allows a company to offer loans to its Danish parent company and to certain non-Danish companies as identified by the national Business Authority. It is also allowed to carry out ordinary business transactions be-

On the other hand, Member States (like Belgium, the Czech Republic, Greece, Ireland, Italy, Poland, the Netherlands, and others) permit a company to "advance funds or make loans or provide security, with a view to the acquisition of its shares by a third party", but make such transactions subject to some conditions (as set out in Art. 64).

They are the following: (1) the transactions must take place at fair market conditions, especially with regard to interest received by the company, the security provided for the financing, the credit standing of the debtor; (2) the transactions must be submitted to the shareholders' general meeting for prior approval[43]; (3) the directors must submit a written report to the general meeting indicating the reasons for the transaction, the interest of the company in entering into it, the conditions, the risks involved for the liquidity and solvency of the company and the price at which the third party is to acquire the shares. This complex process of shareholders' approval is also called the "whitewash procedure", as it is aimed at "washing" the transaction of any risk of conflict of interest and abuse.

Two other conditions must be respected: (4) the aggregate financial assistance granted must at no time result in the reduction of the net assets below the amount of the legal capital plus the reserves, also taking into account any reduction of the net assets that may have occurred through the acquisition by the company of its own shares; finally, (5) the company has to include, under the liabilities in the financial statements, a reserve, unavailable for distribution, equal to the amount of the aggregate financial assistance[44].

---

tween a company and the circle of persons mentioned in Sect. 210, even though such transaction create elements of a credit relationship and thereby effectively a loan. Loans to shareholders must in any case be held within the company's distributable reserves; additionally, the loan must be granted on market terms, meaning that the interest, payment plan, security etc. must be on the same terms as if the loan had been granted by a bank. Under the quoted Swedish provision, loans and securities may be granted, on a general basis, "if they are intended exclusively for the borrower's business operations and the company provides the loan for purely commercial reasons".

43 The quorum requirement to pass the resolution is left to national laws: it is particularly high (the same as that required for the modification of the articles of association) pursuant i.e. to Art. 5.152 B-CA and Art. 2358 It-CC.

44 Exceptions may be made in the case of transactions concluded by banks in the normal course of business, or transactions carried out with a view to the acquisition of shares by or for the company's employees. However, these transactions may not cause the reduction of the net assets below the amount specified in the Directive. Moreover, some national laws, while allowing loans to be made, do not allow securities to be provided as they are deemed riskier: see i.e. Arts. 2.98c Du-CC and 2358 It-CC.

Art. 65 introduces additional safeguards in the case of "related party" transactions (for example, between the company and members of the management body): Member States must ensure through adequate safeguards that such transactions do not conflict with the company's best interests.

The Directive does not govern the consequences of illegal financial assistance. On the opposite, this point (to which domestic laws reserve little attention) has been considered by the EMCA, which makes several distinctions.

Sect. 7.24 provides that any transaction which includes unlawful financial assistance and which has not been executed is invalid; if the transaction has been executed, it must immediately be reversed (advancement of funds or loans must be returned to the company together with interest that accrues annually at the rate specified in national law with the addition of 2%); an unlawful transaction which includes financial assistance in the form of direct or indirect securities is only binding on the company if the contracting party did not know, or should have known, that the transaction constituted illegal financial assistance.

The EMCA also states that if a transaction which includes financial assistance cannot be immediately reversed or financial assistance cannot be immediately returned, directors who have agreed to or allowed it will be liable for any deficits since the amount was not returned.

Similar provisions on the consequences of unlawful financial assistance are particularly useful (and should probably be inserted in national regulations) since many interpretive issues may arise if the law remains silent on this point.

"Leveraged buyout" and "merger leveraged buyout" transactions are also particular types of financial assistance (in the meaning of Arts. 64 ff. Directive): we shall come back to these particular operations below in Chapter 10, § 5[45].

10. (d) Cross-shareholdings

Member States' laws often govern also (beyond the text of the Directive) cross-shareholdings, that is to say the situation where one company has shares of another company that, in turn, is a shareholder of the former company. Basically, pairs of companies exchange shareholdings between each other.

---

45 In any case, it is not always easy to establish which operations constitute financial assistance. While there is no question that the granting of financing falls into the category, other facilities (for example, the payment of costs in relation to certain corporate transactions) may end up under the lens of the provisions (the question of the definition of this perimeter is thus debated).

This is a corporate phenomenon which gives rise to potential problems similar to those of the acquisition of the company's own shares, both from an equity point of view and for the proper functioning of the corporate bodies.

Generally speaking, there may however also be benefits from cross-shareholdings. This practice can strengthen and stabilize relationships between companies, it can provide a steady source of funding for businesses by ensuring that partners will be investors, etc.

The regime contained in the main EU laws on cross-shareholdings can be described as follows (special rules are often laid down for listed companies and companies supervised by administrative authorities, like banks and insurances).

(I) Certain laws prohibit cross-subscription of shares at the stage of the company establishment (or at the stage of subsequent capital increases). In some case this practice is prohibited per se[46], in others it is forbidden when it exceeds a fixed threshold (like 10% of the total capital of the companies involved: i.e. company A subscribes more than 10% of company B, which subscribes more than 10% of company A)[47].

This prohibition extends to indirect holdings established through subsidiaries (i.e. company A controls company B, which invests in company C, which invests in company A)[48].

(II) The reciprocal "purchase" of shares (that takes place at a later stage, after the establishment of the company) is normally unregulated. Some legislations (in particular French, Portuguese and Spanish companies acts) contain however a further rule, regarding this kind of "cross-acquisition" of shareholdings.

Paradigmatically, Sp-CA stipulates that companies which (either directly or through a subsidiary) own over 10% of another company's capital must inform the investee company thereof immediately. In the interim, all rights attached to such holdings shall be suspended. Such notice must be served for each subsequent acquisition exceeding 5% of the capital. The company that first receives the notice shall be bound to reduce its holding in the other company to 10% of such company's capital[49]. If the companies receive these notices simultaneously, both shall be bound to reduce their holdings in the other, unless they agree to a reduction by only one of them[50]. The reduction must be carried out within one year from the date of the notice. Voting rights pertaining to any holdings in excess of the 10% ceiling shall be suspended in the interim.

---

46 See i.e. Art. 2360 It-CC.
47 See i.e. Arts. 233-29 Fr-CC and Art. 151 Sp-CA.
48 See i.e. Art. 2360 It-CC.
49 See i.e. Art. 154 Sp-CA.
50 See i.e. Art. 152 Sp-CA.

Failure to reduce holdings as provided shall prompt a court order mandating the sale of surplus shares where requested by the party concerned and the suspension of all rights pertaining to the noncompliant company's holdings in the other company[51].

The rule is quite complex and cumbersome and perhaps does not take into account the fact that, at this at this stage of the general development of the "corporate model", companies seems less interested in creating structures of cross-shareholdings, at least if not listed (in this case, the scheme can be functional to defend from hostile takeovers)[52].

(III) Finally, if the cross "acquisition" is carried out by a subsidiary and a parent company (i.e., company A controls company B and company B acquires shares of company A), the rules on the – indirect – acquisition of own shares shall apply (see above § 8). This is treated as a case of own shares buy-back by the parent company (even if actually performed by another one, the subsidiary).

As a consequence – pursuant to Art. 67 Directive 2017/1132/EU – the conditions under which the purchase of the parents' shares by the subsidiary is allowed are the same as the ones laid down for a direct purchase by the parent (the transaction must be approved by the parent shareholders' meeting, the parent must have enough distributable reserves, etc.).

11. (e) Relevant losses and compulsory recapitalization (or liquidation)

As noted above, the capital supplied by shareholders at the stage of the set-up of the company (or the capital provided with subsequent capital increases) has to remain at the disposal of the company during its entire lifetime. If the net assets of the company go significantly below that amount (as a consequence of losses deriving from corporate activity), directors must intervene and ask shareholders to provide extra capital in order to cover losses.

More precisely, should it become apparent (in the course of drawing up the annual financial statements or interim documents) – or if it can be assumed when duly assessing the circumstances – that there has been a loss of share capital, the directors will have to call a general meeting without undue delay.

---

51 A similar rule, even if simpler in its main features, is contained in Art. 233-29 Fr-CC; see also Art. 485 Por-CC.

52 See for some factual evidence Drago/Manestra/Santella, *Interlocking directorships and cross-shareholdings among the Italian blue chips*, 2011, at *ssrn.com*.

This is the general principle that can be derived from the directives: Art. 77 Directive 2017/1132/EU states that "the subscribed capital may not be reduced to an amount less than the minimum capital laid down" in the national companies act. Moreover Art. 58 of the Directive adds that "in the case of a serious loss of the subscribed capital, a general meeting of shareholders shall be called within the period laid down by the laws of the Member States, to consider whether the company should be wound up or any other measures taken. The amount of a loss deemed to be serious [...] shall not be set by the laws of Member States at a figure higher than half the subscribed capital".

This is the rule known as "recapitalize or liquidate". It has been implemented in different ways by the Member States and the issue has – notwithstanding the (in fact very laconic) wording of the Directive – not been harmonized to a great extent.

Take, for instance, Germany. If half of the subscribed capital (more precisely, of the net assets, i.e. capital and reserves) is lost, the directors will have to call a shareholders' meeting (Sect. 92 Ge-PuCA). However, there is no duty to recapitalize the company or wind it up. The directors will only have to file for bankruptcy once the capital has been completely lost and the company has become insolvent, at the latest three weeks afterwards (Sect. 15a Ge-InsA)[53].

In other countries the law is more stringent and requires a "mandatory recapitalization" or the winding up of the company. Certain companies acts stipulate that when half of the legal capital has vanished, the directors must instantly (or after a certain period of time) call the general meeting in order to illustrate the financial situation of the company and propose its recapitalization or dissolution[54] (a similar rule is proposed by the EMCA, Sect. 8.30: "if it is established

---

[53] The case of Art. 397 Pol-CC is similar: if a loss higher than the sum of the reserves and one third of the share capital, the management board must immediately convene the shareholders' general meeting in order to adopt a resolution on the company's further existence. However – it has been noted – "the occurrence of a situation referred to in Art. 397 does not mean that a decision to wind up the company must be made in every single case.˙It is also acceptable to implement other measures aimed at improving the company's financial standing. It is only when the adoption of a remedial plan would be purposeless and the loss could not be covered with company's aggregate funds that the decision to wind up the company would need to be passed": see Sójka, in *Company laws*, 680.

[54] See for example Art. 35 Por-CC ("immediately"), Sect. 403 Cz-CA ("without undue delay"). France adopts the same rule, but is much more permissive as far as the time required for intervention is concerned: the recapitalization is required only if the shareholders' equity has fallen to below half of the share capital for a period of two years; if the company fails to recapitalize, anyone can request a court to wind up the company (see Art. 225-248 Fr-CC). Art. 5.153 B-CA require the directors to act even if the loss is only "potential"; the provision stipulates that "when

that the equity of a company represents less than half of the subscribed capital, or in the case of negative net assets, the management of the company must ensure that a general meeting is held within six months. At the general meeting, the board must report the financial position of the company and, if necessary, submit a proposal for measures that should be taken, including a proposal for dissolution of the company").

Other companies acts follow along the same lines and – adopting a slightly more articulated regime – distinguish between losses exceeding a fraction of the legal capital (for instance 1/3), but not affecting the minimum legal capital, and losses that reduce the capital below the legal minimum. In the first hypothesis, the directors have to call the general meeting without delay; the shareholders can however decide, instead of recapitalizing, simply to wait until the date of the annual general meeting to be called for the approval of the financial statements for that year at the latest. On the other hand, in the second case (losses bringing the share capital below the legal minimum), the directors have to immediately call the meeting and ask the shareholders to recapitalize, bringing the capital back to a minimal amount above the legal threshold. If shareholders are not ready to recapitalize, the directors will have to propose either the liquidation of the company or its transformation into a company type which requires lower capital (like a private company) or that does not require any minimum capital (like partnerships)[55].

---

the net assets are likely to become or have become negative, the administrative body must, unless more rigorous provisions in the statutes, convene the shareholders to a meeting to be held within two months from the date on which this situation has been established or should have been established under legal or statutory provisions, with a view to deciding on the dissolution of the company or of measures announced in the agenda to ensure the continuity of the company". For a useful comparative overview see Kalls/Adensamer/Oelkers, *Director's duties in the vicinity of insolvency*, in Lutter (ed.), *Legal*, 112.

55 This is the case of Arts. 2446 f. It-CC. As for Art. 327 Sp-CA, on the one hand, the capital must be reduced where losses have taken the net assets of the company to less than two-thirds of its legal capital and one financial year has elapsed without its net worth having been restored; on the other hand, if losses incurred reduce the net assets to less than one-half of the legal capital, the company will be subject to mandatory dissolution (Art. 363 Sp-CA), unless the capital stock is sufficiently increased – or reduced – and provided that it is not necessary to file for bankruptcy (pursuant to Sp-InsA). Under Sects. 115 and 185 Da-CA, if the equity of the company represents less than half of the subscribed capital, the management must ensure that a general meeting is held within six months. However, regardless of the value of the company's subscribed capital, the obligation shall apply to all cases where the company's equity falls below DKK 62.500 [i.e. around € 8.500]. At the general meeting, the directors must report the financial position of the company and, if necessary, submit a proposal for measures that should be taken, including a proposal for dissolution. See also for a similar rule Ch. 25, Sect. 16, Sw-CA.

Of course, if the company is also insolvent (because it cannot fulfil its obligations as they become due), the directors will normally have to file for bankruptcy (see on that, more extensively, below Chapter 9, § 1). Often, however, the simple loss of capital does not necessarily make the company insolvent; in such a case of mere loss (without insolvency), the directors and shareholders have anyway to take action and ask for a recapitalization.

The rule "recapitalize or liquidate" is normally perceived as more protective for creditors (besides – given the need to call a meeting and disclose the situation – it serves also as a sort of "alarm bell" for all the stakeholders, signalling that the company is losing capital[56]).

On the other hand, the provision becomes more burdensome; the directors have to prepare, *inter alia,* updated interim financial statements to be presented to the general meeting[57].

However, despite Art. 58 of the Directive, the rule is – as we have briefly stated above – de facto absent in certain Member States and, in any case, applied differently. As it has been summarized, "the European approach is quite generous: it only stipulates a duty of the executive board to call a company general meeting and inform shareholders. Apart from this, no further measures are suggested and the general meeting is not even obliged to react to its company financial crisis in any way. A further deficiency lies in the fact that Member States may individually [...] determine the span of time which may elapse after the knowledge of serious losses, until the company general meeting must convene"; moreover, "as there is no European standard definition of serious losses, national legislators have given the term different meanings"[58].

Art. 58 has also been fiercely criticized by scholars since it may act as a disincentive to launching an attempt to reorganize a company in difficulty. The signing by the company of an agreement with creditors, or the completion of a restructuring procedure, may indeed imply an extended period of time. Often these agreements and proceedings require the recapitalization of the company to be temporarily put on hold, for the time necessary to negotiate and reach formal agreements. However, this time frame is often incompatible with the rigid

---

56 Significantly Art. 7.228 B-CA is headed "alarm bell procedure".

57 The approach of Ch. 20, Sects. 27 f., Sw-CA is peculiar: during a period of three years following a resolution regarding a reduction of the share capital to cover losses, a resolution regarding the distribution of profits may not be adopted without authorization from the Swedish companies registration office or a court of law, unless the share capital, after or in connection with the reduction resolution, has increased by not less than the amount of the reduction.

58 See Kalls/Adensamer/Oelkers, *Director's*, 136.

temporal horizon set forth by the rules on mandatory recapitalizations, which may thus potentially jeopardize this sort of restructuring.

This need has recently been addressed by Directive 2019/1023/EU (the "Restructuring Directive"), which sets forth (see Recital 96) that "Member States should be able to derogate from the requirements laid down in Directive 2017/1132/EU (concerning the obligations to convene a general meeting [...]), to the extent and for the period necessary to ensure that shareholders do not frustrate restructuring efforts [...]. For example, Member States might need to derogate from the obligation to convene a general meeting of shareholders or from the normal time periods, for cases where urgent action is to be taken by the management to safeguard the assets of the company, for instance through requesting a stay of individual enforcement actions and when there is a serious and sudden loss of subscribed capital and a likelihood of insolvency [...]. Such derogations should be limited in time to the extent that Member States consider such derogations necessary for the establishment of a preventive restructuring framework"[59].

12. The reduction of capital in excess

The establishment of a certain amount of share capital in the instrument of incorporation produces in any case a sort of (positive) "signalling effect" for creditors. Often, they decide to provide financing – or supply goods or services – deliberately relying on the fact that the company has a "certain" amount of capital, that is to say a definite amount of assets represented by that figure (which are protected by the rules described above).

This is why legal capital cannot be freely reduced by a general meeting resolution amending the articles of association and shareholders cannot be spontaneously repaid by directors. Creditors' legitimate expectations also have to be safeguarded.

---

59 A suspension of the "recapitalize or liquidate" rule has thus recently been introduced, for instance, in Italian law for the case where a company files for admission to the arrangement with creditors procedure or for the approval of a restructuring agreement pursuant to Arts. 161 and 182-*bis* of the Italian bankruptcy law (Royal Decree 267/1942). Moreover – as it has been illustrated in some cases by the CJEU (approached for a request for preliminary ruling) – the rule should be superseded in the face of the exceptional measures taken by national authorities in response to serious economic disturbances (aimed at ensuring EU systemic safety and stability [see, with reference to public companies active in the banking sector, case C-526/14 ("Kotnik") decided by the CJEU in 2017 and case C-41/15 ("Dowling") decided in 2016].

EU rules on this regard are particularly strict. First of all, Art. 73 Directive 2017/1132/EU states that any reduction in the legal capital shall be subject to a decision of the general meeting with at least a supermajority of two/thirds (the notice convening the meeting must also specify the purpose of the capital reduction and how it is to be carried out)[60].

The most important provision is Art. 75. At least creditors whose claims pre-date the publication of the decision on the capital reduction shall have the right to obtain security for claims which had not fallen due by the date of that pub-lication. Member States may not waive this type of right unless the creditor has adequate safeguards (or unless such safeguards are unnecessary having re-gard to the assets of the company). In any event, Member States must ensure that the creditors are authorized to apply to the appropriate administrative or judicial authority for adequate protection, provided that they can credibly demonstrate that due to the reduction in the subscribed capital the satisfaction of their claims is at stake, and that no adequate safeguards have been obtained from the com-pany[61].

The principle is rather clear, but at the same time it needs to be implement-ed. National rules differ greatly. The analysis of these dissimilar provisions is very interesting, since it clearly demonstrates how the issue of the creditor pro-tection can be handled within various legal frameworks and by means of differ-ent technical solutions.

In Sweden, for instance, Ch. 20, Sect. 8, Sw-CA provides for a kind of "sol-vency test". Whenever the directors take action to reduce the legal capital for re-payment to the shareholders, a statement as to whether the proposed repayment is justifiable must be appended to the proposal (the document has to motivate the repayment taking into consideration the size of the shareholders' equity in-volved, the nature, scope and risks associated with the operation, and the com-pany's need to strengthen its balance sheet, liquidity and financial position in general). As a matter of fact, the transaction can be carried out by the directors, even though it is under their own responsibility.

On the other hand, the protection afforded to creditors is very incisive pur-suant to i.e. German law. All creditors holding claims against the company may demand security (under the conditions set in Sects. 224 f. Ge-PuCA). The

---

60 The laws of the Member States may, however, lay down that a simple majority of votes is sufficient when at least half the subscribed capital is represented. This opportunity has been taken by many legislatures.

61 This article also applies where the reduction in subscribed capital is brought about by the total or partial waiving of the payment of the balance of the shareholders' contributions to re-serves.

right to receive security expires six months after disclosure of registration of the resolution. Preferential creditors, moreover, are excluded. Shareholders must not receive any payments from the capital decrease before that period of six months has elapsed and all creditors who claimed in time have received either security or payment. As it has been noted, "the right to demand security does not require any proof from the creditors that their claims are jeopardized by the capital decrease"[62]; the law therefore "gives the creditors an unrestricted right to security"; "in practice, German creditors have a strong position that amounts to a factual veto power. Therefore, ordinary capital reductions rarely take place in Germany"[63].

An intermediate approach has been taken by other companies acts, by giving the right to creditors to "oppose" the reduction, but on the condition that they demonstrate that the transaction is potentially harmful for their credit. For instance, pursuant to Art. 2445 It-CC, creditors may – within a ninety day deadline from the shareholders' resolution approving the reduction – express their opposition and file a suit against the company; the court will decide if the reduction may take place anyway, eventually obliging the company to set forth adequate guarantees for the benefit of the opposing creditors[64].

The EMCA provisions are set out along these latter lines: Sect. 7.32 governs an intermediate period; only once that period has elapsed, the reduction can take place; during that period creditors may apply to a court (or other authority as defined under national law) for adequate safeguards. Creditors have, however, to "credibly demonstrate that due to the reduction in the subscribed capital, the satisfaction of their claims is at stake, and that no adequate safeguards have been obtained from the company" (Sect. 7.30).

In this last regard, therefore, the difference with Sect. 225 Ge-PuCA (but also with Ch. 20, Sect. 8, Sw-CA) is rather noteworthy (other examples may be set forth). One has therefore to conclude that the playing-field of the remedies for creditors' protection in this area of the law is anything but level among the laws of the Member States.

---

62 See similarly i.e. Sect. 178 A-PuCA; Art. 7.209 B-CA; Sect. 518 Cz-CA; Art. 53 Li-CA; etc.

63 See Schall/Machunsky, in *Company laws*, 243. The same Authors notes that "practitioners have however found an escape route via the more accessible tools provided by the [TA], namely split-offs under Sects. 139, 145 [Ge-TA]". The German companies act regulates a simplified capital reduction procedure (than can be carried out by the directors) for the case of compulsory redemption of shares by the firm (cf. Sects. 237ff. Ge-PuCA).

64 Cf. also e.g. Art. 2.100 Du-CC; Arts. 334ff. Sp-CA; for further hybrid systems i.e. Art. 30 Gr-PuCA.

3 Management of the company and controls

Summary:
1. The different governance systems and the failed proposal of the Fifth Directive
2. The "menu" legislative approach adopted in most Member States
3. Main features of the different governance systems: monistic (one-tier), traditional and dualistic (two-tier)
4. A controversial issue: the balance of powers between shareholders and directors
5. "Internal" controls on management: audit committees, statutory auditors and supervisory boards
6. "External" controls on management: audit firms and special examiners
7. Management board and supervisory board meetings and resolutions
8. Shareholders' agreements

1. The different governance systems and the failed proposal of the Fifth Directive

The most widespread – at least internationally – model of corporate governance involves a three-layer structure: shareholders appoint and dismiss directors, directors manage the company, and an external firm audits the accounts.

Notwithstanding the apparent simplicity of this structure, it has not been universally accepted by EU Member States.

The Fifth Directive, aimed at harmonizing national corporate governance systems, has never overcome the mere "draft" stage (as we have seen in Chapter 1): in important EU countries the distance from that basic model of allocation of powers is very significant due to differences rooted in history.

The draft Fifth Directive embraced a model that is very similar to the German one, the "two-tier" (or "dualistic") system. This model has been mandatory for many years (beyond Germany) in important countries like Austria, Denmark, Finland, the Netherlands, Poland, and others.

It is called dualistic because it consists of two separate boards: the "supervisory board", appointed by the shareholders, which supervises corporate actions, and the "management board", governing the company, appointed by the supervisory board. An external audit firm is charged with the task of monitoring the accountability and checking the financial statements.

https://doi.org/10.1515/9783110725025-005

On the contrary, the simpler basic model described at the beginning has been implemented in other European countries which adopt the "one-tier system".

In fact, the one-tier system has matured over time into two different sub-models which are known respectively as the "traditional system" (or "latin") and the pure one-tier system (called also "monistic").

The main difference between those two sub-models regards the fact that in the traditional model, in addition to the board of directors, the shareholders also appoint a board of "statutory auditors" – sometimes called also "censors" – whose main function is to control the activity of the directors. An external audit firm (at least in medium and large companies) audits the accounts and the financial statements.

There are therefore three corporate bodies in the traditional system (shareholders' general meeting, board of directors and board of the statutory auditors), and only two in the pure one-tier system (shareholders' general meeting and board of directors).

In many of the States that adopt the pure one-tier system some of the directors – on the board – are attributed the task of controlling the activity of other directors to a certain extent and therefore forming an internal "committee" with monitoring functions (often named "audit committee").

The powers of the shareholders – i.e.: the shareholders' general meeting – also change extensively in the three models (and in the different versions of those models as implemented by the Member States). The regulations in some States empower them with a strong say on corporate action (shareholders may even advocate important corporate decisions); on the other hand, the laws of other countries categorize the company directors as the sole and exclusive decision-makers.

Finally, the broadness of the controls on corporate action – internal, external – also differs considerably.

In some jurisdictions, for instance, the controllers may take actions in place of the directors and even sue them on behalf of the company (if board members have breached their duties). If serious irregularities are suspected, shareholders owning a certain number of shares may request the courts to issue injunctions, remove the directors, appoint special examiners, etc. On the other hand, in other legislatures, these types of controls are less intense or even absent.

Finally, most States offer companies the option to choose among the alternative models and implement one instead of the other (and change them over time).

2. The "menu" legislative approach adopted in most Member States

(A) The most structured model – the two-tier system – was introduced for the first time in the Netherlands, even though it was later reformulated, particularly in Germany.

Historically Dutch corporations have operated under a "two-board" structure since the establishment of the first public company, the "Vereenigde Oostindische Compagnie" (the "Dutch East India Trading Company"), which adopted a two-tier board in 1623[1].

After its creation in 1602, a significant conflict erupted in 1622 between shareholders and directors. Dissenting participants complained about the numerous conflicts of interests that had arisen between the directors and the company. As a consequence, one year later the company's charter was amended in order to grant certain rights to large investors, including the right to nominate a committee of shareholders entrusted with the supervision of the directors.

From then on, that dualistic model (specifically created in order to overcome the investors' lack of control over the managers) has been maintained in Dutch company law.

In Germany the dual structure was introduced in 1870, right after the country's unification. At that time, the German States were drafting a new company law for the new confederation and, more specifically, were discussing the opportunity to maintain some form of control over companies after the decision to abandon the rule of State authorization for their establishment (the "concession system").

On the one side were the free Hanseatic cities (led by the city of Hamburg), which wanted full freedom of incorporation, arguing that such liberalization would allow for more business associations to arise. On the other end stood Prussia in particular, more skeptical about how far freedom of incorporation could go. Since Prussia carried the majority of German States, it required the in-

---

1 See De Jongh, *Shareholder activism at the Dutch East India Company 1622–1625*, 2010, at *ssrn.com:* the V.O.C. is considered the prototype of the public company because for the first time, it offered limited liability to shareholders and was aimed at operating for a long period of time. That structure superseded other business models which distinguished different categories of stakeholders ("merchants", "tractators", "investors", "commendators"; usually only the latter enjoyed limited liability). Moreover, companies were previously created for the duration of one voyage, after which they were liquidated and the proceeds divided among the participants. See also Schall, *Corporate governance after the death of the king – the origins of the separation of powers in companies*, in *ECFR*, 2011, 478.

troduction of the use of a supervisory board in the newly adopted German code to replace the State authorization and oversight embedded in the concession system (at least in relation to the major form of company, the public company)[2].

Some years later, when the model was called into discussion, its importance was reaffirmed by the political forces: in a society leaning towards socialism, the dualistic system served to also give the workers (company employees) the right to intervene to a certain extent on the management of the company. Starting from 1922, German legislation therefore introduced workers' representation on the supervisory board (representatives were appointed by the work councils, i.e. employee associations or trade unions).

At the end of World War II (under the Allied occupation), general support for the democratization of companies remained: on the one hand, trade unions, which had never been affiliated with the nationalistic movement, were at the centre of the political scene; on the other hand, the German industries of coal, steel and iron (facing strong criticism and the risk of being dismantled because of their involvement in the regime) managed to save themselves by giving unions the right to have representatives on the supervisory boards.

That situation led to the laws of 1951 which granted work councils the right to appoint from one third to one half of the members of the supervisory board (the "co-determination")[3] and, finally, to current legislation that still permits workers' representatives to sit on supervisory boards.

However, the German parliament has always considered it too extreme to have trade unions taking part on the boards of directors and thus directly managing companies: the "two-tier system" has thus provided the right balance.

German trade unions currently appoint representatives to the supervisory boards (one third to one half of the members, depending on the size of the company), thereby taking part in the election of the directors and the controlling activities of the supervisory board. The management board administers – on an exclusive basis – the company.

In the dualistic system the shareholders have thus taken a great step back. The law only provides shareholders with the right to appoint a percentage (as noted, two thirds or one half) of the supervisory board members and, through them, the board of directors[4].

---

2 See extensively Muchlinski, *The development of German corporate law until 1990: an historical reappraisal*, in *GLJ*, 2013, 348.

3 See Muchlinski, *The development*, 371 f.

4 See Sect. 76 – 117 Ge-PuCA; see also Roth, *Corporate boards in Germany*, in Davies et al. (eds.), *Corporate boards in law and practice. A comparative analysis in Europe*, OUP, 2013, 275.

(B) Therefore, when discussions were begun in Brussels in 1972 on the proposal for an EU directive on corporate governance, the documents drafted by the Commission immediately received strong opposition from several Member States with different traditions and no intention of opening the door of company boards – even indirectly – to the workers' representatives.

The seed of discord was, among others, Art. 3 (of Ch. 3, Sect. 1) of the draft Fifth Directive, which expressly stated (clearing the way for union appointees) that "(a) the company shall be managed by a management organ under the supervision of a supervisory organ; (b) the members of the management organ shall be appointed by the supervisory organ", etc.

The proposal for the Fifth Directive was amended twice and eventually withdrawn in 1991.

The presence in the Member States of such different systems has thus stimulated substantial debate among scholars over the possible superiority of each of them over the others.

The example of Italy is straightforward: in extensive debates, some academics portrayed the German model as superior, other criticized it. Therefore, when an important company reform act was adopted in 2003, Italian parliament decided to let the companies establish which model to choose and all the three systems (traditional, one-tier, two-tier) were regulated[5].

The idea has been appreciated by Italian companies. After only a few years from the reform, almost 500 companies – not listed on the stock exchange – had adopted one of the alternative models (monistic or dualistic). Currently, however, the companies choosing these models still represent a small percentage if compared with the number of public companies (around 0,25 %). Moreover, almost all Italian listed companies adopt the traditional system (however, some of the biggest listed banks have recently adopted the one-tier system; a number of them have even shifted to that model after having previously chosen one of the other "new" models).

The "multiple choice" approach provided by Italian law is not new in the EU. France, for instance, has offered a "menu" to entrepreneurs since 1966[6]. In that year a general company law was enacted providing French companies with the option to choose between the two-tier and one-tier models (note: the traditional

---

5 See Ghezzi/Malberti, *The two-tier model and the one-tier model of corporate governance in the Italian reform of corporate law*, in *ECFR*, 2008, 1; Ferrarini/Peruzzo/Roberti, *Corporate boards in Italy*, in Davies et al. (eds.), *Corporate*, 394.
6 See Arts. 225-57 ff. Fr-CC; see Pietraconsta/Dubois/Garçon, *Corporate boards in France*, in Davies et al. (eds.), *Corporate*, 183; Magnier, *Makeup of boards: a new corporate paradigm, for which governance?*, in *EBLR*, 2019, 237.

model has never been available in France: the French menu is, in this regard, poorer than the menu of its Italian cousins[7]). In France, only about 2.700 companies have a two-tier board out of 700.000 public companies even though they are usually bigger ones (0,4%).

In the Netherlands the two-tier system is mandatory. However, since 2013 the law allows larger companies – which fall under the so called "structuurregime" (having more than 16 million euros of turnover or more than 100 employees in the country, or having established a work council) – to opt for the one-tier board[8]. Currently only 49 public companies have a one-tier board, but 31 of them are listed on a stock exchange: on the 140 active listed Dutch public companies, therefore, over 20% have a one-tier board. In the Netherlands bigger companies appear to be shifting to the one-tier board structure.

There is similar flexibility (i. e. possibility of choosing between one or two or more models) currently in several other Member States.

On its part, the Commission's Action Plan of 2003 recommended offering organizational freedom to companies[9]. In the Action Plan of 2012, the Commission also acknowledged the coexistence of different board structures and allocation of powers, which are often deeply rooted in the country's overall economic governance system, and signalled no intention to challenge or modify these arrangements[10]. The EMCA Group shares the view that "Member States should be free to choose between different board structures according to the need of the company and national traditions" (see the general comment on Sect. 8)[11].

---

[7] Hansen, *The Report*, 6, notes that Member States are headed towards "a mutual learning process that appears to bring to each national jurisdiction the main features known in other Member States and remove redundant elements deemed too unpractical. Rather than producing one set of company law options across different jurisdictions, each jurisdiction appears to introduce different options in their company law. The gastronomic equivalence of this effect of cross-border mobility is the variety of restaurants that have appeared in Copenhagen within recent years serving German, French and Italian cuisine [...]. National company law is equally making room for features that used to be available only in foreign jurisdictions, while developing national traditions".

[8] See Arts. 2.153/263 Du-CC. See among others Verkerk, *Modernizing of Dutch company law: reform of the law applicable to the BV and a new legal framework for the one-tier board within NVS and BVS*, in *ECL*, 2010, 113; Nowak, *Corporate boards in the Netherlands*, in Davies et al. (eds.), *Corporate*, 183.

[9] See COM(2003) 284 final, 15.

[10] See COM(2012) 740 final, 5.

[11] Similar conclusions can be found in the literature, see *inter alia* Jungmann, *The effectiveness of corporate governance on one-tier and two-tier board systems – Evidence from Germany*, in *ECFR*, 2006, 426, arguing that each system (especially the dualistic and monistic) has its own strengths and weakness: the one-tier structure is more flexible and less burdensome; however,

The underpinning theoretical vision holds that "the existence of a variety of corporate models should not be viewed as an obstacle to the internal market, but as an asset"[12].

Others may dissent. Entrepreneurs aiming to set up companies in other European countries would probably prefer to rely on similar governance models, maybe taking advantage of regulatory arbitrage with regard to single clauses, but not having to face very dishomogeneous rules and case law. The explanation in the next pages of this book may help you to form your own opinion in this regard.

In any case it is true that legal systems (and enterprises) are already – slowly but inevitably – "converging" towards some models. For instance, the fact that recently some European legislators – as we have seen above – have provided companies with the option to shift to the monistic system and the fact that enterprises (in jurisdictions that do not regulate that model) are choosing the SE type because the SE is allowed to adopt the one-tier system (as we shall see in Chapter 14) appear to be unequivocable signals that the European "market for legal rules" actually requires more convergence, at least to a certain extent[13].

Finally, it should be noted that the participation by workers in the management of the company is not guaranteed exclusively by the dualistic model. Sweden, for instance, is a country that has historically adopted a one-tier regime. Despite this, company employees are entitled to be represented on the board of

---

the directors have to make decisions while simultaneously monitoring these decisions (therefore "a single non-executive director or group of non-executive directors in a meeting of the board may be reluctant to ask for further information, whereas the members of the supervisory board might, collectively, be less reluctant": 460); see for further considerations *inter alia* Hopt/Leyens, *Board models in Europe – recent developments in internal corporate governance structure in Germany, the United Kingdom, France and Italy*, in *ECFR*, 2004, 135; De Groot, *The function of corporate boards: toward a new state of affairs*, in *ECL*, 2007, 4; Davies/Hopt, *Boards in Europe – Accountability and convergence*, 2013, at *ssrn*; see also Gerner-Beuerle/Schuster, *Comparative*, 303 f.; moreover, for an extensive examination of various laws on the functioning of the board of directors, see the essays contained in Birkmose/Neville/Sørensen (eds.), *Boards of directors in European companies. Reshaping and harmonizing their organization and duties*, Wolters Kluwer, 2013, and the general report on the research of the Forum European Corporate Boards (FECB), *Boards in law and practice: a cross country analysis in Europe*, in Davies et al. (eds.), *Corporate*, 3 (with a focus on listed and larger companies).

12 See Hansen, *The Nordic*, 161.

13 Even the German praxis (namely the "German Jurists Forum") has been considering the introduction of the one-tier board for German public companies, at least initially for the ones that are not subject to co-determination; the proposal, advanced in 2008 and 2012, is commented by Roth, *Corporate boards in Germany*, in Davies et al. (eds.), *Corporate*, 280.

directors[14]. If a company has at least 25 employees on average over the latest financial year, it may appoint two ordinary and two deputy board members (as workers' representatives). If the company is active in more than one line of business and has at least 1.000 employees on average over the latest financial year, the employees are entitled to appoint three ordinary and three deputy board members. If the company is a parent company, this applies at group level. However, the number of employee representatives may not exceed the number of other board members[15].

3. Main features of the different governance systems: monistic (one-tier), traditional and dualistic (two-tier)

(A) The one-tier model is the most widespread in the Member States, both as an alternative or as a mandatory model (all States – with the exceptions of Austria, Germany and Poland – allow their public companies to adopt this system, at least as an option; some countries govern it as the sole accepted model such as i.e. Ireland and Spain).

According to this model, the shareholders' general meeting appoints and dismisses the directors (a board of directors; in some jurisdictions it can also be a sole director or more than one director acting separately[16]), for a period which normally ranges from three to six years[17], and approves the financial statements (yearly).

---

14 According to the Swedish Board Representation Act, Private Sector Employees, of 1987.

15 The issue of the mandatory participation by employees on company boards has also been tackled by the Court of Justice. In 2015 the CJEU received a request from the Court of Appeals of Berlin for a preliminary ruling on the "Erzberger case" (C-566/15): the question posed was whether the German co-determination scheme complied with Arts. 18 and 45 TFEU; in 2017, the CJEU ruled that the current German co-determination system does not violate EU law. See Keijzer/Oost/Van Ginneken, *The ECJ Erzberger case: an analysis of German co-determination and EU law*, in *ECL*, 2017, 217.

16 See for instance Sect. 76 Ge-PuCA; the board must comprise at least two people only in companies with a share capital of more than three million euros (the articles of association may however also stipulate that it comprises one person in those larger companies). As noted, a number of three directors is suggested by the EMCA: see Sect. 8.02. The possibility of separate administration is provided for i.e. in Art. 210 Sp-CA. Under many jurisdictions, the members of the corporate bodies (either the board of directors or the supervisory board) may be either natural or legal persons.

17 For example in France, Greece, Slovenia, Spain it is six years; in the Czech Republic five; in Portugal and Sweden four; in Italy three; the EMCA suggests a term of four years (Sect. 8.14). Belgian law allows the term of tenure to be indeterminate: see Art. 5.70 B-CA. A peculiar rule

The shareholders' general meeting can also amend the instrument of incorporation and the articles of association (it deliberates therefore on major corporate transactions: mergers, conversions, etc.). The directors manage the company – basically – on an exclusive basis (but see below § 4).

An audit firm – also appointed by the shareholders' general meeting – checks the accounts and audits the financial statements.

Under some jurisdictions, the directors have to form a committee (called the "audit committee") comprising non-executive directors that has the duty to monitor the activity of the other executive members (see further below § 5).

Even if this type of distinction between directors (and the establishment of a committee within the board) is not mandatory in all States adopting this model, the creation of different positions (executive/non-executive directors) is strongly encouraged both by the EU Commission (see for instance the Green Paper of 2011 and the Action Plan of 2012) and the EMCA, in order to create a "division between supervisory and managing directors within a single-tier board" too[18]. However, not all powers may be delegated; normally, for example, decisions concerning the drafting of the financial statements are deemed to be non-delegable and all directors have to concern themselves with this task.

The figures of "independent" directors is also acquiring importance, including in non-listed companies (in traded ones the appointment of this kind of directors is often mandatory[19]).

An independent director is a non-executive member of the board who does not have a material or pecuniary relationship with the main shareholders (or persons related to them). As stated by the EMCA Group, at least "(1) in traded companies, the board should comprise an appropriate balance of independent non-executive directors. The number of independent non-executive directors should be stated in the rules of procedure. (2) A director should be considered to be independent only if he or she is free of any business, family or other relationship

---

is contained in Sect. 1090 Ir-CA, which sets forth a "rotation of directors" system (unless the articles of association provide otherwise): at the annual general meeting of the company, with one third of the directors (or, if their number is not three or a multiple of three, then the number nearest to one third) retiring from office; the directors that have to retire are those who have been longest in office. A retiring director is however eligible for re-election.

18 See clearly Sect. 9.02 EMCA: "in public companies with a one-tier system, the company shall ensure that there is a division of functions between supervisory and managing functions similar to the functions in the two-tier system. This can be done by separation between executive and non-executive directors".

19 See on this specific aspect below Chapter 12, § 4. See also i.e. the Reccomendation 2005/162/EC (quoted in Chapter 1, § 8).

with the company, its controlling shareholder or the management that creates a conflict of interest such as to impair his or her judgement" (Sect. 8.05)[20].

According to most national laws, the board is also required to establish an adequate internal control system (the duties of executive and non-executive directors may change in this regard, with the former having decision-making power in creating this system and the latter retaining a more restricted monitoring role)[21].

One crucial issue regards the circulation of information among directors and especially the information flows towards the non-executives: in some jurisdictions the right to information is restricted and the latter may receive only information prior to or during the board meeting; however, more often they are entitled to receive any information they require and also to have access to the company's books and employees (see on that further below Chapter 9, § 1).

(B) The "traditional" or "latin" system – despite its name (which leads one to think that it has been implemented in several countries of "latin law" tradition) – is essentially adopted only in Italy, Portugal and Romania (as a system alternative to others in all these countries; it is however often the most widespread).

This system is called "traditional" because the other models – dualistic and monistic – were introduced in those countries at a later stage (or are less significant). The EMCA also refers to it as "traditional".

Its main features are the following. The shareholders' general meeting appoints the directors (usually a board of directors; it can also be a sole director for unlisted companies) for the period set forth in the articles of association (three or four years, depending on the domestic laws[22]), approves the financial statements – yearly – and can amend the instrument of incorporation and the articles of association.

---

20 In this regard for example the Irish companies act is straightforward and stipulates that, where a company is required to establish an audit committee (i.e. it is a "large company"), at least one member of that committee must be an independent non-executive director with competence in accounting or auditing (otherwise the Act does not distinguish between executive and non-executive directors): see Sect. 167 Ir-CA.

21 See i.e. Ch. 8, Sect. 4 Sw-CA and Art. 2381 It-CC. See further below Chapter 9, § 1.

22 Slight differences can be found in the single Member States' companies acts (see i.e. Art. 441 Lu-CA: a minimum of three shareholders has to be appointed unless the company has only one shareholder: see; under Art. 153 R-CA the number of directors always has to be odd, etc.). A number of three directors is suggested – on a general basis for the board of directors (i.e. for all systems) – by the EMCA (Sect. 8.02). The maximal term of tenure is four years in Portugal and Romania, three years in Italy; pursuant to the EMCA the term should not exceed four years (again on a general basis see Sect. 8.14).

The directors basically manage the company on an exclusive basis (but see below § 4). Within the board, some powers may be delegated to one or more directors, with a distinction made between executive and non-executive directors also in this model (an executive committee may also be created).

The shareholders' general meeting also appoints the board of statutory auditors. As already noted, this is the main difference with the monistic system[23]. The number of the auditors is fixed by the law (normally three; some national laws give however the option to increase that figure in the articles of association[24]). Auditors may be freely dismissed by the shareholders' general meeting, even though some domestic provisions state that they can only be removed in certain circumstances and with rigid procedural safeguards (i. e. under control of the court)[25]. The term of tenure is generally three years.

The board of statutory auditors – which has typically to be independent and unrelated to the directors[26] and must include at least one chartered accountant – controls the correctness of the directors' activities, checks the adequacy of the risk management system and may – under some laws – take incisive actions (call meetings of the board of directors or a shareholders' general meeting, file legal actions against the directors, etc.: see also further below § 5). Normally the statutory auditors can – and must – attend meetings of the board of directors and the shareholders' general meetings.

At a different level, the audit firm – also appointed by the shareholders' general meeting – checks the accounts and audits the financial statements (pur-

---

23 Art. 418 Por-CC lays down a rule that also gives the option for minority shareholders (holding at least a 10 % stake) to appoint one member of the board of the directors or one member of the board of statutory auditors: at the request of shareholders holding shares representing at least one tenth of the share capital, the court may appoint one more effective member, provided that the requesting shareholders have voted against the proposals. A similar power is provided for i. e. by Italian law, but only for listed companies (see Arts. 148 f. Legislative Decree 58/1998).

24 Auditors cannot exceed the number of three or five according to Art. 2397 It-CC. Under Art. 413 Por-CC, the company can only have a sole statutory auditor (who must be a chartered accountant); a board of statutory auditors is mandatory only for companies exceeding two of the following thresholds for two consecutive years: a total balance sheet of € 20 million; a total net turnover of € 40 million; an average of 250 employees during each fiscal year; and companies that issue securities admitted to trading on a regulated market.

25 Art. 2400 It-CC is particularly stringent: the revocation resolution has to be approved by a court decree after hearing the interested party. Under Art. 419 Por-CC, the court may dismiss members of the statutory auditors' board (or the sole auditor) for just cause at the request of the board of directors or the shareholders who requested the appointment.

26 This should be a typical feature of the board of statutory auditors; it is however organized differently by each single country with the Romanian law being probably the loosest; see Art. 2399 It-CC and 414 Por-CC.

suant to some laws, smaller public companies may join the two functions and, if the articles of association so provide, the statutory auditors – who will have to be chartered accountants – also perform the role of auditors[27]).

This system may therefore become particularly complex, since (at least in more structured companies) executive directors, non-executive directors (some of whom are independent), statutory auditors and audit firms may all end up working together at the same time, with interconnected roles[28].

(C) Turning finally to the dualistic system, according to this model the shareholders' general meeting appoints and dismisses the supervisory board[29]. The main functions of this board are the election and removal of members of the management board, the monitoring the latter and the assessment of the established risk management system[30].

The management board is entrusted with full responsibility for managing the company (but see below § 4). The board may delegate some of its powers to executive directors or an executive committee (under some laws, however, all members have to act jointly when representing the company, unless otherwise specifically stipulated in the articles of association[31]).

The supervisory board is normally given the important power of approving certain company decisions and examining and agreeing on the company's business plans, annual budgets and financial reports[32]. This is one of the fundamental distinctive features of the dualistic model.

---

27 This is the case of Art. 2409-bis It-CC.

28 Under the Luxembourg companies act, the supervision of the company must be entrusted to one or more "supervisory auditors", who are independent persons who act in a way similar to the auditors, with the exceptions that, on the one hand, they have broader powers and, on the other hand, they do not express an opinion on whether the financial statements submitted to the shareholders for their approval show a true and fair view of the financial situation of the company (see Arts. 443-1 ff. Lu-CA).

29 In smaller companies, the management body may – under certain jurisdictions – comprise a sole director (see i.e. Sect. 76 Ge-PuCA).

30 The term of tenure – for members of both the supervisory and management boards – varies: under French law it is six years, German and Polish five, Danish and Swedish four, Italian three; as noted above, the EMCA suggests a term of four years in these cases (Sect. 8.14).

31 See Sects. 71 A-PuCA and 77 Ge-PuCA. Some non-delegable responsibilities are however recognized (those related to planning, governance, organization, finance and information: see Schall, in *Company laws*, 263). On the comittees within the supervisory board see explicitly i.e. Art. 279 Slove-CA.

32 Normally the board has to meet at least quarterly (see i.e. Sect. 110 Ge-PuCA).

However, the power to vote on these more important matters has to be set forth in the articles of association[33]. As a consequence, the management board is required to report on a regular basis to the supervisory board on all issues important to the company with regard to corporate planning[34].

A possible veto, however, does not shift the competence on these important resolutions from the management board to the supervisory board. The directors remain exclusively responsible for initiating and executing any managerial decisions[35].

Finally, the supervisory board also usually formally approves the financial statements of the company unless the management board – or the supervisory board or the shareholders – require the decision to be made by the shareholders' general meeting.

As far as the composition of the management body is concerned, some companies acts establish that the power to manage companies may even be attributed to a single person; others impose a minimum number of components of the board of directors of two or three members; only some set forth a maximum number.

Regarding the supervisory body, a minimum number of three members is typically required; only some laws fix a maximum number[36].

(D) With regard to the systems of appointment (in all three models), directors are normally elected by the majority of the shareholders (only indirectly, as we have seen, in the dualistic system). That does not, however, mean that shareholders always have to follow the majority rule.

---

33 See Art. 225-68 Fr-CC; Sect. 111 Ge-PuCA; Sect. 294 La-CA, etc.. Similarly, Sect. 8.08 EMCA stipulates that "the articles of association may determine that specific, important transactions may be entered into only with the approval of the supervisory board. The articles of association may also state that the supervisory board shall determine the company's business policy".

34 See in particular Sect. 90 Ge-PuCA ("the management board shall report to the supervisory board on the following topics: (1) the business policy it intends to pursue and other fundamental matters of corporate planning (in particular financial planning, investment planning, and human resources planning) [...]; (2) the company's profitability, in particular the return on equity; (3) the course of business, in particular the sales of the company, and its economic situation; (4) transactions that may have a significant impact on the profitability or liquidity of the company"). The supply of information strengthens the advisory function of the supervisory board, because a more well-informed supervisory board is significantly more capable of advising or intervening on the management board on fundamental issues of corporate strategy.

35 See, with reference to Sect. 111 Ge-PuCA, Schall, in *Company laws*, 267.

36 Under French law i.e. the maximum number of members of the management board is five and, for listed companies, seven. The German companies act maximizes the number of members of the supervisory board according to the size of company's share capital to twenty-one.

That is by far the most common model, but it is not considered mandatory in all Member States. Often different "classes" of shares may be issued – if the articles of association so provide – and the right to appoint one or more directors may be attributed to a class, or more than one class (we shall come back on this issue below in Chapter 4, § 3).

Another technique for electing directors is the "slate voting" system which permits the presentation of "lists" by different groups of shareholders with directors appointed on a proportional basis from the lists that obtain the most votes (minority shareholders can hence pool their shares and obtain the appointment of a number of directors proportional to the share capital held): this type of system, which may always be put into the articles of associations, is expressly regulated in some jurisdictions, including for unlisted companies[37].

A major difference between the Member States' rules regarding the dualistic system is to be found in the fact that only some jurisdictions include provisions for employee representation in their company laws. In other countries, similar provisions on employee representation are contained in the labour code.

In this perspective, the EMCA states that "regarding employee representation [...], national traditions [...] are very strong and the EMCA Group considers that it is not possible to develop a common rule in this area" (see the comment on Ch. 8).

(E) Directors may normally be removed by the shareholders' general meeting (or by the supervisory board in the dualistic system) both "for cause" or "at will"; in the latter case, they will have to be reimbursed for the compensation owed until the end of the tenure[38].

---

37 See i.e. Arts. 80 Gr-PuCA and Art. 243 Sp-CA. A particular provision is contained in Art. 79 Gr-PuCA, which permits that a single shareholder may appoint directly some directors, but not more than 2/5 of the whole board.

38 For cause means, for instance, fraud, criminal conduct, gross abuse of office amounting to a breach of trust, or similar conduct. In the dualistic system, the members of the supervisory board may also be dismissed by the shareholders' general meeting (see i.e. Sect. 103 Ge-PuCA). The rules on the dismissal of directors are rather similar in all national jurisdictions and for all three models (even though the decision is made by the supervisory board in the dualistic system): they are summarized by the EMCA as follows: "(1) A member of the board of directors may resign from the board of directors at any time. (2) A member of the board of directors may be dismissed at any time without cause by those who have appointed the member. (3) A member of the board of directors who is not elected by the shareholders' general meeting may be dismissed at any time by the general meeting for a good cause. (4) If there is no alternate member available to replace the former member, the other members of the board shall take measures necessary to appoint a new member of the board. The new member shall hold office until the next general meeting where his or her appointment must be confirmed by those entitled to appoint the member. The election may be deferred until the next annual general meeting, pro-

The rule of revocation at will is widespread in EU laws (and not as a result of harmonization efforts: it has its historical foundations in the early development of civil law). In contrast, in traditional common law (especially in the US' state legislations), the concept of revocation at will is basically extraneous ("a mandatory rule of removability of directors without a cause" – it has been noted – "is not an American thing. Only three [US] States provide for at will removal without explicitly allowing for deviations in the articles of incorporation"[39]).

This means that directors of American corporations are normally in a stronger position than their colleagues working in EU firms, since the former cannot be dismissed whenever the shareholders feel like it (this clearly shifts the balance of corporate power towards directors in US companies, and towards shareholders in EU companies)[40].

(F) Most EU legislations address the issue of the remuneration of members of the supervisory body (or, in the traditional system, the statutory auditors). The same consideration is also valid for auditors.

On the other hand, the remuneration of members of the management bodies can always be decided upon by the body appointing them (with the exception of listed companies, where special regulations apply, especially with regard to disclosure: see on that below Chapter 12).

Usually the amount of compensation established by the appointing body is later distributed by the board of directors, taking into consideration the role performed (executive, non-executive)[41].

---

vided that the board of directors is quorate with the remaining members and alternate members" (Sects. 8.06 and 8.13).

39 See Cools, *Europe's ius commune on director revocability*, in *ECFR*, 2011, 199.

40 Moreover, in the US the "staggered board" model is widespread; it consists of different classes of directors and only one class is open to elections each term. Generally, one-third of the total board of directors are elected each year, rather than all at once. The adoption of this model is feasible also in most European jurisdictions, but much less frequent (see similarly Sect. 1090 Ir-CA, described above, at fn. 17).

41 Only a few jurisdictions prescribe that the remuneration as a whole (including bonuses, stock options, insurance etc.) must be appropriate in relation to both the tasks and achievements of the board members and the situation of the company, and that the usual remuneration not be exceeded without specific reasons: along these lines see Sect. 87 Ge-PuCA (which also requires, in listed companies, the remuneration policy to be steered towards sustainable business development and that bonuses, options etc. must be connected to the long-term success of the company by using a perennial calculation base; for listed companies see anyway also below, Chapter 12, § 2). Moreover, in the case of a subsequent deterioration of the economic situation of the company, the supervisory board must reduce the remuneration (see again Sect. 87 Ge-PuCA).

(G) As far as the right of representation and the power to bind the company is concerned, members of the board of directors have the power to represent the company in relation to third parties. The company is bound by agreements made on behalf of the company by the entire board of directors or by a single board member.

The power of each member of the board of directors to bind the company may however be restricted by the articles of association so that it can only be exercised by members acting jointly or by one or more specific members acting jointly or alone (a similar rule is laid down by the EMCA, Sect. 8.27).

The issue has been regulated since the First Directive (and it is now addressed by Directive 2017/1132/EU): on the one hand, the Directive makes clear that acts performed by the directors are binding even if those acts are not within the objects of the company. However, Member States may provide that the company shall not be bound where such acts are outside the objects if the company provided that the third party knew it or could not, in view of the circumstances, have been unaware of it (see Art. 9).

(H) The duties and liabilities of the directors and supervisors in the different governance models are analyzed to a greater extent below in Chapter 9.

4. A controversial issue: the balance of powers between shareholders and directors

A very sensitive matter – common to all three governance models – regards the balance of powers between shareholders and directors and the answer to the question of whether shareholders should be vested with some management power in the company.

Actually the matter does not concern the "day-to-day management", which usually remains in the hands of the directors. It has instead to do with the possibility of providing shareholders with a say on (occasional) relevant business transactions – like the sale or purchase of important assets, the execution of complex transactions, etc. – for which the companies acts normally do not require their vote.

The solution offered by domestic provisions to this conundrum – which goes straight to the core of company law[42] – is sharply different and changes to a large extent the "face" of the legislation in each Member State.

---

[42] See, for a general illustration of the theme, *inter alia*, Schall, *Corporate*, 476 ff.; Sáez/Riaño, *Corporate governance and the shareholders' meeting: voting and litigation*, in *EBOR*, 2013, 343;

(A) Beginning with the one-tier model, in some jurisdictions shareholders are expressly excluded from making managerial decisions in any form (this is the case, for instance, in Belgium and France). Art. 225-35 Fr-CC stipulates that the board of directors determines the guidelines of the company's business activities and ensures their implementation. Without prejudice to the powers expressly invested in shareholders' general meetings, and ensuring that they fall within the objects of the company, the board of directors deals with all matters relating to the conduct of the company's business and decides all pertinent issues through its deliberations[43].

According to other companies acts the solution is less clear-cut and the question becomes multifaceted. It regards, simultaneously (1) the "possibility" for the management board to solicit and involve shareholders in business matters; (2) the "duty" of the management board to involve shareholders in such matters; (3) the validity of statutory clauses requiring a shareholder' vote on such matters. In all these cases, a further question arises: (4) when shareholders are involved, may they issue binding instructions to the management board (i.e.: have the directors to decide accordingly on what was established by the shareholders and, if approval is denied, does this denial constitute a kind of "veto")?

The solution adopted, for instance, is rather net in Art. 2380-bis and 2364 It-CC (and it does not differ much – if not for single aspects – from the French one mentioned above). The management of the company's activities lies exclusively with the directors (and they cannot solicit shareholders to participate in business decisions). However – as an exception –transactions indicated in the articles of association may require prior "authorization" by the shareholders' general meeting; this "authorization" in any case does not create a legal power of the shareholders over the directors. According to the main view, this type of vote acts as a kind of "opinion" of the shareholders and it does not have to be followed by the directors, who still may decide under their own responsibility. If the authorization is denied, the directors can execute the transaction, but their decision would be less defendable in court; if the vote is given, they could argue that their action had been endorsed by shareholders and the future judicial scrutiny over the decision could be less severe[44].

Cools, *The dividing line between shareholder democracy and board autonomy: inherent conflict of interest as normative criterion*, in *ECFR*, 2014, 258, also for further references.

43 See Pietraconsta/Dubois/Garçon, *Corporate*, 210; see also i.e. Art. 5.73 B-CA.

44 See, with reference to both the monistic and traditional models, Tina, in *Company laws*, 484 (the "authorization of the shareholders' meeting is in any case accompanied by 'the idea of the power and, therefore, freedom' of the directors 'to carry out the authorized action'; as specified by the same Art. 2364, no. 5 of the c.c., the responsibility of the directors for the actions carried

On the other hand, the powers recognized – or that may be recognized – to shareholders under other Member States' laws are very broad (and the answer to the questions previously raised is positive for all four of them).

In particular, Nordic countries have chosen to endorse a "shareholder-friendly" approach as the paradigm for their legislative system. "The key distinctive feature of Nordic corporate governance" – it has been noted – "is the strong powers vested with a shareholder majority to effectively control the company. This forms the basis for dominant owners to engage in, and take long-term responsibility for their company, but it also offers shareholders of more widely held companies the potential to exert genuine ownership powers, e. g. by forming ad hoc coalitions to deal with issues of common interest. In fact, the model is highly flexible, providing a generally shareholder-friendly governance framework that is functional within a wide range of different ownership structures. The underlying philosophy is that the shareholders should be in command of the company. The board and management are seen as the shareholders' agents for running the company during their mandate period under strict accountability to the shareholders for the outcome of their work"[45].

---

out remains, in any case, "notwithstanding""; the opinion is however debated by other scholars). See also Arts. 111 R-CA and 161 S-CA [referring to the latter provision, Pérez Millán, in *Company laws*, 1207 notes that it "is controversial how the lack of authorization affects the powers of representation of the directors. According to one opinion, any transaction made without this approval would then be null and void, since it would exceed the powers legally conferred to the directors. On the contrary, others claim that the transaction should be treated as an act outside the objects of the company, i.e. it will bind the company with respect to third parties in good faith according to Art. 234.2 Sp-CA]); the Author continues observing that, "this notwithstanding, the directors cannot be *de facto* emasculated, nor transformed into mere executers of resolutions passed at the shareholders' meeting. Moreover, the instructions or authorization by the shareholders' meeting have merely internal effects. A breach of the instructions or a lack of authorization does not affect the powers of representation of the directors (Arts. 161 Sp-CA). Neither following those instructions or having received the authorization of the shareholders' meeting excuses the directors from their responsibility (Art. 236 Sp-CA), since they must identify whether the instructions, they receive break the law, go against the bylaws, or are detrimental to the interests of the company"].

45 See Lekvall et al., *A consolidated Nordic governance model*, in Lekvall (ed.), *The Nordic*, 52; see also Krüger Andersen/Sørensen, *The principle of shareholder primacy in company law from a Nordic and European regulatory perspective*, 2011, at ssrn.com; Dent, *Corporate governance: the Swedish solution*, at ssrn.com, 2012; Bludly Hansen/Lønfeldt, *Corporate governance in Denmark*, in Lekvall (ed.), *The Nordic*, 128, recognize that in Danish corporate governance the general meeting "is almost *omnipotent*" and adds that "shareholders may decide what they want [and] may by resolution interfere with management and take decisions regarding the governance of the company at will. A typical classroom example illuminating this point is to observe that the general meeting may decide the colour of the pencils to be used by the company". Skog/Sjöman,

A more nuanced solution has been adopted, finally, by other companies acts: they do not permit shareholders to participate in business decisions on a general basis, but impose a mandatory vote on important transactions, like the acquisition, disposal or transfer of essential assets to other companies[46]. Moreover, they allow statutory clauses requiring that certain acts – investment plans, relevant contracts, partial asset transfers, etc. – are subject to the prior approval of the shareholders' general meeting, with binding effect[47].

(B) The question of the balance of powers arises also in the dualistic system. Once again, the issue is not clear cut.

As far as the question about whether the articles of association may contain clauses that give the shareholders' general meetings competence in business matters, the answer is clearly "no" – for example – in Germany: management autonomy in public companies is inalienable; the articles of association cannot provide otherwise (see Sect. 76 Ge-PuCA)[48].

As far as shareholders' votes, Sect. 119 Ge-PuCA allows management to ask for a "decision" by the shareholders' general meeting on business matters and shareholders' directives are normally considered binding[49]. However, this provi-

---

Corporate governance in Sweden, in Lekvall (ed.), *The Nordic*, 254, illustrate that, under Swedish law, "the general meeting has a sovereign role over the board of directors and CEO" (with reference to Ch. 7, Sect. 10, Sw-CA). See also, paradigmatically, Ch. 5, Sect. 2, Fi-CA: "the general meeting shall make decisions on matters that fall within its competence by virtue of this Act. It may be provided in the articles of association that the general meeting decides matters that fall within the general competence of the managing director and the board of directors".

46 See Art. 160 Sp-CA: "essential assets" are those valued at more than 25% of the balance sheet assets of the company. Moreover, Art. 81 ff. Sp-LSC requires the shareholders' vote also in case of transfer of all company assets (with a procedure similar to the one set forth for the case of mergers); see also i.e. Art. 330 Slove-CA.

47 According to Art. 153(22) R-CA, the board of directors may not purchase goods or transfer, lease, exchange or give guarantees on behalf of the company, if the value of the transaction exceeds half of the accounting value of the company's assets on the date of its conclusion: in such cases, the approval of the extraordinary general meeting of the shareholders is needed. Art. 421 Cz-CA stipulates that the power of shareholders' general meetings include "any other matters entrusted to the general meeting by law or the articles of association".

48 As we have seen above (§ 3), also in cases where some transactions are subject to the approval of the supervisory board pursuant to the law and the articles of association (Sect. 111 Ge-PuCA), the board can either decide to proceed autonomously (notwithstanding the different position of the supervisory board) or ask for the shareholders' direct approval. See also i.e. Sect. 70 A-PuCA.

49 A more rigid approach is to be found in Poland: board members always have discretionary power and are autonomous while running company's affairs (see Art. 368 Pol-CC). As reported by Oplustil, in *Company laws*, 710, a doctrinal and practical controversy has arisen on the ground of Art. 375 Pol-CC, pursuant to which the relationship of members of the management

sion should not be overestimated: as it has been observed, even if "in theory, the management board has a right to bring items concerning the running of the business to the shareholders", "in practice, it never does, and the shareholders have no way to force them"[50]. In any case, the much debated "Holzmüller/Gelatine" jurisprudence entails however shareholder approval at least of transactions transferring the greater part of the company's assets to other companies[51].

The Dutch two-tier model seems more permissive. Even though the management board is largely autonomous and does not have to accept instructions from other corporate bodies (such as the shareholders' general meeting), important limitations can be found, on the one hand, in the provision which stipulates that the articles of association may grant the right to instruct the management board to another corporate body (such as the shareholders' general meeting: Art. 2.239 Du-CC), and, on the other hand, in the rule that establishes that – even if the articles of association attribute responsibility to the board of directors – any resolution taken that causes major changes in the identity or character of the company must be approved by the shareholders' general meeting (Art. 2.107a Du-CC)[52].

---

board to the company are subject to the restrictions set forth in the law or the articles of association and to the resolutions of the supervisory board and the shareholders' general meeting. According to prevailing opinion, however, Art. 375 cannot be regarded as a legal basis for the shareholders' general meeting to give binding instructions to members of the management board: see Soltysiński, *Corporate boards in Poland*, in Davies et al. (eds.), *Corporate*, 525 ("the general meeting of shareholders and supervisory board may not issue binding instructions to the management board in the area of the management of the company"); Warchol, *The balance of power in Polish company code regulations: an Eastern European perspective on corporate governance*, in ECFR, 2011, 174.

50 See Schall, in *Company laws*, 290.

51 As summarized by Schall, in *Company laws*, 291 "the Holzmüller case has created these rules. In Gelatine, the [Supreme Court] adjusted and clarified them. If more than 75% are transferred, the transaction needs consent by a special resolution with qualified majority"; see also, among others, Löbbe, *Corporate groups: competences of the shareholders' meeting and minority protection – The German Federal Court of Justice's recent Gelatine and Macrotron cases redefine the Holzmüller doctrine*, in GLJ, 2004, 1057; and Böttcher/ Blasche, *The limitations of the management board's directive powers in German stock corporations*, in GLJ, 2010, 493 (cf. respectively German Supreme Court, 25 February 1982 and 26 April 2004).

52 This latter rule more precisely refers to (a) the transfer of business or almost the entire business to third parties, (b) the entering into or discontinuing of long-lasting cooperations between the company or a subsidiary and another company or similar entities, and (c) the company or a subsidiary acquiring or disposing of a participating interest worth at least one-third of the amount of the assets as stated in the company's (consolidated) annual accounts. According to legal scholars, the rule should however be interpreted restrictively and require approval only for resolutions deciding over the (near full) transfer of the company or concluding or terminating

(C) The scenario is thus rather mixed. Usually the choice to empower share-holders originates from the political purpose to make their participation in the life of the company more appealing, and thus to sustain investments in corporations in the long run[53].

In some countries – paradigmatically the Nordic – this also seems to relate to the deeply-rooted economic structure of public companies: since dominant ownership is basically widespread, shareholders require – and do – exercise considerable influence on the management (consider, for instance, that in Sweden there are around 1.000 public companies, one quarter of them are listed and professional investors account for more than 85% of the shareholdings)[54].

On the other hand, the need for companies to give the command to managers only and strengthen their position may be traced back to the goal – expressly declared by some governments – to "enhance the entrepreneurial nature of the

---

partnerships of particular significance (see Roos, in *Company laws*, 1382; see also Oostwouder/van den Braak, *The amended position of shareholders in a Dutch public limited company*, in *ECL*, 2004, 167)

For an important case, ruling that, in principle, the decision to sell a division of the company is up to the board, but whether prior shareholder approval is required will depend on all relevant aspects of the specific case, see the Amsterdam Court of Appeal, Enterprise Chamber, 3 May 2007 (case "ABN AMRO"); the case is commented on by De Groot/van Nood, *The ABN ruling: some commentaries*, in *ECL*, 2007, 168, and by Timmermann, *Application of the Dutch investigation procedure on two listed companies: the* Gucci *and* ABN AMRO *cases*, in Tison et al. (eds.), *Perspectives*, 363. See also the case "AkzoNobel", decided by the Amsterdam Court, Enterprise Chamber, on 10 August 2017: the main arguments of the courts were based on the idea that the decision on a takeover bid is part of the company's strategy, which belongs to the exclusive domain of the board; see Vos, *The AkzoNobel case: an activist shareholder's battle against the backdrop of the Shareholder Rights Directive*, in *ECL*, 2017, 238.

See also Art. 2.128 Du-CC, pursuant to which instructions by the shareholders' general meeting (or another body provided for in the articles of association) of public companies must be limited to instructions concerning the general policy in respect of areas specified in the articles of association. See also i.e. Sect. 421 Cz-CA and Art. 20 Li-CA ("the general meeting of shareholders may also decide on other matters assigned to its powers by the articles of association of a company, unless these have been assigned under this law to the powers of other bodies of the company and provided that, in their essence, these are not the functions of the management bodies").

53 This has been the case for some changes introduced in the Netherlands in 2004, which had the express aim to strengthen the position of shareholders, as the State intended to present itself as being attractive to investors: see Oostwouder/Van den Braak, *The amended position of shareholders in a Dutch public limited company*, in *ECL*, 2004, 166.

54 See Hansen, *The Report*, 6; Id., *The Nordic corporate governance model – a European model*, in Tison et al. (eds.), *Perspectives*, 145; see also Krüger Andersen/Sørensen, *The principle*; Skog/Sjöman, *Corporate*, 618.

companies and define the tasks and responsibilities of the corporate bodies with clarity and precision" (also with a view towards pursuing the objective of promoting the "growth and competitiveness of businesses", by means of more powerful board of directors)[55].

On its part, the EMCA Group states – embracing the view of "shareholders' participation" – that "in public companies, keeping with the principle of shareholders' democracy, decision rights on all-important matters relating to the company should always be reserved for the shareholders".

(D) The question is also a highly theoretical one. In this field the academic debate ("directors' primacy" versus "shareholders' primacy") is very animated.

A line of thinking holds that – since shareholder participation should be meant as a "toolkit aimed at reducing [majority shareholders' or managers'] opportunism" – shareholders' votes should be always endorsed, per se[56].

Others believe that shareholders' approval should be required – more specifically – only in cases of structural changes that may create conflict of interest for shareholders and/or directors, like mergers and takeovers (in such cases directors' decisions could be driven by the fear of losing their jobs), or major investments or disinvestments (those transactions, if successful, have side effects in terms of prestige and remuneration, often based on factors like increases in sales, turnover or company liquidity); beyond that, board authority would remain the more efficient option[57].

The opposite view claims that empowering shareholders to too great an extent, who by definition are irresponsible, may entail severe problems of accountability. Only directors' power may be efficiently constrained. The alignment of managers and directors' interests is always guaranteed by the risk of litigation and by jurisdictions supporting the "market for corporate control"[58].

(E) Finally, it should also be considered that traditional shareholders are being replaced to an increasing extent by a new generation of professional investors, especially – but not only – in listed companies: on the one hand, "insti-

---

55 See for these terms the Italian law 366/2001 delegating the Government for the reform of company law.

56 For an analysis along these lines see for instance Sáez/Riaño, *Corporate*, and Krüger Andersen/Sørensen, *The principle*, also for further references.

57 For this view see especially Cools, *The dividing*, 279 ff., also for further references.

58 Firms whose share prices are lower than they would be if they were managed by more talented or highly motivated managers are attractive takeover targets. By buying up enough shares to vote in a new board of directors, a bidder can then replace an inefficient or ineffectual management team. Jurisdictions favouring takeovers (i.e. the "market of corporate control") thus have an enhancing effect on effective managers' oversight; see also below Chapter 10, § 1.

tutional" investors (asset managers, pension funds, insurance companies, all investing money on behalf of other people); on the other, "activist" or "hedge" funds (which are aggressively managed and make use of leverage and sophisticated financial techniques in order to put pressure on management and increase company profits).

Generally, these investors are more interested in corporate governance and in participating in shareholders' general meetings, also by casting their vote remotely[59]. These funds may also ride on the share under-pricing in the market that is due to corporate governance deficiencies (the reasoning is that weak governance leads to lower prices, so that improving governance benefits market prices). Some funds detect under-pricing due to lack of focus in the business: they will hence insist on a reorganization of the business, spinning off activities, or acquiring other business to achieve a stronger market share.

What are the differences between these institutional and activist investors and traditional shareholders?

Firstly, these investors normally purchase large blocks of shares, allowing them to influence the management, thanks also to their professional skills. Secondly, they often act together with other funds, in concert, and are hence able to multiply their force in the field. Finally, as it has been noted, while small investors usually do not attend the shareholders' reunions, these funds (often with the assistance of top law firms) are – given their interest in enhancing corporate governance – "the masters of the shareholders' general meeting"[60].

---

59 See Wymeersch, *Shareholders in action*, 2007, at *ssrn.com*. On the use by institutional investors of the techniques of remote voting see Van der Elst, *Shareholder engagement and shareholder voting modes: two of a different kind*, 2019, at *ecgi.org*.

60 See Wymeersch, *Shareholders*, 6; see also i.e. Houben/Straetmans, *Shareholder rights and responsibilities in the context of corporate social responsibility*, in *EBLR*, 2016, 618 [affirming that "shareholder activism can have a positive impact on the target company. A striking example is the implementation or improvement of corporate governance rules. The activist expects that such implementation or improvement of corporate governance rules will result in better and more efficient performance of the (management of the) company and will hence increase shareholder value. Therefore, shareholder activism is often associated with the implementation of corporate governance rules in the target company. Activism may, however, also have negative consequences for the target company, for example when activism leads to a higher risk profile of the target company"].

5. "Internal" controls on management: audit committees, statutory auditors, supervisory boards

Meaningful differences between national rules can be found in the ways in which controls over managers' actions are structured, and the extent of the powers conferred to the supervisors.

The differences are really important and they concern both the nature of the controls performed from "inside" the company (i.e. by internal bodies like the audit committee or the supervisory board) and the nature of controls performed from "outside" (i.e. by professionals appointed by the courts on the request of shareholders, by administrative authorities, or even by criminal prosecutors).

(A) Starting with "internal" controls, in the monistic system they are strictly related to the specific features of that model, which however differ among countries.

Some laws adopt a very "basic" one-tier model structure where the shareholders appoint the board of directors and an external auditor who audits the accounts and the financial statements; an internal committee at board level (with a monitoring role) is not mandatory.

This basic model is however sometimes slightly modified in order to mitigate the risk of fraud or negligence. Swedish law presents an interesting example, where – with the aim of counterbalancing the absence of a mandatory audit committee – the powers of the external auditors (i.e. the audit firm) are extended. Ch. 9, Sect. 3, Sw-CA stipulates that "the [external] auditor shall examine the company's annual report and accounts as well as the management by the board of directors and the managing director", and that "where the company is a parent company, the auditor shall also examine the group accounts, where such have been prepared, as well as the relationship inter se of group companies"[61]. This type of control is thus similar – even if carried out from the "outside" (and in any case far less broad) – to the one performed by the statutory auditors in the traditional system (in that case, from the "inside").

Under some jurisdictions, the directors have to form a committee (called – as we have seen above in § 3 – an "audit committee") composed of non-executive directors, with the task of monitoring the activity of the other executive members

---

[61] Under Danish and Finnish law the auditors can call the shareholders' general meeting: see Sect. 93 Da-CA and Ch. 5, Sect. 3, Fi-CA.

(and – to a certain extent – with the power to promote special actions: specific inquiries, etc.[62]).

Normally the committee also has to verify the correctness of the actions of the board of directors[63].

The conclusion is thus that a significant difference can be found between the different Member States' laws – within the same governance model – not only at the level of the body performing the supervision (board, committee, audit firm, etc., and that is more intuitive), but above all at the level of the concrete extension of the controls carried out by the same body, which varies a lot (and that is probably more surprising).

(B) In the "traditional" (latin) system, the statutory auditors are entrusted with supervising the following areas: compliance by the directors with the law and the articles of association of the company; compliance by the directors with the principles of "correct administration"; adequacy and reliability of the organizational and administrative structure of the company; adequacy and reliability of the accounting system.

The function related to monitoring compliance with the principles of correct administration is very important; it entails monitoring the compliance of directors' decisions with the law and good business practices. However, said oversight does not entail verifying the "merits" of the decisions made by the directors, but only involves checking the directors' decision-making process which led to such

---

62 See i.e. Ch. 8, Sect. 4, Sw-CA. Pursuant to Sect. 111 Da-CA, the majority of members of the board of directors of public companies must be non-executive directors. See for listed companies below Chapter 12, § 4. Less frequently the members of the audit committee may be non-executive directors (this is the case of the Irish companies act); this can create a certain level of mixing between controllers and controlees (the situation however changes for bigger companies, where the majority of directors must be independent; see Sect. 167 Ir-CA). As a consequence of a that lack of a formal distinction at legislative level, the jurisprudence does not seem particularly sensitive to this and tends to put non-executive directors on the same level as all other directors [as it has been done by UK judges (Court of Appeal) in the famous case of 2000 "*In Re Barings plc (No 5)*": on that occasion, Judge Parker stated: "(i) Directors have, both collectively and individually, a continuing duty to acquire and maintain a sufficient knowledge and understanding of the company's business to enable them properly to discharge their duties as directors. (ii) Whilst directors are entitled (subject to the articles of association of the company) to delegate particular functions to those below them in the management chain, and to trust their competence and integrity to a reasonable extent, the exercise of the power of delegation does not absolve a director from the duty to supervise the discharge of the delegated functions"].
63 On the other hand, certain provisions limit the duties of the committee to monitoring the company's financial reporting process, the effectiveness of the company's systems of internal control and the independence of the audit firm. See again, for that – more restrictive – direction above all Sect. 167 Ir-CA, for the case where a committee has been established.

decisions. The latitude of the control is, in any case, wide[64] and this width becomes very meaningful considering the further powers that statutory auditors are attributed by some domestic laws.

Normally statutory auditors are obliged to take part in both their own board meetings and those of the other corporate bodies (shareholders' general meetings and, above all, meetings of the boards of directors). They have to request regular information from the directors on the company's operating results or on given transactions, also with reference to subsidiaries. They may carry out inspections which they deem useful for the purpose of the diligent performance of the oversight function[65].

Once they have gained all such information, they may – pursuant to some national laws – also call a shareholders' general meeting in the case of omissions or unjustified delays by the directors or when they detect wrongful acts of a serious nature (or if they are reported by the shareholders), or if there is an urgent need to implement certain measures; moreover they can challenge any resolutions of the board of directors or of the shareholders if they were not passed in compliance with the law and the articles of association, may require judicial review in the case of severe irregularities and may finally file lawsuits against the directors if they believe that the latter have breached their duties and caused harm to the company[66].

---

[64] And may become even wider if some courts' interpretations are followed: there is agreement on the fact that the auditors must ascertain that directors do not carry out any transactions which are outside the company purpose, are aimed at suppressing or modifying the rights conferred by the law or the articles of association to shareholders; are in conflict with the resolutions passed by the shareholders' general meetings or by the board of directors; the statutory auditors have however been sometimes conferred the power to object to decisions by directors that are manifestly imprudent or risky or that may compromise the integrity of the company's assets or pose a threat to the ability of the company to operate as a going concern.

[65] See Arts. 2403 ff. It-CC; pursuant to Art. 164 R-CA the statutory auditors' power to inspect the company is however more limited, since they can obtain information from the directors only on a monthly basis.

[66] That first possibility is provided for by Arts. 420 f. Por-CC and Art. 163 R-CA; that and all the others by Arts. 2406–2409 It-CC; on some of these powers see further below Chapter § 6. The most extreme model may however be found in Italy, where – pursuant to the more recent bankruptcy legislation (law 155/2017) – auditors also have a reporting obligation towards the newly established administrative "corporate crisis settlement authority", which assists companies in the settlement process with their creditors. Once the auditors ascertain the non-sustainability of the debts with the company's cash-flows and/or its inability to operate as a going concern in the following six months, they must write to the directors assigning a deadline of no more than 30 days to report on the solutions identified and the initiatives undertaken. In case of inadequate response or failure to respond in the next sixty days, they have to promptly inform the

(C) Finally, we can examine the characteristics of the controls performed by the supervisory board in the two-tier system.

Taking again Germany as the example, the supervisory board has to check to ensure (also on the basis of well-regulated flows of information) the propriety of the management board's activity, but may only intervene if the directors make mistakes when exercising their discretion[67]. These failures are recognized in certain categories: a) extraneous considerations (such as personal interests); b) illegality (mainly as far as procedural aspects are concerned); c) transgression of economic boundaries (before making any decision, the directors have to weigh the potential benefits against the potential risks; if the risks outweigh the benefits, directors have to omit the targeted action; if however the board of directors still decides to act, the supervisory board may intervene).

The supervisory board may issue (as we have seen, non binding) orders and recommendations; in the most severe cases it can exercise its right to call a shareholders' general meeting, withdraw the appointment of one or more members of the board of directors and file a suit against the directors in the name of the company.

The breadth of control of the supervisory board – also on the company books – is thus pretty large and the monitoring function fundamentally pervasive[68].

---

authority by providing any useful information notwithstanding any duty of confidentiality. The procedure before the authority comprises two distinct phases aimed at the identification of possible measures to remedy the state of crisis and the attempt to settle the crisis, characterized by negotiation with creditors.

67 See Sect. 90 Ge-PuCA.

68 See Sect. 111 Ge-PuCA: the supervisory board may inspect and audit the books and records of the company as well as its assets, particularly the company's cash and the inventory of securities and goods. It may also instruct individual members to perform these tasks, or may commission special experts for certain of them; it is however debated, for instance, whether the supervisory board may have access to employees: see Roth, *Corporate*, 313. The situation is not different i.e. under Art. 225-68 Fr-CC: the supervisory board exerts a "permanent oversight" over the board of directors; it may carry out any verification it considers appropriate and request any document it feels necessary; unlike directors, members of the supervisory board may have direct access to employees of the company. Pursuant to Sect. 95 A-PuCA, the supervisory board may at any time request a report from the management board on the affairs of the company including its relations with a group company, it may inspect and examine the books and records of the company as well as the assets and may also commission individual members or special experts for specific tasks; it may convene a shareholders' general meeting if the welfare of the company so requires. Also, according to Art. 447 Cz-CC the supervisory board is authorized to inspect any and all documents relating to the company's activities.

(D) The duties and liabilities of the members of the supervisory bodies in the different governance systems are analyzed to a greater extent below in Chapter 9.

6. "External" controls on management: audit firms and special examiners

Impressive differences can also be found at the level of the external controls. These controls are the most feared by directors; at the same time, they should be limited as much as possible since they represent – if recognized extensively – an insidious form of external (public) intervention in the sphere of the company's (private) life.

(A) First, in almost all EU jurisdictions, companies must appoint an audit firm (or a single auditor) registered on a ministerial roll of auditors (as we have seen, the appointment of an audit firm may be avoided in the traditional system for smaller companies, which may attribute the audit function to the statutory auditors). Under Nordic laws, the minority shareholders may elect a "minority auditor"[69].

The audit firm must perform a quarterly audit on the accounts and prepare a report on the financial statements that includes an assessment on accounting, the reliability of the financial statements and the results of the audit performed during the financial year. This report must then be submitted to the annual general meeting.

The powers and duties of the audit firms are analyzed more comprehensively below in Chapter 8 (devoted to financial statements and controls on accountability).

(B) Court controls – i.e. controls performed by judges' auxiliaries at the request of minority shareholders – are much more delicate.

As a consequence, many Member States simply do not regulate this type of court intervention. In contrast, they are recognized to a significant extent by other jurisdictions.

---

69 See i.e. Ch. 9, Sect. 9, Sw-CA ("a shareholder may propose that an auditor appointed by [an administrative independent authority] shall participate in the audit together with other auditors. The proposal shall be submitted to a general meeting at which the election of auditors is to take place or at which a proposal set forth in the notice to attend the general meeting is to be addressed. Where the proposal is supported by owners of at least one-tenth of all shares in the company or at least one-third of the shares represented at the meeting, the [authority] shall appoint an auditor)"; see more extensively below Chapter 8, § 5.

Under Dutch and Italian laws, for example, if there is grounded suspicion of mismanagement, shareholders owning 10 % of the shares may request the court to make an order of injunction (for example, order an external inspection of the corporate accounts) and, in more serious cases, remove the directors and appoint a "special administrator" (who acts also like a custodian, manages the company and may even – according to said legislations – file a suit against the directors and the statutory auditors without involving the shareholders' general meeting). The Amsterdam Enterprise Chamber, for example, has been involved in some of the most important (and bitterest) national legal fights by shareholders invoking that remedy[70].

Provisions on "special examiners" to be appointed by courts are also found in Nordic laws (the Danish companies act gives a minority of 25 % the right to ask for a special examiner; the Finnish and Swedish laws reduce the threshold to 10 %), and in many other legislations[71]. In all these cases, however, the special

---

[70] See Arts. 2.345 ff. Du-CC and Art. 2409 It-CC; the power to ask for the appointment can also be reserved to certain shareholders who fulfil the necessary requirements or the statutory auditors (and the criminal prosecutor in listed companies). The powers given to the Dutch court are actually broader: if so requested, the court may order "immediate measures", which are valid for the duration of the proceedings and can take the form (beyond the appointment of new directors) of a restriction of shareholders' rights, a deviation from the articles of association or many other forms, at the discretion of the court itself. At the end of the proceedings, however, the final measurers that may be established by the court are less far reaching and can only take the form as provided for in the Du-CC (see Bisschop/Roelink/Kemp, in *Company laws*, 1322). For the case "ABN AMRO" (2007) see above fn. 52; for the case "Gucci Group" (in particular, Amsterdam Enterprise Chamber, 27 April 1999, and Dutch Supreme Court, 27 September 2000) see Timmermann, *Application*, 367.

[71] See i.e. Ch. 10, Sect. 21, Sw-CA. Pursuant to French law, shareholders holding more than 5 % of the share capital are entitled to pose questions in writing to the board of directors on selected management actions. In the absence of a reply within a month or if the reply is not considered to be appropriate, they may request a Court to nominate an expert to present a report on these actions. This action is also available to the workers' council, the criminal prosecutor and, in listed companies, the supervising authority. The request for an expert should be based on specific acts of management and should not be a criticism of the management in general. Similar rules are also contained in German law: a special audit is a formal procedure set forth under Ge-PuCA, Sect. 142–146 by means of which shareholders are enabled to investigate specified actions as part of the operations of their company. The rationale behind this is closely related to the shareholders' derivative action right in Ge-PuCA, Sect. 148 (on which see below Chapter 9, § 4). The objective is to shed light on possible irregularities within the operations of the company and to provide shareholders with the stock of information needed to evaluate the merits of potential litigation. Where a motion for the appointment of special auditors is not carried at the shareholders' general meeting, the court has to appoint special auditors if a petition to that effect is filed

examiner acts with the narrower goal to shed light on specific corporate actions, having to report finally to the shareholders, who retain the last word on the line of conduct to follow.

The EMCA goes along the same direction: Sect. 11.32 stipulates that a single shareholder may also submit a proposal for a special examiner to assess specific company's operations with a view to preparing a report on their effects for the company and its shareholders, as well as their compliance with the law and good business practices. The motion to appoint the special examiner shall contain at least the information on the scope of the examinations and the reasons for the appointment of the examiner. If the shareholders' general meeting refuses to appoint a special examiner in accordance with the demand of the petitioner, owners of at least 10% of the shares may request the court to order the company to appoint the special examiner. The latter shall submit a report regarding the results of the examination, to be made available to the shareholders and presented at a general meeting[72].

In conclusion, it should be pointed out how some Member States' laws appear to have the directors' action monitored in a much more pervasive way than others.

In this regard, it is worthwhile to put the emphasis on the acknowledgment of the EMCA Group, which has noted that the single States' jurisdictions differ – first of all – "in the degree" to which they place importance on external supervision (and – only at a second stage – "in the way" they govern the controls on management).

7. Management board and supervisory board meetings and resolutions

(A) For the most part, Member States' laws do not set an obligatory frequency for directors' meetings, with a few exceptions. The frequency of meetings may therefore be freely stipulated. A meeting is, however, generally needed at least once a

---

by shareholders whose shares, in the aggregate, are at least equivalent to one hundredth of the share capital, or to a stake of € 100.000. See also Art. 318 Slove-CA; Art. 142 Gr-PuCA; etc.
72 Further specific provisions are set out by the EMCA for companies belonging to groups (see on that below, Chapter 7, § 6). Also, the Action Plan of 2003 recalls that "the High-Level Group made several other recommendations designed to enhance directors responsibilities [among which the] introduction of a special investigation right, whereby shareholders holding a certain percentage of the share capital should have the right to ask a court or administrative authority to authorize a special investigation into the affairs of the company".

year to approve the annual accounts (in the praxis, however, directors meet more frequently in order to diligently fulfil their duty to run the company).

As far as the validity of these meetings is concerned, the general rule is that at least half of the members of the body must be present. Regarding the decision-making process, legislations usually require a simple majority of the directors who are present; however, a few require an absolute majority[73].

Board meeting resolutions may be challenged in court – pursuant to most national laws – by each single director (and by each statutory auditor, in the companies adopting the traditional system).

On the other hand, normally board meetings' decisions cannot be challenged by shareholders. Exceptions are provided in some jurisdictions. For instance, Spanish shareholders may challenge the resolutions of the board of directors provided that they represent 5% of the corporate capital, within thirty days from becoming aware of said resolutions and provided that not more than one year has elapsed since their adoption[74]. Under Dutch law, resolutions of all corporate bodies can be invalidated on the basis of more general private law provisions, such as – for instance – in the case that the resolution is adopted as a result of duress, fraud and/or undue influence or certain creditors of the company are prejudiced and/or in the event of the insolvency of the company[75]. Pursuant to Art. 2388 It-CC, this right to challenge directors' resolutions is given – less broadly – against decisions that "directly" affect shareholders' rights and within a period of three months.

(B) As far as the functioning of the supervisory boards is concerned, specific details are given in national laws both for the frequency of meetings and decision-making, with a certain amount of freedom left to the articles of association, which is nevertheless basically restricted.

Regarding the frequency, the supervisory body must meet whenever necessary, but generally at least once a year to approve (or convey its observations on) the annual accounts.

Most Member States allow shareholders to file lawsuits to challenge the supervisory board meeting resolutions in case of irregularities[76].

---

73 So i.e. Polish law; see Oplustil, in *Company laws*, 712.
74 See Art. 251 Sp-CA. Cf. also for a quite broad provision Arts. 411 f. Por-CC.
75 See Arts. 3.44, 3.45 and 3.59 Du-CC.
76 This is the case also under German law, according the jurisprudence: see Roth, *Corporate*, 349.

Finally, statutory auditors must normally meet with a certain frequency (i.e. quarterly[77]). Statutory auditors' meeting resolutions may only be challenged by members of the same board.

(C) For shareholders' general meetings resolutions – and their invalidity – see below Chapter 6, § 2.

8. Shareholders' agreements

(I) The governance of the company can finally be impacted by the presence of "shareholders' agreements".

The content of these arrangements – which are normally stipulated by only some of the shareholders – may be comprehensive to a greater or lesser extent[78]. They may involve the obligation to consult on some corporate matters, to vote in the same manner, or to give instructions to the directors.

This kind of contract may be also employed to set limits to the transfer of the shares linked by the pact, which assumes thus a different scope.

Shareholders may even acquire the control of the company through these agreements.

The first kind of pacts – on the vote (also called "voting syndicates") – may focus on one or more specific resolutions or even take on an organizational and procedural role, if they are intended to apply to an undetermined number of resolutions. In this latter case, the shareholders may establish that the decision on how to vote in the shareholders' general meeting has to be reached unanimously or by a majority of the shareholders participating in the pact.

The "blocking" effect that can be obtained with the second kind of agreements is also much sought-after. Sometimes shareholders prefer to regulate the circulation of the shares to a more limited extent than what could have been achieved by inserting provisions in the articles of association, and they therefore opt for more definite ad hoc agreements. Also, investors in firms backed by funds are increasingly adopting firm-specific provisions contained in such arrangements.

Finally, agreements which aim at exercising a dominant influence over the company by means of the giving orders to the members of the board are becoming very meaningful. That may trigger wider capital market obligations, like the duty to launch a tender offer (this aspect is considered separately below in Chap-

---

77 See Art. 2404 It-Cc.

78 Less frequently these agreements are signed by all shareholders or with the company.

ter 12). In any case, they may create stable shared control rights among a coalition of shareholders, becoming a tool for alternative governance mechanisms.

Like any contract, these agreements only bind those shareholders who participate in them and are not, therefore, enforceable on the company and investors (current and future) outside of the pact, even if signed by all the shareholders. In the case of breach, the harmed shareholders participating to the agreement may claim compensation against the shareholders acting unlawfully.

Even if shareholders' agreements are known in all Member States and greatly used in practice, they have received little legislative attention: neither the directives nor the EMCA include specific provisions. The approach taken by Member States is thus rather soft and the freedom of contract is the basic principle.

Only a few provisions are to be found in single national laws, sanctioning the exercise of the rights under an agreement that leads to abuse of power[79], or to the violation of law, ethics and public order[80] or the subordination of the will of directors (or other company bodies) to the rules of the pact[81].

---

[79] This is the case of the Netherlands pursuant to Art. 3.13 Du-CC. Among others, the example is the exercise of the rights accorded by the agreement for the sole purpose of harming other shareholders, or in an unreasonable way, etc.). A relevant question however remains open, which is debated among Dutch scholars: whether it is possible to give shareholders' agreements "corporate effect" by using incorporation by reference. The articles of association or the statutes sometimes refer to the fact that certain provisions are further regulated in a shareholders' agreement. The current view is that incorporation by reference is not possible. It is, however, called into question to what extent this is indeed a valid argument, since there are a number of cases in which provisions in shareholders' agreements are given "corporate effect" if all shareholders and the company itself are a party to the shareholders' agreement. Certain case law goes even further and states that even if the company is not a party to the shareholders' agreement it will under certain circumstances be held to comply with the shareholders' agreement: see Steins Bisschop/Roelink/Kemp, in *Company laws*, 1341, fn. 177, quoting the "Chipsol" case of 1996 and the "Versatel" case of 2000.

[80] Some laws, for instance, have chosen to limit themselves to stating that shareholders' agreements are recognized as fully valid and enforceable "inter partes", as long as they respect the limits of the freedom of contracts, namely, law, ethics and public order: see Art. 17 Por-CC and Art. 29 Sp-CA; for further references on the latter see Marín de la Bárcena, in *Company laws*, 1113.

Sect. 82 Da-CA (stating that shareholders' agreements are neither binding on the company nor on decisions taken by the general assembly) was introduced in 2010 de facto in order to overrule a decision of the Supreme Court from 1996 establishing that agreements known to all shareholders were binding on the general assembly and the chairperson would have to regard the shareholder bound to the agreement as having voted according to the agreement; see Werklauff, *New Danish company act on shareholders' agreements: a critical evaluation*, in *ECL*, 2011, 161.

Italian law has taken – apparently as a sole exception – a more regulatory approach. According to the legislative view, these pacts, on the one hand, have the effect of "predeterminating" the vote outside of the shareholders' general meeting and partly diminish the importance of the debate (they can also take by surprise shareholders who do not know of their existence); on the other hand, they risk to put the company directors under the strong influence of some shareholders. Therefore, this national law addresses the issue of their duration and – limited to larger or listed companies – their disclosure.

In unlisted companies, agreements which: i) have, as their objective, the exercise of voting rights in companies or parent companies; ii) place limits on the transfer of shares of the company or parent companies; iii) have, as their objective or effect, the exercise, even jointly, of dominant influence over the company or parent companies, may not have a duration of over five years and are deemed to have been stipulated for five years, even if the parties have envisaged a greater duration (three years in listed companies). If the parties have not envisaged an expiry, each party has the right to withdraw from the agreement with notice of one hundred and eighty days[82].

In other companies, with unlisted shares, but with certain characteristics that make them more open to investors (having more than 200 shareholders, holding together more than 5% of the share capital) the agreements must be communicated to the company and declared at the beginning of every shareholders' general meeting; the declaration must be transcribed in the minutes of the meeting, which have to be submitted to the companies register. In the

---

In France the matter is regulated only by case law: shareholders' agreements are valid as long as they are not in breach of a fundamental "public policy" rule or of a mandatory rule provided for in the by-laws or that contradict the corporate interest; see particularly Supreme Court, 7 January 2004, n. 00 – 11692 (case "Ope Intermarché", quoted in Grossi/Poracchia/Raynouard, in *Company laws*, 87). But see Court of Appeal of Paris, 8 November 2011 (quoted by the latter): in a case where the majority shareholder had breached the voting agreement's provision designed to enable the minority to be represented on the supervisory board, the Court, seized by the minority shareholder, agreed to appoint an "ad hoc representative" to receive all documents, be called and to attend all meetings of the supervisory board and report to the minority (see Grossi/Poracchia/Raynouard, *ibidem*, 88).

81 In Germany the agreements are forbidden only as long they entail the undertaking of a shareholder to exercise the voting right in accordance with the instructions of the company, the management board or the supervisory board of the company or in accordance with the instructions of a dependent company. Likewise, a contract by which a shareholder undertakes to vote for the respective proposals of the management board or the supervisory board of the company is void: see Sect. 136 Ge-PuCA.

82 See Art. 2341-*bis* It-CC and, with slight differences, Art. 122 and 123 of the Legislative Decree no. 58/1998.

event of failure to declare the shareholders' agreement, the right to vote attached to the shares involved in the agreement shall be suspended and the resolutions adopted with their deciding vote may be challenged in court[83].

---

[83] See Art. 2341-*ter* It-CC. In listed companies, agreements regarding the exercise of the voting right in the company and in the controlling companies, within five days from their stipulation, are: a) reported to the supervisory authority; b) published on an excerpt basis in the daily press; c) submitted to the companies register; d) reported to the company with listed shares. In the event of failure to comply with the disclosure obligations, the agreements are again void, the right to vote of the shares may not be exercised and resolutions adopted with a deciding vote are subject to challenge (see again Art. 122 and 123 of the Legislative Decree no. 58/1998).

4 Shares

Summary:
1. Characteristics of shares (bearer, name, paper, dematerialized, par and no-par)
2. Basic and secondary rights of shares
3. Classes of shares: special financial, voting and administrative rights
4. "Golden shares" and the jurisprudence of the CJEU (cases *Elf-Aquitaine*, *BBA*, *Volkswagen* and others)
5. Transferability of the shares (clauses of consent, first refusal, tag along, drag along, change of control). The jurisprudence of the CJEU on national laws preventing investors to pursue cross-border transactions (cases *Tipou*, *Vivendi* and others)

1. Characteristics of the shares (bearer, name, paper, dematerialized, par and no-par)

Shares represent the bundle of rights that the shareholder has with respect to the company as a consequence of the contribution of equity.

Shares also denote the documents that legitimate the shareholder as such.

Even though directives often discuss "shares", "shareholdings" and "shareholders", there is no EU directive devoted to shares and their key features.

At a general level, the main distinctions among shares concern whether they are registered in the company's share register in the name of the shareholders or not ("name-shares" vs. "bearer shares"), whether they physically exist in the form of a share certificate or are dematerialized ("paper-shares" vs. "dematerialized shares") and whether they have a nominal value or not ("par shares" vs. "no-par shares").

(I) The majority of national laws allow public companies to issue either registered (name-shares) or unregistered shares (bearer). Bearer shares are forbidden, however, in some countries, like Belgium, the Netherlands and Sweden; others, like Italy, admit them only on an exceptional basis for listed companies.

While bearer shares are transferred simply by way of transfer of a share certificate (and normally there is a rebuttable presumption in favor of the holder of the paper that said person is the owner of the share), registered shares are transferred according to general rules specified by the laws of each country.

Normally the transfer of a registered share is carried out by way of a written declaration either on the share certificate or in a separate document and requires

https://doi.org/10.1515/9783110725025-006

the delivery of possession of the share certificate[1]. The transfer of the certificate does not however constitute a transfer of the share as such: the share is transferred in accordance with the rules of civil or common law (contract, property law, etc.). If paper certificates representing the registered share are issued, these certificates will mention the name of the shareholder.

(II) On the other hand, a share can be in the form of a share certificate (material form, paper) or can exist without it (as a dematerialized share). In the latter case, the certificate is created and held in an electronic securities account with a financial institution. The many advantages of dematerialization include the reduced costs related to the preparation, storage and transfer of shares and the strengths of transparency and full openness of transactions carried out. Share dematerialization is mandatory when it comes to listed companies.

The holder of the securities account is the person entitled to the rights of the dematerialized securities; the holder can show his right to the shares by means of certificates released by the financial institution holding the account. An agreement (creating an obligation to transfer) will transfer the securities once a record is made on the securities account.

(III) The last distinction is between nominal value shares and no-par value shares.

In the case of nominal value shares, that value will be indicated in the instrument of incorporation, together with the number of the shares issued.

Nominal value shares may not be issued originally at a subscription price that is lower than their nominal value (shares having, for instance, a nominal value of € 1 cannot be subscribed to at € 0,99 or less: see Art. 47 Directive 2017/1132/EU). When the subscription price is higher than the nominal value[2], the part of the subscription price that corresponds to the nominal value must be booked as stated capital in the accounts of the company; the remainder ("share premium") will be booked as a reserve (for example if the company has a capital of € 1 million, shares have a nominal value of € 1 euro and there are no reserves: if the company increases the capital for another € 1 million

---

1 Further formalities may be provided for by the single domestic jurisdictions (for instance, a notary draws up a written declaration). Company law in all Member States also include provisions which require the company to keep a share register; there are however substantial differences regarding the contents of and access to the register, i.e. shareholder identification. In both those regards rules differ, with some jurisdictions being stricter, while other are more relaxed. For an overview see EMCA, general comments to Ch. 5.
2 Shares may be issued at a market price above their nominal value because the economic value of the company is higher than the amount of the share capital.

and the new shares are offered at € 1,50, the post-increase capital will be € 2 million and the reserves € 500.000).

In the case of no-par value shares, the shares have no accountable par. The instrument of incorporation does not state their nominal value. That does not mean that each shareholder cannot calculate their holdings: it is simply given by dividing the figure of the issued capital by the number of issued shares (taking the figures from the previous example, given a capital of € 1 million and 1 million issued shares, if the shareholder owns 100.000 shares, the stake corresponds to 10%).

When the company is established (or later, in case of subsequent capital increases), shareholders determine the price at which the shares will be issued and which part of the subscription price will have to be booked as stated capital in the accounts of the company (this power may be delegated to directors). If no express decision is made, the entire subscription price is booked as stated capital. If only part of the subscription price is booked as stated capital, the remainder must be booked as a reserve.

A debate has arisen over the years about whether the Directive allows capital increases where the par value of the newly created shares is below the par value of the previously issued shares.

An example may clarify. Suppose again a company with a legal capital of € 1 million and 1 million shares, each having a value of € 1. Assume that the company has suffered losses and needs a capital increase of € 500.000. If the company offered the shares at the original price of € 1, investors would buy them reluctantly (or would not buy them at all).

Therefore, the company may decide to approve a capital increase of (say) € 500.000 by issuing 1.000.000 new shares to be subscribed to at the price of (say) € 0,50 each (instead of € 1). The new contribution would still be € 500.000, corresponding to the actual capital increase. The new par value of all shares would however be € 0,75 (2.000.000 shares divided by € 1.500.000 in contributions), which is below the accountable value the shares had before the capital increase (€ 1).

The option to issue new shares with a par value below the value of the previously issued shares is expressly admitted by Belgian, Finnish and Luxembourg law[3].

---

3 See Art. 7.178 B-CA ("shares can be issued below or above the accounting par, or at the accounting par of existing shares of the same category, with or without share premium. Unless the articles of association or the decision to issue shares provides otherwise, the accounting par of all shares without nominal value of the same class is equal, whether they are issued above, below or at accounting par shares of the same class"); Ch. 3, Sect. 5, Fi-CA ("accountable

The literature in other Member States is however much more doubtful, since it is stated that this type of transaction conflicts with Art. 47 Directive 2017/1132/EU, which stipulates that "where there is no nominal value, shares may not be issued at a price lower than their accountable par".

The meaning of "accountable par" (and therefore the minimum limit of the issue price of the new shares) may however have a double meaning: it could be understood to be the result of dividing the pre-existing capital by the number of pre-existing shares (i.e. pre-increase accountable par), or it could be understood to be the result of dividing the "new" capital subscribed to by the number of the new shares subscribed (i.e. the accounting parity of the increase, equal to the amount of the capital increase divided by the number of newly issued shares).

The latter meaning probably makes more sense: in general, the rule on nominal value (Art. 47 of the Directive) should be intended as imposing a limit to protect the capital cover and not the shareholders as such. The interest by shareholders in being able to use this method to implement a capital increase is evident when one thinks of increases approved by companies which – like the example above – are in difficult situations or with poor prospects for the future, and need to encourage third parties to provide equity capital by issuing shares under the old accountable parity.

This kind of capital increase – below the pre-increase par – therefore becomes a tool available to the company which is free to use it whenever it needs it more (obviously within the general limits that require the full payment of consideration, forbid abuses by the majority against the minority, etc.)[4].

The position of the EMCA goes along the same lines: "under such a system" – the Model states – "the no-par value system offers greater simplicity and flexibility without harming any stakeholder's interests", at least as long as the directors correctly price the value of the new shares offered; "the EMCA Group is therefore in favor of such a system" (see Sect. 5.05)[5].

---

par may differ between shares"); Art. 420-14 Lu-CA ("in the absence of a nominal value, shares may be issued below their accounting par value, subject to compliance with the conditions provided for by in Article 420-22, paragraphs 6 and 7"; these latter rules require the directors to draft a detailed report on the issue and state that the directors may also be delegated the power to issue such shares). See also the notarial practice under Italian law (cf. the Recommendation no. 36 of the Notarial Council of Milan).

4 See for all Rickford (ed.), *Reforming*, 934 and Schön, *The future of legal capital*, in *EBOR*, 2004, 447.

5 See De Wulf, *Shares in the EMCA: the time is ripe for true no par value shares in the EU, and the 2nd directive is not an obstacle*, in *ECFR*, 2016, 215: "the truly innovative rule in the EMCA concerning shares is the proposed possibility for companies [...] to use true no par value shares". The Author describes three alternative ways for a company that wants to execute a capital in-

2. Basic and secondary rights of shares

As far as shares are concerned, Directive 2017/1132/EU only sets out a generic principle: "the laws of the Member States shall ensure equal treatment to all shareholders who are in the same position" (Art. 85).

That does not mean that shareholders should all have the same rights and does not preclude disproportionate shareholder rights. The principle serves more as a generic ban on the discriminatory treatment of shareholders by company's bodies.

The modification of the rule of proportionality between the capital stake held and the voting and economic rights attached to the shares can be obtained either by issuing "classes" of shares carrying different rights (and in particular by creating shares with multiple votes or profits) or by allowing the option to allot a disproportionate number of shares compared to the subscribed capital (these arguments are treated extensively below in § 4).

Speaking about shares, in order to understand their legal framework, one should first try to identify the "basic" rights of shares, which are essentially common to all legal systems[6]. Then one should aim to comprehend the "secondary" rights that may be attached to the shares, that is to say the rights whose features are less definite and vary greatly according to the different domestic laws.

Beginning with the "basic" rights of shares (also called "essential" or "key" rights), they are the right: (1) to appoint and dismiss directors; (2) to have the financial statements of the company published (yearly) and to receive dividends, if the directors propose a distribution (and capital repayments when the company winds up, if there is a surplus); (3) to approve lawsuits against directors if they breach their duties; (4) to vote on the main changes of the instrument of

---

crease while the market value is below their nominal value, and illustrates how many of them are more complicated and less efficient. The first one is to call a general meeting to decide on a purely formal reduction of capital and proceed afterwards with the capital increase (in such a case, "if the formal capital reduction entails that losses the company had incurred are set off against legal capital, this may have as a consequence, under certain national tax systems, that these former losses, now gone for accounting and tax purposes, are no longer available to be set off against future profits, a situation the company will regret"). The second possibility is to issue another class of shares, with a different nominal value, provided that the national legal system allows it. The third option is to issue shares with value equal to the previous value, but with preferred rights (new investors in such a case may ask for – and obtain – enhanced economic or administrative rights attached to the shares).

6 Some companies acts even open the section devoted to shares by defining explicitly these "basic" rights (see as an example Art. 93 Sp-CA).

incorporation and the articles of association (and other fundamental issues, like share buy-backs, financial assistance).

The four rights described above – although not regulated by any specific directive – are at the core of EU company law and implied by the various directives.

Also these basic rights are however treated differently by the Member States. The majority of jurisdictions allow shareholders to "directly" appoint directors; vote on the financial statements and receive dividends; participate in the majority decisions to file lawsuits against the directors and change the articles of association.

Deviating from this model, other Member States permit shareholders to only "indirectly" appoint the directors (as is the case in countries adopting the two-tier system); do not allow shareholders to vote on the financial statements of the company (once again, in the dualistic model they are normally approved by the supervisory board, even though there are exceptions); on the other hand, they may permit the shareholders to file lawsuits directly against the directors (on behalf of the company) regardless of the percentage capital they hold (or require that they exceed a certain ceiling, for instance 20% of the share capital).

The other different, "secondary" rights (sometimes called "adjunctive" rights) – i.e. rights that may be recognized beside the basic ones described above, and that are not part of core law – are shaped even more distinctively by each Member State. These rights are diverse in type and extension and in some cases may even not be recognized under some laws (the right to have access to corporate information; to call shareholders' general meetings; to challenge corporate bodies' resolutions in the case of irregularities; to appoint special examiners, etc.).

The features of some of these rights (both core and non-core) have already been discussed (see, with regard to the appointment of the directors, or for special examinations, Chapter 3 above), others will be addressed in later Chapters (for instance, the right to information, the right to challenge general meeting's resolutions, the right to sue the directors: see in particular Chapters 6 and 9).

In this Chapter we shall focus on how these rights may be recognized in a different proportion to the shareholders through the creation of different "classes" of shares, and how they may be modified.

Finally, we shall examine another important right intrinsic to shares: the right to transfer them freely to third parties (this reflect the principle of "free circulation" of the shares). From this point of view, it becomes important to understand how that right may be constrained by means of clauses in the articles of association.

3. Classes of shares: special financial, voting and administrative rights

The option for the company to issue different "classes" of shares with different rights (or shares with "special" rights) is not regulated at EU level.

Some years ago, the EU Commission considered abolishing the possibility for companies to create special classes of shares and special rights, and embracing the principle of full share equality (summarized by the catchphrase: "one share-one vote").

For a while the Commission tought about making this rule mandatory at least for listed companies. In 2007, however, a number of studies on the issue were published and, based on these and the feedback from various stakeholders, the Commission decided to drop its plan for legislation in the area[7].

The positions of the various Member States on this topic have therefore remained assorted; with some States taking a liberal approach and others being more conservative.

(I) Let us consider firstly the case of the so called "loyalty shares": they give shareholders the right to obtain extra shares or extra votes – as a sort of "premium" – if investors remain loyal and hold the shares for a certain period of time (for instance, one year), as set forth in the articles of association[8]. They are com-

---

7 See Ferrarini, *One share - one vote: a European rule?* in *ECFR*, 2007, 147; Psarakis, *One share – one vote and the case for a harmonized capital structure*, in *EBLR*, 2008, 709; Geens/Clottens, *One share – one vote: fairness, efficiency and (the case for) EU harmonization revisited*, 2010, at *ssrn.com*.

8 Cf. i.e. Art. 225-123 Fr-CC and (only for listed companies) Arts. 7.53 B-CA and 127-*quinquies* of Italian Legislative Decree 58/1998 (in all cases shares owned for at least two years obtein double-voting rights). The double voting rights are attached to the "loyal" shareholder, not to the shares. Hence, the double voting rights are lost upon transfer of the shares, so that the beneficiary cannot cash in the extra control rights such shares bestow upon him.

The French example is interesting. As illustrated by Belot/Ginglinger/Starks, *Encouraging long term shareholders; the effects of loyalty shares with double voting rights*, 2019, at *ssrn.com*, the "Florange Act" adopted on 29 March 2014 required listed companies to issue loyalty shares unless they chose to opt out through a shareholder resolution (with a supermajority of two-thirds of the votes) at their general meeting. The Act therefore changed the previous "opt-in" provision for loyalty shares (companies had to vote for that structure) to an "opt-out" provision (the loyalty shares/double-voting structure became the default model). Before 2014 loyalty shares were already popular, especially among small-sized listed family firms (they have been regulated since 1966). Following the Act, of the 455 listed companies affected, 300 (65.93%) already had articles of association that allowed double voting shares and did not have to vote; the remaining 155 called an extraordinary general meeting for the decision. The vast majority (92.11%) did not achieve the two/thirds majority required to maintain the one share/one vote system and there-

mon in some countries and also the EMCA endorses the possibility of issuing this kind of certificates (the model is named also "tenure shares" or "tenure voting" scheme)[9].

Even more frequently "multiple voting" shares are issued: they have the right attached to express more than one vote.

Dutch law, for instance, has long embraced a pioneering attitude and admitted the option to issue shares with up to 6 votes (if the share capital is divided into 100 shares or more), or up to 3 votes (if the share capital is divided into less than 100 shares) (these numbers reflect the current rule: Art. 2.118 Du-CC).

This structure has been widely used by public companies. With an investment of, say, € 100, each shareholder of that special class may prevail with the (6) votes over a shareholder holding common shares (with 1 vote) and having invested up to € 599.

Over the years this multiple voting shares system has been implemented in many other Member States (Belgium, the Czech Republic, Denmark, France, Hungary, Sweden, etc.) and recently also in Italy. This latter case is interesting: multiple voting shares (together with loyalty shares) were introduced in August 2014 in order to intentionally make the legislation more attractive (or, at least, less unappealing) for companies. Indeed, a few months beforehand, in June 2014, the group Chrysler-Fiat (one of the more important Italian multinational corporations) had announced its reincorporation in the Netherlands, also to take advantage of specific governance features of the Dutch "tenure shares / multiple voting" system. The blow of losing a well-known national champion was said to have contributed to the decision by the Italian government to introduce these types of shares[10].

---

fore shifted to the loyalty shares/double-voting structure. Moreover, companies with a one share – one vote structure that solicited a positive vote for the opt out incurred negative market reactions (this suggests that investors had a positive perception of loyalty shares).

The introduction of loyalty shares has been recently proposed in Spain by means of a draft bill (the proposal has however been criticized: see *inter alia* Gurrea Martínez, *The case against the implementation of loyalty shares in Spain*, 9 July 2019, at https://www.law.ox.ac.uk).

9 EMCA (unlike the French model) recommends that multiple voting rights be attached to the loyalty shares (and not to the shareholder), in order to let them circulate.

10 See Ventoruzzo, *The disappearing taboo of multiple voting shares: regulatory responses to the migration of Chrysler-Fiat*, 2015, at ssrn.com; Pernazza, *Fiat Chrysler Automobiles and the new face of corporate mobility in Europe*, in *ECFR*, 2017, 37. The transaction was preceded by another one in September 2013, between CNH Global NV (best known for their agricultural line "New Holland"), which merged with another company related to FCA, Fiat Industrial s.p.a. The new holding resulting from the cross-border merger was registered as CNH Industrial NV with its reg-

Multiple voting structures are used heavily by listed companies in order to strengthen control: around 80% of Swedish listed companies employ that model (followed by around 55% of French ones and around 40% of Dutch and Finnish ones)[11].

Other jurisdictions – on the other hand – forbid multiple voting shares, either expressly (i. e. Sect. 12 Ge-PuCA; Art. 188 Sp-CA) or implicitly[12].

On its part, the EMCA's approach is open: the Model stipulates that shares have voting and profit rights "proportional to their nominal value, unless the articles of association provide otherwise" (Sect. 5.07).

Multiple voting and loyalty shares do not properly constitute "classes" of shares. The same is true for provisions introducing ceilings on voting rights.

(II) Secondly, companies may regulate different "classes" of shares in the articles of association. The greater or lesser freedom depends on the single domestic legislation: i. e. France, Ireland, Italy, the Netherlands and the Nordic countries have followed a liberal path; Austria, Germany, Poland, Portugal, Romania a more conservative one[13].

The former jurisdictions have implemented the option for companies to issue classes of shares with attached special rights of – basically – "any kind".

---

istered office established in the Netherlands. That shift of the registered office was then motivated by the flexibility of Dutch company law allowed by the "tenure voting" model. The majority shareholder of the two companies, Exor s.p.a., was likely to see its interest diluted as a result of the merger. By creating a tenure voting scheme, Exor was able to double its voting rights in the post-merger company, by holding the shares for a fixed period. Although the parties could have chosen a different approach to accomplish this, i. e. converting all or some of the outstanding shares into shares with a double vote, they chose not to and issue, on the contrary, "loyalty" shares. The fact that the shares were not converted into special shares permitted the normal shares to remain listed on a stock exchange. See on that Donders et al., *Longread: tenure voting under Dutch law, a case study of the loyalty voting schemes adopted by CNH Industrial N.V. and Cnova N.V*, at *www.bedrijfsjuridiek.nl*. Exor also become a Dutch company in 2016.

11 See for a summary of data Ventoruzzo, *The disappearing*, 3.

12 See for instance, for Romanian law, Popovici/Bercea, in *Company laws*, 921.The Belgian companies act inhibits multiple voting to listed companies (Art. 7.52).

13 For instance, the Romanian companies act only recognizes two types of shares: "regular shares" (common stocks) and "preferential shares" (preferred stocks). According to Art. 95, the company may decide to issue preferential shares with priority dividends and no right to vote, conferring the following rights on the holder: the right of priority in the distribution of dividends, ahead of any other distribution of profits and all the other rights conferred by regular shares, including the right to participate in the general meetings, except the right to vote. See also Arts. 42 Li-CA and 176 Slove-CA (two classes: ordinary and preference shares). Poland has adopted the principle one share-one vote for listed companies (see Art. 351 Pol-CC).

These rights may have "financial" features, and consist in "preferred dividends", "progressive" or "declining dividends" (distributed to a greater or lesser extent according to the company profits/losses), "postergation" in the sharing of profits or losses; "loyalty dividends" (reserved to shares retained for a certain period[14]), etc.[15].

Special shares may also be issued with particular "voting rights", like the right to vote only on special transactions (mergers, capital increases, etc.), or to approve ordinary resolutions only (the appointment of the directors, the approval of the financial statements, etc.) or to vote upon certain conditions (the presence of losses, etc.). Often when voting rights are limited or excluded, extra financial rights are provided (typically this happens with the "preferred shares": they may not vote at the general meeting, but dividends are paid out to preferred shareholders before the dividends of the common shares are distributed).

"Administrative rights" may also be allotted: increased financial information, allocation of seats in the management and/or control bodies, rights to request the appointment of an auditor, rights to veto some transactions, etc. (or the right to be reimbursed before other shares in the case of the liquidation of the company or the sale of assets: "liquidation preference shares")[16].

Many laws also regulate a further particular class, the "redeemable shares", which may be repurchased at any time – or within the time frame indicated in the articles of association – "at the exclusive initiative of the company"[17]. Some provisions – taking an even more innovative route – allow the possibility for the company to be forced to buy the shares from shareholders who intend to sell and that these shares therefore incorporate a "put option" in favor of the shareholders (instead of a "call option" in favor of the company)[18] (see also Sect. 5.15 EMCA: "redeemable shares may be redeemable at the option of the

---

14 See De Luca, *Higher dividends (for minorities) or equal treatment (of all holders): what do financial markets like more?*, 2010, at *ssrn.com*; Sacco Ginevri, *The rise of long-term minority shareholders' rights in publicly held corporations and its effect on corporate governance*, in *EBOR*, 2011, 587.

15 A specific class of shares with specific profit rights are the "tracking stocks". They carry rights that do not follow the profit distributions of the company as a whole, but only of a certain part, such as a business unit. Tracking stock thus "track" only a part of the equity of the company (e. g. tracking stocks "A" track the business unit A; tracking stocks "B" track the business unit B). There must be a detailed instructions in the articles of association for these kinds of shares. They are known about, i. e., under Dutch and Italian laws (see Art. 2350 It-CC).

16 For paradigmatical examples see *inter alia* Sect. 276 Cz-CA; Arts. 228-11 ff. Fr-CC; Sect. 66 Ir-CA.

17 See i. e. Art. 228-12 Fr-CC; Sect. 66 Ir-CA; see also, for listed companies, Art. 500 Sp-CA.

18 See i. e. Art. 2437-*sexies* It-CC.

company, of the shareholder, or by both, according to the provisions in the articles of association or the terms of issuance of the redeemable shares"). The law may be silent on the issue of the redemption price; in that case it is advisable to predetermine how to calculate it in the article of associations in order to avoid disputes at a later stage (some States require the price to always be determined "fairly"[19]).

(III) Since the freedom to issue special shares is – as seen above – particularly wide-ranging, the problem arises on how to recognize the limits to the options of these types of issues. They have to be found (due to the silence of the laws) in the general principles.

For instance, the possibility to issue special shares with specific financial rights must avoid falling under the prohibition on the "leonine clause" which is often acknowledged (i.e. shareholders may not be put in the position of being totally exonerated from participation in either dividends or losses)[20] and, more in general, the principle of "equality" among shareholders should always be kept in mind at the very end[21].

---

19 See i.e. Art. 2347-*sexies* It-CC. An intermediate position is taken by the EMCA: the articles of association must determine the redemption price or contain rules to fix it and the "redemption is not possible if the articles contain no rules to make the redemption price determinable" (Sect. 5.15)

20 See i.e. Art. 1844-1 of the French Civil Code (and *inter alia* the decision of the Supreme Court of 29 October 2003 on the case "Société Harpax").

21 For instance, the option of issuing "divided loyalty" shares has been addressed by Dutch case law in the light of that principle (set forth in Art. 42 Second Directive, and now in Art. 85 Directive 1132/2017/EU) and the jurisprudence of the CJEU on the principles of "proportionality" and "subsidiarity". In 2007 (on December 14) the Dutch Supreme Court delivered a ruling (in the "DSM" case) on the lawfulness of the issue of shares with attached "loyalty dividends" (a bonus of 30% would be paid to shareholders who retained the shares for at least three years). The argument of the trial and appeal court judges (the Amsterdam Enterprises Chamber) was that the amount of the dividend paid on a share would no longer be determined by the class of the share but by circumstances that concern the owner of the share. As a consequence, the shareholders of the same class would not be treated equally. However, the judges of the Supreme Court stated that this unequal treatment is permitted if reasonable and objective justifications exist, to be identified in accordance with the above mentioned principles of proportionality and subsidiarity. The company had to show that there was a genuine need to introduce the loyalty dividend, that the dividend was a suitable means for attaining the objective stated by the company and it was necessary to introduce that scheme to reach these objectives; if other non-discriminatory means were available, they would have been chosen instead of the loyalty dividend. The Supreme Court thus overruled the decision of the Court of Appeal, which had established that the loyalty dividend violates the principle of equal treatment; see Lennarts/Koppert/van Beek, *Loyalty dividend and the EC principle of equal treatment of shareholders*, in *ECL*, 2008, 173, recognizing however that "opinions on this issue are divided in the Netherlands".

The allocation of shares with special administrative rights – like the right to appoint directors to the board – should not reach the point (even if the issue is often discussed) of completely dismembering the basic corporate governance model according to which the majority of directors must be nominated by the majority shareholders (or by the supervisory board in the dualistic system)[22]. The right of the company to issue special shares may not therefore deprive common shareholders of their basic rights, as acknowledged by core company laws.

As far as the EMCA is concerned, the main features of the special shares that the Model proposes may be summarized as follows (see Sect. 5.06): unless otherwise provided in the articles of association, each share shall carry one vote; unless otherwise provided by the articles of association, each share shall carry voting rights proportionate to its nominal value; the articles of association may provide for shares with multiple voting rights and/or for non-voting shares; non-voting shares shall carry all shareholder rights except voting rights; a company must issue at least one share with voting power[23].

It is has however to be noted that the great freedom currently allowed to many European companies in emitting classes of shares and permitting disproportionate voting powers (especially in the more extreme cases) could come in the future – at least according to a certain view – under the scrutiny of the juris-

---

22 See, with reference to the appointment of directors, paradigmatically Art. 189 Hu-CA: "holders of preference shares carrying entitlement to appoint executive officers are entitled – in the manner and under the procedure specified in the articles of association – to appoint one or more members of the management board, not to exceed one-third of all members of the management board, who will then become members of the management board. The holders of preference shares shall also be entitled to remove the management board members they have appointed".

23 These rules show a rather open-minded approach once again; it is worthwhile noting, however, the provision according to which "non-voting shares shall carry all shareholder rights except voting rights". Such a rule – which seems to recall the "basic rights" that we have examined above ("all shareholder rights") – bans the ability of the company to issue shares that have no voting rights and have fewer rights than other shares at the same time: for instance, non-voting shares which are only postergated in the distribution of dividends. On the other hand, this type of option (non-voting shares with fewer rights) is admitted in some Member States (i.e. by Art. 228-11 Fr-CC); hence, in this regard, the EMCA clause seems to be less accommodating. On the contrary, the EMCA seems more flexible when it allows the majority shares to be non-voting shares; Arts. 228-1 Fr-CC and Art. 2351 It-CC, for instance, stipulate that non-voting shares shall not represent more than 50 % of the share capital (the former law also states that in companies whose shares are admitted to trading on a regulated market, non-voting shares shall not represent more than 25 % of the share capital: see Art. 228-1 Fr-CC); see also, with different approaches, Art. 95 R-CA (preferential shares may not exceed 25 % of the share capital) and Sect. 279 Cz-CA (shares with no voting rights attached may only be issued if the sum of their par value does not exceed 90 % of the registered capital).

prudence of the CJEU, since national laws allowing schemes favoring domestic companies could be deemed as preventing the liberty of investors to pursue cross-border transactions and thus violate Art. 56 TFEU on the freedom of movement of capital. On this issue – raised with reference to rulings on golden shares and sector-specific national provisions – you may read more extensively above in Chapter 1, § 9 and below in §§ 4 and 5 of this Chapter.

(IV) Another important issue regards the kind of protection that must be guaranteed to the holders of special shares. Indeed, they are always exposed to the risk that majority shareholders could amend the articles of association and modify their rights.

Under most national laws, general meeting resolutions that change the rights of a share class must also be approved by the "special meeting" of the class concerned. This special shareholders' general meeting is normally a separate one, although governed pursuant to the provisions of the standard general meeting[24].

The EMCA also follows this scheme, at least with reference to non-voting shares: "non-voting shares" – states the Model – "may vote, with one vote per share, on resolutions proposed to the general meeting concerning any 'change' to the rights attached to these shares" (Sect. 5.06).

The EMCA actually lays down a very broad kind of protection to the special shares in the case of said meetings (embracing, once again, a rather "shareholder-friendly" view, which is not, however, at least in this regard, the one of the majority of the Member States, whose provisions are less far less extensive). The board of directors must draw up a written report, to be made available to shareholders, in which they have to explain the potential consequences of the proposed changes to the class rights. Moreover, any financial data in this report must have been checked by an external auditor (see Sect. 5.09).

Of course, freedom of contract may also play an important role in shaping the protection of special shareholders. Since they have special rights, they often also succeed in negotiating for efficient protection "ex ante".

For instance, the articles of association may govern the appointment of a "representative" of the class and set forth cases in which the special shareholders' general meeting has to be convened (usually by the same representative or

---

24 A few companies acts set forth supermajorities for the approval of both general shareholders' meeting and special class shareholders' meeting (cf. i.e. Sect. 235 E-CA: "rights attaching to a class of shares may be amended by a resolution of the general meeting by at least a four-fifths majority of votes in favour unless the articles of association prescribe a greater majority requirement. At least nine-tenths of the shareholders whose shares belong to the class of which the rights are amended must vote in favour of the resolution").

the directors or a certain percentage of the shareholders themselves), the majority required to pass the class meeting resolutions, etc.

As far as the tasks, duties and responsibilities of the representative, the articles of association usually require the representative to supervise the special shareholders' common interests and give him the right, *inter alia*, to attend (with no vote) the company's general meetings and to exercise, on behalf of the class shareholders, any relevant actions against the company (actually the role of the representative and the functioning of the shareholders' general meeting are expressly governed in some jurisdictions for listed preference shares, but the related provisions may also be inserted in the articles of association of unlisted companies for any kind of special shares[25]).

(V) The question as to what represents a "change" in the rights of the class – triggering the intervention of the special meeting – is one of the most open to discussion.

A widespread opinion only considers the "formal" changes of the rights attached to the shares to be relevant (for instance, a shareholders' extraordinary meeting resolution that modifies the articles of association and reduces the guaranteed dividend for the special shares from, say, 10 % to 5 % of the overall profits: namely, "direct prejudice"), but also the issue of new shares whose rights impair the rights of the older shares, even if the rights of the latter remain "formally" the same (so called "indirect prejudice").

Let us make an example to clarify. Suppose the company has its capital divided into common "Class A" shares (say, 60 %) and special "Class B" shares (40 %), the latter having the right to receive a special dividend (say, a "double dividend": each B share counts as two). If the company intends to distribute € 1 million in profits, the dividend will be shared in the following proportion: € 571.428 overall to special Class B shares and € 428.572 overall to common Class A shares.

Imagine now that the company wants to raise its capital by creating a new class of shares ("Class C") which allows said shareholders to receive dividends in a fixed amount before the outstanding shares (A and B) receive a distribution (i. e. a "preferred dividend"), by introducing for instance the following provision into the articles of association: "all other shares shall receive a distribution only after Class C shares have received a dividend of € 500.000".

---

25 For a particular provision see also Art. 228-19 Fr-CC: "the holders of preference shares, by a special meeting resolution, are empowered to instruct one of the company's auditors to draw up a special report on the company's compliance with the special rights attached to the shares".

In this case, the rights of Class B shares have not been formally impaired (they still have the right to receive a double dividend), but they are indirectly affected since the prior distribution guaranteed to C shares may drain the whole payment, especially in years of poor financial results (and in any case, in our example, assuming that the dividend is still € 1.000.000, Class A and B shares obtain only half of the cake, € 500.000, after Class C has already eaten the other half).

The EMCA considers both direct and indirect prejudice to be relevant (and also the creation per se of a new class, which is deemed – although not detrimental – in any case to be "a "change" of class rights"): all these variations in the right of the classes have to be approved by the special meeting of all the classes of shares (see Sect. 5.09).

This broad perspective is not shared in all jurisdictions (by scholars and/or case law, with the law generally silent or laconic on the matter)[26]. This view believes that the simple introduction of a new class of shares and the indirect damage to their rights does not represent a relevant "change" of the class rights as such. This restrictive opinion holds that the need for approval by all the classes in the case of indirect prejudice would represent too severe a limitation for company activities (for instance, a merger could be blocked only because the indirect harm – which often occurs in those complex transactions – suffered by some of the shares has not been approved by the majority of all the classes[27]).

The issue is made even more complex by the fact that certain – actually few – jurisdictions also allow shareholders (in case of "changes" of the class rights) a right of withdrawal from the company. These provisions therefore re-

---

26 For example, Dutch and German laws follow along the lines of the EMCA: in the case of the issue of new shares, and if there are different types (classes) of shares, pursuant to Art. 2.96 Du-CC, a valid resolution of the general meeting for the issue of shares requires a prior or simultaneous approving resolution by each group of holders of shares of the same class whose rights are affected by the issue of shares. See similarly also Sect. 182 Ge-PuCA with reference to the case of several classes of shares with "voting" rights; if preference shares exist at the time the resolution on the capital increase is passed, a special resolution of those shares is required if new preference shares with equal or superior preference rights with respect to the distribution of profits are to be issued (see Sect. 141 Ge-PuCA).

27 This is the position, for instance, of Italian case law: see paradigmatically Court of Milan, 9 October 2002 ("it does not satisfy the substantial prejudice required by Art. 2376 It-CC for the convening of the special meeting the resolution approving the merger plan which ensures, from a formal point of view, equal treatment of shareholders" (case "Edison") and, more recently, Supreme Court, 20 April 2020, n. 7920 (case "BPAV"). See on that Sbarbaro/Sacco Ginevri, *The role of preferred shareholders in fundamental transactions: preliminary thoughts*, in *EBLR*, 2015, 765. Belgian law instead expressely allows special shares to vote in case of conversions and certain cross-border transactions (see Art. 7.57 B-CA).

quire a coordination of the different kinds of protections accorded by the law: the vote of the special shareholders' meeting, on the one hand, and the right to withdraw, on the other[28].

(VI) Finally, the option for public companies to issue shares in a manner which is "non proportional" with respect to the contributions is seldom regulated, but is permitted by certain Member States, also for public companies[29].

Applying this scheme, for instance, in a company with a share capital of € 1.000.000, two shareholders each providing € 500.000 in capital may agree that one of them will receive, say, 90 % of the shares and the other only 10 %.

Let us make an example, and assume that negotiations are in place to set up a company (Mirage PLC) between the young entrepreneur Jack, possessing strong know-how but limited financial resources, and the financial partner Flamingo PLC. The definition of the internal balance of power in the company could be difficult.

In a context of necessary proportionality between the value of the contributions, the need to leave the industrial partner Jack with 90 % of the shares could only pass through a shareholders' agreements and loans by Flamingo to Jack prior to the establishment of the company, or similar techniques. Under a regime of non-proportionality, on the other hand, Jack may confer cash or assets for 50 % (or less, even 1 %) of the legal capital, but receive the assignment of a higher stake (90 %, or even more), as agreed with Flamingo.

4. "Golden shares" and the jurisprudence of the CJEU (cases *Elf-Aquitaine*, *BBA*, *Volkswagen* and others)

In the field of conceivable "unequal rights" attached to the shares, a related question concerns the validity of inserting "golden shares" into the articles of association of the company.

---

28 Art. 2437 It-CC grants shareholders the right of withdrawal in the case of "amendments to the bylaws concerning voting or participation rights". Various interpretations have been given to this cryptic rule. The most widespread holds that the protection offered by the right of withdrawal has to be added to the protection laid down in Art. 2376 It-CC, which regulates the vote of the class' meeting on the decision, once again basically only for direct prejudices (see on the debate Vicari, in *Company laws*, 638).

29 See for instance Art. 2346 It-CC. Spanish law allows this option for private companies, but forbids it for public ones: see Art. 188 Sp-CA: "in the public company, the creation of shares that directly or indirectly alter the proportionality between the nominal value of the share and the right to vote is not allowed".

These shares "glitter" and are particularly precious since they give their owners (minority shareholders) some "extra-powers" that would be typical of the owner of a majority stake, like the right to block certain transactions or to annul others.

Actually, this case is different from the one examined in the previous paragraph (concerning the possibility of issuing special "classes of shares"). Indeed, the question addressed here regards shares that are allotted (usually in bigger companies operating in national strategic sectors) to one or single shareholders – normally the State or local governments – and provide them with single "personal" rights.

The CJEU has taken a position on this argument deciding a number of cases. The most famous are "Société Nationale Elf-Aquitaine" decided in 2002, "British Airport Authority (BAA)" decided in 2003 and "Volkswagen (WV)" decided in 2007 (and again in 2013).

In the first case (C-483/99), two French legislative decrees came under scrutiny because they provided the national Government with a golden share in the oil company Elf-Aquitaine, according to which (i) any direct or indirect shareholding exceeding the ceiling of 1/10, 1/5 or 1/3 of the share capital of the company should first have to be approved by the Minister for Economic Affairs and (ii) the Government had a right to oppose any decision to transfer or use the most important assets of the company as security.

The Court stated that these rules infringed the principles of the freedom of movement of capital as laid down in the EC Treaty (in particular in Art. 56, now Art. 63 TFEU).

The reasoning by the Court was that these kinds of laws "create obstacles to the right of establishment of nationals of other Member States and to the free movement of capital within the Community, inasmuch as they are liable to impede, or render less attractive, the exercise of those freedoms". Investors of foreign countries – stated the judges – are dissuaded from acquiring shares in a company if they perceive that the State has a veto power on the most important affairs (these rules have a "dissuasive effect").

The decision of the Court on the articles of association of the company BAA, managing the UK airports (C-98/01) was along the same lines[30].

---

30 The Court declared in 2003 that "by maintaining in force the provisions limiting the possibility of acquiring voting shares in BAA PLC as well as the procedure requiring consent to the disposal of the company's assets, to control of its subsidiaries and to winding-up, the United Kingdom of Great Britain and Northern Ireland has failed to fulfil its obligations under Art. 56 EC".

On the other hand, the case concerning the German car manufacturer Volkswagen (VW) SE (case C-112/2005) was more complex[31].

The company's articles of association gave the federal Government and the "Land" (i.e. the federal state) of Niedersachsen (Lower Saxony) a veto against some majority acquisitions while only holding one fifth of all shares of the company: more specifically the articles of association of VW contained three provisions that raised concern. First, the articles of association set a limit to the voting rights of each single shareholder to 20% of the company's voting rights. Secondly, they provided a quorum needed for approval of shareholders' resolutions to 80%. Finally, they granted the right to appoint two members of VW's supervisory board to the Government and to Lower Saxony.

The Court of Justice examined whether these provisions complied with the EU's fundamental principles of free movement of capital and stated that the first two provisions taken together could at least potentially deter direct investors from other Member States to invest in the company and determine a restriction of the freedom of movement of capital.

The right of the government and Lower Saxony to appoint two representatives to the supervisory board also infringed that freedom: the Court found that the provision granted the German authorities a level of influence disproportionate to their actual investment.

The line of defence of the company (and both the government and Lower Saxony) was that the provisions were justified by "overriding reasons in the general interest" (the law was deemed to be "part of a particular historical context", establishing an "equitable balance of powers" in order to "take into account the interests of Volkswagens employees and to protect its minority shareholders").

On this topic, however, the Court recalled its previous case law, based on the principle of proportionality regulated by the Treaty. In order to comply with the latter, the "measures adopted (must) be appropriate to secure the attainment" of the pursued objective and not go beyond what is necessary to attain it. The Court held that the company had failed to provide sufficient justification for the voting restrictions and rejected the argument that they served the protection of interests of employees and of minority shareholders.

---

31 The case is discussed at length e.g. by Zumbansen/Saam, *ECJ, Volkswagen and European corporate law: reshaping the European varieties of capitalism*, in GLJ, 2007, 1027; Ringe, *The Volkswagen case and the European Court of Justice*, in CMLR, 2008, 537; Id., *Domestic*, 1; Van Bekkum, *Golden*, 2008, 6; Van Bekkum/Kloosterman/Winter, *Golden shares and european company law: the implications of Volkswagen*, in ECL, 2008, 6; Winter, Ius audacibus. *The future of EU company law*, in Tison (eds.), *Perspectives*, 43; Rickford, *Free movement of capital and protectionism after Volkswagen and Viking Line, ibidem*, 61; Gerner-Beuerle, *Shareholders*, 97.

The Volkswagen case – and the ones previously decided by the Court – are thus of great importance, since they set forth at least two fundamental principles. The first is that the protection of particular stakeholders (creditors, minority, shareholders) cannot be intended per se as a valid reason of general interest justifying the attribution of these types of extra powers to (only some) shareholders[32]; of course there are some industrial sectors where national laws should

---

32 Other CJEU's judgments related to golden shares were provided under Belgian (C-503/99) and Portuguese (C-367/98 and 171/08) law; see also the Court's ruling on golden share provisions under Italian (C-174/04 and C-326–07) and Dutch (C-282/04) law.

The first case (Société Nationale De Transport Par Canalisations) decided in 2002 regarded the right of the government (i) to oppose any operations to transfer the company's strategic assets if considered against the national interest in the energy field; and (ii) to appoint two representatives to the board of directors of the company and the right of the latter to propose to the Minister the annulment of any decision of the board of directors which they could regard as contrary to the guidelines for the country's energy policy; even though the Court held that "those national rules, although applicable without distinction, create obstacles to the right of establishment of nationals of other Member States and to the free movement of capital within the Community, inasmuch as they are liable to impede, or render less attractive, the exercise of those freedoms", it concluded that "the legislation in issue is therefore justified by the objective of guaranteeing energy supplies in the event of a crisis".

In the second ("Portugal Telecom") and fourth ("Commission vs. Italy"), decided in 2002 and 2005, regarding measures adopted by the Portuguese and Italian governments in the context of privatisations, which *inter alia* limited the overall amount of shares which may be acquired or subscribed to by foreign entities, the Court held that they were in breach of the principles of the Treaty.

In the sixth case ("KPN NV and TPG NV"), decided in 2006, the Court ruled that, by maintaining certain provisions in the memorandum and articles of association of the two companies providing that the capital of the companies was to include a special share held by the Netherlands State, giving it special rights to approve certain management decisions of the bodies of those companies which were not limited to cases where the intervention of that State is necessary for overriding reasons in the general interest recognized by the Court and, in the case of TPG NV in particular for ensuring the maintenance of universal postal service, the Kingdom of the Netherlands had failed to fulfil its obligations under Article 56(1) EC.

In the fifth case (decided in 2009, "Commission vs. Italy") the Italian government had maintained special powers in companies in the fields of oil, electricity and telecommunications to oppose the acquisition by investors of significant shareholdings representing at least 5% of voting rights or a lower percentage fixed by decree of the Minister for Economic Affairs and Finance; to oppose the agreement of contracts or agreements between shareholders representing at least 5% of voting rights or a lower percentage fixed by decree of the Minister for Economic Affairs and Finance; the power to veto resolutions for the dissolution of the company, transfer of the undertaking, merger, demerger, transfer abroad of the company headquarters, alteration of the company's objects, amendment of the articles of association removing or modifying the special powers; power to appoint a non-voting director. The Court ruled the Italian Republic had failed to fulfil its obligations under Art. 56 EC; *inter alia*, the Court Stated that the Italian

allow the government (or public authorities) to participate in certain activities of "vital importance" to the national economy, with the purpose of imposing an economic policy, and give them "golden shares"; these restrictions, however, should be considered permissible only as long as they strictly regard services in the "public interest" or "strategic" sectors and are proportionate.

The second principle (which is probably more important for its expansive potential) is that the attribution of individual extra powers to shareholders cannot reach a level where they may be deemed to "deter" foreign investors from other Member States from investing in that company (and in that State) and therefore cause a restriction of the freedom of capital circulation within the EU.

---

laws contained "no details of the circumstances in which the criteria for the exercise of the power of veto [..] may be applicable. Even if that power may be exercised only in situations of real serious risk or health emergencies, [...] that is to say, for reasons of public policy, public safety, public health and defence, investors do not know, for want of any information as to the actual circumstances permitting the exercise of the power in question, when the power of veto may be applicable. In consequence, it must be considered, as the Commission argues, that the situations allowing the exercise of the power of veto are potentially numerous, undetermined and undeterminable, and that they leave the Italian authorities broad discretion".

In the third case (Portugal Telecom), the Court ruled that by maintaining special rights in the company the Portuguese Republic had failed to fulfil its obligations under Art. 56 EC. In this case, golden shares had been acquired legitimately under Portuguese national law, which provided for the possibility of creating golden shares; nevertheless, national law was no defence to a breach of EU legislation.

These and other cases are discussed in Papadopoulos, *Privatizations of state-owned enterprises in Greece after the third economic adjustment programme published*, in *ECL*, 2018, 205; Id., *Greek legislation on strategic investments; the next golden share case before the European Court of Justice?*, in *ECL*, 2009, 264; Szabados, *Recent golden share cases in the jurisprudence of the court of justice of the European Union*, in *GLJ*, 2015, 1099; Ruccia, *The new and shy approach of the Court of Justice concerning golden shares*, in *EBLR*, 2013, 275; Szabados, *Recent*, 1099; Van Bekkum, *Cross border*, 811; Id., *Golden shares: a new approach*, in *ECL*, 2010, 13; Mukwiri, *Free movement of capital and takeovers: a case-study of the tension between primary and secondary EU legislation*, 2014, at *ssrn.com*; Agranovska, *Italian golden shares – A never-ending story?* 2012, at *ssrn.com*; Gaydarska/Rammeloo, *The legality of the "golden share" under EC Law*, 2009, at *ssrn.com*; Werlauff, *Safeguards against takeovers after Volkswagen – On the lawfulness of such safeguards under company law after the Court's decision in "Volkswagen"*, in *EBLR*, 2009, 1010; Artes, *Advancing harmonization: should the ECJ apply golden shares' standards to national company law?*, in *EBLR*, 2009, 457; Van Bekkum/Kloosterman/Winter, *Golden shares and European company law: the implications of Volkswagen*, in *ECL*, 2008, 8; Vossnstein, *The state of affairs of golden shares, general company law and European free movement of capital*, in *ECFR*, 2008, 115; Andenas/Gütt/Pannier, *Free*, 757; Adolff, *Turn of the tide?: the "golden share" judgements of the European Court of Justice and the liberalization of the European capital markets*, in *GLJ*, 2002, 20. See also the Authors quoted in the previous footnote.

In the Court's view, on the one hand, the VW statutes did not fall into the category of "strategic" companies' ones, since they did not concern one of the country's key branches. Moreover, they had the "dissuasive" effect for foreign investors that has to be avoided.

Notwithstanding the rather clear Courts' conclusion, it is true, however, that it is still highly uncertain as to how "strategic" key branches are to be identified (this issue is of course very sensitive, and cannot be examined further here) and – even more problematic – which laws assume a "dissuasive" effect.

As it has been noted, however, the WV decision – which should be read in line with the cases on the "real seat" jurisprudence started from the "Daily Mail" case (see above Chapter 1, § 7) – "constitutes another formidably challenging contribution to the already complex development of European corporate law. It is this combination of the interplay between the Commission's attempts at moving European company law forward with the different strategies of the Member States to resist or to adopt to the 'pressure to reform'"[33] (and see along these lines also the Court's jurisprudence in the recent case "Vivendi", described in the next paragraph).

As a consequence of the VW judgment, the German company changed the articles of association, but eliminated only the 80% quorum. Therefore, in 2012, proceedings were initiated against the German Government for the alleged failure to fulfil the obligations arising from the 2007 Court judgment. The Government justified itself on the basis that it was just the combination of the three provisions of the VW articles of association that violated the EU Treaty and not each of them taken individually.

The Court accepted that view and hold that "the failure to fulfil obligations established in that judgment results solely from the interaction between the provision relating to the cap on voting rights [...] and that relating to the lower blocking minority"; since the German government amended the rule which blocked the shareholders' resolutions (80% ceiling), the other provisions could remain in force (Case 95/12, decided in 2013, also called "VW II").

A final note. It is interesting to reflect on the occasion that brought the Court to scrutinize the WV golden shares[34].

The law giving the extra powers to the government and Lower Saxony was attacked in the context of the bitter fight between two giant German car manufacturers: Porsche AG and VW AG. The former company had become in 2008 a VW minority shareholder and had secretly built a bigger stake, through the

---

33 See Zumbansen/Saam, *ECJ*, 1044.
34 See Gerner-Beuerle, *Shareholders*, 101 f.

use of derivative securities that were not subject to reporting to the market, of more than 74% of VW ordinary shares.

Considering that the law and the 80% supermajority clause would have impeded Porsche, after the acquisition, from entering into a "group agreement" with VW, aimed at financing the acquisition, that company asked for the repeal of the VW law, denouncing it as "obsolete and no more applicable in a world of free capital exchange".

Notwithstanding the Court's first ruling, VW finally won the match. The context is however meaningful. The attempt by Porsche to acquire the WV group (which was ten times bigger) was de facto frustrated by the VW law (more precisely, by the combination of the VW law and the supermajority provision contained in the WV's bylaws) and the subsequent legal fight.

This observation is not intended as a personal judgment, since the CJEU has already ruled twice on the case (probably with a mixed result). It only aims to highlight how these "golden power rules" and, more generally, the laws impeding investors from freely buying shares – possibly combined also with complex structures (like supermajority provisions) – may play an important role in transactions aimed at changing the control of public companies and therefore radically affect their governance.

5. Transferability of the shares (clauses of consent, first refusal, tag along, drag along, change of control). The jurisprudence of the CJEU on national laws preventing investors to pursue cross-border transactions (cases *Tipou*, *Vivendi* and others)

(I) Most countries rely on the principle of general share transferability, but at the same time accept that the companies' articles of association may restrict that circulation to a great extent.

Art. 4 Directive 2017/1132/EU only stipulates that information on "the special conditions, if any, limiting the transfer of shares" must appear in the instrument of incorporation or the articles of association.

The EMCA also states that there should be no "reason to deal with the issue of transferability through mandatory rules. It should certainly be possible to limit the free transferability of shares [...]. But it should be left to the articles of association to deal with the issue of transferability, with free transferability as the default rule in any type of company" (see comment on Sect. 5.13). The EMCA adds also that "the limitation may entail a total ban on transfers of shares for a fixed period of time or any other kind of limitation such as a right of first refusal and a consent clause" (Sect. 5.14).

The majority of companies acts therefore basically allow most types of restrictions[35]. Some laws, like the Finnish and the Swedish, only permit limitations which are explicitly provided in the law (essentially the "consent clause" and the "right of first refusal", that we will examine below).

(II) One of the most common restrictive clauses is the "consent clause", which subject the transfer of shares to the approval of the company; this approval may be devolved to either the board of directors or the shareholders' general meeting (or the supervisory board in companies with the dualistic system), or even to classes of shareholders.

Since, however, a possible refusal of approval may frustrate both the interests of the prospective shareholder from entering the company and the interest of the incumbent shareholder from selling its shares, some laws stipulate that, within a certain period from the notification of the refusal, the company is obliged to buy the shares[36]. The purchase price has normally to be determined fairly, with the intervention in case of dispute of an expert appointed by the court.

In other companies acts the solution is even more clear-cut (even if less favorable from the point of view of the autonomy of shareholders): share transferability may only be subject to prior company authorization if the articles of association list precisely the cases in which the withholding of such authorization is legitimate: the reasons for the refusal must therefore be laid

---

35 Pursuant to Sect. 270 Cz-CA and Art. 3 Gr-PuCA all restrictions are allowed, provided that the transfer does not become totally impossible; under Art. 2355-bis It-CC the complete restriction to sell the shares has to be maintained within five years. Art. 2.78 B-CA stipulates that "inalienability clauses must be justified by a legitimate interest, in particular with regard to their duration. Inalienability clauses of indefinite duration may be terminated at any time subject to reasonable notice".

36 See i.e. Sect. 272 Cz-CA; Arts. 228-23 f. Fr-CC; Ch. 4, Sects. 6 and 12 Sw-CA. On the other hand, this is not the case for German law for example (more favorable to the company), pursuant to which "the by-laws may make the transfer contingent upon consent being granted by the company. Such consent is to be granted by the management board" (according to scholars, only with the caveat that the restriction on transferability must not be so stringent that is practically impossible to transfer the shares): see Sect. 68 Ge-PuCA, which adds that "the by-laws may specify the reasons for which consent may be refused" and that "the by-laws may stipulate that the supervisory board or the general meeting is to adopt a resolution on whether or not to grant consent". Therefore, if the articles of association do not provide details concerning the reason to grant or withhold consent, the management board will decide in its own discretion.

down "objectively". A permissible refusal will follow only where the purchaser does not fulfil the objective conditions set forth in the articles of association[37].

The consequences of violating the consent clause is normally the invalidity of the share transfer (claims for damages against the seller may be asserted by the purchaser).

(III) Another clause that is often contained in the articles of association is the right of "first refusal".

Shareholders may wish to increase their interest in the company if one of them wants to sell its shares. For this purpose, the articles of association may provide for a clause reserving to all shareholders – or (less often) to a particular class of shareholders (or even to the board of directors or the supervisory board, which will appoint the purchasers itself) – the option to buy all shares whose sale is envisaged on a priority basis.

Usually the selling price is fixed freely by the seller and thus the purchase will be exercised at the same price and conditions as those contained in the proposed transfer to the shareholders. Shareholders could, however, agree in the articles of association that, in case of disagreement, the price will be determined by an independent expert (under some laws the latter is the default regime[38]).

The consequences of violating the clause are regulated differently by different national laws. Pursuant to the great majority of national laws, a sale made in violation of the clause shall be null or void[39]. Similarly, the EMCA: Sect. 5.14 provides that "any transfer in violation of the articles of association is void".

Some jurisdictions however differ: under French law, for instance, in the absence of fraudulent collusion between the seller and the purchaser, the violation of the clause does not in itself invalidate the transfer; the harmed shareholders (who have lost the opportunity to acquire the transferred shares) can obtain compensation for the damage incurred. However, if the purchaser knew of the existence of the clause, the harmed shareholders may act to annul the transfer

---

37 See Art. 123 Sp-CA, which therefore only governs the possibility of an "objective" – motivated – refusal of consent and not also the possibility of a "simple" – unmotivated – refusal (in this latter case with the corrective of the mandatory buy out by the company or by the third party indicated by the company).

38 See Ch. 4, Sects. 18 ff., Sw-CA. The latter legislation also regulates the "post-sale purchase right clause": the articles of association may include a clause pursuant to which a shareholder shall be entitled to purchase the shares which have been transferred to a new owner (usually the transferee of the title through inheritance, testamentary disposition or division of marital property): see Ch. 4, Sects. 27 ff.; see Sund/Andersson/Haag, *Share transfer restriction and family business: the minority shareholders perspective*, in *EBLR*, 2015, 437.

39 That is the case i.e. of Ch. 4, Sect. 26, Sw-CA.

or ask the court to substitute them for the purchaser in the transfer carried out in breach of the clause[40].

(IV) The company's articles of association may also contain "tag along" or "drag along" clauses (even though these clauses are more often contained in shareholders' agreements; see above Chapter 3, § 8).

The tag along clause gives minority shareholders the right to sell (or rather, the right to "co-sell") their holdings to a third investor who intends to purchase the majority of the share capital, from the main shareholder, benefiting from the same economic conditions.

With the drag along clause, on the contrary, the majority shareholder has the right to sell to the third party the shares of the minority shareholders, along with its own shares under the same conditions.

According to some case law, these clauses should only be considered valid on condition that they contemplate adequate mechanisms for setting the fair selling price and they can be substantially likened, from that point of view, to consent clauses. As a consequence, the price can never be lower than the fair value that an independent expert would set[41].

(VI) The articles of association may also try to address the problem of the sale – instead of a stake in the company – of the majority stake of a company that is a shareholder in the company. These clauses are called "change of control" provisions.

Let us make an example. Assume that a company (Flamingo PLC) has three shareholders: Tom, Dick and Mirage PLC (the latter owning, say, 51% of the share capital). Can the articles of association of Flamingo stipulate that, if the control of Mirage is going to change (because its majority shareholder Harry is selling his stake to a third party, Jack), Tom and Dick (or Flamingo) may claim the right to purchase Harry's stake in Mirage or deny Jack's right to purchase the stake in Mirage?

In the former case the Flamingo's shareholders would exercise a right of first refusal on the shares of company which is not theirs (Mirage). In the latter case, they would exercise a right of consent towards a third party buying the shares of a company which is not theirs (Mirage).

---

40 See Art. 1123 of the Civil Code. An action called "interrogation" was introduced in 2016: if a third party was informed of the existence of the preemption clause, it may request the beneficiary in writing to confirm, within a time that it sets and which must be reasonable, whether they intend to use it. The writing must mention that in the absence of a response within this period, the beneficiary will no longer be able to request its substitution for the assignment entered into with the third party or the nullity of the assignment (see again Art. 1123).

41 See in the Italian jurisdiction Court of Milan, 31 March 2008 (case "Design Factory").

The question is debated. Recently it has been argued that "from an objective point of view, in the event of a change of control of the shareholder, the assumption for the validity of the clause of first refusal – consisting of the transfer of shares in the company – is missing, remaining unchanged the person who is attributed the right of ownership over them"; as a consequence, the provision in the articles of association governing a simple right of first refusal by the shareholders should be declared null or void[42].

On the other hand, it may be held that the statutory clauses that provide a right of consent should be considered valid only as long as they provide for the right of redemption by the company of the shares of the shareholder whose control is changing. In our case, Flamingo's shareholders should therefore be entitled to oppose Mirage's change of control if the articles of association of Flamingo obliged the company to buy out the stake of Mirage in Flamingo.

Moreover, the company intending to change control (Mirage) should be forced by the articles of association to make the necessary communications to the directors (of Flamingo), in order to let them evaluate and organize the purchase[43].

(VI) A last issue has to be mentioned. It regards the validity of the legitimacy of national provisions limiting the transferability of the shares to certain shareholders.

Please note that we are now speaking of "legislative" rules (i.e. laid down by a legislator in legislative acts) and not of "statutory" provisions (i.e. inserted by shareholders in the articles of association, like the ones considered in the above text).

The Court has developed its jurisprudence especially in the cases "Commission v. Italy [pharmacies]" (C-531/06, decided in 2009), "Commission v. France [bio-medical laboratories]" (C-89/09, decided in 2010), "Tipou v. Tipou" (81/09, decided in 2010) and – more recently – "Vivendi v. AGCM" (C-719/18, decided in 2020).

In all these cases – that we have already examined above in Chapter 1, § 9 – single Member States' laws limited the possibility for investors to acquire shares in domestic companies.

The Court actually extended the reasoning already followed on the topic of golden shares (see above § 4). In the cases mentioned in this paragraph, however, the overruled provisions did not favour the position of a Member State in the

---

42 See recently in the Italian jurisdiction Court of Rome, 9 May 2017 (with reference to a clause of right of first refusal).

43 See, as far as the Italian praxis is concerned, the Recommendation no. 185 of the Notarial Council of Milan.

relevant companies (by giving him "golden powers"), but created legal mechanisms in sector-specific legislation in order to regulate definite markets, with
the effect of disfavoring perspective investors (in the Vivendi case, for instance –
as you may remember – the Court considered the provisions of Italian law regulating the telecommunication and television sectors preventing Vivendi from
acquiring 28,8% of the capital in Mediaset as contrary to EU law: the provisions
have been judged not appropriate for achieving the objective of protecting pluralism of information and constituting a prohibited impediment to the freedoms
acknowledged by the Treaties).

Beyond the above cases, scholars have reported others, like the one concerning the German steelmaker Thyssen Krupp AG. The case was raised before a German court, but ultimately did not make it to the CJEU[44]. It is anyway interesting
to consider it.

The plaintiffs – minority shareholders of the public company Thyssen
Krupp – had claimed, *inter alia*, that a particular application of Sect. 101 Ge-
PuCA violates European the free movement of capital rules (the said provision
regulates the appointment of the members of the supervisory board). Indeed
Thyssen Krupp's articles of association were amended so as to grant a sole shareholder the right to appoint three supervisory board members (de facto allowing
the controlling power over the company) as long as that shareholder holds more
than 25% of the shares. The plaintiffs alleged that the mere existence of Sect. 101
Ge-PuCA and its concrete use in that case made it less attractive for investors to
acquire shares in the company, because it granted a shareholder holding more
than 25% of the shares an extensive right to control the company, disproportionate to the size of its shareholding. Regrettably – as it has been noted – the German courts hearing this case decided not to refer the question to the Court of
Justice (notwithstanding the plaintiffs' petition)[45].

According to one view, the cases effectively decided by th CJEU (like pharmacies, bio-medical laboratories, Tipou v. Tipou, Vivendi) "firmly support the development of a body of case law by the ECJ in which company law rules may result
in investors being prevented or deterred from making cross-border investments
in undertakings are judged to restrict the freedom of establishment and the
free movement of capital [Artt. 49 and 63 TFEU], regardless of whether these
rules favour the positions of Member States in certain companies" (like the gold-
en shares cases) or do not (as in the Vivendi case), and could affect many other

---

44 See Ringe, *Domestic*, 14 reporting the case discussed before the German Federal Supreme
Court, on 8 June 2009.
45 See Ringe, *Domestic*, 14.

domestic company law rules (like the ones on multiple voting and loyalty shares) in years to come[46].

Other opinions are more prudent. It is howevere clear that "ultimately, the Court will have to draw the line – and thereby decisively design the future diversity or unity of the canon of European company law"[47].

---

46 See especially Van Bekkum, *Cross-border*, 811. The EU Commission seems aware of the sensitivity of the theme and has in 2016 commissioned a detailed document entitled "*Proportionality between ownership and control in EU listed companies: external study commissioned by the European Commission*" (Ref. Ares(2016)140624).

47 So Ringe, *Domestic*, 39 (proposing an "effect-based" test: "the main focus of assessment should be directed towards the question of whether the particular rule at stake actually 'deters' potential investors from other Member States from investing in the company in a way comparable to golden shares"). For more conservative (or, at least, articulated) opinions see i.e. Gerner-Beuerle, *Shareholders*, 97; Szabados, *Recent*, 1099; also Andenas/Guett/Pannier, *Free*, 757. For the description of the academic debate and further references see also above footnotes 30 and 31 and Chapter 1, § 9.

5 Financing

Summary:
1. Capital increases
2. Equity linked instruments (convertible bonds, warrants, options)
3. Hybrid instruments
4. Bonds
5. Shareholders' loans (and reserve contributions)

1. Capital increases

The traditional means used to finance companies include equity capital and different kinds of debt. Over the years public companies have also started to receive financing also by issuing "hybrid" instruments.

While financing by share capital is addressed particularly in the Directive no. 1132 of 2017, EU laws contain no general provisions regarding debt and hybrid instruments. They are, however, regulated by the laws of some Member States (more extensively bonds and, to a lesser extent, hybrid securities).

Beginning with capital increases, any augment in capital has to be decided upon by the shareholders' general meeting. However, the instrument of incorporation, the articles of association or the general meeting may empower the management body to increase capital up to a maximum amount which they shall set ("authorized" capital increase)[1]. That power may be granted for a maximum period of five years (even if it may be renewed one or more times by the general meeting, each time for a period not exceeding five years) (see Art. 68 Directive 2017/1132/EU).

Whenever a previous capital increase is not fully subscribed, the Directive allows the capital to be increased by the amount of the new subscriptions only if the terms of issue provide for this (Art. 71). Some Member States' laws are stricter, and stipulate that the share capital cannot be increased as long as outstanding contributions to a previous capital increase still have to be obtained by the directors[2].

---

[1] Notwithstanding the silence of the Directive on this point, according to majority opinion, the share form that already exists must be chosen: a company whose shares were previously par value shares can therefore only issue par value shares, not no-par value shares, and vice versa.

2 See i.e. Art. 2438 It-CC.

https://doi.org/10.1515/9783110725025-007

Shares issued for cash consideration have to be paid up to at least 25% of their nominal value or, in absence of a nominal value, of their accountable par. If the shares are issued for consideration other than cash, rules similar to those already examined with regard to contributions at the initial stage apply (timing of the payment, assessment by independent experts of the non-cash consideration, etc.: see above Chapter 2, § 2, 6).

The Directive sets also forth that if provision is made for an issue at a "share premium", the related amount has to be paid in full at the date of the share subscription. The price of subscription of the new shares has to reflect the net worth of the company (Art. 69).

This principle is well consolidated in the jurisprudence of the CJEU: since the ruling "Karella and Karellas" of 1991, the Court has affirmed that a national law which leaves the determination of the price of the newly issued shares to the discretion of the directors or administrative authorities (without being set on the basis of the objectively established net worth of the company) violates the principles of the Second Directive and the pre-emptive right of the shareholders provided for by the latter[3].

Indeed the newly issued shares have to be offered on a pre-emptive basis to the "old" shareholders, in proportion to the capital represented by the shares they already own (Art. 72 Directive 2017/1132/EU). The purpose of this "pre-emptive right" is to protect existing shareholders from dilution of capital and loss of voting rights and possible dividends in the event of capital increases.

If the company has several classes of shares (carrying different rights: for instance Class A, Class B and Class C) and it increases its capital by issuing new shares in only one of these classes (say, C), the Directive allows the right of pre-emption of shareholders of the other classes (Class A and Class B) to be exercised only after the exercise of the pre-emption right by the shareholders of the class in which the new shares are being issued (Class C).

For the exercise of the right of pre-emption, companies must provide a period of no less than fourteen days from the date of publication of the offer or from the date of dispatch of the letters communicating the right to the shareholders.

The right of pre-emption cannot be restricted or excluded by the instrument of incorporation or the articles of association. However, this may be done in the case of contributions in kind (on the assumption that in such a case the interest of the company requires the sacrifice of the single shareholders' interest) or by

---

3 Judgment of 30 May 1991, joined cases C-19/90 and C-20/90. More generally, in other cases brought by Greek shareholders, the Court of Justice clearly stated that the fundamental regulation of the Second Directive cannot be waived by national rules. See also the cases C-381/92 ("Melon") and C-441/93 ("Pafitis").

decision of the general meeting. In both these situations the directors are required to present a written report indicating the reasons for the restriction or exclusion, and justifying the proposed issue price.

As for the latter reason, some laws more clearly stipulate that the decision may be taken only if it is proven that the transaction is "in the interest of the company": the exclusion or restriction must then be necessary with reference to that interest and proportionate in relation to the grave interference with the shareholders' rights[4].

Pursuant to the Directive (Art. 72), the laws of the Member States may provide (and normally do) that the instrument of incorporation, the articles of association or the general meeting have to give the power to restrict or exclude the right of pre-emption to directors if they are given the power to decide on a capital increase.

In any case, the exclusion or restriction of the pre-emptive right can only take place after a resolution of the general meeting (voting on the exclusion or empowering the directors with such a power) with a qualified majority as set out in the same Art. 72: at least two thirds of the votes. The same provision, however, establishes that the laws of the Member States may state that a simple majority of votes is sufficient when at least half the subscribed capital is represented.

Many legislations have also adopted a rule according to which the pre-emptive right may be excluded – in listed companies – if the capital increase against cash contributions does not exceed 10% of the share capital[5].

Finally, the right of pre-emption is not considered to have been excluded where shares are issued to banks or other financial institutions, with a view to their being offered to shareholders of the company. These regulations are employed especially for the capital increase procedures for listed companies and structured IPOs (an "initial public offering" refers to the process of offering shares of a non-listed company to the public for the first time on a stock exchange).

If the shareholders do not use their pre-emptive rights, the question arises as to what should be done with the subscription rights. There are basically two different solutions: according to some laws there is a second term which provides

---

4 See i.e. Sect. 488 Cz-CA ("important interest") and Art. 308 Sp-CA ("best interest"). German case law has reached the same result: in 1978 the Supreme Court ruled that shareholders' resolutions that waive the pre-emptive right are only valid if they can be justified by a good reason in the company's interest (10 March 1978, case "Kali und Salz").

5 This rule has been implemented for instance in Art. 2441 It-CC and, as per German law, only if the issue price is not significantly lower than the stock exchange price: see Sect. 186 Ge-PuCA.

an option for the other shareholders to subscribe to the remaining shares[6]; the alternative, which does not involve a second round, is found for example in the Nordic countries' laws (they allow the company to sell the subscription rights and the proceeds are allocated among the people who would have been entitled to receive or subscribe to the new shares[7]).

In the presence of several classes of shares, a decision by the general meeting concerning the capital increase is normally subject to a separate vote at least for each class of shareholders whose rights are affected by the transaction (see above Chapter 4, § 3).

Finally, a different way to effect a capital increase is by using existing company capital reserves. The shareholders' general meeting may resolve to increase the share capital by converting the reserves (and retained earnings) into equity. The shares emitted in this way to all shareholders in proportion of their shareholdings are also called "bonus shares". The requirements for the resolution are the same as for an ordinary capital increase[8].

After the decision on the capital increase has been taken and registered in accordance with the rules illustrated above, the capital increase will be carried out by collecting the contributions and registering the increase in the companies register.

2. Equity linked instruments (convertible bonds, warrants, options)

The issuance of "debt" instruments does not require a decision by the general meeting: the authority for this lies with the management of the company, according to the rules on management powers.

This is normally the case – apart from bank financing (ordinary loans) – when issuing bonds, as a form of split debt represented by certificates (see more extensively below § 4). In some cases, however, the issue of bonds requires the intervention of the shareholders' general meeting, when they are emitted

---

6 See i.e. Art. 2441 It-CC.

7 See paradigmatically Ch. 11, Sect. 9, Sw-CA.

8 German law is however particularly strict in this regard (and goes beyond the rules of the Directive): the annual financial statements to which the resolution refers must be audited and contain an unqualified audit opinion and the effective date may not exceed eight months prior to the application for registration of the resolution in the companies register (see Sect. 209 Ge-PuCA).

with a "conversion" clause that permit the bondholders to change them at a later stage into shares ("convertible bonds").

Convertible bonds are financial instruments which give the owner a right – but not an obligation – to convert bonds into shares (on the other hand, they can also be issued as "mandatory convertible" or "reverse convertible" bonds, obliging the owner to convert at the company's request).

"Warrants" are similar to convertible bonds, and are instruments which entitle the owner to subscribe to new shares (however, without having provided financing, unlike with bonds[9]).

The rules on convertible bonds and warrants (contained in the legislation of many Member States, in the EMCA at Ch. 6, Part 3, and more concisely in Directive 1132/2017/EU at Arts. 68 and 72) are twofold: on the one hand, they seek to ensure that the subscribers to the convertible bonds and warrants receive all the relevant information regarding their rights and duties in connection with the issuance (such instruments – if exchanged on a trading venue – are also subject to the securities laws on prospectuses); on the other hand, they have to protect current shareholders that may see their position affected by the conversion of the bonds or the warrants in the future.

From the latter point of view, the issue of convertible bonds and warrants therefore always requires a decision by the general meeting, with the same majority laid down for raising capital. The resolution of a general meeting shall determine the maximum amount of the capital increase that may be converted or subscribed and the "conversion ratio" of the bonds or warrants into shares. The conversion of convertible bonds is to be regarded as a contribution in cash paid up by set-off against receivables due to the company and will be subject to the same conditions as such a contribution[10].

On the other hand, all other themes – i.e. terms of the bonds and warrants – can be decided by the board (or by the general meeting if the articles of association stipulate this).

---

9 Some laws also regulate bonds that include a preferential right to subscription of shares (so called "preferential bonds"): see i.e. Sects. 286/294 Cz-CA. The regulation of convertible bonds and warrants laid down by the Sw-CA is particularly extensive (see Ch. 14–15). See also, for hybrid instruments regulated under French law, Arts. 228-91 ff. Fr-CC.

10 Some Member States set out quantitative limits to the issue of "conditional capital", like Germany, where it may not exceed half of the share capital. However (pursuant to Sect. 192 Ge-PuCA), this restriction does not apply if the conditional capital increase is decided upon to enable the company to make a conversion that it is entitled to in the event of imminent insolvency or for the purpose of averting it; it is therefore possible to issue convertible bonds that can be converted into shares and by doing so, provide equity capital during the company's crisis, based on the legislator's idea of facilitating the company restructuring.

The shareholders' general meeting may however empower the management body to make decisions about issuing convertible bonds or warrants. The shareholders' resolution (at the basis of the directors' powers) must set a time limit for the authorization and the maximum number of instruments to be issued[11].

As far as the security holders' rights are concerned, owners of convertible bonds or warrants may ask to convert them into shares within the time limit determined by the resolution upon issue. Unless the resolution agrees on another procedure, the security holders may request the conversion at any time. Usually the directors, within the first month of each semester, will issue the shares corresponding to the securities that have requested the conversion in the previous semester and will register the capital increase corresponding to the issued shares the following month in the companies register.

Pursuant to Directive 2017/1132/EU convertible bonds and warrants have preemption rights in connection with later capital increases, if the terms of the issue do not provide otherwise (see Art. 72).

Finally, a company can also issue "call options", which include a right to acquire shares already issued by the company for a pre-specified price ("exercise price"). The decision to issue options does not require a decision taken by general meeting and the resolution, as well as the specific setting of the option conditions, can be taken by the company's board of directors.

Options are mentioned – for instance – by Dutch company law, in Art. 2.96 Du-CC, but only with the aim to exclude them from application of the rules on the pre-emptive right (this right shall not apply to "a person who previously had acquired a right to shares", i. e. a call option).

3. Hybrid instruments

Other securities (ordinary bonds, hybrid instruments) are not regulated – or even mentioned – by the directives. As for the EMCA, the Model states that it generally seeks "to give companies the greatest possible freedom to choose the best suited capital structures. A part of this is to grant companies permission to develop and use the most suitable types of financing" (see the general comments to Ch. 6).

The power to use these other types of instruments should lie, according to the EMCA, with the company's management.

---

11 See for instance Art. 414 Sp-CA: prior to the notice by the board, the directors must draft a report explaining the reasons and mechanisms of the conversion, which must be accompanied by another report written by an auditor, appointed for that purpose by the companies register.

Some national companies acts therefore permit public companies to issue instruments that have features of both bonds and shares, while actually being neither. The most common are the "profit-sharing debt instruments" and the "participative financial instruments".

A regulation on these securities – labelled as "innovative" by the EMCA Group – is contained in Italian law. Pursuant to Arts. 2346 and 2351 It-CC, the company may issue "financial instruments" endowed with special asset and administrative rights (which have to be outlined in the articles of association)[12].

These instruments do not provide the status of shareholder. The contribution made by the subscriber of the instrument is not attributed to the share capital, even if it gives rise to an increase in the company's assets. They may be structured in a way that is more similar to a bond (if the holder of the financial instrument is entitled to the repayment of the capital provided); in that case, the instrument is mainly subject to regulations on bonds. Otherwise, the instrument can be structured in a way that is more similar to a share (if the holder is not entitled to the repayment of the capital and simply risks losing it, like an equity provider); the instrument is therefore mainly subject to regulations on shares.

The contribution of the subscriber can be any kind and it is not restricted like shareholders' contributions: it may also entail the performance of work or services (and that makes these securities more flexible and attractive for a public company).

These instruments may have pure "financial" or also "participative" features. In the latter case, they are attributed administrative rights and even – according to mechanisms to be established by the articles of association – the right to appoint "an independent member of the board of directors or of the supervisory board or of a statutory auditor".

The range of administrative rights that can be given through these instruments is actually far-reaching: for example, they may entail the right to vote on specific topics (however, not including voting in the general meetings of shareholders[13]), the right to attend the shareholders' general meeting or meet-

---

12 See Folladori, in *Company laws*, 473.

13 There are two schools of thought on this aspect: according to the first, the vote must be cast in a separate general meeting reserved to holders of financial instruments, which must be held in a different place from the general meeting of shareholders: according to the second, the vote could also be cast at the general meeting, provided that it is calculated in accordance with a separate quorum.

ings of the board of directors' for informative purposes, the right to have full access to corporate books, etc.[14].

The complexity (and fascination) of these instrument may sometimes reach amazing levels, and they can therefore easily become "paradise" for lawyers and notaries.

The laws that govern "dividend-linked participating loans" and "principal-linked participating loans" (especially known in Sweden) are also remarkable.

The interest on these debentures or the amount that will be repaid is – in whole or in part – dependent on dividends to the shareholders, changes in the price of the company's shares, the company's results or the company's financial position. The option to link the remuneration of these instruments to the company's performance therefore seems to be particularly significant. These contracts have to be agreed by the company by a general meeting or by the board of directors following authorization by the general meeting[15].

Sometimes the line of distinction between a participating loan and an equity instrument becomes difficult to draw: for instance, a recent ruling by a Luxembourg court is of interest, for having re-characterised a profit-participating loan into equity for tax purposes[16].

---

14 These instruments can be governed as securities addressed to the market and capable of being traded, or – alternatively – their circulation may be limited.

15 See paradigmatically Ch. 11, Sect. 11, Sw-CA. Also Spanish law acknowledges the option to issue "profit participating loans", which were introduced by the Royal Decree-Law 7/1996 as an instrument to attract investors. This participation in business risk takes place in two ways: the participating loan imposes a subordinated debt condition in the order of credit priority in the case of insolvency of the borrower or the remuneration of the profit participating loan is established on the basis of the development of the borrower's activity (net profit, turnover, total assets or any other indicator), but it is also possible to agree on an interest rate that is not linked to said activity.

16 See Administrative Court, 26 July 2017, No. 38357C (case "Luxembourg vs. PPL-Co"): "it must be concluded that the sums made available to the two subsidiaries by the appellant were made not as financing from a lender concerned with recovering the capital lent, but as a risk-oriented investment to gains in value of the hotels financed through the two loans, so that these sums are to be assimilated to contributions in cash to the subsidiaries and that the normal way of making these sums available would have been the increase in capital. No other particular economic interest justifying the replacement of capital contributions by loans emerging from the elements in question or having been put forward by one of the parties, it must be concluded that the essential tax interest consisted in the deduction of the 'participative interests' by the subsidiaries in the [foreign country] as charges in relation to the taxable capital gains generated by the said subsidiaries".

4. Bonds

Bonds are not regulated by the directives either (nor are they considered extensively by the EMCA). On the contrary, Member States' laws are often analytical and provide for special laws for listed companies.

Almost all companies acts assign the power to issue bonds to the management body (with the exception of the issue of convertible bonds: see above § 2).

French law – in order to add speed and simplicity to bond issues – has even introduced a provision (Art. 228-40 Fr-CC) which allows the board of directors (or the management board in the dualistic system) to delegate the power to issue bonds to any person of its choice (usually the executive director or the chief financial officer).

At the opposite end, there are more conservative laws whereby the issue of bonds can be decided by an extraordinary shareholders' general meeting only[17]. Some regulations require the issue agreement to be formalized in a public deed, which must have minimum legal elements and be published in the companies register[18].

As far as any presence of quantitative limits, national laws normally give freedom to the companies and do not set out particular ceilings. However, certain company laws impose significant limitations. For example, Art. 2412 It-CC stipulates that the company can only issue bonds for an amount that does not exceed twice the share capital and the reserves resulting from the most recently approved financial statements. That limit can be exceeded if the bonds are intended to be listed on regulated markets or aimed at professional investors subject to prudential supervision by administrative authorities (in this case, if the bonds are subsequently put on the market, the transferor will be liable for the company's solvency towards buyers who are not professional investors)[19].

Other national laws require differently – as a pre-condition to the bond issue – that the share capital has been fully paid up and two sets of financial statements approved by its shareholders have been drawn up; in the absence of financial statements, the company must have its assets and liabilities audited. If the company has not yet approved the two sets of financial statements, it will be exempt from that audit if the bonds are guaranteed by a company that has itself approved two sets of financial statements[20].

---

17 See i.e. Art. 113 R-CA.
18 See i.e. Art. 407 Sp-CA.
19 Also, the issue of bonds guaranteed by first mortgages on real estate owned by the company, up to two thirds, is not subject to the limit.
20 See in this sense Art. 228-39 Fr-CC.

Concerning the character of the bonds, companies generally undertake to repay the bondholders on maturity and repay the capital for the duration of the loan with yields that may be fixed or variable.

The right to reimbursement and remuneration are however natural but not essential elements of the bond loan, where regulations change the rights accorded to bondholders with respect to that basic model. For example, the right to the repayment of capital and interest may be, in whole or in part, subject to the satisfaction of the rights of other creditors of the company (so called "subordinate bonds"); or the times and extent of the payment of interest may vary depending on objective parameters, also relating to the company's economic performance (these kinds of bonds show affinities with the "profit-sharing debt instruments" dealt with in the previous paragraph)[21].

Bonds may be issued in accordance with various models. They can be "registered" or "bearer" bonds; "simple" or "secured" bonds (if they are guaranteed by company's or third parties' assets), etc.

Bonds can also be emitted – only in few jurisdictions – in the form of "exchangeable bonds" (which have to be kept separate from "convertible bonds"): bondholders will not convert their bonds for shares that the company must issue, but will obtain in exchange shares already issued by other companies, that can be arranged by the company issuing the bond[22].

As far as the subscription of the bonds is concerned, the company has to set a period of time within which they have to be subscribed. The terms and conditions of the issue can be amended by a resolution of the bondholders' meeting and with the issuer's consent. Some national provisions require, more stringently, the consent of all bondholders for essential modifications, while others allow the company to change some terms unilaterally[23].

The provisions in individual countries also normally govern the appointment of a bondholders' "representative" and set forth the cases in which the bondholders' meeting has to be called (usually by the same representative or the directors or a certain percentage of the bondholders themselves), the majority required to pass the bondholders' meeting resolutions and, in some cases, the cases where bondholders' resolutions may be challenged[24].

The events that trigger a call of the bondholders' meeting and the powers of the representative vary from State to State. Under Spanish law, for instance, if the

---

21 For this possibility see i.e. Art. 2411 It-CC.

22 See i.e. Art. 144 Sp-CA.

23 See i.e. Art. 2415 It-CC and Art. 7 of the Polish "Acts on Bonds" of 2 February 2015 respectively.

24 For a particularly extensive regulation see Arts. 70 f. of the Polish Act on Bonds.

company delays paying the interest or amortization due on a bond for more than six months, the representative may even call a shareholders' (note: not a bondholders) general meeting. If the bonds are secured by a mortgage or a pledge and the company postpones the interest payment for over six months, the representative, subject to a decision adopted by the general bondholders' meeting, may foreclose on the assets constituting the security to pay the principal and interest due[25].

As far as the tasks, duties and responsibilities of the bondholders' representative, this officer has to supervise the common interests of the bondholders; for this purpose national companies acts normally empower representatives with the competence – among others – to attend (with no vote) the issuing company's general meetings and exercise, on behalf of the bondholders, any relevant actions with respect to the issuing company, directors or liquidators or any party that may have secured the bond issue[26].

5. Shareholders' loans (and reserve contributions)

Despite the rising popularity of bonds and hybrid instruments, European firms still get financing mainly from banks and other lenders[27]. However, companies acts do not regulate the relationship between lenders and the company which is traditionally dealt with by the laws on contracts (or other normative bodies).

(I) However, special treatment has been reserved by some national legislations for loans granted to the firm by a specific category of lenders: the shareholders themselves.

Germany was the first Member State to introduce provisions on "shareholders loans" (in 1990) in order to sanction shareholders who – in case of pre-insolvency – decided to provide financing instead of equity (we have already dealt with this theme above in Chapter 2, § 5).

If the company is healthy, the choice between debt or equity should be neutral. If, on the contrary, the company is illiquid or overindebted (or even on the verge of insolvency), financing makes more sense for shareholders than providing equity. In the case of insolvency proceedings, shareholders are treated as creditors (at least for the money provided as debt). This may induce them to

---

25 See Arts. 428 f. Sp-CA. Pursuant to French law (recently amended), decisions may be taken by the bondholders at the general meeting or in writing: holding general meetings will no longer be the only method for making decisions (see Art. 226-46-1 Fr-CC).

26 See again i.e. Art. 421 Sp-CA.

27 Of course, the matter is different for listed companies, which also raise capital on the market.

take advantage of the situation and provide financing instead of equity any time they feel that the firm is suffering and needs cash, benefitting from any inside information they may have (and that other creditors do not have).

In order to fight this kind of conduct – which also leads to systematic under-capitalization – many companies acts have adopted rules whereby, on the one hand, the loans provided by shareholders must be paid back, in the insolvency proceedings, only after all other creditors have been satisfied and, on the other hand, any reimbursed loans have to be paid back. Shareholders' financing is thus "postergated" (i.e. legally subordinated) to the financing provided by other creditors (some jurisdictions have recently introduced amendments and do not require the company to be in a situation of crisis when the shareholder's loan is granted in order to apply the rules[28]).

---

28 The German law (Sects. 39 and 135 Ge-InSA) was initially restricted, but has subsequently been modified, in order to embrace any loans (see Schall/Machunsky, in *Company laws*, 222). Paradigmatically see also Art. 283 Sp-InsA: loans are always subordinated (independently of the situation of the company at the time they were made) if made by shareholders who hold at least 5% (for companies listed on a stock exchange) or 10% (for unlisted companies) of the company's share capital, or by any person related to the creditor.

On the other hand, see the Austrian "Act on equity substitute payments" of 28 October 2003: a loan granted to a company by a shareholder shall be deemed to be an equity substitute payment, if the loan was granted during a financial crisis of the company receiving the loan. A company is deemed to be in a financial crisis if the company is either (i) insolvent or (ii) over-indebted or (iii) if the equity ratio is less than 8 per cent and if the fictious duration for a payment of all debts exceeds 15 years, unless it can be shown by a certificate issued by a certified auditor that the company does not require a reorganization. In the third case, the loan shall only be deemed to be an equity substitute payment, if at the time when the loan was granted, an equity ratio of less than 8 per cent and a fictious duration for a payment of all debts of more than 15 years could be seen from the current annual 18 accounts or would have been seen, if the annual accounts had been drawn up on time or if the lender knows that the annual accounts or an interim financial account would show these facts. A loan shall not be deemed to be an equity substitute payment if (a) the money loan was not granted for a period longer than 60 days or (b) if a commercial or other loan was not granted for a period longer than six months (this period can be longer if the shareholder can prove that longer terms for payment are common in this trade) or (c) if a loan granted prior to the company's financial crisis was extended or if a moratorium was granted (see Art. 2 ff.). Also pursuant to Art. 2467 It-CC the postergation rule applies however only if the company is in a situation of crisis as a consequence of over indebt-edness or financial stress (or both).

According to the majority of laws, "shareholder" only refers to the controlling shareholders or a person holding a certain percentage of the share capital (50% in Hungary, 25% in Austria, 10% in Croatia, Poland and Romania) or a person who otherwise has the power to exercise dom-inant influence over the company. Art. 2467 It-CC applies only to private companies (and holding companies in groups) but is extended by case law to shareholders in public companies, as long as they are in a position to understand the difficult financial situation of the company and de-

After the adoption of these laws, national courts have coped with many related issues. The German Supreme Court, for example, stated that a loan given by a former shareholder (i.e.: a creditor who is not current shareholder) will be subordinated if the lender had been a shareholder of the company at any point in the previous year and the company goes bankrupt at a stage when the lender is not a shareholder anymore[29]; and also that a loan given by a shareholder is subordinated if the shareholder has sold the loan to a (neutral) third party, but has kept its shares in the company[30]. In all these cases the shareholder is deemed to have been taking advantage of his position. The situation becomes thus highly fact specific.

However, other Member States' legislations have taken an opposite route and simply do not lay down particular rules: shareholders may provide loans to their company basically without limits.

(II) Finally, most domestic laws allow another way of providing liquidity to the company, which is neither equity, nor financing, nor hybrid financing. It is "contribution to reserves".

The liquidity supplied by the shareholders is acquired by the company and recorded in the accountancy and financial statements under the "reserves" (while equity is recorded under "capital" and loans and bonds are recorded under "payables").

Indeed company reserves may be built up (beside of retained earnings) with those contributions made by the shareholders specifically aimed at increasing the net assets (although not the share capital). The company net assets are thus improved and, in the case of losses, the latter may be reduced by using these reserves too. More precisely, such contributions can be used to cover losses or to subscribe to new capital increases; if all debts have been paid, they can be returned to the shareholders.

However, sometimes it may be difficult to interpret the will of the shareholders: did they intend to provide this kind of contribution or, on the contrary, did

---

cide to choose to provide debt instead of equity; that is obviously the case of the majority shareholder. On the other hand, the rule is usually not applied to public companies' minority shareholders, since they are seldom in the position to have a clue about the current situation of the company (at least in that jurisdiction, they receive financial information only once a year, when they participate in the annual meeting voting on the financial statements).

29 See German Supreme Court, 15 November 2011 (case "E. AG").

30 See German Supreme Court, 21 February 2013 (case "U. GmbH"). The recent decisions of the German Supreme Court show that judges maintain a rigorous line concerning shareholder loans and comparable claims.

they just want to provide mere financing[31]? The distinction is obviously important especially from the investors' standpoint since contributions to reserves cannot be returned (unless the reserves are dismantled, and this requires a shareholders' resolution), while financing must be repaid by the company at the simple shareholders' request (or upon the terms of the financing agreement).

The issue has been addressed by the case law: "the qualification, in one sense or another" – it has been stated – "depends on the interpretation of the will of the parties, and the relative proof (of which the plaintiff shareholder is encumbered) must be drawn from the way in which the relationship has been implemented in practice, the practical purposes to which it appears to be directed and the interests that are underlying"[32].

---

31 There can be no confusion instead with reference to the contribution to capital (equity), since in order to increase the latter a resolution of the extraordinary general meeting, or the board, is required (see above § 1).

32 See i. e. Italian Supreme Court, 23 March 2017, no. 7471 (case "Ravenna Beach")".

6 Protection of minorities (right to vote and right to exit)

Summary:
1. Shareholders' voice and exit (and directors' liability). Different approaches of national laws
2. Right to vote in general meetings and to challenge shareholders' resolutions
3. Right to information
4. Right to withdrawal
5. Right to sell out (and to winding up)
6. Shareholders' litigation and jurisdiction: the jurisprudence of the CJEU (case *E-ON Czech Holding*)

1. Shareholders' voice and exit (and directors' liability). Different approaches of national laws

(I) As it has been shown – among others – by the papers prepared by groups of experts appointed over the years by the EU Commission, there is an ongoing international debate on the role of shareholders in public companies.

Part of this discussion has to do with the opportunity to strengthen the "voice" of shareholders in companies by empowering their right to vote at general meetings (this logically implies extending the right to information and the right to challenge invalid general meeting resolutions).

The other paramount issue regards the possible acknowledgment of a right to "exit" the company, i.e. the opportunity of introducing provisions in companies acts that allow shareholders to disagree with certain major corporate decisions (and/or relating to oppression by the majority) to leave the business venture.

The main idea, in both cases, is that if shareholders perceive that they are being properly protected by company law, they will be keen on investing more in firms, reinforcing their financial structure.

On the other hand, giving significant powers to shareholders may weaken both the efficiency of the decision-making process and the same financial structure (if they exit, shareholders' ownership must be liquidated, often at at the company's expense).

There are therefore arguments both "pro" and "con" in recognizing extensive privileges to minority shareholders.

https://doi.org/10.1515/9783110725025-008

The question has not been be treated organically by any directive, plan or single EU legislation.

The EU Action Plans of 2003 and 2012 emphasize, only at a general level, the opportunity to strengthen the position of shareholders in companies. The first document, for instance, specifies – as a statement of principle – that "a sound framework for protection of members and third parties, which properly achieves a high degree of confidence in business relationships, is a fundamental condition for business efficiency and competitiveness"[1].

A (very well done) comparative study – of over 7000 pages – on the legal remedies for the protection of minority shareholders in the Member States was published by the EU Commission in 2018[2].

Legislative action has been more straightforward for listed companies only, with the adoption of Directives 2007/36/EC and 2018/828/EU on the exercise of certain rights of shareholders (the "Shareholder Rights Directives"; see below Chapter 12).

These sector-specific regulations endorse the view that shareholders have to be offered more opportunities to participate in general meetings, oversee directors' remuneration policy and monitor the risks embedded in related party transactions.

Taking a different route, the EMCA Group – from its perspective – has also addressed the issue for unlisted public companies and considers the issue of minority rights rather extensively. The EMCA has divided minority rights into several areas, the most important of which are the right to vote; the right of information at the level of shareholders' general meeting; shareholders' exit; the right to appoint special examiners; derivative liability suits.

(II) In the paragraphs below, we shall thus examine the regulatory solutions adopted by Member States in order to create a protective legal framework for minority shareholders.

Of course, the various techniques are interrelated. As demonstrated by the EMCA, the debate cannot be reduced to a simply "more/less" voice (or exit) dichotomy.

---

1 See COM (2003) 284 final (§ 2.1).

2 *Study on minority shareholders protection. Final report*, prepared by TGS Baltic, 2018, at https://op.europa.eu/en/publication-detail/-/publication/1893f7b8-93a4-11e8-8bc1-01aa75ed71a1/language-en. Significantly the study states that it "embraces 64 categories of minority shareholders rights, which cover extremely broad range of different legal concepts, legal institutes, definitions, frameworks, remedies and measures, often trespassing many different legal sources of both EU and national law".

In each company law system, the right to vote (or to withdrawal, etc.) must be read in connection with the other provisions that provide minorities with other important rights, like the right to sue the members of the corporate bodies, the right to file for the appointment of special examiners, etc.

The corporate governance model (monistic, dualistic, etc.) matters, too. Finally, the underlying "normative philosophy" (more or less shareholder-friendly) is of the greatest importance. Jurisdictions more inclined towards the "shareholders' primacy model" are evidently more ready to bestow remedies and enhanced transparency to investors (see above, Chapter 3, § 4).

The picture is thus rather complex.

In order to proceed in a certain order, we shall first deal with the remedies giving shareholders the option to have their "voices" heard in the company: the right to vote, to challenge invalid resolutions and to information.

We shall then consider the various "exit" remedies. They are governed very differently under domestic laws. Having acknowledged that the problem of minority shareholders who are locked into a company is a core issue of company law, Member State legislators have however adopted regulatory techniques that are very dissimilar (appraisal rights with shares bought back by the company, right to sell out the shares to the majority shareholders or even the winding-up of the company, as a remedy against oppression, etc.).

Please note that – regarding the "other" rights conferred to the minorities (which are, as noted, in any case linked and combined to the ones examined here) – they have either been treated above in this book or they will be examined elsewhere at a later stage[3]. As a consequence, this Chapter should be read in combination also with those other Chapters.

2. Right to vote in general meetings and to challenge shareholders' resolutions

Let us begin by considering how shareholders "vote" in general meetings and challenge invalid resolutions.

---

3 E.g.: the possibility for shareholders to challenge board meetings resolutions has been analyzed above in Chapter 3, § 7 and the right to appoint special examiners above in Chapter 3, § 6. The issue of the place of shareholders in corporate governance (and to vote on certain business transactions) has been addressed above in Chapter 3, § 4. The right of shareholders to sue directors and supervisors for liability will be discussed below in Chapter 9.

(I) The "procedural rules" governing general meetings are basically similar in the Member States. The meeting is normally called via an appropriate notice by the directors[4], each time they deem it necessary.

The calling of the meeting is however mandatory in a series of cases (at least once a year for approval of the financial statements, upon ascertaining a case of dissolution, etc.).

The general meeting may also be called, according to some regulations, by other corporate bodies (like the supervisory board or the board of the statutory auditors, under special circumstances)[5] and when shareholders with a certain aggregate shareholding so require (in this case, if the meeting is not called, the shareholders may ask a court to intervene)[6]. The notice of call may also indicate the day of the second call (for cases where the quorum envisaged on first call has not been reached).

The agenda defines the boundaries of the shareholders' general meeting, outlining the topics on which the meeting may deliberate. The agenda need not necessarily be analytical, but it must be enough to inform each shareholder on the issues to be discussed and allow them to participate in the general meeting in an informed manner[7].

Under many companies acts, the general meeting is considered to have been validly called when the entire share capital is represented and when the majority of members of the administrative and control bodies attend the meeting ("full

---

4 Member States usually permit companies to call the meeting via notice to shareholders through means that guarantee proof of receipt at least eight days prior to the meeting, entering this into their articles of association (e.g., registered letter with return receipt, e-mail, fax or hand delivery). Pursuant to Art. 7.133 B-CA the meeting can be held in writing if all shareholders agree.

5 I.e.: pursuant to Sect. 111 Ge-PuCA, the supervisory board is entitled and even obliged to call the meeting if so required in the interests of the company; under Art. 2406 It-CC, the board of the statutory auditors must call the meeting in the event of a lack of action by the directors, or if all directors are unavailable, or if it identifies facts of considerable severity that must urgently be resolved.

6 See paradigmatically Art. 2.110 Du-CC (10%); Art. 225-120 Fr-CC (5%); Sect. 112 Ge-PuCA (20%); Art. 375 Por-CC (5%), etc. Most (but not all) of these provisions also allow shareholders to put items onto the agenda (the models go from the simplest one – like Ch. 7, Sect. 16, Sw-CA – permitting any shareholder to propose a resolution, to more complex ones, requiring the ownership of a minimum shareholding – like i.e. Sect. 366 Cz-CA, referring to "qualified shareholders"). In accordance with some laws, the supervisory board may also add supplementary items (see i.e. Sect. 25 Li-CA). For a comparative analysis see also Roth/Kindler, *The spirit*, 122.

7 Only few laws provide for the right of shareholders to make proposals and counterproposals, once the meeting is called; i.e. the formulation of Sects. 361 ff. Cz-CA, Art. 25 Li-CA and Sect. 300 Slove-CA is particularly broad.

quorum meeting"). In this case, despite the fact that the participation by all shareholders is not effectively precluded (given the presence of the entire share capital), failure to validly call the general meeting may, however, prejudice the right of shareholders to be fully informed and aware of the items on the agenda. In order to guarantee resolutions that have been passed on an informed and agreed basis, each shareholder can normally object to the discussion and decision of issues on which he does not consider him to be sufficiently informed, thereby making it necessary to call a valid meeting according to the terms and procedures already examined[8].

Quorums are different under different national laws (also taking into consideration the differences between ordinary and extraordinary shareholders' general meetings)[9].

An important question regards the possibility to add "supermajority" or "unanimity" clauses into the articles of association, and their extent, which could block the capability of the meeting to pass resolutions.

This argument is actually very sensitive since it concerns the boundaries of the shareholders' contractual autonomy. Moreover – according to a widespread view (but you may also consider the "Volkswagen" cases decided by the CJEU, examined above in Chapter 4, § 4) – these provisions are of interest also in the perspective of the principles and liberties acknowledged by the Treaties, since they may indeed become obstacles to the freedom of investors to buy stakes in foreign companies[10].

Participation in general meeting is normally possible also by means of proxy.

The general meeting is chaired by the person indicated in the articles of association or, failing that, by the individual elected by the majority of those present. Voting and relative methods are normally governed by the articles of association.

(II) All Member States allow shareholders to file suits to challenge the shareholder's meeting resolutions in the case of irregularities. However, the extent of

---

8 See i.e. Arts. 54 Por-CC and Art. 2366 It-CC.

9 In any case, in order to facilitate decision making and reduce the effects of any shareholder absenteeism, governance of meeting quorums is usually different between the first call and the subsequent calls.

10 That is probably the reason why the EU Commission has also focused its attention on supermajority provisions – beside multiple voting shares, voting right ceilings, golden shares, etc. – as possible mechanisms restricting the fundamental freedom of circulation of capital and services; see the study *Proportionality between ownership and control in EU listed companies*, cited above in Chapter 4, § 5.

this right varies greatly (even though it is – at a general level – broadly recognized as an important tool to protect minorities, along with the rules on directors' liability[11]).

Most domestic laws distinguish between "nullity", on the one hand, and "voidability", on the other, with differences in the severity of the infractions, the parties entitled to enforce them, the terms for the filing of the suit, etc. (sometimes these categories are defined as "absolute" and "relative" nullity or "nullity" and "annullability", etc: for the sake of simplicity, we shall adopt the definition employed by the Fifth draft Directive).

A rather clear distinction – at least on paper – may be found in many companies acts: general meeting resolutions that are not adopted in compliance with the law or with the articles of association shall be "null" if the provisions that are violated are meant to protect a "general interest" (this is the case, for example, of the rules on financial statements, which are significant also for creditors), while "voidability" steps in when the interest protected by the breached provisions is only a shareholders' one (like flaws concerning calling the meeting or the disclosure of information prior to the meeting[12]).

The distinction explains why in cases of nullity, the resolution may be appealed by anyone interested – and also recognized by the court on its own motion – and within a deadline which is usually quite long (for instance three years) or even without time limits[13].

---

11 In many jurisdictions this is probably still the "main" tool of protection: see clearly Sáez/ Riaño, *Corporate*, 355, according to whom "this litigation mechanism – the possibility of nullifying a shareholder resolution, and not an exit right or a direct action against controlling shareholders – is, *de lege lata*, the main tool that Spain, like most continental jurisdictions, has designed to defend shareholders' property rights in the corporation against expropriatory behaviour. This point is particularly pertinent [for instance] in Spain, since several elements make it particularly burdensome to mount a derivative action against directors, which is an important indirect mechanism to monitor controlling shareholders' abuse".

12 The boundaries of the concept of "general interest" may however vary a lot: for instance, under Romanian law, nullity is applicable in the case of breach of the legal requirements established for summoning the meeting (a call which is not published according to the legal requirements, which is issued by a non-authorized person, which does not contain the text of the amending proposals of the articles of association, or the lack of quorum or of the required majority for adopting the resolution); on the contrary, the same cases normally give rise only to voidability according to German and Italian law (nullity is applied for more severe breaches, like i.e. the total absence of the call): compare Starc/Bojin and Schall, in *Company laws*, 957, 294 487. Both Sects. 199 A-PuCA and 214 Ge-PuCA add that a resolution is null whenever "it is incompatible with the nature of the public company".

13 This is the case i.e. with Sect. 241 Ge-PuCA and Art. 2379 It-CC respectively, on the one hand, and Art. 56 Por-CC and 132 R-CA and 1252 of the Romanian civil code, on the other, in accordance

On the other hand, in the case of voidability, resolutions may be appealed within a shorter deadline (ninety / thirty / fifteen days, etc., depending on the legislation) from the date of the resolution and only by absent, dissenting or abstaining shareholders (as well as by the directors)[14].

Normally the rights acquired by third parties in good faith in the execution of the resolution affected by voidability remain valid[15]. Moreover, the principle that shareholders may ratify a voidable (or even a null) resolution also seems to be generally accepted.

Sometimes the scope for invalidation is further reduced with regard to particularly important resolutions (the increase and reduction of share capital, issue of bonds, approval of the financial statements, conversions, mergers[16]) and even simply negated in the case of minor flaws[17].

A challenge in court does not automatically suspend the effects of the resolution in question; however, suspension may be ordered by the court subject to comparing the damage that the claimant would suffer upon implementation of

---

with how the provisions are also interpreted by case law. Notwithstanding the deadline of three years, resolutions that modify the corporate purpose by including illegal or impossible activities may be appealed without any time limits under Art. 2379 It-CC. Art. 1252 of the Romanian civil code establishes a presumption in favour of voidability when there are doubts about the nature of the interest protected by the breached provision.

14 See i.e. Art. 2377 It-CC and Art. 132 R-CA. Under the former body of law, the challenge may only be proposed by a number of shareholders (holders of the right to vote) that possess, even jointly, at least five percent of the share capital or one part per thousand in listed companies (the articles of association may reduce, but not increase or exclude this requirement). To compensate for the loss of the right to challenge the resolution, shareholders who do not reach the indicated thresholds – and those who do not have the right to vote or in any case are not entitled to challenge the resolution – have the right to compensation for the damage suffered from non-compliance of the resolution with the law or the articles of association.

15 See Art. 2377 It-CC; this solution has, however, also been recently extended to the case of nullity by Art. 2379 It-CC.

16 See Arts. 2379-*ter*; 2434-*bis*; 2500-*bis*; 2504-*quater* It-CC.

17 Like the infringement of minor procedural requirements, insufficient information deemed unessential, participation at the meeting by non-entitled persons (unless decisive), invalidity of one or more votes and the erroneous calculation of those cast (unless decisive): see i.e. Art. 204 Sp-CA. The aspect of the lack of information at the general meeting is specifically addressed by Sect. 243 Ge-PuCA stating that "an action for avoidance may be brought where inaccurate or incomplete information has been provided, or a request for information has been refused, only if a shareholder assessing the situation objectively would have regarded the provision of the information as a significant pre-requisite for the appropriate exercise of his participatory rights and rights as a member"; the provision has given rise to a considerable amount of case law (on which see Gerner-Beuerle/Schilling, *Comparative*, 434).

the resolution against the damage that the company would suffer in the event of suspension[18].

The distinction between nullity and voidability in some Member States' laws is less clear-cut[19]. Certain companies acts contemplate only one category (reducing the importance of the difference between nullity and voidability) and simply state that breach of the law or the articles of association may be challenged within a certain time frame (for instance, one year)[20].

Finally, many laws consider resolutions which are adopted by shareholders that involve a conflict of interest or are harmful to the company – or to other shareholders – to be void (or null)[21].

As far as the EMCA is concerned, the Model states – along the lines set forth by the Nordic jurisdictions[22] – that a resolution may be challenged if it has been unlawfully passed or is contrary to the law or to the company's articles of asso-

───────

18 For explicit provisions along these lines see Art. 2378 It-CC.

19 For instance under Art. 2.14 Du-CC a resolution is null if it breaches the law or the articles of association, unless otherwise provided for by law (like in the following cases: breach of provisions in the articles of association that govern the powers of the different bodies of the company, adoption of a resolution despite the absence of notice to – or authorization by – the corporate bodies, etc.). See however Art. 2.15 Du-CC for exceptions (cf. Steins Bisschop/Roelink/Kemp, in *Company laws*, 1333).

20 This is the case of Arts. 204f. Sp-CA, which stipulates that resolutions which are contrary to the law or to the articles of association may be challenged within one year (except resolutions which are contrary to public order: in such a case the action is not time-barred). However, the dissenting shareholders (owning at least 1% of the shareholding), directors and third parties showing a "legitimate interest" are also entitled to take action. See also Sects. 428ff. Cz-CA.

21 This is the case i.e. of Sect. 125 A-PuCA ("nobody can exercise the voting right for himself or for another person if a resolution is passed on whether he is to be discharged or released from a liability or whether the company should assert a claim against him"); Sect. 108 Da-CA ("the general meeting may not pass a resolution if it is clear that that resolution is likely to give certain shareholders or others an undue advantage over other shareholders or the company"); of Sect. 243 Ge-PuCA (in the case of violation to the detriment of the company or to other shareholders); of Art. 2373 It-CC (a resolution approved with the decisive vote of those who have, on their own behalf or on behalf of third parties, an interest that is in conflict with that of the company can be declared void if detrimental; the resolution can also be declared void pursuant Art. 2377 It-CC if it is abusive against the minority in violation of the rules of fairness and good faith, according to case law); of Art. 422 Pol-CC, as interpreted by the judiciary: according to the position of the Supreme Court, a resolution of the general meeting, taken in violation of the requirement of loyalty to the shareholder, holding a significant block of shares, may be regarded as contrary to good practices and affect the interests of the company; the Court confirmed the existence of a duty of loyalty both in the relationship between the company and a shareholder, as well as among the shareholders: see Oplustil, *in Company laws*, 732); of Art. 204 Sp-CA (in case of harm to the company's interest); of Ch. 7, Sect. 50, Sw-CA; etc.

22 See Sect. 109 Da-CA and Ch. 7, Sect. 50 Sw-CA.

ciation. The legal proceeding must be taken no later than three months from the date of the resolution.

However, this general rule does not apply when "(a) the resolution could not be passed lawfully even with the consent of all shareholders; (b) [the law or the] articles of association require the consent of all or certain shareholders and such consent has not been obtained; (c) there has been a serious failure to comply with the rules governing notice of general meetings" (Sect. 11.28). The EMCA thereby draws a distinction between less serious and more serious violations, which is reminiscent of the distinction between nullity and voidability.

3. Right to information

One of the most important rights of minority shareholders – linked to the right to vote (but also to the right to exit) – is probably the right to corporate information (beyond the one disclosed in the financial statements)[23], which is approached very differently by the various national companies acts.

(I) Pursuant to some laws that right is practically almost non-existent, at least for unlisted companies (the regulation regarding the latter is obviously more specific and we shall return to that in Chapter 12).

Take the example of Italian law: shareholders in public companies only have access to the register of shareholders and the book of general meeting resolutions. Additionally, before and during the general meeting, they have no specific right to information (apart from major transactions like mergers and certain capital increases) and the duty of directors to provide some disclosure has had to be crafted – to a marginal extent – by case law[24]; this legislative choice reflects the fact that under this law the powers of the general meeting have been (intentionally) reduced over the years.

On the other hand, the right to corporate information is very broad in other jurisdictions (and not only in the ones that empower the general meeting with important decisions). Under the French commercial code, for instance, share-

---

23 As recognized, for instance, by Sáez/Riaño, *Corporate*, 383: "pivotal elements" are disclosure and information rights: "disclosure in itself has a relevant deterrent effect but, to a certain extent, might be also seen as a complement to voting and litigation: it is a prerequisite for these core strategies' effectiveness".

24 The question is rather different in listed companies, where shareholders have the right to examine corporate documents, prepared by the managers for the general meeting, and the right to ask questions before the general meeting, according to the Second Shareholders' Rights Directive (Directive 2017/828/EU).

holders have a sort of "permanent" right to information, i.e. they are entitled to obtain at any time disclosure of documents they consider to be important and are allowed to make copies. This disclosure right covers the last three complete accounting periods (financial years); if the information is not duly disclosed, the shareholders can file a lawsuit and have their rights enforced by the court. These documents include the reports by the board of directors, the auditors' reports that were presented to the board meetings, the text of – and the objects and reasons for – the proposed resolutions, information concerning candidates for the board of directors, the total amount of remuneration paid to the highest-paid persons[25].

In Nordic countries's law, the directors must provide information at the general meeting, upon request by any shareholder, on the matters on the agenda and "any circumstances which may affect the assessment of the company's financial position" (if the information cannot be promptly disclosed, it will have to be made available in writing at the company's offices within two weeks and sent to any requesting shareholder). Moreover, in public companies of reduced dimensions, each shareholder is afforded an opportunity to access the company's offices and review any documents related to the company's operations, to the extent necessary to be able to assess the company's financial position and results or a particular matter which is to be addressed at the general meeting[26].

The majority of the Member States (e.g. Austria, Belgium, Denmark, Germany, et al.) stipulates – taking an intermediate stance – that shareholders may obtain information if (and only if) the matter is included on the agenda of the general meeting. During the meeting, shareholders may however request any information or clarification they deem necessary, in any case concerning – once again – only the items on the agenda. The directors are normally obliged to provide the requested information (orally) to a large extent, unless said information is deemed unnecessary for recognition of the shareholders' rights or

---

25 See Art. 225-117 Fr-CC; similarly, Art. 288 Por-CC and Sect. 92 Slove-CA ("each company member, including a company member who is not entitled to conduct business, may be informed of the company's affairs and shall have the right to inspect the company's books and documents and documentation. If a company member believes, based on a well-founded reason, that business is being conducted dishonestly, they may exercise the right under the preceding paragraph even if it has been excluded or restricted by the memorandum of association").

26 See Ch. 7, Sects. 32f., Sw-CA; Sect. 102 Da-CA (at least as long as the board of directors believes that it may take place without significant harm to the company). For a particularly broad view see Andersson, *Minority shareholder protection in SMEs: a question of information ex post and bargaining power ex ante?*, 2010, at *ssrn.com*.

there are objective reasons to consider that the information may be used for purposes detrimental to the company's best interests[27].

From its perspective, also the EMCA seems more concerned with the information to be provided "during" (and even "after") the meeting than to the one which could be obtained "before" the same. Sect. 11.23 EMCA – following the Nordic companies acts – states that "upon request from a shareholder (and when deemed by the board of directors not to cause material damage to the company) the company's board shall disclose to the general meeting the pertinent information at the meeting in respect of any circumstances which may affect the evaluation of a matter on the agenda. If the answer to a request requires information that is not at hand at the general meeting, such information shall be made available to the shareholders no later than two weeks after the meeting"[28].

(II) In some cases the right to information becomes a more stringent right to "inspection", which may be exercised usually through special examiners appointed by a court.

These inspections, however, usually take place in more "occasional" and less ordinary moments of the corporate life. The boundaries of this right have thus been examined elsewhere, speaking of the "controls on management" (see above Chapter 3, § 6).

---

27 See i.e. Sects. 118 A-PuCA and 131 Ge-PuCA. A peculiar (and rather analytical) position is taken by Spanish law: until the seventh day before the general meeting is due to be held, shareholders may request in writing any information or clarification they deem necessary from the directors, regarding the items on the agenda. The directors shall be obliged to facilitate the information in writing, by the day on which the general meeting is held (Art. 197 Sp-CA). The directors can only refuse to provide that information if, in their opinion, its disclosure damages the interests of the company, unless the information was demanded by shareholders holding at least 25% of the share capital (Art. 196 Sp-CA). However, not all inaccurate or insufficient information supplied in response to the exercise of the right to prior information is sufficient to challenge a shareholders' general meeting resolution: this possibility is only provided for if the incorrect or missing information would have been essential for the reasonable exercise of the shareholders' right to vote or any other rights regarding their participation in the meeting (Art. 204 Sp-CA). Also Sect. 16 Li-CA stipulates that "a company must reply to the questions related to the issues on the agenda of the general meeting of shareholders and submitted by a shareholder to the company in advance before the general meeting of shareholders, where the questions were received by the company not later than three working days before the general meeting of shareholders".

28 See similarly Sect. 358 Cz-CA.

4. Right to withdrawal

(I) The right to withdrawal is the right that shareholders mature – upon particular events – to have their shares bought out by the company at a price reflecting
the value of their investment (if necessary, as determined in a judicial proceeding).

EU legislation does not address the issue. Member States' laws differ (some
simply do not recognize it). The EMCA Group considers the remedy as a viable
mechanism for the protection of minority shareholders, but does not provide a
general framework.

Typically some companies acts lay down the right of withdrawal in the case
of – legitimate – shareholders' resolutions impacting on members' rights like i.e.
the conversion (transformation) of the company, the transfer of the registered office abroad, the modification of the corporate object clause (when it allows a significant change to the company's business), etc.[29]

This should be intended as the "proper" right of withdrawal (an equivalent
of the US "right of appraisal"): it consists in the right to demand the redemption
(buy-out) of the shares by the company at a fair price.

The right to withdrawal however is also sometimes laid down for the case of
change of control. Under some laws – as we shall see more extensively below (in
Chapter 7, § 6) – that right is accorded to shareholders if their company stipulates
an agreement giving birth to a group of companies, thereby becoming the parent
company. The shareholders of that parent company are entitled to have their
shares redeemed by the latter (in some cases the right is accorded, on the
other hand, to the shareholders – instead of the parent company – of the companies becoming subsidiaries)[30].

---

29 This is the case of Art. 2437 It-CC. Other reasons pursuant to the law are: revocation of the
resolution to wind up the company, modification of the criteria for determining the value of the
shares in the event of withdrawal, the extension of the company term (if the articles of association do not provide otherwise), the introduction or removal of restrictions on the circulation of
shares (if the articles of association do not provide otherwise), the amendment of administrative
and voting rights. If the company is established for an indefinite period, shareholders may withdraw with at least one hundred and eighty days' notice; the statute may provide for a longer
term, not exceeding one year. See similarly Art. 346 Sp-CA and, with reference to the change
of objects, Art. 416 Pol-CC.

30 A similar rule applies under Italian law when a company is attracted under the sole management of a holding company or that sole management changes: in this case, the purchase of the
shares of the subsidiary's shareholders is mandatory for the parent company; see below Chapter 7, § 6.

Finally, an interesting hypothesis of right of withdrawal has been recently introduced in Spanish law: shareholders may demand to have their shares bought out by the company in the case of failure to distribute dividends. More precisely, five years after the date of the company's registration, any shareholder who voted in favor of the dividend distribution shall have the right to exit the company (who has to buy the shares) if the general meeting does not agree to distribute at least one third of the legally distributable profits of the previous financial year[31].

(II) The above examples show how the right to withdrawal is granted by some (evidently not all) domestic jurisdictions in order to respond to different needs of protection; however the various companies acts are evidently not all in agreement.

A common underpinning rationale for this kind of exit right may be found in the fact that minority shareholders should be given the opportunity to leave the company whenever its "basic features" are impacted by majority shareholders' decisions. This argument holds that people who buy shares in a company with a certain identity and set of characteristics may rightfully expect to continue as an investor in "that" enterprise and that no one should be able to force them to become investors in a "different" business. Major organic changes also pose a risk to shareholders of being unfairly treated.

This remedy is however often criticized, since providing shareholders with the opportunity to leave may result in blocking important transactions or weakening the company financial structure (an outflow of cash is registered anytime a shareholder withdraws and the legal capital has to be reduced if the company does not have disposable reserves, etc.). This is why some laws even allow creditors the right to object to shareholders withdrawing if they can demonstrate that the consequent reduction of capital may put their claims at risk[32].

The vagueness of the legislative wording of the rules on the right of withdrawal may also create great uncertainty. This is the case, for instance, with the provisions that establish that shareholders may withdraw in the case of "amendments to the articles of association concerning voting or shareholding rights" (i.e. Art. 2437 It-CC). In a recent national case, for instance, a national Supreme Court has ruled that the right of withdrawal from the company should be recognized if the articles of association are modified and the entity of amount of dividends distributable in favor of the shareholders is even reduced (in the case examined by the judges, the percentage thresholds of profits to be allocated

---

31 See Art. 348-*bis* Sp-CA.
32 See Art. 2437-*bis* It-CC.

to the legal reserve was raised from 5% to 12%, and those to be attributed to the extraordinary reserve from 5% to 40%)[33].

At this point, however, which "amendment to the articles of association concerning voting or shareholding rights" should be considered material? For instance, even within the boundaries of the specific right to obtein a vote on the distribution of dividends from a given pool, which percentage has to be considered material when that pool is reduced: 50%, 30%, 15% less, more? The contours of the matter risk to become evanescent. This is an interpretative question – that inevitably give raise to different opinions – of no small importance (like many related others regarding the right of withdrawal).

Notwithstanding, a different view states that the danger of having important transactions blocked by dissenting shareholders exercising their right to withdraw should not be overestimated. The greater the number of shareholders who have the perception that the proposed deal is problematic (irrational, unfair) and the greater the number of dissenters, the more likely it is that management will reconsider its position. This should lead to more efficient decisions and corporate transactions.

Moreover, the exit option might have the effect of making the company even financialy stronger. The reasoning is that prospective investors are normally attracted by the possibility of withdrawing in important cases and prefer to invest in companies whose bylaws grant that right to a large extent. It is more probable that the right "attracts" investors than not. Legislators sharing this view are thus inclined to allow also the option to increase the numbers of exit options by means of clauses inserted in the articles of association (and even to accept the introduction of cases of withdrawal "at will"[34]).

---

33 Ruling of 22 May 2019, no. 13845 (case "Banca Sella").
34 For instance, Italian notarial practice affirms that "the articles of association of public companies can legitimately provide for the right of withdrawal, as well as in the cases provided for by law: (i) upon the occurrence of (other) certain events, whether they are represented by resolutions of corporate bodies, or by different acts or facts, of any nature; (ii) upon the occurrence of a 'just cause', not specifically determined by the articles of association; (iii) at the mere will of the withdrawing shareholder ('ad nutum' withdrawal)" (see the Recommendation no. 74 of the Notarial Council of Milan).

5. Right to sell out (and to winding up)

(I) In any case, the criticalities of the withdrawal remedy are significant.

This is why many companies acts have refused to insert provisions on the right of withdrawal (at the cost of the company) into their companies acts and have preferred to lay down rules obliging the majority shareholders to buy out – at their cost – the other shareholders in the case of unfair treatment. Creditors should not be involved in the process.

Certain national laws regulate therefore this right for minority shareholders to "sell-out" their shares (or to "be bought out") in the case of abusive / illegal actions; under such circumstances it is the "oppressive" shareholder who is forced to buy the shares of the "oppressed" shareholder(s).

An example is to be found in the Dutch and Nordic companies acts[35]. Paradigmatically, under the former law, a shareholder who, as a result of the conduct of one or more of his co-shareholders, is harmed in a way that precludes his continuing status as a shareholder may file a legal claim against his co-shareholders, claiming that the latter must buy up his shares[36]. The price is fixed by the court[37]. The court may not have to appoint experts if the parties agree on the value of the shares or if the articles of association or an agreement between the parties contains clear criteria for an assessment of the value of the shares[38].

The EMCA runs along the same lines: Sect. 11.37 stipulates that if any shareholder has – intentionally or by gross negligence – caused a loss to another shareholder and there is a risk of continued abuse, the court may order that shareholder to redeem the shares belonging to the shareholder who suffers a loss. The redemption shall be made at a reasonable price.

(II) According to a different scheme, exit is provided for by some States when the majority shareholders reach a certain threshold of share capital in the company (90% or 95%); usually this right arises after a takeover bid (and without

---

35 Within two weeks from when a copy of the judgment in which the price of the shares is set has been served officially on the defendants, each of them is obliged to take over (buy up) the number of shares determined by the court against simultaneous payment of the fixed price, while the plaintiff is obliged to transfer these shares to the defendants; see Art. 2.343 Du-CC; Sects. 362f. Da-CA; Ch. 29, Sect. 4, Sw-CA.

36 Actually this type of claim can also be filed against the company on the basis of the conduct of one or more shareholders or of the company itself; in such a case the cost of the buy out are borne by the company.

37 See Arts. 2.337, 2.339 and 2.340 Du-CC.

38 See Art. 2.343a Du-CC.

the requirement of abuse[39]). In some cases, however, the right is recognized independently from the outcome of a takeover and also in unlisted companies.

Noteworthy examples are (i) Ch. 22, Sect. 1, Sw-CA I, pursuant to which – both in listed and non-listed companies – "a shareholder who holds more than nine-tenths of the shares in a company shall be entitled to buy-out the remaining shares of the other shareholders of the company; any person whose shares may be bought out shall be entitled to compel the majority shareholder to purchase his shares"; and (ii) Art. 418 Pol-CC, giving – in non-listed companies – to minority shareholders holding less than 5% of the shares the right to demand that no more than five shareholders controlling at least 95% of the share capital buy them out; if the resolution on sell-out is not adopted, the company itself is obliged to carry out the purchase (the clause is interesting since the relevant shareholding can be owned – instead of by a single shareholder – by many shareholders, even unrelated, and not linked by shareholders' agreements)[40].

The EMCA also offers minority shareholders a similar right to sell-out. When a parent company owns, directly or indirectly, more than 90% of the shares and the voting rights, the minority shareholders may ask for their shares to be purchased by the parent or another person designated by it in court.

(III) A further exit remedy is provided for by some national companies acts in the case of major severe abuses towards shareholders.

In such a hypothesis, the minority shareholders may ask the court to dissolve the company, which is therefore wound up as a consequence of the acknowledgment of the actual loss of trust among all the members.

This is the case, again, in the Nordic laws (normally requiring that shareholders own a certain minimum shareholding like 10%)[41]. Sect. 11.33 EMCA

---

39 The right to sell out after a takeover in listed companies is examined below in Chapter 12, § 3.
40 Similar provisions are recognized by other national laws, like Art. 490, n. 5 and 6, Por-CC ("right to be bought"); Sects. 3.53 and 3.324 H-CA; Art. 46 Gr-PuCA; see generally Van der Elst/Van der Steen, *Balancing interest of minority and majority shareholders: a comparative analysis of squeeze out and sell out rights*, in *ECFR*, 2009, 391.
41 See Sect. 230 Da-CA ("where any shareholders in a limited liability company have wilfully contributed to passing a resolution by the general meeting that is in contravention of Sect. 108, or have otherwise abused the influence that they have over the company or contributed to a contravention of this Act or the company's articles of association, the court may, upon request from shareholders representing no less than one-tenth of the share capital, order that the company be dissolved if special grounds exist because of the duration of the abuse or other circumstances"; Sect. 108 states that "the general meeting may not pass a resolution if it is clear that that resolution is likely to give certain shareholders or others an undue advantage over other shareholders or the limited liability company"); see also similarly Ch. 23, Sect. 2, Fi-CA

also permits a minority representing 10 % of the share capital to request the company to be dissolved[42].

6. Shareholders' litigation and jurisdiction: the jurisprudence of the CJEU (case *E-ON Czech Holding*)

All the above described rights, once enforced, give rise to legal disputes on the applicable law whenever shareholders and the company have different nationalities.

The question is usually answered on the basis of the Regulation 2001/44/EC (as recast by Regulation 1215/2012/EU), which tackles the issue of the jurisdiction and the recognition (and enforcement) of judgments in civil and commercial matters.

By way of example, Art. 24 of the Regulation states that "in proceedings which have as their object the validity of the constitution, the nullity or the dissolution of companies" or "of the validity of the decisions of their organs", the courts of the Member State in which the company has its seat has exclusive jurisdiction, regardless of the domicile of the parties. In order to determine that seat, the court must apply its rules of private international law.

The provision is therefore very clear with reference to lawsuits brought by shareholders that challenge the validity of the company or general meeting resolutions, with the object of the action evidently being the instrument of incorporation or the decision of a company organ. The jurisdiction is hence the State where the company has its seat.

On the contrary, the answer is less obvious whether the above provision also applies to the cases regarding the compulsory acquisition of shares as a consequence of a fact triggering the shareholders' right of withdrawal or the right to sell out. Does Art. 24 have to be interpreted as covering also proceedings for the acknowledgment of those rights and the review of the reasonableness of the consideration which the company (or the principal shareholder) is required to provide?

(no minimal shareholding is required) and Ch. 25, sect. 21, Sw-CA (10 % shareholdings); Art. 2.356 Du-CC.

42 On the other hand, other national companies acts (or courts) are rather reluctant to allow the liquidation of a company on the basis of a breach of equality among shareholders, except in extreme circumstances, where it may (more difficult) be proven that the functioning of the corporate bodies has become impossible (see on that below, Chapter 11, § 1).

The case was addressed by the CJEU in 2016, with regard to a claim concerning the reasonableness of the consideration which – in a procedure for buying out minority shareholders – a German company (E.ON Czech Holding AG) was required to pay them following the compulsory transfer of the shares which they held in a Czech company (Jihočeská Plynárenská a.s.). The preliminary ruling was released in 2018 (case C-560/16)[43].

The Court observed that – even if, under Czech law, proceedings on the acknowledgment of the grounds for selling out the shares and their fair value may not lead to a formal decision which results in invalidating a resolution of the general assembly – the scope of Art. 24 cannot depend on the choices made in national law by Member States or vary depending on them.

Moreover, the attribution of the jurisdiction to the courts of the State where the company has its seat is consistent with the objectives of predictability of the rules of jurisdiction and legal certainty pursued by the Regulation No. 44/2001 (as the Advocate General observed in point 35 of his opinion, the shareholders in a company, especially the principal shareholder, must expect that the courts of the Member State in which that company is established will be the courts having jurisdiction to decide any internal dispute within that company relating to the review of the partial validity of a decision taken by a body of a company).

As a consequence, the answer to the question was that the proceedings to review the reasonableness of the consideration that the principal shareholder of a company is required to pay to the minority shareholders of that company in the event of the compulsory transfer of their shares comes within the exclusive jurisdiction of the courts of the Member State in which that company has established its seat (in that particular case, it was thus Germany, the state of incorporation of E.ON Czech Holding AG).

Other similar issues (which cannot be addressed here) arise at the border between national company laws and Regulation 1215/2012/EU.

---

43 See extensively Rammeloo, *Forum societatis: jurisdiction concerning the reasonableness of consideration resulting from a squeeze-out resolution in a cross-border context: CJEU C-560/16 (E.On Czech Holding),* in *ECL,* 2018, 131.

7 Groups

Summary:
1. A brief history of company groups in Europe and their regulation
2. The legal definition of group: "control" and "unitary direction"
3. Main issues addressed by Member States' laws: (a.1) unitary direction, binding instructions, group interest and parent company's liability: the German model (followed by other Member States) of "contractual groups" and "de facto groups"
4. (a.2) unitary direction, binding instructions, group interest and parent company's liability in other Member States. The position of the EMCA
5. (b) the disclosure of the existence of the group and the results of the unitary direction
6. (c) rights of the minority shareholders of the subsidiaries (to special investigation, to withdrawal)
7. (d) rights of the minority shareholders of the parent company (to information, to withdrawal, to vote)
8. (e) cross-shareholdings, intercompany loans and group financing
9. Cross-border groups and applicable law: the CJEU judgment on the *Impacto Azul* case

1. A brief history of company groups in Europe and their regulation

(I) Groups of companies have been traditionally widespread in Europe[1]. The reasons are manifold.

Companies look for diversification: different companies, under a sole main ownership, may be created in order to operate in different business areas (for instance, food, pharma, construction, etc.).

The financial results of each business unit may be effectively monitored if each entity, in the form of a separate company, has its own accounting system and presents its own financial statements.

---

[1] It is recognized, for example, that around 70% of the total capital and reserves of German companies belong to companies in group relationships: see Werlauff, *Group and community – the European Court's development of an independent community law concept of the group and its significance in company law*, in *ECL*, 2007, 201.

https://doi.org/10.1515/9783110725025-009

The group structure may also help attract partners: minority shareholders (and creditors) can be easily involved if they are allowed to choose whether to provide capital (or financing) to a single business only or to more (i.e.: only the food sector, pharma sector, etc.).

Tax laws and the effects of taxation are also a frequent driver.

In Europe, groups have developed over time – more than in other continents – also as a consequence of the supranational borders: the founding of branches was often either legally impossible or difficult, considering the various regulations; in such cases, it generally became (and is still often) easier to set up distinct companies in each foreign country, often with local partners as minority investors.

Groups of companies in Member States can comprise hundreds of subsidiaries (normally, however, fewer), headed by a parent company (the holding company). The parent often owns the main shareholding in a company, which owns the main shareholding in another, and so on: the group is thus formed of a chain of "vertical" shareholdings. Alternatively, the group can have a "horizontal" structure, with the parent owning the main shareholdings in many companies, which remain separated from the others. Commonly, a group has a mixed structure (both vertical and horizontal).

The existence of a group increases the risks for both minority shareholders and creditors of the various companies.

Since the parent company owns a majority stake in many subsidiaries, usually it is induced to consider the interest of all the companies that form the group instead of (or beside) the interests of each single company. Sometimes it may be in the wider interest of that overall multitude to impose sacrifices on a single company for the benefit of others.

One of the companies in the group may be particularly healthy and others may be facing difficulties. It may be beneficial for the distressed companies – but also for the companies forming part of the group as a whole – to have the company that is doing well agree to actions that are burdensome but may help the other companies. A classic example is the provision of a loan from an economically fit company to another in crisis. Normally (i.e., for a company not belonging to a group), such a transaction would make little sense and would not be carried out by the directors; in the context of a group, however, it may become rational to sustain sister companies and grant loans, even if risky and below market conditions.

This simple example may be replicated (and become more sophisticated): for instance, companies belonging to a group may sign a "cash-pooling agreement", by which they transfer the liquidity from their accounts to the holding company's account and give it the power to distribute the funds as needed by the group; the subsidiaries pooling their liquidity run the risk of the company where the pool is located and of the management of the latter.

However, this "overall view" does not necessarily coincide with the vision of the minority shareholders and creditors of the impacted subsidiary. They receive no gain from the fact that other group companies are sustained at the cost of the subsidiary of which they are shareholders or that they have financed. There is hence a mismatch between the interests of the parent company and the interest of the stakeholders – minorities, creditors – at the level of the single subsidiary (the problem loses importance in the case of wholly owned subsidiaries, although in that case, the position of the creditors remains relevant).

At the core of the group phenomenon are, therefore, on the one hand, the main shareholding of the parent company and its relationship with the subsidiaries and, on the other hand (and as a consequence), the capability of the parent company to make decisions at the level of the single subsidiaries that could harm some of these companies and benefit others and the group itself.

That capability to make decisions at the level of the single companies derives from the fact that the parent company, by holding the majority of the votes in each subsidiary, can appoint the board of directors of the subsidiaries and induce them to make decisions (for instance, granting a loan to a sister company) by issuing instructions.

Beyond the risks illustrated above, a group also generally entails a higher level of opaqueness, both from a financial point of view and with regard to the ownership structure.

(II) Notwithstanding this problematic picture, one should recognize that big enterprises are nowadays often managed in the form of a group of companies, and the group has definitely become the typical form of the larger business organization.

Establishing rules that are too rigid and pervasive in order to protect the interests of investors or creditors may create unjustified impediments and burdens which could harm the efficiency of these kinds of modern esterprises.

These are, currently, the two sides of the coin when considering corporate groups. On the one hand, there is the need to "protect" investors and creditors, and, on the other hand, the necessity to "organize" the group as flexibly as possible and give managerial freedom to the directors running the enterprise. Frequently it is said that the rules on corporate groups may be intended either as a law of "protection" (entity approach) or as a law or "organization" (enterprise approach); the view of legislators – as well as judges and scholars – often reflect these two different starting points in approaching the theme[2].

(III) As we have seen (Chapter 1, § 5), the EU tried to regulate groups, with the draft Ninth Directive, dating back to the early 1970s. However, that proposal has never been approved by the Member States and has been abandoned.

The EU has however continued to deal with issues relating to groups, by having expert groups analyze the state of company law and develop appropriate suggestions.

The Commission's Action Plan of 2003 (on the basis of the result of an experts' report) stated that, while no overall directive may be needed, specific provisions are required.

In 2011, a report drafted by another group of experts established by the Commission concluded that some points required special attention: the disclosure of information on the main features of the group structure, its functioning and management and, subject to further evidence, the adoption of a recommendation on the recognition of the "group interest" in company decision making. On the basis of this report, the Commission also launched a public consultation. Two-thirds of the responses from the business community expressed support for EU intervention, especially in the area of better information on groups and the recognition of the group interest. Protection of the interests of minority shareholders and creditors was also endorsed. On the other hand, the idea of a comprehensive legal EU framework covering groups of companies was met with caution[3].

---

2 The CJEU has often ruled on cases involving groups of companies, in fields however other than company law (for an exception see the "Impacto Azul" case described below in § 9). It treats the group basically as a sole enterprise, for instance, addressing competition law issues. See on that Sørensen, *Groups of companies in the case law of the Court of Justice of the European Union groups*, in *EBLR*, 2016, 393.

3 As a follow-up, in 2016, another group nominated by the Commission (the "Informal Company Law Expert Group" or "ICLEG") issued a report on information on groups with recommendations on the improvement of the information available both to stakeholders in the parent company and in the subsidiary; in the same year the Group also presented "*A proposal for reforming group law in the European Union – Comparative observations on the way forward*", 2016, at ssrn.com. Over the years, apart from the ICLEG, the main groups of experts that have presented proposals are the "Forum Europaeum Konzernrecht" (2000), the "High Level Group of Company Law Experts" (2002), the "Reflection Group on the Future of EU Company Law" (2011), the "Forum Europaeum on Company Groups" (or "FECG", 2015), the "European Company Law Experts" (or "ECLE", 2016). For an overview see Chiappetta/Tombari, *Perspectives on group corporate governance and European company law*, in *ECFR*, 2012, 261; Conac, *Directors' duties in groups of companies: legalising the interest of the group at the European level*, in *ECFR*, 2013,

(IV) Beside these attempts at EU level (and the abortion of the draft Ninth Directive), over the years Member States have taken basically four major legislative approaches: comprehensive regulation, partial regulation, case law recognition of the interest of the group, and lack of treatment.

The first approach entails a global and comprehensive regulation of groups of companies. This line originates in Germany (1965), and has been followed (in chronological order) by Portugal, Hungary, the Czech Republic, Slovenia and Croatia.

A second method consists in partial or selective regulation, which deals with some major questions of groups without aiming to regulate it in a comprehensive manner. This is the case for instance in Italy which adopted a new regime for groups in 2003. It is significantly influenced by German law but is considered to be more flexible.

The third approach is traditionally the French one. It derives from the 1985 "Rozenblum decision" of the French Supreme Court and is concentrated on the issue of the "interest of the group" and the question of whether the directors of a subsidiary may consider this interest when making a decision that harms the subsidiary provided that several conditions are satisfied. This flexible case law approach is recognized in the majority of the Member States (e.g. Belgium, Estonia, Luxembourg, the Netherlands, the Nordic countries, Poland, Romania, Spain, etc.), even if the position of the national courts differs significantly as far as the relevance of the "interest of the group" is concerned.

Finally, some companies acts contain no specific provisions on groups (beyond the ones mandated by the directives like the ones on consolidated accounts). This approach is followed for instance in Ireland.

2. The legal definition of group: "control" and "unitary direction"

(I) As we pointed out above, at the core of the phenomenon of company groups (and the risks raised by that legal structure) is the possibility that the parent company gives instructions to the directors of the subsidiaries that may be detrimental for one or more of the subsidiaries but beneficial for the group as a whole.

194; and more recently Sørensen, *Recognising the interests of the group – another attempt to harmonise the rules regulating groups of companies in the EU*, 2020, at *ssrn*.

This possibility arises from the fact that the parent company usually owns the majority stake (51%) – directly or indirectly – in all the subsidiaries and is thus in a condition to appoint the board of directors and call for their obedience[4]. These directors (of the subsidiaries) are the ones who actually take the harmful / beneficial decisions for their company, but they operate de facto under the influence of the instructions received by the parent company's directors. The subsidiary's directors defer to these instructions since the parent company has the power to re-appoint them at the end of their tenure or to dismiss them at any time.

These features are duly described by the EMCA, which – in the absence of a directive – is very helpful (also in its descriptive parts) in pursuing the legal analysis of groups.

The Model – which does not seek a regulatory definition of "group" (which would be actually redundant) – focuses instead on the main substantial aspects. Sect. 15.01 EMCA states in short that a group is the entity comprising the parent company and all its subsidiaries (one may doubt whether a group is actually an "entity" per se; the answer is probably no, at least on a general level, but we can accept this definition for the sake of simplicity).

The same Sect. 15.02 EMCA states that a "subsidiary" is a company subject to the "control" of another company, the "parent" company (either directly or indirectly through another subsidiary). "Control" (ownership of 51% or more of the shareholdings) is thus decisive (a stake of more than 51% gives rise to the "de jure control"). Control is defined as the "power to govern the financial and operating policies of a subsidiary" (Sect. 15.04).

Control may, however, also exist even if the parent company owns less than 51% of the subsidiary's shares as long as that shareholding permits the parent – actually – to appoint the directors of the subsidiary (or, in the dualistic model, the supervisory board). This may happen when some shareholders regularly do not show up at the general meeting of the subsidiary and hence the number of shares needed to pass resolutions in that meeting is less than 51% (for instance, giving an example, if the shareholders' presence normally registered at a general meeting is – say – 80% of the share capital: in such a situation, the ownership of only 41% of the shares ensures control of the company). This situation is known also as "de facto control".

Control may finally also derive from a situation where a company does not even own shares of another company, but is in the condition – on the basis of

---

4 In jurisdictions with dual board structure, control is exercised with respect to the appointment of the members of the supervisory board which appoints the members of the executive in turn.

a commercial agreement – to appoint its directors (or the supervisory board), once again on a de facto basis. Take the example of a licensing agreement and suppose that the licensee company produces almost solely for the licensor company. In this case, the licensor acquires de facto a very incisive position: the licensee, fearing that the production may be shifted to other suppliers, is normally ready to accept orders and directives from the licensor, including the choice of directors. The licensee company becomes thus de facto "controlled" by its client, on the sole basis of the commercial agreement in force (another paradigmatical example is loan agreements by which the lender may come to exercise control).

Finally, control (de jure and de facto) may also be "joint", when several persons are in the position to obtain – by "acting in concert" – the appointment of the directors (or the supervisory board) of the subsidiary and govern its financial and operating policies.

(II) From this type of situation of "control" (i.e. ownership of the relevant shareholding or existence of a particularly unbalanced commercial agreement) it normally follows the managerial influence of the parent on the subsidiary: the "unitary direction".

More precisely, the unitary direction generally emerges from resolutions officially sent out from the parent's board of directors to the subsidiary's board of directors, but it may also take the form of informal instructions (or even mere oral "pressure") delivered by the parent's directors to the subsidiary's directors.

"Control" and "unitary direction" normally coexist (it is not common for a company to spend money to purchase a majority stake without intending to appoint directors and exercise actual influence). It may, however, happen – but this should be considered rather as an exception – that the parent company chooses to give managerial freedom to the subsidiary's directors and refuse to impose its will (in such a case there will be control, but not unitary direction).

3. Main issues addressed by Member States' laws: (a.1) unitary direction, binding instructions, group interest and parent company's liability: the German model (followed by other Member States) of "contractual groups" and "de facto groups"

(I) The main problem tackled by domestic laws on corporate groups is whether the parent company has the right to give binding instructions to the directors of a subsidiary that may be detrimental for that company but beneficial for the group as a whole.

Do the directors of the subsidiary always have to obey the directives of the parent company directors even if they are harmful for the company they manage? Or must they, on the contrary, reject these disadvantageous instructions on the basis that they are expected to manage the subsidiary for the exclusive benefits of its shareholders and considering the interest of its creditors?

The solutions provided for by the companies acts – and case law – of the single Member States differ significatively on this point (national rules have historically been dissimilar; that is the reason – to put it simply – for the failure of the directive on corporate groups).

(II) German legislation has traditionally been the most complex. Companies can follow two different paths which are regulated by the German public companies act[5].

Firstly, companies involved in the activity of a group can enter into a "domination agreement" whereby each subsidiary company formally agrees – i.e. by means of a binding contract – to the unitary direction of the parent company management.

A slightly different form of agreement is the "profit transfer agreement" whereby a company agrees to regularly transfer all its profits to another company.

These inter-company agreements are rather similar and give birth to a "contract-based group" (this more complex structure is normally implemented by bigger groups, like – for instance – Volkswagen AG or Deutsche Lufthansa AG).

The agreements have to be approved by a majority of three-quarters of the share capital represented at the general meeting of each company, with the companies agreeing to submit to the will of another. In practice this is usually a mere formality because the parent company already holds this majority; however, the law requires the directors of the subsidiary to prepare a report on the agreement to provide minority shareholders with a sufficient basis for their decision; furthermore, the agreement must be audited by an expert.

The first consequence of creating a contract-based group is that the subsidiary's capital is exempt from the standard capital maintenance restrictions set

---

5 Respectively by Sects. 291-310 (and 319-328) and 311-318 Ge-PuCA. For a brief but detailed sketch of the German regulation see Scheuch, *Konzernrecht: an overview of the German regulation of corporate groups and resulting liability issues*, ECL, 2016, 191; see also Hommelhoff, *Protection of minority shareholders, investors and creditors in corporate groups: the strengths and weakness of German corporate group law*, in EBOR, 2001, 61. For Portuguese law see Antunes, *The law of corporate groups in Portugal*, 2008, at https://core.ac.uk/download/pdf/14505698.pdf. For Czech law see Havel, *Czech corporate law on its way*, in ECFR, 2015, 27.

forth by the law for individual companies (for instance, the rules on financial assistance are disapplied, also in order to facilitate cash-pooling agreements[6]).

Secondly, the autonomy of the subsidiary's directors is replaced by the parent company's authority to issue binding instructions, which have to be complied with by the subsidiary's directors and may be detrimental for that company as long as they serve the interests of the parent or the group of companies (although they cannot be so pervasive that they force the board to change the line of business or endanger the economic existence of the subsidiary).

The duties of the parent company's directors are extended to the operations of the subsidiaries and they are held liable to the subsidiary for violations of these obligations, particularly in issuing instructions. On the other hand, the subsidiary's directors cannot be held liable if they have been following the binding instructions from the parent company.

As a corrective for those very invasive powers attributed to the parent company, the law lays down protective measures for minority shareholders and creditors of the subsidiary. The most important is the obligation of the parent company to compensate the subsidiary for any net loss suffered during the financial year. It is not important whether the loss was caused by the parent or not.

At the same time, minority shareholders of the parent company also deserve protection: they actually could raise objections against the decision to have their company enter into such a dominion contract which obliges their company to stand for the losses of other companies. Therefore, the law stipulates that they may either ask for compensation for their negatively impacted position (in the form of recurring payments) or decide to have their shares bought out by the parent company at a fair price (if they feel that the price is not fair, they may ask the court to intervene)[7].

(III) The other group structure – which is used much more by German companies – is the "de facto group".

---

6 See on that supra Chapter 2, § 9.
7 The rules on adequate compensation and on the sell out rights are set forth by Sects. 304 and 305 Ge-PuCA respectively; see Lieder, in *Company laws*, 387 (also for a description of the provisions concerning the amendment, cancellation and termination of the inter-company agreements).
A timid approach towards adopting legislation on contract-based group has also been made by Art. 7 Pol-CC; the provision is however considered practically useless by scholars since it is deemed to lack a series of further rules which should be indispensable for the correct functioning of a contract-based group regime (see Opalski/Moskala, in *Company laws*, 835: the model "remains almost exclusively a theoretical figure discussed by academia, with little practical importance").

At the basis of this type of structure there is not any contract by which a company submit to the power of the other. On the contrary, the group is established on a de facto basis as a consequence of the acquisition by the parent of the control (de jure or de facto) in one or more subsidiaries and the exercise of unitary direction over them.

The law admits that the influence of the parent may cause disadvantages to the subsidiary, but at the same time requires any resulting harm to be promptly compensated (see the important rule of Sect. 311 Ge-PuCA). The main differences from the "contract-based group" examined above sub point (II) concern (besides the absence of an undersigned "contract" of dominance) the fact that the directors of the subsidiaries are not obliged to accept the instructions from the parent company's directors (they are required to act firstly in the interest of their own company) and that the compensation in cases of harm caused as a consequence of the unitary direction may not happen on a general and indeterminate basis (like for contract-based groups) but must follow a rather "analytical" approach, which considers each single disadvantage and compensation.

The legal model is perceived as rather flexible since it allows the subsidiaries to take into consideration also their own interests and, if harmed, to obtain an accurate compensation, but at the same time leaves the parent company free to exercise its unitary direction (the prevailing opinion tolerates the compensation being deferred to the end of the financial year; however, this compensation has to be made following – as noted above – a rather precise calculation[8]).

If the parent fails to provide compensation, its directors will be held liable (together with the directors of the subsidiary) if the damages and failure to compensate derives from a unitary direction that has been wrongly exercised; in this regard an act performed by the directors may be deemed to have been wrongly exercised if it can be ascertained that a prudent and conscientious manager of an independent company would not have carried it out.

The action for damages against the parent (and its directors) can be brought by individual shareholders or creditors of the subsidiary (see Sect. 317 Ge-PuCA).

An argument which is debated in German literature is whether the rules on parent company's liability supersede the capital maintenance provisions also in de facto groups. The German Supreme Court has stated, since 2009 (along the lines of the law on contract-based groups), that Sect. 311 Ge-PuCA takes precedence over these rules on capital maintenance as long as the negative effects

---

8 Sometimes this requirement is interpreted in a stricter way; for instance, in the case "HVB/UniCredit", the German Supreme Court held that if the parent company approves a disadvantageous transaction it must provide compensation for the subsidiary's disadvantage in the very resolution: see Supreme Court, 26 June 2012 (quoted in Lieder, *Company laws*, 394).

on capital are adequately and promptly offset by the compensation resulting from the membership in the group[9].

4. (a.2) Unitary direction, binding instructions, group interest and parent company's liability in other Member States. The position of the EMCA

Other Member States have taken a less structured approach and decided either to provide only partial regulation of groups or to leave it substantially untreated.

(I) The Italian civil code has chosen a path close to the German company act, even if not as elaborate. The law has refused to duly regulate the case of "contract-based" groups, but has introduced legislation which is very similar to the one on the "de facto" groups contained in the German provisions[10].

---

9 See Supreme Court, 1 December 2008 (case "MPS"); see especially Cahn, *Intra-group loans under German law*, in *ECL*, 2010, 44. Since a deferred claim for compensation may be considered as a kind of distribution from the subsidiary to the parent company, the Supreme Court ruled that such financial support may be accepted in the light of the advantages resulting to the company from belonging to the group itself, as long as it is actually obtained within the financial year. Another example is provided by the rules on financial assistance which is generally not allowed under German law (see above Chapter 2, § 9), but is basically permitted within groups (see, among others, Gerner-Beuerle/Schillig, *Comparative*, 777, fn. 474).

10 See e.g. Corapi/Benincasa, *The law on groups of companies in Italy*, in *ECL*, 2019, 121; Baccetti, in *Company laws*, 609.

Often the lack of a precise law on the functioning of the groups (and practical organizational reasons) stimulates holding companies to create – on a total voluntary basis – "group codes" (or "group regulations"), which provide all the companies belonging to the group with a framework of rules for the group structure, including provisions on common management, flows of information, etc.; those codes are usually "presented" at the general meetings of the subsidiaries (or even approved by means of a resolution, provided that it maintains the relevance of a sort of "acceptation for use"). They are widespread in some Member States; see i.e., for Polish law, Opalski/Moskala, in *Company laws*, 836, summarizing that "the codes can specify group leaders for particular segments of group activity (e.g. production and distribution) as well as service companies (in practice often taking form of shared services centres) supporting the lead activity companies in fields such as financing, accounting, HR or IT. Secondly, they may determine the process of developing the strategy of the group and facilitate its implementation by the parent company. […] Thirdly, groups usually tend to maximise the synergy effect achieved in intra-group cooperation. Therefore, they generally adopt instruments of stricter integration in certain fields of their operations […]. For this purpose, groups may enter into specific mechanisms ensuring higher efficiency of cash flows or insurance coverage. Fourthly, members of the group may find themselves in a regulatory necessity to introduce internal audit systems ensuring their compliance with increasing amount of public law duties (e.g. GDPR group-wide compli-

A parent company that – while exercising unitary direction on subsidiaries – acts in its own interest and in breach of the principles of correct corporate and business management, is held to be responsible towards the shareholders of the subsidiaries for any harm caused to the profitability and value of their shareholding, as well as to the creditors for the damage caused to the company assets. There is no liability if there is no damage in light of the overall result of the unitary direction or it such a damage has been wholly eliminated as a consequence of operations expressly aimed at it[11].

Anyone who has taken part in the damaging event (like, for instance, the directors of the subsidiary or of other sister companies) and – within the limits of the advantage obtained – who has consciously benefited from it (for instance, the sister companies) shall respond jointly and severally.

The shareholders and the creditors of the subsidiary can take action against the parent, however, only if they have not previously been compensated by the subsidiary.

On such a legal basis, it is debated among scholars whether the directors of the subsidiary may refuse to accept the instructions given by the parent or if they have to accept and execute them even if they are detrimental to their company's interest. The main opinion – like the one widespread in Germany with reference to the de facto groups – holds that the directors of subsidiaries are not obliged to follow harmful instructions and are permitted to only execute such orders as long as they have ascertained that the parent is prepared to compensate for the resulting disadvantages.

(II) On the other hand, most Member States – as noted above – have chosen not to regulate the activities of groups (and the liability of the parent company) and left the matter open to developments in case law.

In the Netherlands – paradigmatically – the courts follow a rather clear track (which substantially follows the same lines as the domestic laws on de facto groups described above). The basic interpretation of the Dutch judges is that the duties of directors are primarily owed to the company itself and not to the group as such. The main relevant interest has been defined in particular

---

ance)"; "the group structure may also provide for establishment of group committees (councils, steering boards) or other group-wide bodies with formally only advisory functions, but in reality capable of adopting certain important decisions regarding the group which are then almost automatically adopted on the corporate level of relevant companies. Lastly, the group management systems often reinforce flow of information between the companies which is crucial for implementing all other mechanisms".

11 See Art. 2497 It-CC (but see similarly also, for instance, Art. 71 Cz-CA).

in the "Cancun case" of 2014, when the Supreme Court stated that directors essentially have to promote the lasting success of their own enterprise even if embedded in a group[12].

The Court has also emphasized that, although shareholders may appoint directors, the latter have to serve the interests of the company regardless of the source of their appointment (i. e. they must not fulfil the parent's interests simply because they have been appointed by the parent itself). As far as the parents' instructions, the principle of board autonomy applies: the subsidiary's board of directors may take these instructions into consideration only if they are not detrimental to the company.

It is usually noted, however, that the company interest may be so entangled with the interests of the group that this can be taken into account when determining what constitutes the interest of the company. In company groups, the interest of the company as a group member will generally run parallel to the interest of the group as a whole and therefore, an instruction that serves the group interest will often also serve the company interest of the subsidiary involved. The Supreme Court reasoned similarly in the "Bruil" case of 2007 (which is the landmark in this particular respect): in situations in which a person acts in his capacity as a director and shareholder of several legal persons which together constitute a company group, it will be unlikely that there is a conflict of interest; after all, the entire goal of establishing such a group is to centralize the power and the balancing of all interest involved[13]. Recently, there have been however several cases in which the Dutch courts have been more willing to affirm the relevance of the conflict of interest in company groups[14].

These are the main guidelines set forth by case law; in practice, however, some singularities of the Dutch legal system on corporate governance can be used in order to give to the parent company some extra powers. These singularities show – in general – how the legislation on groups is, as a matter of fact, also strictly dependent on the more general corporate governance rules that are in place.

---

12 See Dutch Supreme Court, 4 April 2014; the case is discussed – with others – by Bartman, *Dutch Supreme Court at a loss over groups*, in *ECL*, 2016, 123; more extensively see Olaerts, in *Company laws*, 1409.

13 See Dutch Supreme Court, 29 June 2007. See on that particularly Bartman, *From autonomy of interests to concurrence of interests in Dutch group company law*, in *ECL*, 2007, 207 and Olaerts, in *Company laws*, 1412.

14 See i.e. Amsterdam Court of Appeal, Enterprise Chamber, 30 April 2018 (case "De Seizoenen").

Firstly, the parent and the subsidiary can enter into a contract on the basis of which the parent can give instructions not to the directors individually but to the board of the subsidiary as such. It can be questioned whether this type of construction is allowed under the Dutch law on public companies and this is a point of discussion in the literature (see above, Chapter 3, § 4). Considering, however, that the articles of association of a subsidiary which is a private company can contain that right to give and receive instructions[15], a contract between the parent and the subsidiary can be used in order to further implement this flow of instructions at least if one of the parties is public and one is private.

Secondly, the parent can be granted an important power over its subsidiary by putting a clause in the articles of association of the latter company requiring shareholder approval of certain board decisions. This is possible under such national law, as the residual power – as we have seen (above Chapter 3, § 4) – lies with the general meeting from this standpoint. The granting of approval rights cannot however reach so far that the board is no longer able to manage the company[16].

---

15 See Olaerts, in *Company laws*, 1410. With regard to private companies, the right to give specific instructions was introduced in 2012: Art. 2.239 Du-CC now stipulates that the articles of association may provide that the board of directors is subject to the instructions of another body or organ of the company. This is lawful and binding on the board of directors of the subsidiary as long as there is a basis for these instruction rights in the articles of association and as long as they do not go against the interest of the subsidiary and the enterprise connected to it. According to Bartman, *Dutch*, 128, "in this respect one could say that Art. 239(4) of the Dutch Civil Code, in combination with and even stronger recognition of the group interest in [the Dutch] system of company law, forces the holding company to be clearer about the nature of its relationship with subsidiaries".

16 See Olaerts, in *Company laws*, 1411. Under Spanish law – to mention another Member State that resolves the problems of company groups at case law level – the Supreme Court has recently recognized that the interest of the subsidiary must be conceived as necessarily "coordinated" with the global interest of the group within a framework (of protection) that has to grant compensatory advantages: "The integration of company into a corporate group, even as subsidiary or dominated company, does not mean" – the Court has stated – "the total loss of identity and autonomy. The subsidiary not only retains its own legal personality, but also its specific objectives and its own specific corporate interest, nuanced by the interest of the group, and coordinated with it [...] Indeed, the existence of a group of companies means that, when there are conflicts between the interest of the group and the particular interest of one of the companies, a reasonable balance must be sought between one interest and another, that is, between the interest of the group and the particular corporate interest of each subsidiary, which makes possible the efficient and flexible operation of the business unit that the group of companies represents, but prevents in turn the plundering of the subsidiary companies and the unnecessary postponement of their corporate interest, so as to protect external shareholders and creditors of any kind, public, commercial or labour. This balance can be sought in the existence of compensatory ad-

French law – on the other hand – has remained substantially faithful to the so called "Rozenblum doctrine" over the years, deriving from the already mentioned "Rozenblum decision" of the criminal chamber of the Supreme Court (addressing a case of intra-group financing) which tends to be more in favour of recognizing the "group interest"[17].

The Court held that financial assistance provided by the parent company to another company of the same group must be ispired by a common interest, assessed in the light of a group policy.

The conditions emerging from the Rozenblum ruling are the following: all companies must be members of the same group of companies (there must be

---

vantages that justify that some action, considered in isolation, could be a detriment to company" (Supreme Court, 11 December 2015: the Court confirmed that the administrator cannot be exonerated from responsibility on the grounds that he was acting under the instructions of the management of the group, and ruled that he would be responsible on the basis of infringement of his duty of loyalty to the corporate interest of the subsidiary).

The absence of statutory law on the parent's liability for damages caused has led scholars to rely also on the theory of "de facto director liability" (Art. 236 Sp-CA) and on the duty of loyalty of the controlling shareholder (implicitly recognized in Arts. 7 and 1258 of the civil code). As far as the position of the subsidiary's directors, the main opinion holds that they have a duty to act as a diligent "filter" and to demand information from the parent company about the legitimacy of the instructions (this duty should be inferred – according to scholars – from Arts. 225 and 226 Sp-CA, that impose on directors the duty to demand and gather sufficient information, as well as to act in accordance with an appropriate decision-making procedure). See extensively Fuentes, in *Company laws*, 236; see also Girgado, *Legislative situation of corporate groups in Spanish law*, in *ECFR*, 2006, 363.

Also under Polish case law similar results could be achieved: according to Opalski/Moskala, in *Company laws*, 843, "considering that the interest of the company should be a product ("resultant") of interests of all groups of shareholders (also minority shareholders), a condition for legitimizing actions in the interest of the group which cause costs or burdens for the subsidiary should be securing of an adequate compensation to the company for such burdens or costs. The adequacy of such compensation should be measured in reference to justified expectations of the minority (outsider) shareholders (e. g. reasonable policy towards achieving profits and distributing dividends), as well as safeguarding the company's creditors from possible insolvency caused by actions made in the group interest". The Authors note however that the above requirements risk to be "very vague" (they "do not provide a formula for determining even the approximate amount of compensation and the deadline when it should be rendered to the subsidiary", "lack a satisfying level of legal certainty and may be rejected by courts (for instance, in a judgment of 20 March 2014 [...] the Regional Court in Bialystok only pointed out the issue of compensation without more detailed remarks on its form and timing)".

17 See Schiller/Barsan, in *Company laws*, 147, clearly affirming that "this lack of regulation is not the result of an omission. It is precisely in line with this deliberate approach", which rely also on other rules (above all on accounting and cross-shareholding); and Pariente, *The evolution of the concept of "corporate group" in France*, in *ECFR*, 2007, 317.

structural links between the companies); the sacrifices imposed on the subsidiary must be done in the interest of the group in order to maintain its equilibrium or to pursue a coherent overall policy; the group must be based on non-artificial elements that contribute to the achievement of its overall purpose (thus, if companies in the same group exercise their activities in very different sectors and there are cash flows between the group companies whose sole aim is to conceal the deteriorating financial situation of one group company, there is no economic coherence in such a group); the sacrifices made must not place the company concerned at too great a risk; the sacrifices must be made for consideration and must not exceed the financial abilities of the company making them.

Actually, the French model (considering that the Rozenblum doctrine was formulated in the area of criminal law) also relies on other bodies of law, like the one on the "de facto directors": thus, if the parent company, or any other company in the group, acts as a de facto manager of another company, the civil liabilities regulated by those provisions will apply[18].

(III) Finally, there are few companies acts that do not contain any specific provisions on groups and the group interest (see, for instance – as noted above – Ireland, where no specific case law has developed, either). In those jurisdictions the problems raised by groups structures are mainly addressed by the laws on directors' conflicts of interests and the rules on related party transactions[19].

(IV) The EMCA has basically chosen to follow the "French" approach and recognizes the interest of the group[20].

The Model "is focused on the issue at the heart of group reality: the management of the group"; it adds that "protection of subsidiary companies and related

---

18 See Art. 651-2 Fr-CC; see Schiller/Barsan, in *Company laws*, 162.

19 While Sect. 239 Ir-CA simply prohibits the granting of loans to directors and "connected persons" (and that such arrangements are voidable), at the same time Sect. 243 Ir-CA (entitled "intra-group transactions") adds that "Sect. 239 does not prohibit a company from (a) making a loan or quasi-loan to any body corporate which is its holding company, subsidiary or a subsidiary of its holding company, or (b) entering into a guarantee or providing any security in connection with a loan or quasi-loan made by any person to any body corporate which is its holding company, subsidiary or a subsidiary of its holding company", and that "does not prohibit a company from (a) entering into a credit transaction as creditor for any body corporate which is its holding company, subsidiary or a subsidiary of its holding company, or (b) entering into a guarantee or providing any security in connection with any credit transaction made by any other person for any body corporate which is its holding company, subsidiary or a subsidiary of its holding company". See Thuillier, *Company law in Ireland*, 2nd ed., Clarus, 2014, 89.

20 See for a comment Conac, *The chapter on groups of companies of the European Model Company Act (EMCA)*, in *ECFR*, 2016, 301, correctly recognizing that however the "EMCA chapter on groups of companies is much more elaborated than the Rozenblum approach".

interests (shareholders, creditors) should not be ignored, of course, but it should not be achieved through excessively burdensome rules"[21].

The basic principles of the EMCA are thus the following: the parent company has a right to give binding instructions to a subsidiary; there is no specific liability on the parent for the damages suffered by a subsidiary; the subsidiary must fulfil the instructions given by the parent, otherwise the directors of the subsidiary must resign; the right of the parent to issue binding instructions to subsidiaries is limited by conformity with the interests of the group (see Sect. 15.09 EMCA and comments)[22].

However, the EMCA introduces a further distinction and regulates the figure of "nominee" directors, who are the ones appointed – "nominated" – by the parent company. As a matter of fact – so the EMCA Group's reasoning goes – these directors are always aligned to the interests of the parent company and should be bound to its board's instructions. On the contrary, the other board members should not be bound to these instructions: they are "(a) directors and managers who were not appointed by the parent company or by the controlling shareholder, but as a result of provisions in the articles of associations, or a shareholders' agreement or of any law or regulation [i.e. were elected de facto by minority shareholders] (b) directors who are defined as 'independent directors' [...]; (c) directors who are employee representatives".

The solution adopted by the EMCA is rather clear, as are the underlying reasons[23]. It remains true, however, that other Member States have taken very different routes. Moreover, the distinction drawn by the Model between "nominee" directors and "other" directors may contribute to dismantle long established concepts and add further complications.

---

21 See the general comments to Sect. 15: "companies acts which entitle the parent company with a legal power of direction over subsidiaries only on the condition that an over-reaching protection is granted to creditors, minority shareholders and the subsidiary itself, have proven to provide a legal regime which is deemed to be too rigid and with little practical efficacy".

22 More precisely Sect. 15.16 stipulates that "if the management of a subsidiary [...] acts in a way contrary to the interests of the subsidiary, a director or manager shall not be deemed to have acted in breach of their fiduciary duties if (a) the decision is in the interests of the group as a whole, and (b) the management, acting in good faith on the basis of the information available to [...] may reasonably assume that the loss/damage/disadvantage will, within a reasonable period, be balanced by benefit/gain/advantage, and (c) the loss/damage/disadvantage [...] is not such as would place the continued existence of the company in jeopardy".

23 There is widespread agreement towards acknowledging, to a larger extent, the concept of "group interest": see for instance Conac, *Directors'*, 194, Teichmann, *Towards a European framework for cross-border group management*, in *ECL*, 2016, 151; Sørensen, *Recognising*, 1.

(V) Finally, the EMCA contains a section on the parent company's liability, but with an approach which is, once again, rather original (see Sect. 15.17).

Whenever a subsidiary company, which has been managed according to instructions issued by its parent in the interest of the group, has no reasonable prospect, by means of its own resources, of avoiding being wound-up (i.e. it has reached a "crisis point"), the parent company is obliged without delay to carry out a fundamental restructuring of the subsidiary or to initiate the winding-up procedure.

If the parent company does not act in this way, it shall be held liable for any unpaid debts of the subsidiary company incurred after the crisis point.

The right to claim compensation can, however, be invoked only by the liquidator or administrative receiver of the subsidiary (the liquidator is obliged to exercise this claim if creditors holding 10% of the debts of the subsidiary request it; the insolvency court may itself promote the claim).

This section is clearly inspired by the concept of "wrongful trading" which originates in the UK (see currently Sect. 613 Ir-CA), but there is a significant difference: instead of making the directors liable for "wrongful trading", it makes the parent company liable.

5. (b) The disclosure of the existence of the group and the results of the unitary direction

(I) The Member States' laws that are more focused on the interest of each subsidiary than on the interest of the group itself (since they perceive that the group regulation should primarily be intended to act as a regime of "protection": Germany, Italy, the Netherlands, etc.) are also more concerned about the need to provide "disclosure" of the existence of the group and the results of the unitary direction. They adopt therefore rules aimed at reducing the intrinsic opaqueness that can be typical of the structure of groups.

As it has been clearly noted (from the viewpoint of countries which do not provide for any publicity requirements relating to the setting up and existence of a group) "in the absence of publicity regulations, from a third party's perspective, every company within the group appears as a distinct and autonomous company, with its activity regulated by the company contract/articles of association, having its own administrative, control and other governing bodies and its own assets"; this may distort the perception that investors and creditors have of that company even though it is under the influence of a parent company and maybe has tens or hundreds of sister group companies[24]

German law – with reference to the de facto groups – requires, when a company is under the unitary direction of another, its directors to prepare yearly reports detailing, among others, the existence of the group, all transactions with the parent company and other group companies and their results (see Sect. 312 Ge-PuCA). The report is meant to enable outside shareholders of the subsidiary to pursue a claim against the controlling enterprise and, more generally, to prevent mismanagement[25].

Italian legislation is more extensive. Pursuant to Arts. 2497-bis f. It-CC, the subsidiary must first indicate the name of the parent company in its letterheads and register it in the applicable section of the companies register. Secondly, the subsidiary must display a summary of the essential data from the latest financial statements of the parent company and the relationships with the holding and the other group companies in its financial statements, as well as the effect the unitary direction has had on the performance of the company and its results. Finally, the decisions of the subsidiaries' boards of directors, when influenced by the parent company, must be analytically motivated and registered in the company's books[26].

Dutch law also requires financial information on the relationships within a group, beyond those that has to be contained in the consolidated accounts (see Arts. 2.376 ff. Du-CC). Creditors and minority shareholders are protected by the requirement to disclose transactions with related parties in the financial statements and the explanatory notes. Debts to other group companies have to be set out in the financial statements. The same goes for a liability that the company has relating to the debts of others. The profit and loss account should also con-

---

24 See for example Tec/Doroga, in *Company laws*, 1020, with reference to Romanian law (acknowledging that a general regulation in that country regarding the formation of groups is absent).

25 See Lieder, *Company laws*, 395. It is usually noted among scholars that the usefulness of this report for outside shareholders and creditors is impaired by the fact that it is not made directly available to them for reasons of non-disclosure of sensitive information. However, since that report is audited by an external auditor, the shareholders may gain indirect knowledge of it as the supervisory board is obliged to comment on it as well as on the auditor's findings at the general meeting: see Scheuch, *Konzernrecht*, 196. Art. 82 Cz-CA states as well that directors have to prepare a written report on relations between the controlling company and the controlled one and on relations between the latter and other companies controlled by the same.

26 These reports will not usually be available to shareholders and creditors, but may become of great importance if the company goes bankrupt and a court receiver is later appointed, with the task of reconstructing the intercompany activities that have occurred.

tain the returns on shareholdings and the proceeds and losses stemming from relations with group members[27].

It is actually difficult to disagree with this approach of enhanced transparency on the existence and functioning of the group, since the aim of these rule is – first of all – the improvement of the corporate governance[28].

Notwithstanding, legislations with a more heightened sensitivity towards the primacy of the "group enterprise" may perceive them as redundant burdens.

6. (c) Rights of the minority shareholders of subsidiaries (to special investigation, to withdrawal)

Other provisions contained in some companies acts are headed in the same direction towards shareholders' "protection". Some promote more transparency, even if on a more "occasional" basis. Others strengthen the option for shareholders to leave the company if they feel that their investment is put at risk by the presence of the group.

---

27 See Olaerts, in *Company laws*, 1404. See however also Ch. 7, Sect. 32, Sw-CA, according to which, with reference to general meetings, "upon request by any shareholder and where the board of directors believes that such may take place without significant harm to the company, the board of directors and managing director shall provide information at the general meeting in respect of the following: (1) any circumstances which may affect the assessment of a matter on the agenda; and (2) any circumstances which may affect the assessment of the company's financial position. In a company which is included in a group, the duty to provide information shall apply also to the company's relationship to other group companies. Where the company is a parent company, the duty to provide information shall also apply to the group accounts and such circumstances regarding subsidiaries as specified" above. Sect. 33 adds that "where information which has been requested pursuant to Sect. 32 may only be provided on the basis of information which is not available at the general meeting, such information shall be made available to the shareholders in writing at the company's offices within two weeks thereafter and shall be sent to any shareholder who requests such information".
28 See for a similar view Tec/Doroga, in *Company laws*, 1020, "Romanian law does not provide for other types of transparency requirements even though transparency within the group is vital for the protection of the rights of third parties (creditors, employees, public authorities). Such useful disclosure conditions could relate to the very existence of the group and intra-group relationships, to the effects of the contracts concluded between the members of the group (for instance, whether or not the group's contracts may be relied upon by third parties), or to the shift of liability between the members of the group".

(I) The right attributed by the first group of rules to the minority shareholders of the subsidiaries is the right to "special investigation" (see paradigmatically Art. 351 Du-CC and Sect. 351 Ge-PuCA[29]).

This right is particularly important for shareholders because it allows them to obtain the most valuable element in the field of corporate groups first hand: information on specific transactions.

According to the EMCA, shareholders of a subsidiary may even request a special "investigation" – to be carried out by a special examiner – of the parent company in relation to a specific decision which has affected that subsidiary (see Sect. 15.14 EMCA). Since the result of the investigation is, however, brought to the attention of the general meeting of the subsidiary (and, therefore, to the final decisions of the parent company), the remedy becomes effective only as long as the legislation also gives to the minority shareholders the right to bring a suit against the directors on behalf of the company (this right is punctually provided for by the EMCA: see Sects. 11.38 and 39).

(II) Other jurisdictions – as anticipated – are more focused on providing shareholders of the subsidiary with an "exit" option and establishing the mandatory obligation (by the subsidiary or the parent) to buy out their shares.

This is the choice, for instance, made by Italian law, in three cases (see Art. 2497-*quater* It-CC; each of them may be qualified as a right of withdrawal with the exit costs charged to the subsidiary).

Firstly, the subsidiary shareholders may withdraw when the parent company approves a transformation that implies a change of its corporate object, allowing the exercise of activities that significantly alter the economic conditions of the subsidiary. In such a case the minority shareholders of the latter company are

---

29 See however – under a regime which could be considered less shareholder friendly – also Arts. 225-231 and 254 Fr-CC. Pursuant to Art. 225-231, one or more shareholders representing at least 5% of the share capital, either individually or as a group of any kind, may submit written questions to the chairperson of the board of directors or the executive board on one or more of the company's management operations; in the case of controlled companies, the application must be evaluated in light of the group's interests. The reply must be sent to the auditors. If no reply is received within one month, or if the information contained in the reply is unsatisfactory, these shareholders may file a claim for the appointment of one or more experts to submit a report on one or more management transactions. The public prosecutor, the works council, and, for listed companies, the financial markets authority may file a similar claim. The report is sent to the petitioner, the public prosecutor, the works council, the auditor and the board of directors and must also be attached to the auditors' report prepared for the next general meeting. Art. 225-254 Fr-CC also permits all shareholders to file a lawsuit against the directors on behalf of the company. See Schiller/Barsan, in *Company laws*, 153.

given the right to leave since they may refuse to remain in a group that has changed its main entrepreneurial features.

Secondly, the subsidiary shareholders may withdraw when a court's decision has been issued in their favor, recognizing that the parent company has abused its management powers; in this case, the fiduciary relationship among shareholders is lost and the harmed ones should be given the opportunity to leave[30].

Thirdly, the subsidiary shareholders may withdraw "at the beginning and on the termination" of the unitary direction, "when an alteration of the risk conditions of the investment results". This is the case in which an individual company enters a group or the group is dissolved: being part of a group or not alters the perspectives of the shareholders and thus – once again – the disagreeing minority shareholders should be given the chance to sell out their shares[31] (the latter rule does not apply where the subsidiary is a listed company and a public tender offer has been promoted on the market by the main shareholder or a third party, since the same exit option is given by means of that offer).

(III) Conclusively, as we can see, the regimes described above – in this and in the previous § 5 – may be defined as "upstream" (or "bottom-up") models: the most important shareholders' rights are provided for by the law at the level of the subsidiary where the need for protection is felt to be stronger.

Within this model, we may make a further distinction and observe that the kind of safeguard provided by each domestic law reflects the fundamental legislative techniques employed at a more general level: Member States with (broadly speaking) "shareholder-friendly" regulations tend to rely on – more participatory –

---

30 See similarly Art. 2.343 Du-CC (on which see also above Chapter 6, § 5): as noted by Olaerts, in *Company laws*, 1428, "on the basis of this article a shareholder can request to be bought out if this shareholders is harmed in such a way in his interests or rights that a continuation of his shareholdership cannot reasonably be expected of him and if this harm is the result of the conduct of either one or more of his co-shareholders or the company itself". The obligation to buy is on the parent company in this case.

31 This provision is interpreted by the doctrine to having been extended (beyond the situation in which the company enters or exits from a "group situation") to the case of the simple change of the parent company (i.e. of the "group" to which the subsidiary belongs, as a consequence of the purchase of the majority of the subsidiary's shares by another company); see Baccetti, in *Company laws*, 626. The rule – or at least its extensive interpretation – has been criticized by some scholars on the grounds that it imposes heavy economic burdens on a company any time it establishes a group or wants to buy companies belonging to other groups, hence discouraging acquisitions (and more generally the "market for corporate control", on which see below, Chapter 10, § 1).

"information rights". Member States less well-disposed to the involvement of shareholders in the business prefer to recognize "exit rights".

7. (d) Rights of the minority shareholders of the parent company (to information, to withdrawal, to vote)

(I) On the other hand, jurisdictions endorsing a more "organizational" – enterprise – view seem more interested in rules concerning the rights owed to shareholders at the level of (not surprisingly) the parent company. This is a more "downstream" ("top-down") model: the main rights are afforded to the shareholders of the holding company (instead of to the shareholders of the subsidiary, as we have seen in the previous paragraphs).

This model is reflected in the most relevant organizational system, the German law of "contract-based" groups. As already explained, parent company shareholders may legitimately intend to reject the decision of having their company enter into such a group agreement (which brings radical changes in the functioning of the company); therefore, they are given the right to be bought out by the controlling shareholder at a fair price (see above § 3).

The parent's shareholders may also be given the right to vote on the creation of a group: once again this occurs under the German law on contract-based groups. The "domination agreements" and "profit transfer agreements" have to be approved by a majority of three-quarters of the share capital represented at the general meeting of each company accepting that they will submit to the will of the other (see above § 3).

The right to information and to request a special investigation may also be given to the shareholders of the parent company (this occurs again in the domestic companies acts which are more sensitive to shareholders' disclosure, in general[32]).

This right is particularly important, especially since relevant information may be frequently available only at the level of the subsidiary (and thus be constantly ignored by the parent company's minority shareholders).

(II) At this point, another conclusion may be drawn. One should recognize how dramatically the underpinning economic and political vision of corporate

---

32 Similar provisions can be found i.e. in Sect. 102 Da-CA; Ch. 7, Sect. 32, Sw-CA; and Sect. 15.12 EMCA; see however also Arts. 2.346 Du-CC and 290 Por-CC (under a law which is far more protective also for the shareholders of the subsidiaries).

groups contributes towards shaping the laws devoted to them by the Member States.

There is a long way to go before convergence is achieved (if convergence is deemed important).

At the current stage, the choice by a company on whether to incorporate in one Member State or another may be rendered heavily dependent on the different group regimes put in place by each single State.

In any case, the low level of knowledge of how corporate groups are governed in the different countries (and the very different principles underpinning each domestic law) currently represent a significant hurdle for cross-border mobility.

In this light, it has thus been noted that – even if the CJEU has mainly been called upon to rule on national laws governing group in specific sectors (tax, antitrust, etc.) – it cannot be excluded that in the future the Luxembourg judges may be also asked "to assess whether company law rules on groups of companies conflict with the freedom of establishment" or of movement of capital acknowledged by the EU Treaties[33].

Actually the Court has already ruled in an important case of group company law, the "Impacto Azul" case of 2013, however with a mixed result. We shall examine it below, in § 9.

8. (e) Cross-shareholdings, intercompany loans and group financing

Companies that belong to groups frequently execute very complex transactions. Group companies, for instance, may subscribe to or purchase other companies' shares or lend each other money; they also may guarantee the transactions of sister group companies with third parties; etc.

(I) As we have already seen above (in Chapter 2, § 10), Art. 67 Directive 2017/1132/EU stipulates that the subscription to and acquisition of shares in a public

---

[33] In this light, it has thus been noted that – even if the CJEU has mainly been called upon to rule on national laws governing group in specific sectors (tax, an-titrust, etc.) – it cannot be excluded that in the future the Luxembourg judges may be also asked "to assess whether company law rules on groups of compa-nies conflict with the freedom of establishment" or of movement of capital acknowledged by the EU Treaties: see Sørensen, *Groups*, 393.

Actually the Court has already ruled in an important case of group company law, the "Impacto Azul" case of 2013, however with a mixed result. We shall examine it below, in § 9.

company by a subsidiary must be regarded as having been carried out by the parent company itself.

As a consequence, the majority of national laws allow subsidiaries to subscribe to and acquire the parent company's shares under the same conditions prescribed for the acquisition of own shares by the company itself.

A particularly complex law on cross-shareholding has been laid down furthermore, for instance, by the French commercial code, which relies – as we have noted (§ 4) – more on "selective" regulations (like that one) than on more structured laws in dealing with groups (for further details on that cross-shareholding regime see above Chapter 2, § 10).

(II) Intra-group credit operations are obviously allowed, but they are either regulated pursuant to the "catch all" rules on the unitary direction (and the case law on the "interest" of the group) – see above § 4 – or addressed according to selected laws on "related party transactions".

An extensive regulation of "related party transactions" has been laid down, once again, by French legislation (from act no. 2001–420 onwards[34]). Two types of intra-group related party transactions are covered: agreements between the company and one of its shareholders owning more 10% of the voting rights and agreements between the company and the parent company's controlling shareholder that has more than 10% of the voting rights in the company[35].

The required procedure is twofold: the board needs to authorize the transaction and the general meetings must approve it. The auditors have to draft a special report on the related party agreements in order to provide the shareholders with the relevant information for their vote. The related party cannot take part in this vote and its shares are not taken into account for the quorum or the majority of the vote. An unauthorized agreement may be void if it causes harm to the company; it can, however, be confirmed by a vote by the shareholders at the general meeting. If a related party transaction causes harm to the company, the consequences of this harm will be borne by the related party and might also be ascribed to the board members[36].

---

34 See especially Schiller/Barsan, in *Company laws*, 157.

35 There are however exemptions, i.e. cases to which the law does not apply: on the one hand, transactions agreed under normal conditions and, on the other, transactions agreed between a parent company and wholly owned subsidiaries. For a similar provision see Art. 150 R-CA.

36 Also pursuant to Dutch law, relevant transactions with affiliated or "linked" parties that have not been entered into under normal market conditions have to be disclosed (although not approved by the general meeting). Information has to be provided concerning the scope of the transactions, the nature of the relationship with the affiliated party and other information about those transactions that is necessary in order to have an insight into the financial position

The EMCA shares this position in principle. As a matter of fact, however, it opposes it, at least for unlisted companies. "The problem" – the Group observes – "is that such rules usually are very complex in their nature, will cause excessive transaction costs compared with the level of shareholder protection they effectively provide and, in the end, are usually circumvented by individuals who choose to do so. For that reason, the EMCA Group does not propose any rule in this regard" (see the general comments to Ch. 7). In accordance with the great majority of Member States, the EMCA has thus stayed in line with the laws and jurisprudence on unitary direction[37].

(III) Finally, it is worth to recall some provisions expressly dedicated to intra-group financing: by way of example Art. 283 s. Sp-InSA and Art. 2497-*quinquies* It-CC. Pursuant to these rules, a loan provided by the parent company to a subsidiary is postergated (i.e. legally subordinated) if conceded in a situation of crisis of the latter (moreover, in case of bankruptcy, any loan that has already been repaid to the parent must be returned to the subsidiary, if made within a certain period from a declaration of insolvency[38]).

These provisions – which mimic the rules on the postergation of loans provided by shareholders in companies that do not belong to groups (see Chapter 2, § 5, and Chapter 5, § 5) – act as a disincentive to grant loans and encourage a parent company to provide equity any time that liquidity is needed by the subsidiary.

---

of the counterpart. Disclosure of transactions is not required if the subsidiaries that are party to the transaction are 100% subsidiaries of one or more members of the group. Cf. Art. 2.381 Du-CC; smaller companies are exempted from this requirement: see art. 2.396. Cf. Olaerts, in *Company laws*, 1407.

37 Finally Swedish law is rather firm: it states that a company may not lend money to a parent company, but only to sister companies and exclusively for commercial reasons: Ch. 21, Sect. 1–2, Sw-CA: "a company may not lend money to (1) any person who owns shares in the company or another company within the same group; (2) any person who is a member of the board of directors or managing director of the company or another company within the same group", unless "the borrower is a company within the same group as the lending company [and] the loan is intended exclusively for the borrower's business operations and the company provides the loan for purely commercial reasons".

38 Spanish rules are actually more articulated; see extensively Fuentes, in *Company laws*, 1245.

9. Cross-border groups and applicable law: the CJEU judgment on the *Impacto Azul* case

Frequently enterprises operate as a group in different Member States, with the parent company's seat in one country and the subsidiaries' seats in others. In such cases it becomes important to identify the applicable law whenever a lawsuit is filed by a shareholder or a creditor.

Let us make the example of a company located in Portugal (a country – as noted above – that has adopted a comprehensive law on groups) and let us assume that the parent company is headquartered in France (a State which, on the contrary, has not implemented "group-specific" provisions). May the creditors of the Portuguese subsidiary claim that the French parent company has to be held liable pursuant to the Portuguese rules on the unitary direction?

The example is, in fact, a real one. The case has been decided by the CJEU in 2013 ("Impacto Azul": C-186/12).

The Court was asked for a preliminary ruling on whether national laws precluding the application of the principle of joint and several liability (of parent companies vis-à-vis the creditors of their subsidiaries) to parent companies who have their seat in the territory of another Member State are contrary to the European freedom of establishment as regulated by Art. 49 TFEU[39]. Domestic laws on groups are actually let free to fix the boundiaries of application of their national provisions and Portuguese law stipulates that its liability regime applies only to companies incorporated in that State.

Impacto Azul LDA was a Portuguese private company which had signed a promissory contract for the sale of a building to another Portuguese private company (BPSA9 LDA) in 2006. BPSA9 was wholly controlled by another Portuguese private company (SGPS LDA), which was wholly controlled by a public company with seat in France (Bouygues Immobilier s.a.).

Impacto Azul, claiming that the purchaser BPSA9 had not fulfilled its contractual obligations, brought a lawsuit before a Portuguese court for damages, suing BPSA9, SGPS and Bouygues Immobilier, the latter as (direct and indirect) parent companies, in accordance with Portuguese law regulating the joint and several liability of parent companies for the obligations of their subsidiaries.

The defendants contended that the domestic rules on joint and several liability of parent companies did not apply to parent companies having their seat

---

39 The case has been extensively analyzed by Rammeloo, *The judgment in CJEU C-186/12 (Impacto Azul): company law, parental liability and article 49 TFEU – a plea for a 'soft law' oriented EU law approach on company groups*, in *ECL*, 2014, 20.

in another Member State. Since Bouygues Immobilier had its seat in France, it could not therefore be held liable vis-à-vis the creditors of BPSA9 under Portuguese law.

The Court started by observing that Art. 49 TFEU (on the freedom of establishment) precludes any national measure which, even if applicable without discrimination on grounds of nationality, is liable to hinder or render less attractive the exercise by EU nationals of the freedom of establishment. Subsequently the Court observed that it is necessary to consider whether the Portuguese legislation at issue – the rules on joint and several liability of parent companies for the debts of their Portuguese subsidiaries not applying to parent companies having their seat in another Member State – constitutes a restriction within the meaning of Art. 49 TFEU.

As laws concerning corporate groups are not harmonized at EU level, the Court affirmed that Member States still have, in principle, jurisdiction to determine the law applicable to a debt of a related company.

Art. 49 TFEU acknowledges that companies set up in any Member State exist only by virtue of the national legislation which determines their incorporation and functioning. This fundamental right implies that it is exclusively for the law of the Member State where the company was set up to decide on matters of formation, structure, powers and – what most interests us here – liabilities.

Therefore, a national law (like the French one) constraining the parent company liability only to some areas and not to others, and a national law (like the Portuguese one) limiting the application of the rules on groups only to domestic companies do not constitute a restriction of the freedom of establishment within the meaning of Art. 49 TFEU.

This ruling has been criticized[40]. If – according to the core concepts of EU company law – a parent company from a different Member State (France) must have the same rights (information, possibility to exercise the unitary direction, etc.) as the parent company from the subsidiary's own state (Portugal), "there is however" – it has been stated – "a legal asymmetry", if that same parent company from another Member State (France) "cannot be imposed the same obligations as the parent company from the subsidiary's own State" (Portugal). Rights and duties should go hand in hand. As a consequence, it has been concluded, "in the light of the widespread use of company groups, it must be asked

---

40 See Rammeloo, *The judgment*, 23 ff.

how to face the consequences of the legal vacuum resulting from the CJEU's interpretative ruling in Impacto Azul"[41].

Bringing the reasoning to its logical consequences (and reversing the perspective), if a French company is exonerated from the parent liability typical of the Portuguese groups' regime, the same French company should be prevented from exploiting the scope for group management in Portuguese law. This deprivation (first of an obligation, but logically, consequently, also) of a right may be a relevant restriction of the freedom of establishment and of the movement of capital[42].

This is currently one of the several complex – and fascinating – questions under the lens of EU company law.

---

41 So Rammeloo, *The judgment*, 27. See also Teichmann, *Towards*, 151f. ("what the Court did not take into account was a considerable side effect of this provision: the liability of the Portuguese parent is accompanied by a right to give instructions to the subsidiary in the interest of the group [;] the national court only asked for a preliminary ruling on the liability rule, but the reasoning could have been more cautious and elaborated").
42 See Sørensen, *Groups*, 393.

8 Accounting and financial statements

Summary:
1. An overview on EU companies' financial reporting
2. Layouts and principles of financial statements
3. Consolidated financial statements
4. Audit of the financial statements
5. Approval and publication of the financial statements
6. Financial statements in listed and other companies using the "International Accounting Standards" and "International Financial Reporting Standards" ("IAS/IFRS")
7. Profit and dividends (and the "right to dividend" acknowledged by some jurisdictions)

1. An overview on EU companies' financial reporting

National laws on accounts – and the auditing of those accounts – are among the most harmonized. This has to do with the implementation of the Fourth and Seventh Directives, later replaced by the "Accounting Directive" (2013/34/EU, further amended by Directive 2014/95/EU)[1].

All public companies have to draft annual financial statements to monitor the condition of their business and provide a true and fair view of their financial position.

Groups of companies must publish consolidated financial statements.

As far as listed companies are concerned, Regulation 1606/2002/EC requires these undertakings to prepare their financial statements in accordance with a

---

[1] The Directive amended Directive 2006/43/EC, repealing Directives 78/660/EEC and 83/349/EEC. For extensive descriptions see, *inter alia*, Beckman, *The new EU-Directive on annual and consolidated financial statements and related management reports*, in *ECL*, 2013, 199; Strampelli/Passador, *Is the harmonisation of the accounting law in the EU feasible?*, 2016, at *ssrn.com*; Hommelhoff, *Chapter 12 "Annual accounting and auditing" of EMCA: a critical review*, in *ECFR*, 2016, 254; Cisi, *Differences and similarities between IAS/IFRS regulation and the new directive*, in Grandinetti (ed.) *Corporate tax base in the light of IAS/IFRS and EU directive 2013/34. A comparative approach*, Kluwer, 2016, 39; Strampelli, *The EU issuers' accounting disclosure regime and investors' information needs: the essential tole of narrative reporting*, in *EBOR*, 2018, 541; Seehausen, *European Model Companies Act (EMCA): a critical review of Chapter 12 – Annual accounting and auditing*, in *EBLR*, 2019, 633; Id., *Audit reports – Balancing harmonisation, standardisation, and customisation*, in *EBLR*, 2020, 359.

https://doi.org/10.1515/9783110725025-010

single set of international standards, the "IFRS" ("International Financial Reporting Standards"), previously known as "IAS" ("International Accounting Standards").

EU Member States may opt to extend the use of IFRS to annual financial statements and non-listed companies as well.

The principles and more specific rules regulating the drafting of the financial statements are laid down in the above-mentioned Directive and regulation and have therefore been implemented into the legislation of each State.

On the other hand, the EMCA Group has chosen not to implement the Auditing Directive in the Model; this effort would have gone beyond the scope of the EMCA. However, the Model contains some basic rules regarding the general meeting's choice of auditors, the auditors' duties, etc. (Ch. 12).

The scope of financial disclosure is manifold.

It helps managers and shareholders to constantly be aware of the health of their companies and allows them to operate pursuant to standards of good accountability. Financial statements give the idea of the effectiveness of management: how well a company is performing depends on its profitability, which these statements show.

Financial disclosure lets creditors know if the company they have financed is still worthy of credit and whether prospective creditors should provide financing to that company or not. The statements also provide information on the company's cash flows; creditors can use this data to predict the company's liquidity and cash requirements.

In companies open to the market, financial data gives investors signals on whether to buy or sell shares in the company. Investors use the information contained in the financial statements to make their financial decisions.

On a more general level, the rules on accounting promote the convergence of standards and ensure consistent and comparable financial reporting across the EU. In this way, they facilitate cross-border investment and improve Union-wide comparability and public confidence in financial statements.

Mandatory disclosure should however avoid putting excessive administrative burdens on smaller companies and should provide for disclosure that is proportionate to the size of the company. For this reason, the Directive allows a simplified reporting regime for small and medium-sized enterprises and a very light regime for micro-companies (those with less than 10 employees). The Directive includes a definition of micro, small, medium and large companies based on thresholds concerning turnover, total assets and number of employees; these thresholds are periodically updated to keep pace with inflation[2].

The various goals of the legislation are explained in the Directive: according to Recital 4, "annual financial statements pursue various objectives and do not merely provide information for investors in capital markets but also give an account of past transactions and enhance corporate governance. Union accounting legislation needs to strike an appropriate balance between the interests of the addressees of financial statements and the interest of undertakings in not being unduly burdened with reporting requirements".

In two interesting cases from 2003 (C-435/02 and C-103/03), the CJEU also explained the rationale behind the rules on accounting. The Court stated that all shareholders and also third parties have the right to urge any company covered by European accounting rules to file its accounts with the companies register.

Both proceedings had been brought by the publisher Axel Springer AG before the German courts against small competitors for non-compliance with financial disclosure rules. These small companies, fearing the moves of the far bigger company Springer, aimed to maintain their numbers secret. The regional courts put the case before the CJEU. The Court ruled that, even if the disclosure obligations "have a sufficiently direct and significant effect on freedom to exercise a trade or profession, the restriction they impose, in particular the restriction on the right of an undertaking to keep secret certain potentially sensitive information, appears on any analysis to be clearly justified" in the light of the need of "protection of third parties against the financial risks involved with those types of companies which offer no safeguards to third parties beyond the amounts of their net assets" and in order to establish in the Union "minimum equivalent legal requirements as regards the extent of the financial information" (for current and perspective investors)[3].

The Court saw very limited room in this Directive to deal with the confidentiality of business information in the competitive environment of incorporated enterprises. From then onwards the route to more financial disclosure has been downhill.

---

2 See above Chapter 1, § 1, fn 4.
3 Cases are commented in Schön, *Corporate disclosure in a competitive environment – the ECJ's Axel Springer case and the quest for a European framework for mandatory disclosure*, 2006, at *ssrn.com*.

2. Layouts and principles of financial statements

(I) Financial statements have to include the "balance sheet", the "profit and loss account", the "explanatory note" and the "cash flow statement" (the four documents constitute the annual "financial statements"). Companies also have to publish management reports.

The annual financial statements have to be drawn up in accordance with the provisions – and layouts – of the national regulations adopting the Directive.

On the one hand, the balance sheet shows the company's assets, while on the other, contains the details of the liabilities; it has to be prepared in accordance with Annex III of the Directive[4].

---

4 HORIZONTAL LAYOUT OF THE BALANCE SHEET
Assets
A. Subscribed capital unpaid of which there has been called (unless national law provides that called-up capital is to be shown under "Capital and reserves", in which case the part of the capital called but not yet paid shall appear as an asset either under A or under D (II) (5))
B. Formation expenses as defined by national law, and in so far as national law permits their being shown as an asset. National law may also provide for formation expenses to be shown as the first item under "Intangible assets".
C. Fixed assets
I. Intangible assets
1. Costs of development, in so far as national law permits their being shown as assets
2. Concessions, patents, licences, trade marks and similar rights and assets, if they were:
(a) acquired for valuable consideration and need not be shown under C (I) (3); or
(b) created by the undertaking itself, in so far as national law permits their being shown as assets.
3. Goodwill, to the extent that it was acquired for valuable consideration
4. Payments on account
II. Tangible assets
1. Land and buildings
2. Plant and machinery
3. Other fixtures and fittings, tools and equipment
4. Payments on account and tangible assets in the course of construction
III. Financial assets
1. Shares in affiliated undertakings
2. Loans to affiliated undertakings
3. Participating interests
4. Loans to undertakings with which the undertaking is linked by virtue of participating interests
5. Investments held as fixed assets
6. Other loans
D. Current assets
I. Stocks
1. Raw materials and consumables

2. Work in progress

3. Finished goods and goods for resale

4. Payments on account.

II. Debtors (amounts becoming due and payable after more than one year shall be shown separately for each item)

1. Trade debtors

2. Amounts owed by affiliated undertakings

3. Amounts owed by undertakings with which the undertaking is linked by virtue of participating interests

4. Other debtors

5. Subscribed capital called but not paid (unless national law provides that called-up capital is to be shown as an asset under A)

6. Prepayments and accrued income (unless national law provides that such items are to be shown as assets under E)

III. Investments

1. Shares in affiliated undertakings

2. Own shares (with an indication of their nominal value or, in the absence of a nominal value, their accounting par value), to the extent that national law permits their being shown in the balance sheet

3. Other investments

IV. Cash at bank and in hand

E. Prepayments and accrued income (unless national law provides that such items are to be shown as assets under D (II) (6))

Capital, reserves and liabilities

A. Capital and reserves

I. Subscribed capital (unless national law provides that called-up capital is to be shown under this item, in which case the amounts of subscribed capital and paid-up capital shall be shown separately)

II. Share premium account

III. Revaluation reserve

IV. Reserves

1. Legal reserve, in so far as national law requires such a reserve

2. Reserve for own shares, in so far as national law requires such a reserve, without prejudice to point (b) of Article 24(1) of Directive 2012/30/EU

3. Reserves provided for by the articles of association

4. Other reserves, including the fair value reserve

V. Profit or loss brought forward

VI. Profit or loss for the financial year

B. Provisions

1. Provisions for pensions and similar obligations

2. Provisions for taxation

3. Other provisions

C. Creditors (amounts becoming due and payable within one year and amounts becoming due and payable after more than one year shall be shown separately for each item and for the aggregate of those items)

1. Debenture loans, showing convertible loans separately

2. Amounts owed to credit institutions
3. Payments received on account of orders, in so far as they are not shown separately as deductions from stocks
4. Trade creditors
5. Bills of exchange payable
6. Amounts owed to affiliated undertakings
7. Amounts owed to undertakings with which the undertaking is linked by virtue of participating interests
8. Other creditors, including tax and social security authorities
9. Accruals and deferred income (unless national law provides that such items are to be shown under D)
D. Accruals and deferred income (unless national law provides that such items are to be shown under C (9) under "Creditors")
VERTICAL LAYOUT OF THE BALANCE SHEET
A. Subscribed capital unpaid of which there has been called (unless national law provides that called-up capital is to be shown under L, in which case the part of the capital called but not yet paid must appear either under A or under D (II) (5))
B. Formation expenses as defined by national law, and in so far as national law permits their being shown as an asset. National law may also provide for formation expenses to be shown as the first item under "Intangible assets".
C. Fixed assets
I. Intangible assets
1. Costs of development, in so far as national law permits their being shown as assets
2. Concessions, patents, licences, trade marks and similar rights and assets, if they were:
(a) acquired for valuable consideration and need not be shown under C (I) (3); or
(b) created by the undertaking itself, in so far as national law permits their being shown as assets
3. Goodwill, to the extent that it was acquired for valuable consideration
4. Payments on account
II. Tangible assets
1. Land and buildings
2. Plant and machinery
3. Other fixtures and fittings, tools and equipment
4. Payments on account and tangible assets in the course of construction
III. Financial assets
1. Shares in affiliated undertakings
2. Loans to affiliated undertakings
3. Participating interests
4. Loans to undertakings with which the undertaking is linked by virtue of participating interests
5. Investments held as fixed assets
6. Other loans
D. Current assets
I. Stocks
1. Raw materials and consumables
2. Work in progress
3. Finished goods and goods for resale

4. Payments on account
II. Debtors (amounts becoming due and payable after more than one year must be shown separately for each item)
1. Trade debtors
2. Amounts owed by affiliated undertakings
3. Amounts owed by undertakings with which the company is linked by virtue of participating interests
4. Other debtors
5. Subscribed capital called but not paid (unless national law provides that called-up capital is to be shown as an asset under A)
6. Prepayments and accrued income (unless national law provides that such items are to be shown as assets under E).
III. Investments
1. Shares in affiliated undertakings
2. Own shares (with an indication of their nominal value or, in the absence of a nominal value, their accounting par value), to the extent that national law permits their being shown in the balance sheet.
3. Other investments.
IV. Cash at bank and in hand
E. Prepayments and accrued income (unless national law provides that such items are to be shown under D (II) (6).)
F. Creditors: amounts becoming due and payable within one year
1. Debenture loans, showing convertible loans separately
2. Amounts owed to credit institutions
3. Payments received on account of orders, in so far as they are not shown separately as deductions from stocks.
4. Trade creditors
5. Bills of exchange payable.
6. Amounts owed to affiliated undertakings
7. Amounts owed to undertakings with which the company is linked by virtue of participating interests
8. Other creditors, including tax and social security authorities
9. Accruals and deferred income (unless national law provides that such items are to be shown under K)
G. Net current assets/liabilities (taking into account prepayments and accrued income when shown under E and accruals and deferred income when shown under K)
H. Total assets less current liabilities
I. Creditors: amounts becoming due and payable after more than one year
1. Debenture loans, showing convertible loans separately
2. Amounts owed to credit institutions
3. Payments received on account of orders, in so far as they are not shown separately as deductions from stocks
4. Trade creditors
5. Bills of exchange payable
6. Amounts owed to affiliated undertakings
7. Amounts owed to undertakings with which the company is linked by virtue of participating

The layout of the profit and loss account must also follow Annex IV of the Directive[5].

---

interests

8. Other creditors, including tax and social security authorities

9. Accruals and deferred income (unless national law provides that such items are to be shown under K)

J. Provisions

1. Provisions for pensions and similar obligations

2. Provisions for taxation

3. Other provisions

K. Accruals and deferred income (unless national law provides that such items are to be shown under F (9) or I (9) or both)

L. Capital and reserves

I. Subscribed capital (unless national law provides that called-up capital is to be shown under this item, in which case the amounts of subscribed capital and paid-up capital must be shown separately)

II. Share premium account

III. Revaluation reserve

IV. Reserves

1. Legal reserve, in so far as national law requires such a reserve

2. Reserve for own shares, in so far as national law requires such a reserve, without prejudice to point (b) of Article 24(1) of Directive 2012/30/EU

3. Reserves provided for by the articles of association

4. Other reserves, including the fair value reserve

V. Profit or loss brought forward

VI. Profit or loss for the financial year

5 LAYOUT OF THE PROFIT AND LOSS ACCOUNT

1. Net turnover.

2. Variation in stocks of finished goods and in work in progress

3. Work performed by the undertaking for its own purposes and capitalised

4. Other operating income

5. (a) Raw materials and consumables

(b) Other external expenses

6. Staff costs

(a) wages and salaries

(b) social security costs, with a separate indication of those relating to pensions

7. (a) Value adjustments in respect of formation expenses and of tangible and intangible fixed assets

(b) Value adjustments in respect of current assets, to the extent that they exceed the amount of value adjustments which are normal in the undertaking concerned

8. Other operating expenses

9. Income from participating interests, with a separate indication of that derived from affiliated undertakings

10. Income from other investments and loans forming part of the fixed assets, with a separate

The notes to the financial statements provide additional information pertaining to the company's operations and financial position. They contain both a summary of the company's significant accounting policies and the details of items such as – *inter alia* – the existence of any financial commitments and guarantees, the remuneration given to members of the administrative and supervisory bodies, the average number of employees, the number and nominal value for each class of shares (where there is more than one class), the existence of any convertible debentures, warrants, options or similar securities or rights, with an indication of their number and the rights they confer, etc.

The cash-flow statement reports the aggregate amount of the cash paid or received as purchase or sale consideration.

Directors have to prepare a management report (and in groups also the consolidated management report). As stated in Recital 26 of the Directive, "a fair review of the development of the business and of its position should be provided [by the directors], in a manner consistent with the size and complexity of the business. The information should not be restricted to the financial aspects of the undertaking's business, and there should be an analysis of environmental and social aspects of the business necessary for an understanding of the undertaking's development, performance or position".

In member States adopting the one-tier system in the latin version, a report drawn up by the statutory auditors also has to be provided.

(II) Recitals 9 and Article 6 of the Directive are very important, since they lay down the general financial reporting principles.

Annual financial statements should be prepared on a "prudent basis" and give a "true and fair view" of the company's assets, liabilities and profits or losses.

The company is assumed to be carrying out its business as a going concern and accounting policies and measurement bases have to be applied consistently from one financial year to the next.

---

indication of that derived from affiliated undertakings

11. Other interest receivable and similar income, with a separate indication of that derived from affiliated undertakings

12. Value adjustments in respect of financial assets and of investments held as current assets

13. Interest payable and similar expenses, with a separate indication of amounts payable to affiliated undertakings

14. Tax on profit or loss

15. Profit or loss after taxation

16. Other taxes not shown under items 1 to 15

17. Profit or loss for the financial year

Prudence requires that, on an ordinary basis, the assets should be represented at the most cautious value, their "historical cost". That is to say, the price the company has paid to buy or produce each single asset: the "purchase price" or the "production cost".

Let us assume, for example, that a company purchases a piece of land for building some apartments, paying € 100.000 in cash. The company will enter € 100.000 as the cost of the land in its accounting records. In a booming real estate market, the fair market value of the land five years later might be € 500.000. Although the market price of the land has significantly increased, the amount entered in the balance sheet and other accounting records would continue to be unchanged at the cost of € 100.000.

An important advantage of the historical cost concept is that the records kept on the basis of it are considered consistent, comparable, verifiable and reliable. Any valuation basis other than historical cost may create serious issues for companies. For example, if a company uses current "market value" or "sales value" rather than historical cost, each director could likely suggest a different value for each asset of the company.

The same principle of prudence implies that financial reports should avoid presenting unrealized gains and should include all foreseeable losses.

In any case, Member States may permit the adoption of a "fair value" (IFRS) system of accounting, which is less prudential but more willing to represent the current effective economic and financial situation of the company. Following on from this, the Directive – on a general level – permits the company to opt out and extend (as we have already seen) the use of IFRS to the whole set of financial statements (see also below § 6).

At a more specific level, the Directive already requires – also for financial statements that are drafted pursuant to the historical cost concept – that some assets have to be entered in the balance sheet at fair value and allows the adoption of the fair value criteria for many more assets.

Art. 7 stipulates that "Member States may permit or require, in respect of all undertakings or any classes of undertaking, the measurement of fixed assets at revalued amounts".

The Directive also explicitly allows for the inclusion of unrealized gains in profit or loss: Art. 8.9 states that "Member States may permit or require, in respect of all undertakings or any classes of undertaking, that, where assets other than financial instruments are measured at fair value, a change in the value be included in the profit and loss account".

Just to make one example, financial instruments (like shares or bonds) should be recorded with reference to their market value (if a reliable market value can be identified), or alternatively to the value of their components or a similar instrument (Art. 8.7).

3. Consolidated financial statements

Similar principles also apply to consolidated financial statements, which have to be drawn up as at the same date as the annual financial statements of the parent company in a group context.

The consolidated financial statements have the function of representing the economic and financial situation of an entire group, considered as a single company, thus overriding the distinct legal personalities of the individual companies that make it up. The latter are practically considered as "divisions" or "branches" of a single large company.

The characterising element in the group configuration is – as we have already seen (Chapter 7, § 1) – control (see also Art. 22 of the Directive).

The controlling (parent) company prepares the consolidated financial statements by consolidating the values of the assets, liabilities, costs, revenues and cash flows of the companies directly and indirectly controlled and by eliminating intragroup items. Art. 24 states that, "in particular, the following shall be eliminated from the consolidated financial statements: (a) debts and claims between the undertakings; (b) income and expenditure relating to transactions between the undertakings; and (c) profits and losses resulting from transactions between the undertakings".

It follows that the economic elements that derive from internal relations must be eliminated as they lose relevance when companies are considered as a single entity. For example, in the case of a sale of goods between two companies of the same group, the revenue of one equalling the cost of the other will be eliminated by means of specific consolidation records.

The consolidated financial statements – like the financial statements – are made up of the following documents: consolidated balance sheet; consolidated profit and loss account; cash flow statement; consolidated explanatory note. A consolidated management report also has to be drawn up.

4. Audit of the financial statements

(I) Recital 43 and Art. 34 of the Directive state that the financial statements of "medium-sized and large undertakings are audited by one or more statutory auditors or audit firms approved by Member States to carry out statutory audits".

Moreover, the statutory auditors or audit firms must also: "(a) express an opinion on: (i) whether the management report is consistent with the financial statements for the same financial year, and (ii) whether the management report has been prepared in accordance with the applicable legal requirements; (b) state whether, in the light of the knowledge and understanding of the undertaking and its environment obtained in the course of the audit, he, she or it has identified material misstatements in the management report, and shall give an indication of the nature of any such misstatements".

The audit opinion (also called audit report) must therefore declare whether the annual or consolidated financial statements give a true and fair view in accordance with the relevant financial reporting framework.

Notwithstanding the rules of the Directive, audit reports still vary across Member States, with the variance depending upon both the degree of harmonization of the rules on audit reports and the degree of freedom in these rules in each single State[6].

In any case, the auditors must also comply with the "International Standards on Auditing" ("ISA"), which are professional standards – issued by the International Federation of Accountants ("IFAC") through the International Auditing and Assurance Standards Board ("IAASB"), both headquartered in New York – which are generally accepted worldwide.

The annual financial statements of small undertakings should not be covered by this audit obligation, as auditing can be a significant administrative burden for that category of company, while for many small companies both shareholders and managers are actually the same persons and, therefore, have a limited need for third-party assurance on financial statements. However, the Directive does not prevent Member States from imposing audits on smaller companies, taking into account the specific conditions and needs of small companies and the users of their financial statements.

Auditors are elected by the general meeting (also in companies adopting the dualistic system[7]: see above Chapter 3, § 3).

Some Member States provide that minority shareholders may request a Court or an administrative authority to appoint an additional approved auditor to participate in the audit with the other auditors (the provision on minority auditors is adopted by the companies act of the Nordic countries and is suggested by the

---

6 See Seehausen, *Audit*, 391.
7 See i.e. Sect. 119 Ge-PuCA. In that case, however, it is the supervisory board which commissions the audit; the auditor forwards the audit report to the supervisory board after having given the management board the opportunity to comment.

EMCA, at Sect. 12.04, setting the threshold of shareholdings needed to bring the request at 10%[8]).

In groups of companies, the subsidiaries must normally engage the same auditor as the auditor engaged by the parent company. Directive 2014/56/EU indeed states that the group auditor bears the full responsibility for the audit report in relation to the consolidated financial statements, and further that the group auditor must evaluate and review the audit work performed by third country auditors (see Art. 27). The aim of this provision is to ensure that the auditor engaged by the parent company gets an insight into the subsidiary's financial situation in order to assess the group's financial situation as a whole.

The appointment remains in force until a new auditor is elected by the general meeting. An auditor engaged to audit the company's financial statements may only be removed before its term of office expires if this removal is based on reasonable grounds (divergence of opinions on accounting treatments or audit procedures is not sufficient grounds for dismissal).

Under some domestic laws, shareholders representing 5% or more of the voting rights of the share capital are permitted to bring a claim before a court for the dismissal of the auditors or the audit firm where there are proper grounds (a similar rule is contained in the EMCA, at Sect. 12.07).

5. Approval and publication of the financial statements

Normally the financial statements have to be signed by all directors and have to be approved by the annual general meeting.

In companies adopting the two-tier system, however, it is the supervisory board that approves the documents. If the supervisory board does not approve the directors' proposal or if the management board and the supervisory board seek formal approval from the general meeting, the latter body however votes[9].

The financial statements then have to be submitted to the companies register according to the individual national laws.

Art. 30 Directive 2013/34/EU stipulates that "Member States shall ensure that undertakings publish within a reasonable period of time, which shall not exceed twelve months after the balance sheet date, the duly approved annual financial

---

8 See Sect. 144 Da-CA; Ch. 7, Sect. 5 Fi-CA; Ch. 9, Sect. 9 Sw-CA.
9 See Sect. 173 Ge-PuCA. Pursuant to other legislative models, the general meeting is involved and votes if a minority of the members of the supervisory a board (one third) so require: see Art. 2409-*terdecies* It-CC.

statements and the management report, together with the opinion submitted by the statutory auditor or audit firm".

Recital 41 of the same Directive states that "liability for drawing up and publishing annual financial statements and consolidated financial statements, as well as management reports and consolidated management reports, is based on national law. Appropriate liability rules, as laid down by each Member State under its national law, should be applicable to members of the administrative, management and supervisory bodies of an undertaking. Member States should be allowed to determine the extent of the liability".

The consolidated financial statements are, on the contrary, not approved by the general meeting and the duty remains with the directors (in the monistic system) or the member of the supervisory board (in the dualistic system).

As far as objecting to the financial statements is concerned, if they are approved by the general meeting, the resolution passed by the members of that body may be challenged and set aside according the ordinary rules regarding this matter (see above Chapter 6, § 2).

The consolidated financial statements may also be challenged in court and declared invalid, even if they were not approved by the general meeting.

6. Financial statements in listed and other companies using the "International Accounting Standards" and "International Financial Reporting Standards" ("IAS/IFRS")

The "International Accounting Standards" ("IAS") and "International Financial Reporting Standards" ("IFRS") – that we have already mentioned above in § 1 – provide a common accounting language used by several countries, also beyond Europe. They make company accounts understandable and comparable across international boundaries.

Recital 2 of Regulation 1606/2002/EC stipulates that "it is important that the financial reporting standards applied by [EU] companies participating in financial markets are accepted internationally and are truly global standards. This implies an increasing convergence of accounting standards currently used internationally with the ultimate objective of achieving a single set of global accounting standards".

The IAS/IFRS are developed by an independent body based in London, the "International Accounting Standards Board" ("IASB"). The IASB is part of the "IFRS Foundation", a nonprofit accounting organisation[10].

When a new standard is issued by the IASB, the EU needs to endorse it before it comes into force. Regulation 1606/2002/EC establishes a specific endorsement process under the responsibility of the European Commission together with consultative and advisory organizations[11].

IAS 1 sets out the overall requirements for the presentation of financial statements, the guidelines for their structure and the minimum requirements for their content.

It requires the company to present a complete set of financial statements at least annually; the set comprises: (i) a statement of financial position as at the end of the period; (ii) a statement of profit and loss and other comprehensive income for the period (other comprehensive income includes those items of income and expense that are not recognized in profit or loss in accordance with IFRS standards) (iii) a statement of changes in equity for the period; (iv) a statement of cash flows for the period; (v) notes, comprising a summary of significant accounting policies and other explanatory information.

As far as the principles that have to be followed in drafting the statements, they can be grouped into two categories.

The first category includes the principles that we could define as fundamental: understandability, significance, reliability, comparability. The other category includes further principles that can be defined as secondary, that is, relevance, faithful representation, prevalence of substance over form, neutrality, prudence, completeness. Compared to the approach of the Directive, we note that some principles are not covered by the latter. It is the case, for example, for relevance and neutrality[12].

---

10 The IASB must be kept separated from the IAASB, that we mentioned above in § 5. The two boards work closely together on their respective plans, on the development of standards, etc., but they act at different levels and with diverse goals.

11 The "European Financial Reporting Advisory Group" ("EFRAG"), an independent organization providing expert advice to the Commission, and the "Accounting Regulatory Committee" ("ARC"), composed of representatives of EU countries and chaired by the European Commission.

12 Information should be relevant to the decision making needs of the user, helping them in predicting future trends of the business (predictive value) or confirming or correcting any past predictions they have made (confirmatory value). Neutrality implies that information contained in the financial statements should be free from bias and reflect a balanced view of the affairs of the company, without attempting to present them in a favored light.

On the other hand, other principles appear to take on a different weight in the view of the Directives compared to the IAS/IFRS principles. This is the case, for example, with the principle of prudence, which constitutes a cardinal principle in the perspective of the Directives but is considered to be a secondary principle in the IAS/IFRS system.

Anyway, the core of the IAS/IFRS regulation relies in the current ("fair") value measurement of the assets and liabilities.

As it has been noted, "it is clear that one of the main advantages of fair value accounting is the market-based representation. This measurement contemplates a hypothetical transaction between market participants on a specific date and, therefore, 'captures the essence' of the company's performance in its dynamic and continuous process of evolution [...]. Fair value accounting should aim to assure the reliability of the accounting representation of the performance that evolves continuously along with the process of business management. In this context a financial information system based on fair value can assure consistency between the characteristics of the continuous process of business management and its accounting representation"[13].

Information therefore has to be updated every year in order to reflect the fair value. According to the "Conceptual framework for financial reporting" issued by the IASB in September 2010 (and revised in March 2018), "because of the updating, current values of assets and liabilities reflect changes, since the previous measurement date, in estimates of cash flows and other factors reflected in those current values. Unlike historical cost, the current value of an asset or liability is not derived, even in part, from the price of the transaction or other event that gave rise to the asset or liability".

7. Profit and dividends (and the "right to dividend" acknowledged by some legislations)

Once the financial statements show that the company has realized a profit, the shareholders' general meeting may decide to distribute it – in full or in part – as dividends[14].

---

13 See Cisi, *Differences*, 41.
14 Most Member States also have provisions which allow for the adoption of a decision to distribute dividends more than once a year in the form of "interim" dividends.

In many jurisdictions, the general meeting votes on a proposal of distribution made by the directors and, therefore, the decision-making power to distribute is first assigned to them[15].

As a consequence, in almost all Member States, minority shareholders may only exert indirect control over dividend distribution through their voting at the general meeting, and in several jurisdictions provided that the distribution has been proposed by the directors.

However, some companies acts have introduced provisions aiming to grant to the minority shareholders a kind of "right to dividend". The Finnish and Swedish laws merit consideration in particular: at the request of the holders of at least 1/10 of the shares, the general meeting must adopt a resolution to pay dividends from the profit for the financial year remaining after making allocations to cover previous losses, if there are no other available reserves. However, the general meeting shall not be obliged to resolve upon a distribution in excess of 8% – 5% (respectively) of the company's shareholders' equity[16].

Portuguese law also goes along these lines (even more generously): 50% of financial year profits must be distributed among the shareholders unless otherwise specified by the instrument of incorporation or the articles of association, or else agreed upon by a qualified majority of 75% of the votes (see Art. 348-bis Por-CA).

Finally – as we have already seen (Chapter 6, § 5) – the Spanish companies act has recently introduced the right for shareholders to have their shares bought out by the company in the case of continued failure to distribute dividends: any shareholder who voted in favour of dividend distribution shall have the right to exit the company if the general meeting does not agree to distribute at least one third of the legally distributable profits from the previous financial year.

In some Member States a similar right to sell out the shares is acknowledged by case law, provided that the an oppressive conduct of the majority is proved (see Chapter 6, § 5), while under other legislations the repeated refusal by the

---

15 For instance, under Danish, French and Italian laws, a board's approval and/or recommendation is required for dividend distribution. Pursuant to Sect. 58 Ge-PuCA, the board has the right to allocate a maximum of 50% of company profits to the reserves, thereby depriving shareholders of their right to decide on the distribution of this amount; only the remaining amount may be distributed according to the general meeting's decision (without any further involvement from the board).

16 See Ch. 13, Sect. 7, Fi-CA and Ch. 8, Sect. 11, Sw-CA.

majority to distribute dividends allows the minority to bring an action for damages against the majority shareholder(s)[17].

Of course – as already discussed – shareholders may always obtain a permanent "right to dividend" by negotiating the issue of specific classes of shares with priorities attached with respect to dividend distribution (see above Chapter 4, § 3).

---

17 See for instance, under Italian law, Court of Turin, 19 April 2017 (case "Pencil"): "even if there is no shareholder's right to the net profit for the year until a resolution of the shareholders' general meeting has been passed on the allocation of the profit itself as a dividend, there is certainly a legitimate expectation on the part of the shareholders to receive an adequate remuneration for the investment made, i.e. fair and reasonable, which does not depress the value of the shareholding. Also in this matter, it is therefore possible to re-examine the exercise of the power of the shareholders' general meeting, which may lead to the annulment of the resolution if it is demonstrated – also on the basis of presumption – that an extra-social interest has led the majority to preempt the individual rights of the individual shareholders, making a distorted use and abusing the discretionary power that it is entitled to by law".

9 Duties and liabilities of directors and supervisors

Summary:
1. Directors' duties
2. Supervisory board members' and statutory auditors' duties
3. Auditors' duties
4. Liabilities and proceedings
5. Liability rules between "company" and "insolvency" law: the CJEU judgment on the *Kornhaas* case
6. Shareholders' liability

1. Directors' duties

The competencies of the board of directors, of the supervisory board (in the two-tier system) and of the statutory auditors (in the one-tier system, in the latin version) have been already outlined in Chapter 3.

In this Chapter we shall focus on the specific duties of the members of these corporate bodies, their liabilities and the way in which the latter can be enforced by the company, the shareholders and third parties.

Beginning with the directors, they are the responsible for the management of the company's affairs.

(I) In all Member States, the laws provide that directors have firstly a duty to act with the care and skill that can reasonably be required in the conduct of business. Even if the wording may be slightly different, the core meaning is that they have to follow a regulatory standard of "diligence", which may be further developed by the courts[1] (taking into consideration, for instance, the personal skills, the profession, etc., of each single director)[2].

---

[1] As noted by Gerner-Beuerle/Schuster, *The evolving structure of directors' duties in Europe*, in *EBOR*, 2014, 191 ff., in spite of differences in regulatory technique and legal tradition, the effect of the legal strategies employed by the Member States in this field "is often remarkably similar and legal systems exhibit interconnections in the form of mutual learning across borders"; in any case, a "point of difference between Member States is the level of detail with which duties are formulated in statute or case law. Some jurisdictions provide for a largely exhaustive list of narrowly defined duties, and others rely on a general clause that lays down the behavioural expectations of directors in broad terms"; for similar conclusions see also Dotevall, *Is a common structure of company directors' duties evolving in EU?*, in *EBLR*, 2016, 285.

https://doi.org/10.1515/9783110725025-011

In shaping that standard, courts are usually required to apply the "business judgment rule", a tool acquired from US corporate law. This rather pragmatic criterion holds that directors will not be deemed liable for their actions in cases where it is clear that they had made their decisions in an informed manner, within the boundaries of rationality and free of any interests of third parties or themselves.

Many national companies acts have therefore developed a system close to the US one, introducing a duty of care at a legislative level (as a "standard of conduct"), while endorsing – at a more informal level – the development of the business judgment rule (as a "standard of review", to be mainly employed by the judges)[3].

As a consequence, directors normally know that they must act with care and skill, but they are aware at the same time that they will not be held responsible by the courts for company losses as long as they have acted loyally and on an informed and rational basis. This should encourage a more risk tolerant attitude, while allowing the most negligent directors' actions to be sanctioned.

---

2 Some jurisdictions, however, do not allow distinctions to be drawn on subjective elements. On the objective/subjective standards see especially Gerner-Beuerle/Schuster, *Mapping directors' duties: strategies and trends in the EU*, in Birkmose/Neville/Sørensen (eds.), *Boards*, 17 (affirming however that the difference between the two standards "should not be overstated").

3 The business judgment rule has been incorporated into the regulation of a few Member States, like i.e. Germany (Sect. 93 Ge-PuCA), Romania [Art. 144(1) R-CA], Portugal (Art. 72 Por-CC) and Spain (Art. 266 Sp-CA). In the majority of the jurisdictions it remains a rule that has to be inferred from the general principles of law (see i.e. Jastrzebski, *Corporate directors liability in Polish law*, in EFCR, 2017, 82; see also Werlauff, *How to try cases on board and management liability after a financial crisis*, in ECL, 2020, 72, illustrating the Danish Supreme Court's decision in the "Capinordic Bank" case of 15 Januar 2019, that has acknowledged the existence of the rule); cf. also Gerner-Beuerle/Schuster, *The evolving*, 203ff.; Gerner-Beuerle/Schillig, *Comparative*, 506ff.; Told, *Business judgment rule. A generally applicable principle?*, in EBLR, 2015, 713.

From its side, the EMCA, although rather generic, is very clear in recognizing the provision: on the one hand it states that it "should be formulated in such a way, that a director or managing director will not be deemed liable for their actions in cases where it is clear that they had a justifiable basis for making a decision and that they had an overview of the company's financial position" (see the general comments to Ch. 10); on the other hand it stipulates that "a director who makes a business judgement in good faith fulfils the duty under this Section if he or she: (a) is not interested in the subject of the business judgement; (b) is informed with respect to the subject of the business judgement to the extent that the director or managing director reasonably believes to be appropriate under the circumstances; (c) rationally believes that the business judgement is in the best interests of the company" (Sect. 10:01 EMCA; see for a comment Engrácia Antunes/Fuentes Naharro, *Director's' duties and conflicts of interest in the EMCA*, in ECFR, 2016, 269; Cebriá, *The Spanish and the European codification of the business judgment rule*, in ECFR, 2018, 41).

The duties of directors have to be interpreted in relation to the specific position they hold on the board and the information they receive (from the other directors and/or the company's employees, as the case may be[4]): therefore the distinction between executive and non-executive directors is important and the issue of the information flows is paramount (see also above Chapter 3, § 3).

The chairman of the board may also be attributed – and it is often imposed by law – extra specific duties like the one to collect information to be circulated prior to the board meeting and to make sure that the board operates in an efficient manner[5].

(II) Secondly, directors must avoid acting in conflict situations to the detriment of the company's interest. The regulatory techniques adopted by Member States in order to pursue this aim are rather different[6].

---

4 Normally each director has full access to information on the company in order to fulfil his duties defined under the law. In some countries, however, this right is restricted and non-executive directors may only receive information prior to or during the board meeting, essentially from the chairperson (prior) or the executive directors (during). The underpinning rationale is that non-executive directors should not be given the responsibility to constantly monitor company activity and they should be asked to monitor only as long as they participate in the meetings, in order to limit their subsequent possible liability (see along these lines Art. 2381 It-CC: information is restricted to the documents previously circulated by the chairperson and the ones disclosed – during the meeting – by the executive directors). On the contrary, e.g. Spanish law recognizes the director's right to obtain the adequate and necessary information to fulfil his duties from the company (see Art. 225 Sp-CA): although it is generally accepted that this right includes the right to have access to all the documents of the company and to interview the staff (which is actually often very important), "it is controversial as to whether the right to information includes the right to obtain a copy of the documents of the company including the minutes of the meetings of the management committees or the minutes of the board of directors" (see Marín de la Bárcena, in *Company laws*, 1142). Regarding French law, Pietrancosta/Dubois/Garçon, *Corporate*, 207 notes instead that normally a director may not request information and documents directly from employees; however, if the information is urgently required, he may obtain a court decision ordering that the relevant documents are immediately delivered.
5 See i.e. Ch. 8, Sect. 17, Sw-CA ("the chairman shall preside over the work of the board of directors and monitor that the board performs the duties set forth" in the companies act); Art. 2381 It-CC ("the chairman calls the board of directors, sets the agenda, coordinates its work and ensures that adequate information on the items on the agenda is provided to all directors"); also under French case law, the chairman of the board of directors must provide "in council" all the information necessary for an informed deliberation of its members on the questions debated in meeting (cf. Pietrancosta/Dubois/Garçon, *Corporate*, 207). The role of the chairperson is emphasized also by the EMCA: see Sect. 8.03, pursuant to which "the chairman is responsible for the leadership of the board and ensuring its effectiveness in all aspects of its role".
6 For a comparative overview see Krüger Andersen/Balsøj, *Directors' conflicts of interest: a contribution to European convergence*, in Birkmose/Neville/Sørensen (eds.), *Boards*, 57; Hopt, *Conflict of interest, secrecy and insider information of directors, a comparative analysis*, in *ECFR*,

Some companies acts simply impose a duty of loyalty on directors, other set forth rules (more or less specific) aimed at tackling situations of conflict[7].

Usually national legislations require prior disclosure to other directors anytime the transaction sees the company as a counterpart and the director has a relevant interest[8]; more frequently – in addition to disclosure – directors in conflict will have to refrain from taking part in the decision, which is referred to the board[9]. In some cases, the transaction also has to be approved by the general meeting (or the supervisory board in the dualistic system[10]; the decision is normally transferred to the next level in the case of a sole director). More complex rules are set forth for listed companies (see on that below Chapter 12, § 2).

Rather pragmatically, Sect. 9.05 EMCA takes an approach that embraces the various possible solutions, stating that "(1) directors shall inform the board of directors or, in the absence thereof, the other directors or, in the event of a

---

2013, 167; Gerner-Beuerle/Schuster, *The evolving*, 206 (observing that "the duty of loyalty has a long tradition in the common law world, where it can be traced back to the partnership and trust roots of company law. A considerable body of case law has given it well-defined contours. The duty applies comprehensively to any situation giving rise to a conflict, or potential conflict, of interest between the director and the company. Legal systems belonging to the civil law tradition, in contrast, often have not developed an all-encompassing no-conflict rule or have not included an express formulation of the duty of loyalty in their company law statutes. This does not necessarily indicate gaps in the legal system, because all jurisdictions are familiar with fiduciary principles derived from general civil law, for example, the law on agency. These fiduciary concepts inform much of company law and can be relied on where the rules on directors' duties do not address a particular conflict").

7 A noteworthy exception is German law, where the duty of loyalty has not been codified in the companies act (and must be inferred from the duty of care: according to Schall, in *Company laws*, 272 "this may well explain why the law on directors' duties of loyalty and good faith is still considered underdeveloped in Germany"). Also, Finnish law limits itself to state that "the management of the company shall act with due care and promote the interests of the company" (Ch. 1, Sect. 8, Fi-CA).

8 See i.e. Sect. 231 Ir-CA and Art. 2391 It-CC (in the latter case also the statutory auditors have to be informed).

9 See i.e. Arts. 5.76 B-CCA; 441-7 Lu-CA; 397 Por-CA and 229 f. Sp-CA; Ch. 8, Sect. 23, Sw-CA.

10 This is the case of Art. 225-38 Fr-CC: "any agreement entered into, either directly or through an intermediary, between the company and its general manager, with one of its assistant general managers, one of its directors, [...] with the company which controls it [...] must be subject to the prior consent of the board of directors". Moreover, according to Art. 225-40 Fr-CC, the chairperson of the board of directors shall notify the statutory auditors of the agreements and commitments authorized and finalized in application of Art. 225-38 Fr-CC, within one month from the finalization of these agreements and commitments. It also states, for each agreement and commitment authorized and finalized, the reasons justifying their interest for the company, adopted by the board of directors in application of the last paragraph of Art. 225-38 Fr-CC. Normally, however, the shareholders' general meeting is also asked to approve the agreement.

sole director, the general meeting, of any situation that may involve a conflict of interest between their own and the company's interest. Directors in such a situation shall refrain from taking part in the agreements or decisions relative to the operation/transaction around which the conflict has arisen. (2) This duty to inform [...] is not breached if the matter has been authorized by the disinterested directors or the general meeting".

A resolution passed by the board with the participation of one or more conflicted directors (or in the case of lack of disclosure) is normally voidable and may give rise to liability[11].

(III) The reference to the "interest of the company" raises the question of what such an interest is (we have already made reference to this issue above in Chapter 2, § 1). The topic is relevant for both the duty of care and loyalty since it affects the decisions that directors have to take whether there is a conflictual interest or not.

Take for instance the decision to buy an asset with a bank's loan (in the simplest case, from an unrelated third party, not in a situation of conflict), which could be deemed positive for shareholders since it could increase the prospects of dividends and maximize the value of their shares, but much less appealing for creditors, because it increases the company's debt. It is of course very different from the directors' point of view to have complete freedom to decide whether to pursue the deal (taking into consideration only the effect on shareholders) or, on the opposite, to have to comply with laws that require to ponder also the interest of creditors and/or of other stakeholders.

Most Member States do not specify the concept of company's interest, and therefore leave the option of interpreting it as the interest of the sole shareholders as long as specific laws do not constrain them and require to consider also other stakeholders, like creditors, employees, etc.

Other States take the opposite view and permit or require directors to also consider the interests of other stakeholders (some laws, for instance, ask directors to observe "duties of loyalty, in the interest of the company, taking into account the long-term interests of shareholders and concerning the interests of other stakeholders relevant to the sustainability of the company, such as their employees, clients and creditors"[12]).

---

11 This solution is normally provided for directly by the laws (see i.e. Art. 2.15 Du-CC); alternatively, it is set out by case law (see i.e. for Ireland, Thuillier, *Company*, 92).

12 As already mentioned (see above Chapter 2, § 2), paradigmatical in this regard are Art. 64 Por-CC (where the quotation in the text comes from) and Sect. 70 A-PuCA. This view is also shared in Germany (although not reflected in the law): see Schall, in *Company laws*, 264: "according to the traditional, still prevalent view, the management has to conduct the business

The question is much debated among scholars. Usually it is held that the broader concept of company's interest (i. e. long term, many stakeholders) is less efficient, since it does not provide a clear driver for directors, who could have to face too many complications in taking care of different stakeholders' interests before deciding (this model also makes managers less accountable). On the other hand, the customary criticism is that if only the short-term interests of shareholders are considered, directors could employ a riskier and more short-sighted management style.

The EMCA Group adopts basically a "pluralist" approach and holds that the directors should operate for the "success of the company" (which is actually also a different concept from the more precise one of company's "value" or, even better, shareholders' value[13]).

This notion does not bring much to the discussion. The same Group appears to be conscious of this and states that "the word 'success' is used because not all companies are aimed at maximizing the financial interests of their members. In such cases, maximizing the value of the company is not the primary objective of its members and perhaps not even an objective at all" (thus is, however, not fully

---

with a view to the interests of all the company's stakeholders that are the shareholders, the employees, the creditors and the general public"; "in line with the stakeholder approach, the German Corporate Governance Code expresses in 4.1.1: 'the management board assumes full responsibility for managing the company in the best interests of the company, meaning that it considers the needs of the shareholders, the employees and other stakeholders, with the objective of sustainable value creation'. Those interests need to be balanced out fairly against each other by the management board. This is not to say that there can never be any priority. To the contrary: since the corporation is fuelled by the money of the shareholders, it is understood that their interests need to be given, and will often be given more weight than those of other constituencies in the balancing exercise. But: the balancing needs to be done!". On the opposite side, see, for instance, under Swedish law, Skog/Sjöman, *Corporate*, 258: "a board member owes his or her duties to the company as a whole (i. e., to all shareholders)"; "nevertheless, specific legislation in other segments together form a comprehensive network for the protection of external stakeholders and society at large – for example, employment law, work environmental law, environmental law, competition law, marketing law, tax law, etc. – with which a company must comply".

13 The latter concept is reminiscent of the exclusive "shareholders' value" idea (see Chapter 2, § 1). See however also Sect. 9.04 (and the comment), where, more explicitly, the Group states that "the director should have regard to a range of factors such as the long-term interests of the company, the interests of the company's employees, the interest of company's creditors and the impact of the company's operations on the community and the environment". Some Member States' laws maintain their focus on a wider company interest also with reference to the specific takeovers regulation (see below Chapter 12, § 3).

true, since it is difficult to deny that in the practice most companies are aimed at maximizing their shareholders' financial interests).

As far as timing is concerned, the EMCA Group believes "that the interests of the company in the medium to long term should be the focus of the directors' attention" (and this is another very critical issue, since the concept of "long term" is inevitably very vague; we shall come back to the dispute between "long-term value governance" vs. "short-terminism" in Chapter 12, § 2).

In the end, the question seems to be political. Member States considering that the interests of all stakeholders are important, and that the time-horizon in which they should be realized must be medium-long, may introduce regulations along these lines; other Member States will not. And this is actually the current state of the art in the various national laws[14].

In any case, one should recognize that shareholders' primacy is still the dominant view, at least among scholars, for the reasons described above.

(IV) Special provisions are often devoted to the issues of "corporate opportunities" and "competition with the company"[15].

As far as the corporate opportunities are concerned, usually a director may not personally (or on behalf of third parties) exploit a corporate opportunity (i.e. a possible business that has been originated by the company). Some Member States have introduced specific rules on corporate opportunities, while others seek to protect the company's business only through the director's duty of loyalty.

Competition with the company is instead normally addressed by means of rules stating that a director may not carry out a competing activity with the company (or be a manager or director of a competing company) without prior appro-

---

14 Hansen, *The Report*, 15, notes that "to remove the pressure on management from shareholders, who might be eager to press for short-term gains in an irresponsible way, it was suggested [by the Reflection Group in 2009] that the company could adopt in its articles a provision that the company should be run in the long-term interest of the company and that this aim should have priority over shareholders in case of a conflict. This is known from Dutch company law. From a Nordic perspective, this is an acceptable proposition, because the adoption in the articles should be decided by the shareholders, though it is not very likely to occur".

15 There is sometimes controversy (but probably unfounded) as to whether the business judgment rule is applicable to decisions concerning the establishment of such a system (and, more in general, to the fulfilment of "oversight" functions: see for instance Marín de la Bárcena, in *Company laws*, 1140; Schall, *ibidem*, 276, illustrating how "some writers suggest a liability-free zone of managerial discretion when organising the company's compliance system by way of analogy to the business judgement rule" (adding, however, that the argument is challenged).

val by the disinterested directors or the general meeting. On the contrary, some Member States do not regulate the matter and prefer to leave it to the case law[16].

The EMCA governs both corporate opportunities and competition with the company (see Sect. 9.06 and 9.07).

(V) Many companies acts contain provisions which compel directors to build and regularly evaluate the adequacy of the company's risk monitoring system (under some laws, this organization is called the "internal control system" or the "organizational, administrative and accounting" framework of the firm)[17]. Actually this type of duty should be considered to be in any case in place as a specification of the general duty of care.

As a consequence, the directors must implement structures and policies that enable them to promptly detect events or behaviors which may put the company at risk and which allow them to adopt adequate countermeasures.

These specific provisions are gaining more and more importance, in order to both manage risk and enhance the company's efficiency[18].

(VI) Some Member States' laws impose duties on directors that are expressly aimed to protect creditors[19].

In Ireland, for example, a liability rule on "wrongful trading" is set out in Sect. 610 Ir-CA, to the effect that the directors may be held liable to the creditors for carrying out the business of the company in a reckless manner, or with the intent to defraud creditors. Danish and Swedish laws (but also, i.e., the Italian) include other rules with a creditor perspective, namely that directors have a re-

---

16 The case law solution is preferred in many Member States such as the Netherlands and the Nordic countries. A special provision on competition is for example to be found in Germany (Sect. 88 Ge-PuCA). In any case, as observed by Gerner-Beuerle/Schuster, *The evolving*, 213, in all Member States "the law seems to be elastic enough to address conflicts of interest where regulatory intervention is deemed expedient, notwithstanding the regulatory technique employed by the legal system. Even jurisdictions with no express regulation of corporate opportunities and no comprehensively codified duty of loyalty have achieved results driven by case law and judicial innovation that are similar to that" of the Member States with more specific provisions.
17 See paradigmatically Sect. 91 Ge-PuCA (see Gerner-Beuerle/Schillig, *Comparative*, 548) and Ch. 8, Sect. 4, Sw-CA. Italian law is also particularly extensive, according to which, on the one hand, the board of directors must "evaluate", based on the information received, the adequacy of the company's organizational, administrative and accounting structure; while, on the other hand, the executive directors must "ensure" that such a structure is adequate for the nature and size of the company (Art. 2381 It-CC); see Tina, in *Company laws*, 510.
18 See extensively Van der Elst, *The risk management duties of the board of directors*, in Birkmose/Neville/Sørensen (ed.), *Boards*, 129.
19 For a useful general description, see Gerner-Beuerle/Schuster, *Mapping*, 43.

sponsibility to ensure that the company has an adequate capital base in order to carry on business or to preserve the integrity of the corporate assets[20].

Also the EMCA lays down rules designed to protect creditors, by ensuring that the company has an adequate capital base or, as in the case of wrongful trading, by imposing a duty on the directors to avoid acting in a reckless manner and recalling some domestic provisions on wrongful trading (see Sect. 10:04: "directors may be liable if the company continues its business at a time when the directors knew or ought to have concluded that there was no reasonable prospect of the company being able to pay its creditors").

(VII) As we have seen (above Chapter 2, § 10), Directive 1132/2017/EU (and also the EMCA) set forth rules introducing specific directors' duties in case of relevant losses.

As a prototype (along the lines set out by Art. 58 of the Directive), we may recall Sect. 8.30 of the EMCA, pursuant to which "if it is established that the equity of a company represents less than half of the subscribed capital, or in the case of negative net assets, the management of the company must ensure that a general meeting is held within six months. At the general meeting, the board must report the financial position of the company and, if necessary, submit a proposal for measures that should be taken, including a proposal for dissolution of the company".

Please refer to Chapter 2, § 10 above for more information on the subject.

(VIII) Some laws expressly instruct directors to file for bankruptcy in the case of insolvency of the company[21] (however, a similar duty may be inferred from the duty of care in the absence of a specific provision).

The recognition of the duties of directors in the earlier phase of "pre-insolvency" (which may also occur in the absence of losses) is more delicate. In such

---

20 See Art. 2394 It-CC (devoted to the liability suit that creditors may file): "the administrators are liable to the corporate creditors for the non-compliance with the obligations inherent to the preservation of the integrity of the corporate assets". See also, for a domestic liability regime functionally equivalent to the "wrongful trading" one sketched above, Antunes, *"Law"*, 365 ("Portuguese law of insolvency provided for a direct and joint liability of directors of a corporation once it has been ascertained they had a significant contribution to the corporate insolvency").

21 This is particularly the case under Estonian, French, German, Portuguese and Spanish laws: for instance, according to Sect. 15a Ge-InsA, managing directors of a German company are obliged to file for insolvency if the company is illiquid or over-indebted; the petition must be filed without undue delay, at the latest, however, within three weeks of the occurrence of the illiquidity or over-indebtedness. See e.g. Schmidt, *Ground for insolvency and liability for delays in filing for insolvency proceeding*, in Lutter (ed.), *Legal*, 144; see above all the particularly extended essay of Kalls/Adensamer/Oelkers, *Director's*, 112.

a case, it is highly debated if the escalation of the financial and economic difficulties which may bring the company to the verge of insolvency should result in a shift of the director's duties and oblige them to consider solely the interests of creditors[22].

The discussion has recently been impacted by the promulgation of Directive 2019/1023/EU (the "Directive on restructuring and insolvency"). Recital 70 reads as follows: "to further promote preventive restructuring, it is important to ensure that directors are not dissuaded from exercising reasonable business judgment or taking reasonable commercial risks, particularly where to do so would improve the chances of a restructuring of potentially viable businesses. Where the company experiences financial difficulties, directors should take steps to minimize losses and to avoid insolvency, such as: seeking professional advice, including on restructuring and insolvency, for instance by making use of early warning tools where applicable; protecting the assets of the company so as to maximize value and avoid loss of key assets; considering the structure and functions of the business to examine viability and reduce expenditure; refraining from committing the company to the types of transaction that might be subject to avoidance unless there is an appropriate business justification; continuing to trade in circumstances where it is appropriate to do so in order to maximise going-concern value; holding negotiations with creditors and entering preventive restructuring procedures".

Recital 71 (which emphasizes creditors' interests) affirms that "where the debtor is close to insolvency, it is also important to protect the legitimate interests of creditors from management decisions that may have an impact on the constitution of the debtor's estate, in particular where those decisions could have the effect of further diminishing the value of the estate available for restructuring efforts or for distribution to creditors. It is therefore necessary to ensure that, in such circumstances, directors avoid any deliberate or grossly negligent actions that result in personal gain at the expense of stakeholders, and avoid agreeing to transactions at below market value, or taking actions leading to unfair preference being given to one or more stakeholders".

Notwithstanding – probably aware of the delicacy of the debate – the same Recital 71 states that "the Directive is not intended to establish any hierarchy

---

22 For an illustration of the debate see recently Henriques, *The duties of directors when there is a likelihood of insolvency and the proposal for a new directive*, in *ECL*, 2019, 50. The position of the German literature, for instance, is illustrated by Schall, in *Company laws*, 274, as follows: under German law, "unlike under some common law jurisdictions [...], there is no general concept of shifting fiduciary duties towards the creditors in times of crisis. If the company enters troubled waters, the director will still have to act according to the interests of the enterprise".

among the different parties whose interests need to be given due regard. However, Member States should be able to decide on establishing such a hierarchy".

Article 19 – called "duties of directors where there is a likelihood of insolvency" – stipulates that Member States have to ensure that, where there is a likelihood of insolvency, directors must have due regard to "(a) the interests of creditors, equity holders and other stakeholders; (b) the need to take steps to avoid insolvency; and (c) the need to Notwithstanding avoid deliberate or grossly negligent conduct that threatens the viability of the business".

Therefore, the issue of the relevant interests to be considered by the directors is still open, also with reference to the critical company pre-insolvency phase.

(IX) Some laws provide for special duties for the directors of the parent company (in a group) and related specific responsibilities, both towards minority shareholders of the subsidiaries and their creditors. For these more complex liability regimes, see above Chapter 7, §§ 3, 4[23].

(X) A final note. As one can easily see, the system of the rules on the duties of the directors is very complex; many duties cross and often add up.

In general the situation may be simplified the closer you get to a model in which the directors must operate only in the interests of the shareholders, unless some external rules require that the interests of other categories are taken into account, and these latter external rules – thought for other stakeholders – are simple and clear-cut.

This presupposes, however, also that other systems of rules set forth by the broader legislation aimed at protecting other stakeholders and in first place creditors (like contractual and bankruptcy rules) are also efficient.

The liability rules necessary to enforce sanctions against directors and supervisors should be simple and effective, too (we will return to this below in § 4). A net solution is not, therefore, easy to find.

2. Supervisory board members' and statutory auditors' duties

The competencies of the supervisory board (in the two-tier system) and of the statutory auditors (in the one-tier system, in the latin version) have already

---

23 Some companies acts expressly regulate these kinds of duties and liabilities, even though similar results may also be achieved in jurisdictions which do not contain explicit provisions, on the basis of the general principles of the law: see i. e., with reference to Dutch case law, Borrius, *Directors liability: the Netherlands*, in *ECL*, 2011, 247.

been examined in Chapter 3, § 4. In this paragraph we shall briefly consider the duties of the members of these corporate bodies and their liabilities.

(I) Starting from the supervisory board in the two-tier model, their main duty is to act with skill and care in performing the various tasks for which they are empowered (from monitoring management to the decisions on significant transactions, and so on).

For instance, Sect. 116 Ge-PuCA refers to Sect. 93 Ge-PuCA, which in turn determines the duty of care to which the members of the board of directors are subject. The respective rules that apply to members of both bodies may therefore generally said to be equivalent[24].

The duties of the supervisors have, however, to be interpreted in relation to the information they receive – from the management board or the auditors – on corporate planning, the company's financial situation and significant transactions[25].

Beyond the duty of care, the members of the supervisory board are normally subject to a duty of confidentiality (for instance, Sect. 116 Ge-PuCA determines both the supervisory board member's duty of care and their duty of confidentiality). Supervisory board members must not disclose confidential information and secrets of the company, in particular trade and business secrets which have become known to them as a result of their supervisory board membership.

Finally, the supervisory board members are subject to fiduciary duties which require them to be loyal to the company and to protect its interests.

(II) As far as the duties of the statutory auditors are concerned, they must carry out their obligation with the skill and diligence required by the nature of the assignment.

Moreover – pursuant to some national laws – statutory auditors are also responsible for the truthfulness of their statements and shall keep all facts and documents they are informed about in connection with their office confidential (see, for instance, Art. 2407 It-CC).

---

24 See Poelzig/Bärnreuther, in *Company laws*, 306.
25 See for the German companies act, Schall, in *Company laws*, 286. In general, this standard of care applies to all members of the supervisory board to the same degree, the exception being a higher standard of care for those members that bring special skills with them when taking office.

3. Auditors' duties

The main tasks of the auditors – in all the governance systems – have already been examined in Chapter 8, § 5. In this paragraph we shall consider the duties of the auditors and their liabilities.

(I) The main task of the auditors is to examine the company's accounts and the annual financial statements in accordance with the national laws.

The "Auditing Directive" (2013/34/EU, as amended by Directive 2014/95/EU) contains comprehensive rules on auditing, including the scope of the statutory audit, use of auditing standards, audit reporting, etc. and detailed rules on auditing have been implemented in national laws. The auditors must operate in accordance with all these provisions.

The auditor must ensure that the company's management fulfil their obligations to draw up rules of procedure and prepare and keep books, records and minutes, and that the rules on the submission and signing of audit records are complied with (see for instance EMCA, Sect. 12.8).

If the auditor finds that the requirements are not met, he must prepare a declaration to that effect to accompany the company's annual report (the declaration may also be contained in the auditor's report).

Special rules are usually laid down for the auditors' activities in company groups.

(II) A sensitive issue is whether the audit firm's tasks go (or should go) beyond the audit of financial statements and the assessment of whether the management has undertaken all the measures incumbent on it for adequate accountability.

Pursuant to some companies acts, the auditor must also check whether a risk monitoring system is operating efficiently. Neither the Auditing Directive nor the EMCA contain similar provisions; on the other hand, they are found in the Danish and Swedish laws which tend to support broader action by the auditors ("the auditor shall examine the management by the board of directors and the managing director"[26]).

One should, however, consider that auditors must operate on the basis of international auditing standards, or "ISA" (see above Chapter 8, § 5). Among these standards, ISA 250 requires auditors – as part of their duty to comprehend the company and its environment – to obtain a general understanding of the legal

---

26 See i.e. Ch. 9, Sect. 3, Sw-CA. But see in both directions, for instance, also German law: see Hommelhoff, *Chapter 12*, 259.

and regulatory framework applicable to the firm and the industry or sector in which it operates and how the company is complying within that framework.

Therefore, the auditor must inquire from management (or, as appropriate, those charged with governance) whether the company is in compliance with all the laws and regulations that may have a material effect on the financial statements. During the audit, the auditor may request management to provide written representations that all known instances of non-compliance or suspected non-compliance with laws and regulations have been disclosed[27].

If the auditor becomes aware of information concerning an instance of non-compliance or suspected non-compliance, it must obtain an understanding of the nature of the act and the circumstances in which it occurred, and further information to evaluate the possible effect on the financial statements. If the auditor suspects there may be non-compliance, the auditor must discuss the matter with the appropriate level of management.

If management does not provide sufficient information and, in the auditor's judgment, the effect of the suspected non-compliance could be material to the financial statements either quantitatively or qualitatively, the auditor must consider the need to obtain legal advice and in any case, it will have to communicate the matter to the next level up of authority at the company, if it exists (e. g. an audit committee).

At this point, a question arises: must the auditors also report their findings to the public authorities?

Once again, neither the Auditing Directive nor the EMCA contain similar provisions. In some countries, like Denmark, however there are regulations requiring auditors to mention certain breaches of laws and regulations in their audit report to the general meeting (and thus give external evidence to them) if these breaches could give rise to civil liability or criminal liability for members of the management. The provision (which is very critical) is pragmatically interpreted in the following way: is civil or criminal liability a "possibility" because of the breaches? If the answer to this question is affirmative, then the auditor should mention the breaches in the audit report[28].

A liability for damages regime similar to the one set forth for directors and supervisors applies to auditors. If an audit firm has been engaged as auditor, both the audit firm and the auditor performing the audit are liable to the audited

---

27 The EMCA gives the auditor the right to demand that the members of the board provide relevant information that is deemed to be of importance for the assessment of the company and, if the company is a parent company, its group. The Auditing Directive does not set forth a similar provision, which is, however, contained in many companies acts.

28 See for further references Seehausen, *Auditors*, 89.

company and any third party entitled under national law to bring a claim for compensation[29].

4. Liabilities and proceedings

(I) In the majority of Member States, directors and supervisors are held to be jointly liable for the damage caused as a consequence of the breach of their duties[30].

Joint and several liability is only imposed on those who neglected their duties. A director who claims not to be liable must prove that he has acted diligently, for example by ensuring that any objections made to the decisions taken by

---

29 See Beckman/Nass, *Auditors' liability in the European Union*, in *ECL*, 2007, 103; Seehausen, *European*, 391, who reminds us that the European Commission has issued a few relevant recommendations, especially Recommendation 2008/473/EC, concerning the possible limitation of the civil liability of statutory auditors and audit firms. Formally, the recommendations are limited to auditors and audit firms carrying out audits for listed companies; but their provisions might also be relevant for auditors and audit firms carrying out audits for other companies. However, auditors' liability should not be limited to cases of intentional breach of duties. The recommendations are discussed i.e. by Flores, *New trends in auditor liability*, in *EBOR*, 2011, 415; Id., *Auditors' multi-layer liability regime*, in *EBOR*, 2012, 501; Foged-Ladefoged/Werlauff, *Limitation of auditors' liability: some comparative comments, and considerations under EU law, on the choice of method to limit liability*, in *ECL*, 2014, 271.

For a provision limiting auditors' liability see Art. 57 Slove-CA: "the auditor shall be liable to the company and to its shareholders as well as its company members for any damages resulting from a violation of the auditing rules laid down by the Act governing auditing. The auditor shall be liable for damages referred to in the previous sentence up to an amount of € 150.000 for small companies limited by shares, up to an amount of € 500.000 for medium-sized companies limited by shares and up to an amount of € 1.000.000 for large companies limited by shares. The liability for damages referred to in the preceding sentence may not be limited if damages were caused intentionally or through gross negligence".

30 The amount of liability is potentially unlimited; as an exception, one has to mentions the recent innovation of the Belgian companies act, which has set forth a maximum sum for which a director can be held liable (a concept relatively unique in the world of directors' liabilities). The threshold of the director's liability depends on the size of the company, which is determined in function of the turnover and the balance sheet total: see Art. 2.57 B-CA. This limitation is however subject to a number of important exceptions, in which case the director is liable for all the damages; the most important regards serious errors, fraudulent acts, and the like. As a counterbalancing measure to the limitation of the liability of directors, the B-CA introduces a prohibition for companies to exonerate their directors from directors' liability. So-called "hold-harmless agreements" will no longer be valid.

the board are documented in the minutes. The liability of a director (or a supervisor) is therefore dependent on an individual assessment[31].

Usually directors' (and supervisors') duties are "owed to the company". The company therefore has the right to take action against them. That means that the shareholders' general meeting has to table a resolution and vote in favour of the action[32]. In some national companies acts, once the resolution has been passed with a certain percentage of votes, the directors will lose office[33].

If the company does not want to table the resolution or it does not pass with a majority vote at the general meeting, some legislations provide minority shareholders with a so-called "derivative action". Normally the standing is given to shareholders who represent a certain percentage of the share capital or other amount envisaged in the articles of association[34]; sometimes even to a single

---

31 Interesting comparative remarks are to be found in Gerner-Beuerle/Schuster, *The evolving*, 203, with reference to the question of the burden of proof. The Authors observe that "less coherence exists with respect to the question of who bears the burden of proving due care. A number of Member States stipulate that the claimant shall bear the burden of proving lack of due care, for example, [...] Ireland, France, Spain, the Netherlands, Denmark and Sweden, while a roughly equal number of jurisdictions provide for a reversal of the burden of proof, for example, Germany, Austria, the Czech Republic, Italy, Slovenia and Portugal. However, the divide between these two approaches is not necessarily clear-cut" (see ibidem for some examples).

32 Normally the company may waive its claims to compensation, or make a settlement regarding these claims, provided that a certain number of shareholders approve the deal (20% of the share capital under Art. 2393 It-CC; 10% under Sect. 93 Ge-PuCA, but in this latter case only once three years have lapsed since the claim arises).

33 See i.e. Art. 2393 It-CC.

34 1% under Art. 7.157 B-CA and Sect. 148 Ge-PuCA, 5% under Art. 77 Por-CA, 20% under Art. 2393-*bis* It-CC, etc.. In this case, the action is filed by the minority through one or more common representatives, appointed by the majority of capital held. However, Sect. 148 Ge-PuCA provides that the court must refuse the application if there are "overriding interests" of the company that prevent the enforcement of the claim. The reference to overriding interests is meant to operate as a filter to effectively screen out frivolous and vexatious shareholder actions; to do so, the court will have to apply a test of proportionality in which all arguments relevant to the admission decision will have to be objectively weighed against one another (cf. Paul, *Derivative actions under English and German corporate law – shareholder participation between the tension filled areas of corporate governance and malicious shareholder interference*, in ECFR, 2010, 81). In Spain, on a subsidiary basis, a corporate liability action can be brought by shareholders holding, individually or jointly, at least 5% of the share capital if the directors have not called a general meeting for this purpose; the company has not brought the action within one month from the adoption of the resolution; or the resolution was contrary to bringing the liability action. In any case, if the action is based on the directors' breach of their duty of loyalty, shareholders also holding at least 5% of the share capital can directly bring this action irrespective of any resolution of the shareholders' meeting (Art. 239 Sp-CA). For further analysis cf. especially Gerner-Beuerle/Schuster, *Mapping*, 36; and Latella, *Shareholder derivative suits: a com-*

shareholder[35]. If the claim succeeds, the company will reimburse the claimant shareholders for the costs of the proceedings and those incurred in ascertaining the facts.

The EMCA also regulates suits for damages against directors – and supervisors – that must be passed by the general meeting and shareholders' derivative suits (see Ch. 11, Sects. 38 and 39)[36].

Certain domestic laws lay down regulations that permit also creditors to file a suit against the directors (and supervisors). As said above (§ 1), board members may be liable to creditors for wrongful trading or for having eroded the net assets of the company. In such cases, those laws provide for a lawsuit that may be filed by single creditors[37].

Moreover, widespread are also other rules which permit individual shareholders or third parties to file suit against the directors (and supervisors) upon the condition that the shareholders/third parties have been "directly" harmed by the directors or supervisors (for example, when the latter have been induced by the the former to subscribe capital or provide financing on the basis of false financial statements)[38].

A company may purchase and maintain insurance on behalf of an individual director (or all directors) against liabilities asserted against him (or them) in that capacity. One possibility for the company to obtain compensation for an injury that directors have caused is therefore to take out liability insurance. This type of insurance is permitted in all Member States, although the matter is not always regulated in the companies acts (in certain cases insurance is, on the opposite,

parative analysis and the implications of the European shareholders' rights directive, in ECFR, 2009, 307

35 This is the case of Art. 225-252 Fr-CC. See Grelon, Shareholders' lawsuits against the management of a company and its shareholders under French law, in ECFR, 2009, 205

36 See Kalss, Shareholder suits, common problems, different solutions and different steps towards a possible harmonization by means of a European Model Code, in ECFR, 2009, 324.

37 See Sect. 93 Ge-PuCA, Art. 2394 It-CC and Art. 240 Sp-CA, in any case if the equity of the company is insufficient to settle the money they are owed. The action will be filed by the creditors in their own name but in the interests of the company according to Art. 240 Sp-CA; on the other hand, under German law the action will be brought in the interest of the creditor, provided that a gross breach is recognized; pursuant to the Italian civil code, since the specific provision is silent on the matter, both interpretations are covered by legal doctrine. However, normally it is difficult to prove that the equity of the company is insufficient.

38 This is the case of Art. 107 Gr-PuCA; Art. 2395 It-CC and Art. 241 Sp-CA. See also, for Dutch case law, Bisschop/Roelink/Kemp, in Company laws, 1327.

mandatory[39]). The insurance premium is generally paid by the company (see on that Sect. 10.06 EMCA).

(II) Finally, as far as the civil liability of the auditors is concerned, auditors who, in the performance of their duties to check the annual accounts and financial statements, have intentionally or negligently caused damage to the company, are liable to pay damages. The same applies where the damage is caused to shareholders or any third party.

The legal basis for liability and the extent of liability is normally covered by national contract or tort law, which varies and which the Directive does not try to harmonize (see on that EMCA Sect. 12.12).

5. Liability rules between "company" and "insolvency" law: the CJEU judgment on the *Kornhaas* case

Insolvency law is not a subject analyzed in this book.

Restructuring and insolvency proceedings are regulated by Directive 2019/1023/EU. Cross-border insolvencies are governed by Regulation 2015/848/EU (repealing the previous Regulation 1346/2000/EC).

A clear separation between the two areas – company law and insolvency law – is however not always possible (or, at least, simple). That is demonstrated by the Kornhaas case (C-594/14) decided in 2015 by the CJEU, regarding the application of the rules on directors' liability.

As a general rule, if the company goes bankrupt, the applicable insolvency law is the one of the state of the "real" seat (more precisely, the insolvency proceedings is brought before the courts of the Member State where the debtor has its "centre of main interests" or "COMI", defined as "the place where the debtor conducts the administration of its interests on a regular basis and which is ascertainable by third parties": see Art. 3 of Regulation 2015/848/EU).

The basic statement of the Court in the Kornhaas case is that the rules (or at least certain rules) on directors' liability should be classified as pertaining to "insolvency laws"; as a consequence, directors' liability should be covered by the provisions of the State where the company has its real seat (or the COMI), even if it is incorporated in another State.

The case regarded a private company (Kornhaas Ltd.), entered on the companies register in Cardiff (UK), with a branch established in Germany, which had gone bankrupt in 2006. On that basis, a suit against the sole director of

---

39 See i.e. Arts. 396 and 418 Por-CC respectively for directors and supervisory board members.

the company (Ms. Kornhaas) was brought before the Court of Jena, in Germany, by the judicial liquidator.

Claiming that the company had been insolvent and the director had made payments on some of his debts, the liquidator sought reimbursement from Ms. Kornhaas on the basis of Sect. 64 Ge-PrCA (now Sect. 15 Ge-InsA), which holds directors liable if they do not file for bankruptcy within three weeks from when the company becomes insolvent.

Ms Kornhaas' attorneys were instead trying to attract the case in the UK, as the State of incorporation of the company, and claimed that German courts had no jurisdiction.

After some proceedings, the case was finally brought before the CJEU. The Court held that the purpose of the German law (which is now identical both for public and private companies) was, in essence, "to prevent the assets of the insolvent estate being reduced before the opening of the insolvency proceedings and to ensure that those assets are available, so that the claims of all the company's creditors can be satisfied in the insolvency proceedings on equal terms". "That provision" – according to the judges – "although formally integrated in legislation on company law, falls, therefore, within insolvency law and is enforceable against a managing director of a limited liability company".

The Court affirmed that Regulation 1346/2000/EC (now Regulation 2015/848/EU) on insolvency proceedings must be interpreted "as meaning that an action directed against the managing director of a company established under the law of England and Wales, forming the subject of insolvency proceedings opened in Germany, brought before a German court by the liquidator of that company and seeking, on the basis of a national provision such as [Sect. 64 Ge-PrCA], reimbursement of payments made by that managing director before the opening of the insolvency proceedings but after the date on which the insolvency of that company was established, falls within its scope".

The important passage of the ruling is the one where the Court states that "the personal liability of the managing directors of a company on the basis of [Sect. 64 Ge-PrCA] is related, not to the fact that the capital of that company does not reach the minimum [share capital] amount laid down by the German legislation or by the legislation in accordance with which that company has been established, but only to the fact that, in essence, the managing directors of such a company have made payments at a stage when they would have been required, under [Sect. 64 Ge-PrCA], to apply for the opening of insolvency proceedings". In other word, it was not question of rules on capital, but of rules on insolvency.

The statement may however give rise to a high degree of arbitrariness (and uncertainty), since the liability of directors in the vicinity of insolvency (and even in the phase of actual insolvency) is, in some Member States, strictly linked to the rules on capital maintenance (see also above 1, and in Chapter 2, § 11), in other it is not.

In any case, the extent to which a liability rule belongs to "company law" or "insolvency law" may be debated at length; the ruling has therefore been strongly criticized[40].

6. Shareholders' liability

We shall finally deal with the issue of "shareholders' liability". Can shareholders be held liable for corporate actions performed by the company, notwithstanding the – much (and duly) celebrated – principle of the "limited liability" of the shareholders?

The argument is very sensitive, complex and could take us very far away. We shall therefore treat it only briefly.

The answer is basically no.

However there are some areas of law – and reasons – that justify exceptions.

Firstly, as we have seen, the regulation on groups of companies require – pursuant to important domestic laws – the parent company (in its status of main "shareholder" of the subsidiaries), under certain conditions, to be considered liable for the abusive actions carried out to the detriment of the minority shareholders and creditors (see above Chapter 7, § 3 and 4).

Secondly, investor-friendly legislations which recognize broad decision-making powers to shareholders in corporate matters (i.e. especially the Nordic countries: see above Chapter 3, § 4) seem more disposed to admit that shareholders may be obliged to compensate for damages caused as a consequence of their actions. In this regard, we may recall – paradigmatically – the sample of Ch. 29, Sect. 3, Sw-CA (entitled "liability in damages of the shareholders"), which reads as follow: "a shareholder shall compensate damage which he or she causes to the company, a shareholder or another person as a consequence of participating, intentionally or through gross negligence, in any violation of this Act,

---

40 See Lindemans, *The walls have fallen, run for the keep: insolvency law as the new company law for third parties*, in *Eur. rev. priv. l.*, 2016, 877; Wessels, *CJEU case note: CJEU 10 December 2015, C-594/14 (Kornhaas v. Dithmar)*, in *ECL*, 2016, 82; Szydło, *Directors' duties and liability in insolvency and the freedom of establishment of companies after* Kornhaas, in *CMLR*, 2017, 1853; Ringe, *Kornhaas and the challenge of applying Keck in establishment*, in *ELR*, 2017, 270; Lombardo, *Regulatory*, 188; Krawczyk/Giehsmann, *Shareholders' liability for ruining a company in light of the CJEU's judgment in Kornhaas*, in *EBOR*, 2020, 475.

the applicable annual reports legislation or the company's articles of association"[41].

Thirdly – and most importantly at a general level – almost all national legislations contain rules (of common or civil law tradition) compelling shareholders to act in "good faith" and "fairly" towards other shareholders, above all in the decision-making procedures.

As a consequence, (especially) the right to vote at the general meeting must be exercised without fraudulent intent towards the minority or without the aim of unjustifiably favoring the majority to the detriment of the minority. Resolutions adopted that breach these standards may be both invalid and grounds for liability.

Also the conduct of the minorities can be scrutinized in the light of the principle of good faith (for example, when they misuse their rights to inspect company's books or to challenge shareholders' meeting resolutions).

Finally, some Member State's companies acts and/or their case law also rely on the "piercing the corporate veil" doctrine.

Particularly serious case of fraud, wrongdoing, or injustice to third parties may be considered red flags allowing a court to find the liability of the (usually majority) shareholder for the company's debts (indeed, to "pierce the corporate veil").

As anticipated, the various applications made by each Member States' laws (and case law) are, however, too different and motivated by too dishomogeneous (nation-specific) underlying principles to be further examined here.

---

41 A similar provision is, however, also contained in other laws; see i.e. Sect. 117 Ge-PuCA: "anyone who intentionally compels, by exploiting his influence on the company, a member of the management board or of the supervisory board, [...] to act to the detriment of the company or its stockholders shall be under obligation to provide compensation to the company for the damage it has suffered as a result. Such party shall also be under obligation to compensate the stockholders for the damage they have suffered as a result, insofar as they have suffered damage above and beyond the damage that has been caused them by the damage caused to the company". See also i.e. Sect. 289 E-CA and Sect. 264 Slove-CA.

10 Extraordinary transactions

Summary:
1. Basic principles on extraordinary transactions
2. Mergers
3. Divisions, spin-offs and carve-outs
4. Leveraged buyouts
5. Sales of company's assets
6. Shares purchases
7. Squeeze-outs and freeze-outs
8. Conversions
9. Cross-border transactions

1. Basic principles on extraordinary transactions

Some extraordinary transactions have been expressly regulated at EU level, as we have seen in the previous Chapters. That is the case of mergers and divisions (originally in the Third and Sixth Directives and now in Directive 2017/1132/EU) and cross-border conversions, mergers and divisions (mergers in Directives 2005/56/EC and 2017/1132/EU; the three of them in Directive 2019/2121/EU).

Other transactions have not been addressed by EU regulations (with the partial exception of takeovers, for listed companies: see Directive 2004/25/EC, illustrated below in Chapter 12, § 3).

The EMCA only deals with few transactions (basically the same as those considered by the Directive of 2017).

On a general level, literature on corporate law tends to draw a line among extraordinary transactions, distinguishing between "asset deals" and "share deals". The former concern principally the company and its assets (i.e.: the company sells part of its asset to another company); the latter principally the shareholders (i.e.: a shareholder buys some of the shares from another selling shareholder).

As a matter of fact, although such a distinction is important, it should not be overestimated. Transactions are frequently both asset and share deals (like mergers and divisions); share deals may impact the company and – on the other hand – asset deals may require shareholder involvement[1].

---

[1] For instance, shareholders may be called to vote on the sale of major company assets (see above Chapter 3, § 4 and below § 6) or on the purchase of some of them (like the case of

https://doi.org/10.1515/9783110725025-012

Some "general" principles may be therefore summarized from the EU directives handling corporate deals, which may be considered also for unregulated transactions. Those principles may be inferred essentially from Directive 2017/1132/EU (and 2019/2021/EU) and, partially, from Directive 2004/25/EC[2].

The Directives of 2017 and 2019 set forth (i) the principle of "adequate information" for shareholders ("in as objective a manner as possible"); (ii) the goal of suitable protection for their rights (and also for the rights of creditors, in order to avoid transactions "adversely affecting their interests"); and (iii) the need for "certainty in the law" as regards relations between shareholders, companies and third parties, therefore limiting the cases in which invalidity can arise and the restriction of the period within which proceedings can be commenced (see, respectively, Recitals 50 ff. and 17 ff.).

The Directive 2004/25/EC on takeovers sets out – for listed companies – (iv) the principle of the necessary facilitation (or, at least, of no hindrance) of "takeovers", i.e. the purchase by third parties of the majority stake of the company (see Recital 19: "Member States should take the necessary measures to afford any offeror the possibility of acquiring majority interests in other companies and of fully exercising control of them").

As long as these "change of control" transactions are encouraged – or, at least, not hindered – by the law, they will be pursued actively (as has been demonstrated by economic literature) by those entrepreneurs who believe that they can manage the company more efficiently than incumbent shareholders and directors. At the same time, incumbent directors will be driven to perform optimally in order to enhance the market price of their company shares; if this is not the case, they risk becoming easy targets for corporate raiders (and shareholders aiming to sell their shares) and thus exposed to the peril of losing their jobs (as everyone knows, new owners usually replace management after the acquisition). This facilitation of takeovers may stimulate the "market for corporate control", which could improve companies' corporate governance[3].

---

share deals financed with debt, as leveraged buyouts: see below § 5); on the other hand, just as an example, consider the "consent clause" that may be contained in some articles of association (see above, Chapter 4, § 5): pursuant to some laws, if the transfer of the shares that a shareholder intends to sell is forbidden by the board of directors, the company has to buy out the shares. **2** See also Teichmann, *Corporate restructuring under the EMCA*, in *ECFR*, 2016, 277, outlining similar basic principles that are common to all the operations.
3 See *inter alia* Enriques, *European takeover law: the case for a neutral approach*, in *EBLR*, 2011, 623; Benocci, *Purposes and tools of the market for corporate control*, in *ECFR*, 2016, 55; Mukwiri, *Protectionism and the EU market for corporate control: is it possible to get the best of both worlds?*, in *ECFR*, 2017, 308.

In the set of these main principles – as laid down by the above-mentioned Directives – one should therefore search for (some) guidelines on the interpretation of national laws on extraordinary transactions.

2. Mergers

(I) The merger is an extraordinary transaction by which only one company replaces a plurality of companies, and this is done either by forming a new company or by incorporating one or more companies into another company. The regulation (originally implemented through the Third Directive) is currently contained in Directive 2017/1132/EU (see Arts. 87 ff.). These rules are basically similar to the ones of the EMCA (see Sects. 13.07 ff. EMCA).

After negotiations between the companies involved have reached an agreement, the management bodies jointly prepare a merger plan. The plan indicates, on the one hand, the essential characteristics of the post-merger company (name, headquarters, share capital, statutory clauses, etc.); on the other hand the exchange ratio of the shares (i.e. how many shares of the post-merger company will be assigned to the shareholders of the merged companies) and the "cash adjustment", if any.

According to widespread legal theory, this adjustment (cash compensation) – which pursuant to the Directive cannot exceed 10% of the face value of the assigned shares (or, where they have no nominal value, of their accounting par value) – serves to solve the case of an exchange ratio that gives rise to residual fractional shares, pursuant to the equal treatment principle, and cannot permit a cash payment to just some of the shareholders.

The plan is filed for registration in the companies register, with the option, as an alternative, of publication on the company's website (a solution introduced firstly by Directive 2009/109/EC and now by Directive 2017/1132/EU to simplify and reduce costs).

Thirty days have to elapse between filing the plan for registration and the general meeting resolution. The plan must be accompanied by the annual accounts of the merging companies for the preceding three financial years (and, pursuant to many laws, also by a more recent supplementary financial statement[4]).

---

4 Drawn up on a date which shall not be earlier than the first day of the third month preceding the date of the merger plan, if the latest annual financial statements relate to a year which ended more than six months before that date: see i.e. Sect. 63 Ge-TA; Sect 1134 Ir-CA; Art. 98 Por-CC;

The plan is then explained in a detailed written report drawn up by the directors. Moreover, experts appointed by the court must prepare a report on the fairness and reasonableness of the exchange ratio and provide an opinion on the adequacy of the methods adopted for calculating it.

A copy of all the preparatory documents is filed at the registered offices of the companies participating in the merger in the thirty days prior to the meeting[5]; the preparation of the documents may however be waived by unanimous consent of the shareholders (only the merger plan has to be drafted in any case).

The merger is decided by each of the participating companies through approval of the plan by a general meeting resolution (in the dualistic system, the proposal must have been approved also by the supervisory board)[6]. The decision

---

etc. According to the prevailing opinion, this document – consisting of the balance sheet and income statement – must also be accompanied by the notes, the directors' report (and the statutory auditors' report), without however requiring explicit approval by the general meeting. The merger supplementary statement can be replaced by the most recent financial statements provided that the year did not end earlier than six months prior to the deposit of the plan with the company.

5 Often with the alternative of publication on the company's website; some national laws also allow for the possibility of the shareholders obtaining electronic transmission of the documents upon request. The possibility of waiver of the merger accounting statement, provided for pursuant Art. 2501-*septies* It-CC for example, is particularly criticized in legal theory since the document also contains important information for creditors. The document is not, however, mandatory, as per the Directive (see Art. 97).

6 Pursuant to some provisions, the management body must report to the general meeting and to the management bodies of the other companies participating in the merger on any significant changes in the assets and liabilities starting from the date when the merger plan is deposited with the company's registered office (i. e. Art. 2.315 Du-CC; Art. 236-9 Fr-CC). The directors should draw up and publish a new merger accounting statement in the case of "extraordinary" changes. Should these "extraordinary" changes occur after the general meeting and before the merger deed is registered, shareholders nevertheless should have the right to be informed of them at a special general meeting (only extraordinary changes generating increases may be considered an exception, and could be reported in the company's post-merger financial statements; see on all these profiles Vicari, in *Company laws*, 634).

A discussed issue in some countries regards the option for shareholders to amend the merger plan: in this regard, for instance, Art. 2502 It-CC allows "only amendments that do not affect the rights of the shareholders or of third parties" to be introduced to the drawn up and published plan. This rule (considerably discussed in legal theory and which is, according to experts, meant to reiterate – at the level of principle – the "centrality" of the general meeting in the procedure) is in effect, however, interpreted in a very restrictive sense, so the options for actually amending the plan are very few. See also, i.e., Art. 506 Pol-CC; although the provision is rather clear in permitting only a yes/no vote (complete approval/complete rejection), a debate is ongoing whether modifications are allowed: see Mataczyński/Jerzmanowski, in *Companies laws*, 860.

is taken by the shareholders in compliance with the quorums required to amend the articles of association (as far as the possibility to withdraw is concerned, Member States vest shareholders with that option on an exceptional basis only)[7].

(II) Art. 94 of the Directive permits an important exception from the requirement of such approval by the shareholders' general meeting, even if only with reference to the general meeting of the "acquiring" company (i.e. the company into which the other or others are merged, which usually already owns a shareholding into the other or others).

This occurs in the case where at least one month before the date of publication of the merger plan, all shareholders of the "acquiring" company have been entitled to inspect the relevant documents (merger plan, annual accounts, directors' report, etc.) at the registered office of the acquiring company (by means of a special announcement). One or more shareholders of the acquiring company holding a minimum percentage (to be fixed at no more than 5% of the share capital) may however require that the general meeting of the acquiring company is called, in order to vote on the merger.

This opportunity has been implemented by a few (but important) Member States. This is the case of the Nordic countries, Germany and the Netherlands[8]: unless the articles of association provide otherwise, it is the board of directors of the acquiring company that may decide to merge (as noted, an announcement must give notice that the merger plan will be filed for inspection, also allowing disagreeing minority shareholders to request a general meeting).

The same possibility – of a decision at board level – is provided for by Art. 113 of the Directive for "simplified mergers" (or "special mergers"), i.e. mergers where the acquiring company holds the whole share capital or 90% of the share capital of the acquired company.

Finally, some laws also require the post-merger company to draft "post-merger financial statements" in order to ensure the continuity of financial statements and to allow control over the post-merger company's capital calculation (see Ch. 16, Sect. 17, Fi-CA; Sect. 17 Ge-TA); in the jurisdictions where such a document is not mandatory, the issue of the opportunity to draft it is being debated among scholars: see again Vicari, in *Company laws*, 634.

7 The right of withdrawal is recognized, for instance, pursuant to Ch. 16, Sect. 10, Fi-C and Sect. 1140 Ir-CA (see also, more restrictively, Sect. 29 Ge-TA). The EMCA holds that "shareholders in general are sufficiently protected by the merger procedure, in particular by the expert's report confirming the share exchange ratio to be fair and reasonable. The group therefore considers that there is no need to suggest a mandatory sell-out right as a general rule in the Model Act. It should be left to the articles of association to provide for a sell-out right in such cases" (see comment to Sect. 13.07).

8 See Sect. 247 Da-CA; Art. 331 Du-CC; Sect. 62 Ge-TA; Ch. 23, Sect. 15, Sw-CA.

In such cases the articles of association may allow the decisions (both for the parent and the subsidiary company) to be made by the respective management bodies since it would not make much sense to involve the general meetings (especially the meeting of the acquired company, where the acquiring company would express 100% or 90% or more of the votes). However, once again, the shareholders of the acquiring company representing at least 5% of the share capital may ask that the decision to approve the merger is adopted by the general meeting. This procedure has been introduced in many companies acts[9].

However – as one can easily notice – there is a significant difference between the exceptions provided for by Art. 94 and Art. 113 of the Directive. The latter model (Art. 113) basically concerns cases of infra-group companies (where the parent holds from 90% to 100% of the shares of the subsidiary); the former model (Art. 94) also relates to cases where there may even be no share-relationship between the merging companies and it is simply agreed in the merger plan that one company will "acquire" the other (or others). Both exceptions – but especially the one provided for in Art. 94 – are noteworthy: they allow an incisive alteration to the articles of association (the merger) to be decided by the directors instead of the shareholders (and without the directors having been previously empowered by a shareholders' resolution, as in the case of capital increases delegated to directors: see on that Chapter 5, § 1).

This new approach – which is very innovative for Member States' legislations (and is actually not shared by the EMCA Group[10]) – implies that, in place of a "right to vote", shareholders are given a simpler "right to information" (and a right "to require a vote" at the general meeting, as long as they own the minimal shareholding required by the law)[11].

---

9 See Art. 236-11 Fr-CC; Arts. 49 ff. Sp-LSC; etc.; see also Sect. 13.07 EMCA.

10 See the general comment to Ch. 13: "regarding the different types of protection, the EMCA Group decided that shareholders should be protected by the requirement that mergers and divisions have to be approved by a qualified majority in the general meeting. In connection with a merger, the EMCA Group has decided not to take up the option of derogating from the requirement of the general meeting, except for intra-group mergers".

11 In case of "simplified mergers" (where – as noted – the acquiring company holds from 90 to 100% of the merged one), moreover, even this right to information may be sacrificed. Pursuant to the Directive (Art. 114 ff.) the reports by the directors and the reports by the experts may not be drafted if the merger takes place between a company holding the whole capital of the other (that is in fact easily understandable, since there is no exchange ratio to be fixed and thus no exchange ratio to be examined and assessed by the directors and the experts).

If the acquiring company holds instead less than 100% but more than 90% of the share capital of the acquired subsidiary, the same documents can be waived if the minority shareholders of the subsidiary are entitled to have their shares bought out by the acquiring company (in

No Member State has, moreover, availed of a further possibility introduced by Directive 2017/1132/EU (which is – on the other hand – endorsed by the EMCA, at comment to Sect. 13.05).

Art. 116 of the Directive states that the laws of Member States may allow the possibility to arrange "a cash payment to exceed 10%" of the nominal value of the assigned shares for shareholders; in this case (cash payment above 10%) the minority shareholders have to be provided with the right to sell out their shares.

That is not actually a proper "cash merger" (which, on the contrary, entails a model where it is the company that has the "right" to oblige minority sharehold-ers to accept cash instead of shares). In any case, whenever shareholders are given fewer shares than they were entitled to obtain (and receive a relevant amount of cash instead of shares), they may prefer to leave the company and agree to sell out their entire shareholding (and be fully cashed out). Therefore, even if the Directive does not introduce a "proper" cash merger model, it allows companies de facto to "prepare the field" for shareholders preferring to have all their shares cashed out in occasion of the merger; this may be – as a matter of fact – a situation not too far from a "real" cash merger.

These latter rules (even if not currently implemented) are very significant from a regulatory point of view: they break with the traditional framework adopt-ed by national laws (which have been historically inspired by the principle of equal treatment and have allowed shareholders the right to vote on major trans-actions). They also give more space to decision-making by directors and shift the protection of shareholders from the right to vote to the right to exit.

(III) Coming back to the merger proceeding, after the merger resolution has been adopted, it has to be filed with the preparatory documents in the compa-nies register. Finally, a "merger deed" has to be agreed by the directors of the companies involved (in many jurisdictions under a notary's control) and that document also has to be filed in the companies register.

---

the event of disagreement regarding the consideration, the relative value has to be determined by a court). In such a case, the minority shareholders of the acquired company (which represent a small percentage of the capital: less than 10%) may "de facto" be squeezed out by the parent company, which, if it is ready to buy their shares, can avoid illustrating the exchange ratio (and having it assessed by the experts) (in any case, the exchange ratio has to be fixed since the mi-nority shareholder of the acquired company may still chose to retain stakes in the post-merged company).

Both these opportunities provided for simplified mergers (the option to renounce drafting the documents in 100% mergers and renouncing it in 90–99% mergers if a sell out right is granted to minority shareholders) have been introduced in some Member States' law (paradig-matically Art. 236-11-1 Fr-CC).

(IV) Legislation of EU Member States is rather similar with regard to the above-mentioned areas (with the described exceptions) since the rules laid down by the Directive are rather detailed. However, for other areas, national regulations diverge, above all with reference to the characteristics of the protection granted to shareholders and creditors.

Art. 108 of the Directive sets forth the conditions for the "nullity" of the merger. After having stated that mergers "may be declared void only if there has been no judicial or administrative preventive supervision of their legality, or if they have not been drawn up and certified in due legal form, or if it is shown that the decision of the general meeting is void or voidable under national law", it provides that "nullification proceedings may not be initiated more than six months after the date on which the merger becomes effective as against the person alleging nullity or where the situation has been rectified".

The rationale behind this rule is the need for the stability that legislation pursues in regulating key extraordinary transactions, and in particular in supporting mergers as a tool for business growth and economic development. Easy attempts to annul the merger have to be avoided (it would also be very difficult to bring things back to the "ex ante" situation). Member States have however implemented this type of rule in different ways.

Under some laws, for instance, the provision is clear-cut: after the registration, the merger resolution and the merger deed can no longer be invalidated, with only a right to compensation for damages remaining for injured shareholders, creditors or third parties[12]. Shareholders can try to avoid the preclusive effects of registration by challenging the merger shareholders' resolution (for reasons of nullity or voidability pursuant to the general rules) and requesting a suspension of its effects[13].

---

12 See i.e. Art. 2504-*quater* It-CC. In any case, there is still the opportunity to pronounce the invalidity of single clauses in the articles of association amended at the time of the transaction (if illegitimate).

13 To my best knowledge, this suspension has only seldom been granted in the case of a merger, as the court is called upon to make a comparative assessment of the damage that the petitioning shareholder sustains it will suffer under the merger and that the company would suffer due to the interruption of the transaction (see the ruling of the sole Arbitrator, 10 January 2008, that has decided on a merger that would have diluted a shareholder depriving him of a qualified shareholding, stating that "the prospect of mere compensation would not appear fully satisfactory"; case "DB vs. A s.p.a. & IL s.r.l."). According to a minority opinion, after filing the application for registration of the merger deed with the office, the shareholders could – in extreme cases – present complaints and petitions aimed at spurring judicial control and calling attention to irregularities emerging from deeds officially scrutinized in order to prevent the registration or, if it has already been registered, a petition to the judge in charge of the companies register. See

On the contrary, in most Member States, the merger may still be declared null and void after its completion (the transaction is therefore "rescinded"); however, the procedures to annul the merger may not be initiated after expiry of a three (or six) months deadline from the date on which the merger became effective[14].

Moreover, if the irregularity which could lead to declaring the merger null and void can be remedied, the judge will afford the companies a deadline to rectify such irregularity. In any case, in those States, the definitive decision to declare the nullity or voidability of the merger does not affect the validity of the obligations undertaken by (or the rights pertaining to) the companies involved, which arose between the date when the merger became effective and the publication of the judicial decision concerning the invalidity of the transaction (which remain to be ascribed to both or all the pre-existing company).

(V) The solution provided for compensation for damages caused by the merger also differs considerably.

German law, for instance, is analytical: while shareholders can always challenge the merger resolution under the general rules on damages, they cannot claim this remedy on the grounds of unfair exchange ratios (Sect. 14 Ge-TA); indeed there is a specific procedure in place to review the valuations made by the directors and assessed by the experts (see Sect. 14 and 34 Ge-TA)[15]. The underlying justification is that the transaction itself should proceed for the benefit of the company and not be delayed by a dispute that can be simply settled by dishing out more money. Moreover, the German Transformation Act grants the right to make a special claim against the directors and the supervisory board members of the merged company (under Sects. 25, 26 Ge-TA): unless they apply due care, they are liable to compensate for all damages arising from the merger to the company, the shareholders or the creditors, who however, must act through a specially appointed common "agent"[16].

---

also, for the possibility of a suspension of the merger resolution under Polish law, Mataczyński/ Jerzmanowski, in *Companies laws*, 865.

14 See Art. 2.323 Du-CC; Art. 117 Por-CC; Art. 251 R-CA; Art. 47 Sp-LSC; Ch. 23, Sect. 36, Sw-CA; etc. Actually not all Member States set forth explicitly a term of six months: cf. i.e. Art. 12.19 ff. B-CA and Art. 235-8 Fr-CC.

15 See also i.e. Sect. 225c A-PuCA; Art. 398 E-CA and Art. 509 Pol-CC.

16 This claim has some noteworthy features. First, it is a controversial deviation from general company law principles that would only accept the company as claimant for damages due to breaches of directors' duties. To make up for this, the claims can only be brought by a special representative who is to be appointed by a court (Sect. 26 Ge-TA). The aim is to avoid a race by the various claimants and to facilitate dealing with the case in one trial. The right to have the special agent appointed lies with any shareholder and creditor. However, the right by cred-

Other companies acts have chosen to remain generic and refused to lay down specific rules (or have stipulated short ones pursuant to which shareholders and third parties harmed by the merger simply may "obtain compensation for damages"[17]).

These laconic provisions obviously raise problems and are highly debated (it is discussed whether they might be executed in a specific form, i. e. with delivery of shares or only by cash; whether they provide for indemnity or a true compensatory remedy[18], etc.).

In any case, in all national laws, if there are grounds for their liability, normally the post-merger company, the directors, the statutory auditors, the experts and the auditing company can be called upon to answer, once again according to the general provisions of the law (see also Arts. 105 f. Directive 2017/1132/EU and Sect. 13.20 EMCA).

---

itors to petition is conditional upon their claims not being satisfied by the receiving company. Second, Sect. 26 Ge-TA creates a legal fiction whereby the transferring company is still deemed to exist despite having been merged. This is done so that it can receive the award of damages and thus to prevent the shareholders of the absorbing company from sharing the proceeds that are only meant to benefit the shareholders of the old company. In contrast to this peculiar liability regime against the directors of the transferring company, the directors and supervisory board members (if any) of the absorbing company will only be liable for breaches of directors' duties under general law (Sect. 27 Ge-TA); see on all these aspects Schall, in *Company laws*, 412.
17 See respectively, i.e., Ch. 23, Sect. 36, Sw-CA (which only regulates the "invalidity" of the merger and not the aspects of the harm caused by the transactions), and Sect. 1147 Ir-CA (which makes generic reference to the right of shareholders and third parties to bring a suit for damages). A particular procedure is governed under Sects. 249 f. Da-CA: shareholders may claim compensation if they deem that the consideration offered for the shares is not fair and reasonable (if they made a complaint to this effect at the general meeting at which the merger resolution was passed). Proceedings must be commenced within two weeks from adoption of the merger by all of the merging companies. If a complaint is made, the merger resolution may only be registered after expiry of the aforesaid time limit unless the valuation experts conclude that the consideration offered is fair and reasonable. However, the merger will only be considered to have been completed when "the shareholders' claims for compensation [...] have been settled [...]. If valuation experts have drawn up a statement on the plan, including the consideration, and the statement is based on the assumption that the consideration is fair and reasonable, the valuation experts must also have declared that their statement on the consideration is not disputed to any significant degree". Also the EMCA is rather laconic about the issue of damages (see Sect. 13.20).
18 Adopting the first interpretation, the shareholder may obtain a monetary benefit from the post-merger company once both the defect in the procedure or deed of merger and the damage have been proven (however, without the need to demonstrate wilful intent or wrongdoing of the directors); for the second interpretation, on the other hand, the shareholder must also prove the wilful intent or wrongdoing of the directors in addition to its damage.

The limitation period for filing the suits for damages is usually deemed to be the common one as fixed by national laws.

(VI) As far as the protection of creditors is concerned, since the completion of the transaction may put their claims at risk, Member States' laws address the issue extensively. At a general level, all the companies acts agree that creditors of the merging companies (whose claims predated the publication of the merger plan and had not yet fallen due at the time of publication) have to be protected[19]. The same principle also applies to debenture-holders. However, the domestic provisions set forth very different legal responses as far as the legislative technique is concerned.

Basically, the main differences regard the "kind" of protection that creditors receive and whether they can block the merger if they do not receive adequate protection (there are similarities with the issue of the safeguard owed to creditors in the case of reduction of capital in excess seen above in Chapter 2, § 12).

On the one hand, there are States (i. e. Austria, Belgium, Germany, Hungary, Poland, similarly France) which protect creditors by basically allowing them the right to "seize" the – old – company's assets, which are considered as a separate pool in the post-merger company. In any case, the action brought by the creditors may not block the merger. Paradigmatically, the German Transformation Act offers creditors the right to make a specific claim to receive collateral from the company (Sect. 22 Ge-TA), on condition that proof is given that the satisfaction of the claim is potentially jeopardized by the transaction. The same specific liability regime which is in place against the directors of the transferring company (Sects. 25, 26 Ge-TA) directly protects also creditors, provided however, that the absorbing company cannot fulfil their claims (the main examples are transactions that cause damage which exceeds the coverage of the collateral to be provided under Sect. 22 Ge-TA[20]).

---

19 As for the concept of creditor, the Directive, legislations and the EMCA Group tend to consider it legitimate to only protect creditors who hold claims on the date the merger plan was filed for registration in the companies register (or for publication in the company website). Subsequent creditors are not given said right on the grounds that they supplied credit to a company that had already made its plan to merge public and were (at least formally) aware of the transaction and of the risks that it might entail.

20 A similar system is laid down by Art. 236-14 Fr-CC. The merger may not be carried out until one month has elapsed from the date of publication of the merger. During this time creditors may raise objections, which shall be brought by the creditor before the court. The court decision shall either reject the objection or order repayment of the claims or the formation of guarantees if the acquiring company is ready to offer them and if they are deemed sufficient. In the case of failure to repay the claims or set up of the guarantees, the merger shall not be binding on the claiming creditor. Nevertheless, in any case, the objection raised by a creditor shall not have

Then there are the laws (i.e. of Italy, Ireland, Portugal, Romania, Spain, Sweden) which allow creditors to "object" to the merger and even block it in court; if the court, however, approves the transaction, they may obtain, at best, only a security on the post-merger assets. For instance, creditors may oppose the merger within (say, sixty days) from the last registration of the shareholders' resolutions in the companies register. The objection (made by filing a suit) focuses on the ability of the post-merger company to fulfil the creditor's claims and aims to obtain the suspension of the merger procedure for all participating companies, thus preventing the directors from registering the merger deed without court authorization[21]. Registration of the merger deed before the sixty-day term elapses (or pending a court decision on the opposition) leads to the deed becoming void. It is, on the other hand, possible to complete the transaction even before the sixty-day term under some conditions: (i) there is consent by the creditors; (ii) the creditors that did not give their consent are paid; (iii) the corresponding amounts are deposited with a bank; (iv) an auditing firm draws up a statement, declaring – under its own liability – that the merger accounting statement of the companies participating in the merger makes creditor protection guarantees superfluous[22].

---

the effect of preventing completion of the merger operations and creditors may not obtain the suspension of the procedure by using their right of objection. Bondholders may only empower their representative to raise a similar objection (Art. 236-15 Fr-CC).

21 The provision, which refers to the "guarantees" of creditors and the "risk of prejudice", persuades some scholars that the basis of the challenge is to be seen in the risk that completion of the transaction may threaten the claims "of all creditors considered collectively". According to others, however, only the risk of prejudice for the opposing creditor is relevant since the rule also refers to the guarantee aspect, "only such a prejudice can be 'compensated' by 'guarantees' suitable for that purpose". See Vicari, in *Company laws*, 635.

22 See Art. 2503 It-CC. A similar system is regulated, for instance, in Spain and the Netherlands. Creditors are entitled to object to the merger (within 30 days from publication of the merger) and the transaction may not be carried out until the company has offered security to the creditors' satisfaction, or otherwise, until the creditors have been notified of a joint and several surety bond in the company's favour issued by a duly approved credit institution, for the amount of their claim and for the duration of their entitlement to make the claim (Art. 2.316 Du-CC; Art. 44 Sp-LSC). Under Sect. 1193 Ir-CA (which lays down a similar right to objection), if the court deems it necessary in order to secure the adequate protection of creditors, it may determine a list of creditors entitled to object and the nature and amount of their debts or claims, and may publish notices fixing a day or days within which creditors who are not on the list can claim to be put on the list or are to be excluded from the right of objecting to the confirmation. Normally the standing to object is also acknowledged to the bondholders unless the merger is approved by the bondholders' meeting (see i.e. Art. 2503-*bis* It-CC).

Finally, other countries (the Nordic ones) basically rely on a statement by an auditor (or an audit company): if the auditor states that the merger is not harmful, creditors may not make any claims; otherwise they have to be notified and may object to the merger (note that also according to other laws auditors may be implicated to a certain extent: hybrid solutions are possible)[23].

Therefore – as noted, among others, by the "Report of the the Reflection Group on the future of EU company law" of 2011 – "there is no harmonization of the consequences of creditors' rights on completion of the merger. In practice, this is a source of uncertainty"[24].

(VII) The last issue that has to be address regards national laws on the treatment of "special" (i. e. class) shares and "hybrid" instruments.

Normally, each domestic law states that the holders of those securities must be granted rights basically equivalent to those they held in the pre-existing company (see i. e. Sect. 23 Ge-TA). A "special" meeting of these security holders has to be called and the transaction is passed if the majority approves it.

Whats does, however, "equivalent rights" mean? An aspect of considerable uncertainty is whether special shareholders (and securityholders) should be also protected by means of a vote of the special meeting when their rights are harmed as a consequence of an "indirect" effect, not represented by a "formal" ("direct") amendment of the articles of association worsening their rights, but by assignment of predominant rights to other shareholders (or securityholders) in the post-merger company.

The right to withdrawal is also a remedy that is sometime acknowledged to special shareholders under some national laws, but not pursuant to others.

The above issue has been treated more generally above in Chapter 4, § 3, and may therefore be referred to.

---

23 According to the Swedish companies act, creditors may only be involved if they are notified after one or more auditors have been encharged for each of the merging companies (or, in the event of a merger by acquisition, the company being acquired: see Ch. 23, Sect. 11). If the auditors found that the merger would jeopardize the payment of claims held by creditors of the company being acquired, the creditors must be notified (see Ch. 23, Sect. 19). The creditor protection works so that creditors can prevent the merger if they do not receive payment or get security for their claims (see Sects. 22–23). Sect. 242 Da-CA provides for a similar solution.

24 The Report – that we have already mentioned in Chapter 1, § 8 – reproduces the work of the "Reflection Group on the Future of EU Company Law" set up by the European Commission in December 2010; see § 2.6.2.

3. Divisions, spin-offs and carve-outs

(I) The division (also called "demerger") comprises a company (divided company) "assigning" assets to one or more pre-existing or newly-formed companies (recipient), whose shares are passed to the shareholders of the divided company.

Directive 2017/1132/EU fully regulates the transaction (see Arts. 137 ff.). The provisions of the EMCA are very similar to the ones contained in the Directive (see Sect. 13.49).

Whereas the Second Directive (Directive 82/891/EEC) required the Member States to introduce only "total division" (which takes place when the divided company assigns all of its assets to two or more pre-existing or newly-formed companies and at the same time is wound up), the more recent Directive also regulates the "partial" division, which occurs when the divided company transfers only a portion of its assets, and therefore survives. This is due to the recognized adequacy of the transaction to meet multiple needs for restructuring and reorganizing the companies.

The two basic elements of the division are therefore: (1) the assignment of the assets – or part of them – by the divided company to one or more other recipient companies; (2) the assignment by the recipient (or recipients) of shares to the shareholders of the divided company, which therefore become shareholders of the recipient (or recipients).

The Directive – and national laws accordingly – regulate the division plan which defines the first phase of the procedure. The contents of the plan, and in broader terms the procedure's regulations, are determined in reference to provisions laid down for mergers (see above, § 2), even if with a few significant differences.

The purpose of the division plan is to account for the factors characterising the transaction: the assignment of the divided company's assets to the recipient companies and the allocation of their shares to the shareholders of the recipient company. The Directive therefore requires that the demerger plan precisely describes the assets and liabilities to be assigned to each of the recipients.

A sensitive aspect governed by the Directive and national laws concerns the case where certain assets or liabilities are not mentioned in the plan. Art. 137 sets out a specific rule for this type of omission: with regard to the assets (i) in the case of total division, the omitted property is split up between the recipients in proportion to the portion of shareholders' equity assigned (as measured when determining the exchange ratio); (ii) in the case of partial division, the property remains with the divided company.

With regard to any liability items omitted, the rule states that: (a) in the case of total division, the recipients are jointly liable; (b) in the case of partial division, the divided company and recipients are jointly liable. The provision states that Member States may provide that this joint and several liability is limited to the net assets allocated to each company; therefore, some national companies acts have introduced this limitation.

Shareholders, creditors and third parties must be given adequate information, which is provided by filing the division plan at the registered office in the thirty days preceding the general meeting called to vote on the transaction and publication in the companies register of where the companies involved have their registered offices[25].

The plan also has to be evaluated in light of the directors' report that explains the transactions in legal and economic terms and offers an assessment of the assets of the divided company, explaining the criteria adopted to assign shares and determining as many exchange ratios as there are recipient companies.

Then the experts' report on the adequacy of the exchange ratio is required. This is however unnecessary in the case of division by formation of one or more new companies which adopt the criteria of assigning strictly proportionate shares to each shareholder in each company (so there is no risk of damage for the shareholders who will keep their original percentage of investment in all the companies resulting from the transaction).

A cash adjustment is allowed, based on the rebalancing of an exchange ratio which gives rise to fractional shares; this cash payment must not exceed 10% of the nominal value of the shares allocated.

With the unanimous consent of the shareholders, the experts' report, the accounting statement and the explanatory report prepared by the directors can be waived. The division plan is approved through a general meeting resolution[26].

---

25 As for a merger, the plan can be (under some national rules) published on the website of the company as an alternative to filing, and the shareholders are entitled to unanimously waive the above-mentioned thirty-day term, which is in the sole interest of the shareholders.

26 Also, in the case of division (like in the case of merger: see above § 2), an exception from the requirement of approval by the general meeting of a recipient company is provided for by the Directive whether the laws of the Member States require the following conditions to be fulfilled: (a) the publication of an announcement, for each recipient company, at least one month before the date fixed for the general meeting; (b) at least one month before the date specified in point (a), all shareholders of each recipient company are entitled to inspect the preliminary documents at the registered office of that company; (c) one or more shareholders of any recipient company holding a minimum percentage of the subscribed capital is entitled to require that a general meeting of such recipient company be called to decide whether to approve the division (such minimum percentage may not be fixed at more than 5%). See i.e. Arts. 2.334-a ff. Du-CC.

After the transaction is approved, the management bodies of the companies involved in the transaction must then draw up the division deed in public form. Once the publicity obligations have been fulfilled, the division deed can no longer be invalidated pursuant to the same rules seen above for the merger (seen above at § 2).

The question of whether or not a division can be subject to revocatory action has been debated in the case law of many States since the demerger is a transaction that can defraud creditors. As we have already seen, however, the CJEU has taken a firm position on this topic in 2020, with an interpretation which is now binding for individual national courts (case C-394/18, IGI; see Chapter 1, § 3). The Court holds that neither the protections remedies granted before the division is implemented, nor the rules establishing the cases in which "nullity" of a division may be declared preclude creditors from bringing a revocatory action, in cases where this is appropriate. Indeed, such a clawback remedy does not affect the validity of a division but merely allows for that division to be rendered unenforceable against the acting creditors[27].

As far as the general protection of creditors' interests is concerned, they are usually outlined by the national provisions in a way that is similar to the ones set out for mergers (see above, § 3).

(II) A few domestic laws explicitly regulate two specific types of division: "non-proportional" and "asymmetric" divisions, which are of particular interest. On the contrary, most Member States do not lay down specific rules on those specific transactions, with the consequence that it is may be not clear if they they should considered forbidden or not (actually Art. 137 Directive 2017/1132/EU states that the division plan has to include "the terms relating to the allotment of shares in the recipient companies" and seems thus rather flexible on this regard).

An example of a "non-proportional" division is the following.

Assume a company (Flamingo PLC), where Tom owns 80% and Dick owns 20%, is going to be split into two new companies (Mirage PLC and Bellagio PLC). One should expect that both Tom and Dick would receive a shareholding of 80–20% after the division in both recipient companies. However, the non-proportional model allows Tom, for instance, to own 99% of Mirage (and Dick 1%), while Dick obtains 51% of Bellagio (and Tom 49%). The distribution criteria depends both on the value of each company and the proposal made by the board of directors.

---

27 See De Luca, *Actio*, 97.

Pursuant to the Member States' laws which regulate the transaction, dissenting shareholders (in our case, for instance, Dick) are given either a veto right – since all shareholders must be entitled to opt for the shares of each of the divided or recipient companies – or the right to sell their holdings to the subjects "specified" in the plan (i.e. other shareholders or the company itself) for an amount determined at a fair value, if necessary to be set by a court[28].

On the other hand, an "asymmetric" demerger occurs when shares in one of the recipient companies are not distributed to all the shareholders, but only to same of them, while some shareholders are only assigned only shares in the divided company.

Let us go back to the example of Flamingo, where Tom owns 80% and Dick owns 20%. The asymmetric model permits, for instance, Tom to own 100% of Mirage and Dick 100% of Bellagio. In such a case the individual consent of all shareholders is required pursuant to all domestic laws (each of them has thus a "veto right")[29].

The reason for the diverse regulations between the cases of "non-proportional" and "asymmetric" divisions under some companies acts lies in the different impact each transaction has on shareholders' rights (asymmetric division is more radical because it entails denying some shareholders the option of remaining as shareholders in all participating companies). The unanimous consent serves to protect the minority shareholder, which has the power to block the transaction when it expects to be totally excluded from a stake in the recipient or divided companies.

(III) The word "spin-off" may be used to define different transactions. Here we shall consider a spin-off the operation by which the parent company distributes shares of the subsidiary that is being spun-off to its existing shareholders on a pro-rata basis, in the form of a special dividend[30].

Let us make the case: MGM PLC – participated by Phil and Alan – owns shares in Red Rock PLC and distributes as dividend to the same Phil and Alan

---

28 The first solution is provided for by i.e. Sect. 128 Ge-TA; the second one, by Art. 2506-*bis* It-CC. Prior identification of the parties obliged to purchase is essential in order to prevent the search for a buyer from blocking and delaying the transaction. This obligation is an irrevocable purchase proposal to be sent to the directors, who will attach the declarations received to the plan. See also Art. 541 Pol-CC.
29 See i.e. Art. 2506 It-CC and Art. 76 Sp-LSC.
30 The situation may arise also when the company sets up a company, transfer parts of its asset to it in exchange of shares of the subsidiary, which are subsequently transferred to the parent corporation's shareholders.

part of it shares in Red Rock, allowing the former to become shareholders of the latter.

The parent company typically receives no cash consideration for the spin-off. Existing shareholders benefit by holding shares of two separate companies after the spin-off instead of one.

A few companies acts – like the Ge-TA – extend the regulations on divisision also to spin-offs (see i. e. Sect. 125^{31}). Most domestic laws, on the contrary, govern these transactions with a more liberal regulatory approach.

(IV) "Equity carve-outs" are a specific type of "asset sale", regarding the partial sale of the shares owned by a company in a subsidiary to new investors via a public offer. Indeed, the parent company sells some of the shares it holds in the subsidiary through an "initial public offering" ("IPO"). The parent may sell only a minority stake, mantaining control, or all its shares, effectively establishing the subsidiary as a standalone company. Since the shares are sold to the public, a carve-out in any case originates a new set of shareholders in the subsidiary.

Considering that the minority shareholders of the parent company are not involved in the proceeding, the rules on divisions should not be applied.

Only if the carve-out is preceded by the intentional creation of the subsidiary and the transfer of assets to the latter with a view of pursuing the second transaction, this may be considered a kind of division: some national laws apply therefore also to this scheme the provisions on demergers (see i.e. Sect. 123 Ge-TA); this model is also called "two-step" carve-out. The general assembly of the parent as well as of the subsidiary must therefore approve the first step of the carve-out, the transfer of assets and liabilities, by a three-quarters majority of the share capital represented at the respective shareholders' meetings (Sects. 125, 13 and 65 Ge-TA apply). For the second step of the transaction, the IPO, the general assembly of the parent company must agree if the carve-out reflects a considerable share of the parent company (according to the general rules on the distribution of powers between directors and shareholders, that we have see above in Chapter 3, § 4).

In other jurisdictions, however, the creation of the subsidiary and the following floatation on the market is considered a simple formation of a new company by the parent by means of contributions in kind, followed by an IPO; as a con-

---

31 Both the parent and the subsidiary's shareholders must approve the spin-off by a threequarters majority of the share capital represented at the respective shareholders' meetings (see also Sects. 13 and 65 Ge-TA).

sequence, most national companies acts do not treat the transaction as a division[32].

The term "carve out" is sometimes employed in the praxis to describe other kind of transactions. Above all, this deals are often very complex and characterized also by "mixed" schemes[33]. For the sake of simplicity, we can accept here the above definitions.

4. Leveraged buyouts

(I) A leveraged buyout ("LBO") is the acquisition of a controlling stake in a company (also called "target") by another one through the use of debt. After the acquisition, the debt is reduced by using the resources of the acquired company, which provide loans or guarantees to the acquiring one, or sell assets and distribute dividends, etc.

An example may help. Flamingo PLC acquires 51% of Mirage PLC for € 1 million, fully financed by a bank. After the acquisition, the new replaced board of Mirage grants a loan of € 1 million to Flamingo, which immediately uses it to repay the bank. Conclusion: the bank has been paid, Flamingo is satisfied with the deal, and Mirage has € 1 million in outstanding credit owed by its parent company (previously it had € 1 million in cash).

Sometimes the debt incurred by the buyer is subsequently charged to the target by means of a "debt pushdown": the acquired company – instead of the acquiring – may apply for a loan, which is then used for a dividend payment to its main shareholder, the acquiring company. The acquiring company then uses the dividend payment to pay off its own debt.

Let us clarify. Flamingo acquires 51% of Mirage, with its own money. The new directors of Mirage ask the bank for a € 1 million loan. They then call a general meeting where Flamingo – as majority shareholder of Mirage – approves the distribution of an "extraordinary dividend" of € 1 million to Flamingo. The situation is only similar to the previous one, and is actually a little worse: this time Mirage has a debt towards the bank.

---

32 However, the outflow of a relevant part of the company assets may trigger the shareholders' vote pursuant to those laws that require their involvement in case of relevant company asset deals (see again above Chapter 3, § 4).

33 An evolution of the carve-out is the "split off": in this case, the shareholders of the parent company are offered shares in the subsidiary. The parent's shareholders thus have two options: either continue to hold shares in the parent company or exchange some (or all) of them for shares in the subsidiary (see Sects. 139, 145 Ge-TA).

Similar – and often more articulated – schemes may be employed, with the same basic substantial effect: the shifting of the debt agreed for the acquisition from the acquiring company onto the acquired one. The business objective is, however, usually that of paying back the debt with the increased efficiency of the acquired company. Flamingo in not necessarily a looter, it may also be owned by a brilliant entrepreneur. Mirage can profit from the arrival of Flamingo.

The legitimacy of this kind of transaction is highly debated and addressed from various perspectives in the Member States. Indeed the transaction may trigger application of different laws: on the change of control (the acquiring company takes over the majority stake of the target company and becomes its parent company); on corporate groups (at a general level) and on loans and guarantees provided by the subsidiary to the parent (at a more specific level); on the distribution of dividends; on the duties of directors; on the financial assistance for the acquisition of the company's owns shares; etc.

(II) No directive openly addresses the transactions. National laws do not lay down specific rules either (some regulate the more limited transaction represented by the "merger LBO", which we shall examine at the end of this paragraph).

Let us therefore analyze the transaction from the different perspectives mentioned above, beginning with the dividend payment.

Directive 2017/1132/EU stipulates – as we have already seen (Chapter 2, § 7) – that no distributions to shareholders may be made when the net assets (as set out in the company's annual accounts) are – or would become – lower than the amount of the subscribed capital plus the reserves. An LBO may therefore be carried out only in compliance with this provision (in our case, Mirage may well pay an extraordinary dividend only as long as its financial position is positive and in an amount corresponding to the distributable profit or reserves).

(III) Secondly, the question of the validity of an LBO is often treated in the context of regulations on corporate groups (this is no surprise: remember that Flamingo has acquired control of Mirage and has immediately begun to exercise the unitary direction, by providing instructions to Mirage's directors to grant loans, make debts, call meetings, etc.).

Italian law is a striking example. Since the acquiring company operates as a parent company, this circumstance triggers application of the "group regulation", that is to say the series of rules provided for in Art. 2497 ff. It-CC (special liability of the parent company, enhanced disclosure, etc: see above Chapter 7, § 4).

Moreover, the LBO may give rise to the target (Mirage) minority shareholders' right of withdrawal: pursuant to Art. 2497-*quater* It-CC, the shareholders of a subsidiary have the right to sell out their shares to the company when unitary direction begins if the investment risk conditions are altered (see again Chapter 7, § 6).

Since the LBO actually entails changing the parent company, the beginning of a new unitary direction and normally the alteration of the risk profile of the company (more debt is at the horizon), shareholders of the target company often withdraw.

(IV) The third issue – probably the most debated among Member States' scholars – concerns the application to LBOs of the rules on "financial assistance".

The prevailing opinion is affirmative. The shares of the target are actually purchased by the acquiring company by means of loans and guarantees provided by the same target company. The target thus financially assists a third party (the acquiring company) in buying its own (target) company shares (actually financial assistance is not provided "before" the acquisition of the shares, but "after" it, since the purchase of the shares takes place with the support of other financiers, usually banks; this is however considered sufficient to trigger the application of rules on financial assistance).

Put simply: Mirage's shares are acquired by the third party (Flamingo) with the – subsequent – financial assistance of Mirage itself.

This means that decisions concerning loans and guarantees given by the target to the acquiring company after the leveraged acquisition are either banned (in Member States which have not implemented the right of companies to provide financial assistance, according to Directive 2017/1132/EU) or subject to the strict "whitewash procedure" and quantitative limits set forth by national laws which have adopted the rules of the Directive on financial assistance (see above Chapter 2, § 9)[34]. Since the legal provisions regulating financial assistance do not specify the consequences of infringement, actions that breach the regulation on financial assistance are normally considered null and void. This state of things may – and often do – render LBO impossible in many Member States[35].

However, even some of the more "orthodox" States that generally prohibit financial assistance have introduced some correctives. On a theoretical basis, this has to do with the fact that the leveraged acquisitions, even if they may

---

34 See especially Schlumberger/Ansault, in *Company laws*, 172.

35 See for such a restrictive result – under Art. 225-216 Fr-CC – Schlumberger/Ansault, in *Company laws*, 172. Moreover, as we have seen above (Chapter 2, § 9), the concept of "financial assistance" is rather vague and is not always clear which operations constitute this kind of support: see, i.e., with reference to LBO and Art. 345 Pol-CC, Mataczyński/Jerzmanowski, in *Companies laws*, 872 ("the concept of financial assistance should be interpreted broadly, with the protective nature of the quoted provision in mind"); other interpretations may be more restrictive.

be considered risky, are not negative per se, at least from the perspective of the "market for the corporate control". As we have analyzed above (§ 1), this market should be sustained (or at least not hindered); transactions should be permitted even if the acquirer takes over control of the target with borrowed money.

This approach is followed by Spain for example: on the one hand, the law prohibits companies from providing financial assistance on a general basis; on the other hand, however, if the assistance is given in order to acquire control and exercise unitary direction, the ban is relaxed somewhat. The prohibition only applies if there is a real risk to the interests of shareholders and creditors, and the financial assistance is not provided within a corporate procedure (for instance, the one tackling the conflicts of interests of shareholders and directors) which includes mechanisms of safeguard for those stakeholders. Attention is thus shifted to the presence of "a real risk" for shareholders and creditors as a result of the financial assistance, which – under certain circumstances – may be considered absent[36].

---

36 See Gutierrez, in *Company laws*, 1267. The Italian literature also presents the opinion that decisions concerning financing and guarantees by the acquired company to the buyer after the leveraged acquisition should not be subject to the whitewashing procedure (directors' report, approval of the extraordinary general meeting, etc.) and the application of very strict quantity limitations. In the opinion of some authors, this interpretation risks resulting in the "end" of LBOs through intercompany loans: the financial, economic and procedural limitations and the conditions that must be met for the target company to give guarantees to purchase the target shares are not compatible with execution of this type of transaction. The legislation therefore appears – if interpreted in the sense of needing to apply all the mentioned regulations simultaneously (on financial assistance, groups, etc.) – to be an example of redundant rules that conflict with the interest of fostering the corporate control market and the need to reduce procedural costs for companies. See Vicari, in *Company laws*, 640.

Another paragdimatical example may be found under Romanian law: as reported by Doroga/Sitaru, *ibidem*, 1049, "according to the provisions of [Art. 106 R-CA], a company may not offer advance payments or loans, nor may it set up guarantees for the purpose of subscription or acquisition of its own shares by a third party. However, this prohibition is 'not applicable in the case of transactions performed during the normal operations of credit institutions and of other financial institutions, nor to the transactions performed for the purpose of acquisition of shares by, or for the company's employees, under the condition that such transactions do not lead to a decrease of the company's net assets below the cumulative value of the subscribed social capital and the reserves which may not be distributed according to the law or according to the constitutive act of the company'. In the view of a part of the doctrine, the derogatory norm in paragraph 2 of article 106 [R-CA] would make it possible for LBOs to be performed under Romanian legislation. However, other voices in doctrine disagree, quoting the fact that Romania failed to implement the amended provisions of Art. 25 of the Second Company Directive, which would have made it possible for LBOs to be performed under conditions similar to those concerning the acquisition by a company of its own shares".

Other laws are also inclined to focus on different rules besides the laws on financial assistance. Dutch case law is emblematic: the Netherlands – as we have seen above (Chapter 2, § 9) – permits financial assistance only in accordance with the strict conditions set forth by the Directive. Notwithstanding this, in the case of an LBO emphasis seems to be put (beyond the rules on financial assistance, that are somehow disapplied) on the regulations on directors' duties and liabilities. In an important case of 2010 (realized by using a debt-push-down scheme), the Amsterdam Court of Appeal ruled that the board of directors (and the supervisory board) of the target did not consider the consequences of the LBO to a sufficient extent: the conduct of the board (and supervisory board) in the period leading up to the LBO was qualified as mismanagement[37]. The Court stated that "the principles of reasonableness and fairness require the acquiring company to not only consider its own interests, but also the interests of the company that it wants to acquire"; since an LBO will always create a considerable financial burden on the target company, special consideration should be expected from the parties who have fiduciary duties towards the companies involved and those who make decisions that ultimately lead to the LBO[38]. Even though the directors were sanctioned in the end, in that type of case the financial assistance – and thus the LBO – were considered to be legitimate (even in absence of a strict whitewash procedure, etc.).

(V) A case apart is the LBO executed by means of a merger subsequent to the acquisition: this is the so called "merger leveraged buyout" ("MLBO").

After the target has been acquired, the acquiring company initiates a merger with it in order to obtain access to the liquidity that the target has in its coffers (in our example, Flamingo and Mirage, after the acquisition, merge and become a sole company; frequently, it is – for tax reasons – a "reverse" merger that takes place: Mirage incorporates Flamingo).

Since this transaction is already protected by the rules laid down for mergers by national regulations implementing Directive 2017/1132/EU, some Member States tend to judge it less harmful for shareholders and creditors and regulate it accordingly.

Let us consider once again the Spanish legislation, which has introduced a specific exception for merger LBOs. The Spanish law on structural changes regulates merger LBOs within the regime on common mergers, in a specific provision, Art. 35 ("merger subsequent to leveraged acquisition"). This rule states that when, in a merger between two or more companies, one of them has

---

37 See Amsterdam Court of Appeal (Enterprise Chamber), 27 May 2010 (case "Group PCM").
38 See on that Renssen, in *Company laws*, 1441.

taken out loans in the three immediately preceding years in order to purchase the control of another company, the following rules apply: 1) the merger plan must indicate the resources and the deadlines provided for the company resulting from the merger to pay off the debts incurred to take control; 2) the directors' report on the merger plan must indicate the reasons justifying the acquisition of control, and set out an economic and financial plan specifying the resources involved and describing the aims to be achieved; 3) the expert report on the merger plan must give an opinion on the reasonableness of the merger plan and the directors' report (see Arts. 49-52 Sp-LSC)[39]. The merger LBO may take place, provided that it is duly demonstrated that it does not raise considerable risks for the involved stakeholders.

One may therefore draw a general – interpretative – conclusion: as long as the laws contain enough provisions that adequately protect shareholders and creditors (beyond the ones on financial assistance)[40], LBOs should be accepted and not necessarily discouraged (for instance, by a strict application of said regime on financial assistance)[41].

5. Sales of company's assets

The company may sell part or all its assets to other companies. This type of transaction is not regulated at EU level and neither is it treated in the EMCA. National regulations hence differ.

The sale per se does not impact directly on the position of the shareholders of the companies involved. In any case, it may – pursuant to some domestic laws

---

39 Art. 2501-*bis* It-CC runs along same lines and has probably acted as the model for the more recent Spanish provision (see Silvestri, *The new Italian law on merger leveraged buy-outs: a law and economics perspective*, in *EBOR*, 2005, 101; Strampelli, *Rendering*, 561). Also according to Maczyński/Jerzmanowski, in *Companies laws*, 876, MLBOs should be considered exempt from the application of Art. 345 Pol-CC on financial assistance.

40 Like, for instance – beside the provisions on groups – the ones on the duty of loyalty and on related party transactions: see on this topic Hopt, *Conflict*, 181 ff. and Vicari, *Conflicts of interest of target company's directors and shareholders in leveraged buy-outs*, in *ECFR*, 2007, 346.

41 For a similar reasoning see also e. g. Strampelli, *Rendering*, 568, who advocates for more flexibility in this field of law: "the risk that financial assistance gives rise to market abuse or discrimination amongst shareholders should be limited by the remedies already applicable in the legislation of the various Member States. For example, the regulation of financial services or, more in general, the fiduciary duties of the directors and their duty to act in good faith or conflict of interest regulations".

(like the Belgian, German and Spanish) – require the disclosure of information and general meeting approval, like in the case of merger decisions[42].

Some of these transactions have been already examined above – in Chapter 3, § 4 – discussing the situations that trigger a shareholders' meeting vote in cases of sales of assets.

Certain companies acts, however, go further and explicitly regulate in a more articulate way the case of the sale of the "totality" of the company assets. Under Sp-LSC, paradigmatically, in case of "total assignment", the directors of the assignor company (the vendor) must draw up a proposal containing some necessary information (name, type and registered office of the assignee company, information on the valuation of the assets and liabilities; the consideration to be received by the company; the possible consequences of the assignee on employment; etc.) and a report on the proposal.

The assignment must then be decided on by the general meeting of the assignor company in strict accordance with the proposal, and with the requirements provided for adoption of merger agreements[43].

The assignment shall not be made until one month has elapsed from the publication date of the most recent announcement of the decision, or in the case of written notice to all shareholders and creditors, of the service of notice to the last one. Within this period the creditors of the assignor company and of the assignee company may object to the assignment, on the same terms and with the same effects as are provided for mergers (Art. 88 Sp-LSC).

The total assignment will become effective on its registration by the assignor company in the companies register. In case of multiple assignee companies, anyone of them will be jointly and severally liable for any unfulfilled obligations taken on by each assignee, up to the limit of the net worth allotted to each one in the assignment; when applicable, the assignee company itself if it has not ceased to exist, will be liable for the full amount of the obligation. The joint and several liability of assignees and shareholders lapses after five years (Art. 91 Sp-LSC)[44].

---

42 See Art. 12.7 B-CA; Sects. 176 ff. Ge-TA; Arts. 81 ff. Sp-LSC.
43 The announcement should mention the right of shareholders or partners and creditors to obtain the full text of the decision adopted and the right of objection pertaining to creditors. It will not be necessary to publicize the agreement if a written notice is sent individually to all the shareholders or partners and creditors by a procedure that guarantees receipt at the address appearing in the company's files (Art. 87 Sp-LSC).
44 A similar approach is taken by Sects. 237 A-PuCA and 174 ff. Ge-TA, which govern the "asset transfer" transaction; and Art. 1033-1 Gr-PuCA.

6. Shares purchases

Purchases of shares are regulated by national companies acts only when they give the power to obtain control of a listed company.

In these cases the Takeover Directive (2004/25/EC) – and individual national laws on listed companies – apply. Laws are often supported by a further set of secondary takeover rules setting out more detailed provisions on how takeover bids should be governed (once again only in case of listed companies).

We shall consider these provisions in the chapter devoted to listed companies (see Chapter 12, § 3).

On the contrary, specific safeguards for shareholders of unlisted public companies in case of shares purchase agreements normally are not considered by national companies acts (an exception may be found in the provisions facilitating or limiting the transfer of shares, which were examined above in Chapter 4, § 5).

7. Squeeze-outs and freeze-outs

Several companies acts grant the main shareholders the right to buy out under certain conditions the shares of the minorities ("squeeze out").

(I) For listed companies, the right is set out in the Takeover Directive (2004/25/EC), which allows any shareholder acquiring 90% (or more, depending on the Member State) of the voting shares of a listed company through a tender offer the right to cash out minorities at a fair price (see on the takeover procedure below Chapter 12, § 3).

Some authors have suggested that the threshold of 90% for the squeeze out may be too high to eliminate the problems of the "free rider" investors, who decide not to tender their shares and aim at remaining in the company hoping for increased profits or an improved bid at a later stage (it is rather frequent that the bidder obtains control, but not 90% of the shares after a takeover)[45].

In such a situation the controlling shareholder may employ some tecqniques to try to get rid of the minority shareholders after the takeover. Famous in this

---

[45] As illustrated i.e. by Vos, *'Baby, it's cold outside...' – a comparative and economic analysis of freeze-outs of minority shareholders*, in *ECFR*, 2018, 173, beside the "free rider" problem (the shareholders keep their shares, in order to free ride on the profits that they assume the bidder will make), there may ba also an "holdout problem": shareholders consider the takeover bid sufficiently high, but still hold on to their shares in order to extract a higher portion of the value created by the bidder.

regard are the "Versatel" and "Shell" cases, decided by the Dutch courts starting in 2005 (and in 2007 for Shell).

Tele2 AB (a Swedish operator) launched a takeover bid on Versatel Telecom International NV (a Dutch telecom company) and acquired 83% of the shares, not enough to proceed with a squeeze-out. However – as it was announced in the offer documents – Tele2 decided to "freeze out" the remaining minority shareholder (Centaurus Capital PLC) through a "triangular merger" that would dilute them below the 5% threshold (i.e. Tele 2 and Versatel voted to merge with another company, reducing the stake of the Versatel minority shareholder).

The Versatel minorities filed a request for an investigation procedure with the Amsterdam Enterprise Chamber in order to have the postbid freeze-out technique prohibited. However, the Chamber ruled that the triangular merger did not violate the law. It considered the desire of the majority shareholder to eliminate the minority shareholders a legitimate one, especially since it was also announced in the offer documents for the bid, which was accepted by many of the shareholders. In addition, the Chamber stated that the triangular merger was justified for other reasons, like tax advantages for the Tele2 group.

In a decision in the same case, the Dutch Supreme Court confirmed however a previous decision of the Enterprise Chamber, which ruled that independent directors should remain on the supervisory board of the target company (Versatel) after the takeover in order to negotiate the freeze-out merger and protect the minorities' interests[46].

In another ruling of 2007 on the merger between Royal Dutch Petroleum Company NV and its subsidiary Shell Petroleum NV aimed at freezing out the minorities (Trafalgar Catalyst Fund Inc. and Trafalgar Volatility Fund Inc.), the Amsterdam Enterprise Chamber decided on the contrary – having ascertained that the "freeze out" merger was used with the sole intention of diluting the minorities – that this was an illegitimate use of the procedure and it violated the principle of reasonableness and fairness. The case was later settled by the parties while pending before the Court of Appeals[47].

---

[46] The case – decided on 14 September 2007 – is discussed by Vos, '*Baby*', 173 (reporting that "these decisions have been criticized in [Dutch] legal scholarship for unnecessarily slowing down the process"). The Author notes also that in US laws the threshold for a squeeze out is often not higher than 50%.

[47] See Vos, '*Baby*', 174 (Amsterdam Commercial Chamber, 20 December 2007).

In any case – at it has been noted – "in the Netherlands, the threshold for [squeeze]-outs has in practice been lowered by allowing alternative freeze-out techniques", like the post-takeover merger, although under certain conditions[48].

(II) As far as unlisted companies are concerned, the squeeze out right is also recognized in some national laws (even if far less frequently) outside the scope of the Takeover Directive and thus also for unlisted companies.

Sometimes this remedy is called "corporate squeeze out" in order to distinguish it from the "takeover squeeze out" (the one regulated by the Takeover Directive) and emphasize the fact that they are treated under different areas of the law[49].

Taking again the Netherlands as an example for the "corporate squeeze out" model, a shareholder owning at least 95% of the share capital (exercising at least 95% of the voting rights) may file a legal claim against the other shareholders to demand a compulsory transfer of their shares. The same applies if two or more shareholders together have reached this threshold.

However, the court may still reject the claim (and the right may thus be overruled) if the minority shareholders would suffer a serious material loss as a result of the transfer despite the compensation (or if one of the minorities holds shares to which, according to the articles of association, particular rights are attached in respect of the exercise of control in the company)[50].

The right to a squeeze-out is also set forth by the EMCA: both in Ch. 11, when the majority shareholder holds more than 90% of the shares and a corresponding share of the votes (Sect. 11.34), and in Ch. 15 (on corporate groups), allowing

---

48 See Vos, *'Baby'*, 183, who concludes as follows: "the threshold of 90–95% for freeze-outs in the European Union seems excessively high, as it increases takeover premia to inefficiently high levels and fails to eliminate the free rider problem and the holdout problem completely. Setting a lower threshold for freeze-outs would facilitate (efficient) control shifts, as acquiring complete control becomes easier. On the other hand, there are sound policy reasons, based on the property rights of shareholders and the concentrated shareholder structure in the European Union. In my view, it would make sense in a European context to put the threshold for freeze-outs at an equal level as for other fundamental changes, i.e. two thirds or three quarters of the shares in most European countries".
49 See paradigmatically Sect. 70 Da-CA; Ch. 18, Sect. 1, Fi-CA; Sects. 327a-327 f Ge-PuCA; Art. 47 Gr-PuCA; Sect. 490 Por-CC; Ch. 22, § 1 Sw-CA. For a useful summary see Van der Elst/Van der Steen, *Balancing*, 391.
50 An example of serious material loss as a result of the transfer is if the minorities transferring their block of shares would have to pay special income taxes. See Renssen, in *Company laws*, 1439; Vos, *'Baby'*, 170. However, the possibility of a court overruling it is not provided for in the other jurisdictions indicated in the previous footnote.

the parent company, which controls more than 90% of the shares and votes of the subsidiary, the right to purchase the remaining shares (Sect. 15.11).

One of the most important issues regarding a squeeze-out relates to the consideration for the targeted shares. Usually companies acts require the application of appropriate valuation methods and procedures in order to safeguard the position of minority shareholders[51].

8. Conversions

(I) A conversion is an amendment of the articles of association whereby the type of company is changed without terminating it or generating a new entity (for instance – in the simplest case – a private company changes its form into a public company).

Almost all Member States' laws adopt a very pragmatic approach with reference to this kind of transaction, allowing fundamentally any kind of conversion[52]. As a consequence of the lack of harmonization, some laws are however very detailed (and regulate most cases of conversion); others are more generic. The EMCA does not consider conversions.

Given the purpose of this book, we shall only consider the conversion affecting a public company.

(II) The core of the phenomenon is the "continuity" of the company under another legal type. The transformed company maintains its legal identity, retains its rights and obligations and continues in all its relationships.

Limits to conversions usually involve the legal type that it turns into. For instance, in jurisdictions where bonds can only be issued by public companies (and not by private ones), a public company as such cannot convert into a private company as long as it still has bonds outstanding[53].

---

51 See for further analysis Vos, *'Baby'*, 149.

52 Some exceptions may however be found. See for instance Dutch law, where it is provided that where the transaction concerns a conversion of (or into) a foundation or a conversion of a limited liability company into an association the authorization of the court is required. After the conversion of a foundation, the articles of association must show that the assets of the foundation, as they were upon conversion, and related benefits, may only be used in another way besides the way required prior to the conversion with court authorization; see Renssen, in *Company laws*, 1449.

53 See i.e. paradigmatically Art. 13 Sp-LSC (referring to bondholders) and Art. 131 Por-CC (referring to shareholders with special rights).

Other specific limits are set forth by the individual national laws, like the laws prohibiting the conversion of a company in liquidation or while undergoing an insolvency proceeding[54].

A shareholders' resolution is always required, since the conversion implies – as noted above – an amendment of the articles of association. The majority required to transform a public company into a private company, a partnership or another entity is often set higher than the majority required for simple modifications of the articles of association[55].

Normally it is also stipulated that shareholders who lose the benefit of limited liability – as when a public company is converted into a partnership – have to personally approve the transaction.

Laws are more or less permissive regarding the set of information that has to be provided to shareholders. A great diversity of provisions can also be found with reference to the features and extension of the protection accorded to shareholders and creditors.

(III) Beginning with information, on the one hand, you may find national laws which do not expressly lay down any conditions for the conversion of a public company; therefore, no particular information is required. On the other hand, there are the companies acts stating that, when the meeting is called, the directors have to make a series of documents available to shareholders, unless the decision is taken unanimously (these documents include: a directors' report illustrating the transaction; the company's financial statements, drawn up in the six months prior to the date scheduled for the meeting; the auditor's report on the financial statements if the company is obliged to submit its accounts to audit; the proposed instrument of incorporation or articles of associ-

---

54 See i.e. Art. 551 Pol-CC. For other countries, as far as the liquidation is concerned, see Art. 5 Sp-LSC, which forbids the transaction if the distribution of the company assets has already begun; as far as the insolvency proceedings is concerned, see Art. 2499 It-CC, according to which the conversion is allowed only if the "purpose" or the "state" of those proceedings are compatible with the conversion; therefore, procedures involving the liquidation of companies, such as bankruptcy, are deemed less suited to conversion than those with the purpose to preserve the companies such as agreements with creditors.

55 Unanimous consent is required for the transformation of a public company into a partnership pursuant Art. 225-245 Fr-CC; at least nine tenths of the votes cast are required according to Ch. 26, Sect, 6, Sw-CA and Art. 2.18 Du-CC (in the case of conversion of a public company into a type other than a private company). At the opposite end of the scale are the Member States where no supermajority is required: unless otherwise stated in the articles of association, the simple majority required for amendments of the articles of association are all that is needed (see for instance Art. 321 Da-CA and Ch. 19, Sect. 3 Fi-CA).

ation that will result from the conversion, etc.[56]). Under other legislations – much to a lesser extent – the directors' obligation to prepare a report explaining the reasons and effects of the conversion is only required if a public company is converted into a partnership (or, more generally, an entity that is not a limited liability company, like a consortium, a foundation or an association)[57].

(IV) The protection accorded to shareholders varies a lot. First of all, some laws vest the shareholders with a right of withdrawal if they vote against the transaction[58]; others do not.

Secondly, many regulations provide that, once the deed of conversion has been entered into the companies register, it may only be invalidated within a short time period[59]. Shareholders may still bring a suit for damages: however, this kind of protection involves considerable drawbacks in light of how difficult it is to prove damage (of course it will not be easy to demonstrate the acutal harm suffered as a consequence, for instance, of a conversion from a public company into a partnership, which has deprived shareholders of the benefit of limited liability)[60].

(V) Finally, as far as the protection of creditors is concerned, domestic laws vary again. Creditors simply have to passively accept the conversion, pursuant to some companies acts. According to others they may either present a claim for security or file a suit in order to oppose the transaction under certain circumstances[61].

---

56 See i.e. Sects. 326 ff. Da-CA; Art. 1010-2 Lu-CA; Art. 560 ff. Pol-CC; Art. 9 Sp-LSC.

57 See i.e. Art. 2500-*sexies* It-CC and Art. 565 Pol-CC.

58 See i.e. Art. 2437 It-CC and Art. 15 Sp-LSC.

59 Three months according to Art. 20 Sp-LSC; two months – but only for creditors that object to a conversion of a public company into other entities besides companies and partnerships – pursuant to Art. 2500-*novies* It-CC.

60 An exception in this regard – which is partly at odds with the principle of "certainty" set forth in the directives regulating extraordinary transactions – is represented, for instance, by the French provisions: it is always possible to annul a decision of conversion on the general grounds regulated by the code of commerce (which provides that a decision to amend the company's articles of association can be considered void if the circumstances for annulment fall within those expressly provided for in the same code or if the nullity can be sought on the basis of the law governing contracts). It is however noted that it is very rare in practice to nullify an invalid conversion since a validation procedure is provided for in Art. 220-7 Fr-CC and 1839 of the French code civil. A validation could be requested where a formality prescribed has been omitted or improperly done; see Schlumberger/Ansault, in *Company laws*, 190. The Polish legislator, for example, also only refers to the general provisions which govern the challenge to (all) the resolutions of public companies, which are to apply accordingly: see Art. 422-427 Pol-CC.

61 See paradigmatically for the three different approaches: French law ("rights of the creditors are not affected by the transformation. The creditors are entitled to request from the sharehold-

These latter remedies differ greatly. Under the former, if the creditor proves that his credit will become substantially less recoverable due to the conversion, he is entitled to demand an additional – supplemental – security as collateral to be provided by the company, even before the conversion is entered in the companies register.

On the contrary, the "objection" remedy may even block the conversion unless the court believes that there is no significant harm for creditors or the company provides security which is accepted by the creditor raising the objections.

The absence of convergence in these regards is thus remarkable (as it is for the case – discussed above – of the protection of creditors in mergers: see § 2 [62]).

That situation may also be detrimental for cross-border conversions. As we shall see below (§ 9), shareholders and creditors in case of cross-border transactions may request additional guarantees to the company or the court if they feel that the legislation of the foreign Member State where the company is headed by means of the conversion does not offer sufficient safeguards.

9. Cross-border transactions

The EU released a directive in 2005 with the aim of facilitating cross-border mergers of limited liability companies (Directive 2005/56/EC). In 2017 the Directive was replaced by Directive 2017/1132/EU; in 2019 that Directive was also amended by Directive 2019/2121/EU, which extended the legislation to divisions and conversions (the Directive must be implemented in national laws by 31 January 2023).

The core principle of cross-border operations law is contained in Recital 60 of Directive 2017/1132/EU: "in order to facilitate cross-border merger operations, it should be provided that monitoring of the completion and legality of the decision-making process in each merging company should be carried out by the na-

---

ers of the converted company the payment of the debts incurred prior to the conversion. The same applies for the guarantees attached to the debts": see Schlumberger/Ansault, in *Company laws*, 190); Sects. 204 and 22 Ge-TA (if creditors of the company demand satisfaction of their claims security is to be provided if they file their claims within six months after the date of the transaction); Art. 2500-*novies* It-CC (the conversion from a public company into an entity which is not a limited liability company takes effect sixty days after the mandatory public disclosure; during this period the creditors may oppose it on the grounds that the transaction puts at risk their credit).

62 Actually the remedies offered to creditors are similar to the ones established for the case of merger (and division); and see explicitly Sect. 204 Ge-TA.

tional authority having jurisdiction over each of those companies, whereas monitoring of the completion and legality of the cross-border merger should be carried out by the national authority having jurisdiction over the company resulting from the cross-border merger. The national authority in question could be a court, a notary or any other competent authority appointed by the Member State concerned"[63] (the same is valid also for divisions and conversions).

Therefore, two stages may be identified: the "decision making" stage and the "monitoring of the completion and legality" stage. Each company taking part in a cross-border operation, and each third party concerned, remains subject to the

---

63 See *inter alia* Schindler, *Cross-Border Mergers in Europe – Company law is catching up – Commentary on the ECJ's decision in SEVIC systems AG*, in *ECFR*, 2006, 109; Siemns, *SEVIC: Beyond Cross-Border Mergers*, in *EBOR*, 2007, 307; Gesell/Riemer, *Outbound cross-border mergers protected by freedom of establishment*, in *ECFR*, 2007, 308; Ventoruzzo, *Cross-border mergers, change of applicable corporate laws and protection of dissenting shareholders: withdrawal rights under Italian law*, in *ECFR*, 2007, 47; Schindler, *Discussion report: cross-border mergers*, in *ECFR*, 2007, 43; Doralt, *Cross-border-mergers – A glimpse into the future*, in *ECFR*, 2007, 17; Decher, *Cross border mergers: traditional structures and SE-merger structures*, in *ECFR*, 2007, 5; Ugliano, *The new cross-border merger directive: harmonisation of European company law and free movement*, in *EBLR*, 2007, 585; Myckaert/Geens, *Cross-border mergers and minority protection: an open-ended harmonization*, in *ECL*, 2008, 288; Pellé, *Companies crossing borders within Europe*, in *ECL*, 2008, 284; Raaijmakers/Olthoff, *Creditor protection in cross-border mergers: unfinished business*, in *ECL*, 2008, 305; Szydlo, *The right of companies to cross-border conversion under the TFEU rules on freedom of establishment*, in *ECFR*, 2010, 414; Roelofs, *Cross-border divisions of SEs*, in *ECL*, 2010, 142; Van Eck/Roelofs, *Ranking the rules applicable to cross-borders mergers*, in *ECL*, 2011, 17; Bekkum, *Cross-border investments in undertakings and the future of EU company law*, in *EBLR*, 2014, 811; Bartman, *10 years cross-border mergers directive: some observations about EU border protection and minority exit rights*, in *ECL*, 2017, 214; Stephan, *A French-German company conversion (KG Berlin 21 March 2016): another call for harmonizing the laws on cross-border company migrations in Europe*, in *ECL*, 2017, 177; Biermeyer/Meyer, *Corporate mobility in Europe: an empirical perspective*, in *ECL*, 2018, 64; Garcimartín/Gandía, *Cross-border conversions in the EU: the EU Commission proposal*, in *ECFR*, 2019, 15; Fabris, *European companies' 'mutilated freedom'. From the freedom of establishment to the right of cross-border conversion*, in *ECL*, 2019, 106; Binard/Schummer, *The case for further flexibility in matters of cross-border corporate mobility*, in *ECL*, 2019, 31; Schmidt, *Cross-border mergers, divisions and conversions: accomplishments and deficits of the company law package*, in *ECFR*, 2019, 222; Id., *The mobility aspects of the EU Commission's company law Package: Or – 'The Good, the Bad and the Ugly'*, in *ECL*, 2019, 13; Winner, *Protection of creditors and minority shareholders in cross-border transactions*, in *ECFR*, 2019, 44; Garcimartín/Gandía, *Cross-border conversions in the EU: the EU Commission proposal*, in *ECFR*, 2019, 15; Corbisier/Bernard, *Cross-border mobility within the EU and specifically in Luxembourg and Belgium: same destination, different roads*, in *ECL*, 2019, 18; European Company Law Experts, *The Commission's 2018 proposal on cross-border mobility – An assessment*, in *ECFR*, 2019, 196; Verbrugh, *European company law in 2020: mobility and sustainability*, in *ECL*, 2020, 4.

provisions of the national law which would be applicable in the case of a national transaction: the law of the "departure Member State".

On the other hand, the execution of the transactions is dealt with by the national laws of the resulting company and the scrutiny of legality is carried out by the authority designated for the purpose by the "destination Member State" (that authority must ensure that the provisions of all national laws have been complied with)[64].

The rights of information for shareholders and creditors are clearly at the core of the Directive: on top of everything, they must receive – beyond the information they would obtain in case of an ordinary "national" operation under their domestic legislation – detailed information on "the implications of the cross-border [transaction]" for their position (see Art. 86(e)).

The Directive of 2019 has added some extra-protection for shareholders and creditors. Shareholders of the company ceasing to exist in case of a cross-border merger or division, and shareholders of the company subject to the cross-border conversion, must have the right to dispose of their shares and receive adequate cash compensation if they disapprove the cross-border operation. Such compensation must be examined by an independent expert unless the shareholders waive their right thereto (Art. 86(i)). Put simply, they must have the right to withdraw from the company at a fair value (such a right is currently already granted by some domestic laws)[65].

---

64 Other types of rules are also contained in the directives, on the solution of specific conflicts. An example is the following: "if the law of a Member State to which a merging company is subject provides for a procedure to scrutinize and amend the ratio applicable to the exchange of securities or shares, or a procedure to compensate minority members, without preventing the registration of the cross-border merger, such procedure shall only apply if the other merging companies situated in Member States which do not provide for such procedure explicitly accept, when approving the draft terms of the cross-border merger [...], the possibility for the members of that merging company to have recourse to such procedure, to be initiated before the court having jurisdiction over that merging company. In such cases, the authority [...] may issue the certificate [...] even if such procedure has commenced. The certificate shall, however, indicate that the procedure is pending. The decision in the procedure shall be binding on the company resulting from the cross-border merger and all its members" (Art. 127 Directive 2017/1132/EU). In all other cases (which are ruled neither by the directives nor by the national rules) private international law applies.

65 However, a certain view holds that permitting Member States to introduce additional protection mechanisms for minority shareholders may pose further obstacles to cross-border transactions and thus result in the frustration of the aim of the Directive: see e.g. Kurtulan, *Minority shareholder protection in cross-border mergers: a must for or an impediment to the European single market)?*, in *EBOR*, 2017, 101.

The creditors of the company concerned also have to be assured of more incisive protection, pursuant to the Directive. The directors' proposal needs to contain information about the safeguards offered to the creditors whose claims predate the publication of the proposal. If a creditor is dissatisfied with the safeguards offered, he can request additional guarantees from the court within three months from disclosure of the proposal (Art. 86(j)). This provision is also important, since – as we have seen (above, § 8) – not all Member States provide actual safeguards to creditors for conversions.

Shareholders and creditors must also be given the opportunity to submit comments to their company with regard to the proposed cross-border operation. A notice informing the stakeholders about their consultation rights needs to be disclosed in the companies register when filing the cross-border operation proposal (Art. 86(g)).

In any case, the main obstacles to cross-border transactions – which have been clearly pointed out by the Directive – have not been (and may not be) overcome by the Directive itself: the highest barrier remains "the lack of harmonization of safeguards for members [and] creditors". Shareholders and creditors face – notes the Directive – "a wide variety of different forms of protection [in the various Member States] leading to complexity and legal uncertainty" (Recital 17).

That is hard to deny. Imagine a cross-border merger between a Portuguese company (say, Red Rock PLC) and an Irish one (MGM PLC), with the former incorporating the latter (destination Member State is thus Portugal). Suppose Red Rock already owns 51% of MGM and that Phil, Stu and Alan are, respectively, two minority shareholders and a creditor of MGM.

Phil, Stu and Alan must agree that "their" company will cease to follow laws that – among others – do not regulate the corporate groups and will become subject to laws that, on the other hand, address corporate groups extensively. During the process they may be adequately informed of "the implications of the cross-border merger" for their position and given specific exits and safeguards. However, they will inevitably submit their rights to laws that for them are uncertain in many aspects.

11 Dissolution and liquidation

Summary:
1. Causes for dissolution and directors' duties
2. Liquidators' powers and duties
3. The liquidation proceedings and the cancellation of the company

1. Causes for dissolution and directors' duties

In the absence of any directive on the dissolution and liquidation of the company (the original proposal of 1987 was not adopted[1]), common causes for winding up under Member States' laws (and the EMCA: see Ch. 14) are the following: expiration of the duration of the company, achievement of the corporate objects or evident impossibility of their achievement, inability to operate or continued inactivity by the members of the general meeting, capital reduced to below the legal minimum limit, nullity of the company declared by the competent court, opening of insolvency proceedings, etc., and – in any case – the other reasons set out in the articles of association[2] (according to Nordic laws – and the EMCA – a dissolution may also result from cases of mismanagement or abuse by the dominant shareholder[3]).

---

1 See the draft proposal DOC XV/43/87-EN. The rules on the insolvency proceedings are not addressed in this book (see for some references however see above Chapter 9, § 5). Similarly, the EMCA does not include insolvency law within the boundaries of the Model and explains the choice as follows: "company law and insolvency law can constitute (and in fact they do constitute) one single topic or at least a 'continuum' and therefore insolvency law should/might be included in the EMCA. However, this has the inherent risk of burdening EMCA with a very large amount of legislation, not always connected with company law considerations, which might discourage the states from adopting it".

2 In some Member States, like the Nordic States, the company may also be dissolved at the initiative of the chamber of commerce or the companies register if the company is inactive for a certain time (for instance, the directors appear to be unreachable for at least one year at the addresses mentioned in the companies register or the company has failed for at least one year to comply with its obligation to disclose its annual accounting records or the balance sheet): see on that Renssen, in *Company laws*, 1450. On the other hand, in other States, like Germany, liquidation is basically a "rare" event because – as it has been noted "defunct or dormant companies need not necessarily be removed from the register but can exist for good as empty shell companies"; moreover the main reason for dissolution of companies is the opening of insolvency proceedings: see Schall, in *Company laws*, 420.

3 For cases of mismanagement, see i.e. Art. 2.355 Du-CC and Sects. 12.11 and 14.05 EMCA; for cases of abuse of the dominant shareholder see more extensively above Chapter 6, § 5.

https://doi.org/10.1515/9783110725025-013

When a cause of dissolution arises, the directors must ascertain it without delay and, if a general meeting is needed, call it. They also have to arrange disclosure through registration in the companies register. In the above cases of mismanagement or abuse, the dissolution may also be invoked by the affected shareholders.

In the event of delay or omission, they are – under most Member States law – personally and jointly liable for damages borne by the company, shareholders, company creditors and third parties[4].

Moreover, if the procedures are not promptly opened, directors (and individual shareholders, and the statutory auditors in companies adopting the traditional system) may normally file a claim with the court, which will check why it was wound up[5]. The time specification referring to both the verification of the cause (and the call of the meeting) and its publication may pose serious problems if it is left vague; therefore, under some laws the term is fixed on a mandatory basis[6].

When a cause for dissolution occurs, the directors normally retain the power to manage the company for the purpose of preserving the integrity and value of the shareholders' equity. Therefore, they are also allowed to perform "dynamic" transactions (since the equity of a company is not just a simple accumulation of assets, but rather an organization of assets aimed at running the firm). More specifically, they must perform the existing contracts in order to continue business with regard to the inventories, contracts, employees, network of external agents present at the time of the winding up, etc., in view of the possibility of the company assets being transferred as a whole so as not to lose their goodwill[7]. On the other hand, the directors cannot specifically liquidate the equity as this task is reserved for the liquidators.

Once again, the directors are personally and jointly liable for damages caused to the company, the shareholders, the creditors and third parties deriving from actions or omissions performed in breach of the above obligations.

Few other companies acts take a different, more limiting (and, as a matter of fact, more severe) approach and prohibit the directors, once the winding up be-

---

4 See i.e. Art. 367 Sp-CA; see also Sect. 14.06 EMCA.

5 See i.e. under Art. 2485 It-CC. Less frequently the winding up may be initiated by any person interested (creditors, etc.); see Ch. 20, Sect. 6, Fi-CA.

6 For instance the period is sixty days pursuant to Art. 365 Sp-CA.

7 See paradigmatically Sect. 14.07 EMCA ("until the liquidator assumes his/her duties, the management board of the company shall continue to manage the company with a view to avoid detriment to the integrity and the value of the company's assets"); e. g. Sect. 229 Da-CA and 265 Ge-PuCA

comes effective, from carrying out "new operations", that it to say, the company may no longer engage in any dynamic activity[8].

The general meeting resolution to wind up the company, when needed, must be adopted by the majority required for the amendment of the articles of association (in some States, even with a higher majority[9]).

Should the directors take no action, generally any individual shareholder or director (or a statutory auditor, for companies adopting the latin model) may submit a petition to the court, which will make the necessary decisions if the general meeting has not been called in the meantime or does not pass a resolution[10].

After the liquidation process starts, the general meeting may however decide to revoke the winding up if the grounds for dissolution have disappeared. Under some national laws, however, shareholders who do not vote in favor of that are entitled to withdraw. The company's creditors may also object to the decision on the same terms and with the same effects as provided by law for capital reductions[11].

During the liquidation process, shareholders maintain their rights and the rules concerning the functioning of the bodies, including the auditors and the general meeting, as well as the organization and operation of the company will continue to apply unless the law provides otherwise or such rules are inconsistent with the manner and the purpose of the liquidation.

---

8 See i.e. Art. 233 R-CA. The reason for this provision is that the winding up operation represents the first step in the process of ending the legal personality of the company and it should entail, as a rule, the cessation of its normal course of business. The activity of the company after the winding up comprises only such operations which are strictly necessary for wrapping up any current ongoing commercial activity. The company may no longer seek to gain profit, but its activity must exclusively be aimed towards liquidation. If, acting contrary to the law, the directors of the company continue to pursue new commercial activities on behalf of the latter, they will be personally and jointly liable for their actions. See on that law extensively Doroga/Sitaru, in *Company laws*, 1056.

9 See i.e. Sect. 262 Ge-PuCA and Art. 115 R-CA, which set out a mandatory majority of at least – respectively – three quarters and two thirds of the voting rights held by the shareholders who are present, under the quorum requirements for the meeting of the extraordinary general meeting.

10 See i.e. Art. 227 R-CA.

11 See i.e. Art. 370 Sp-CA; Art. 235 R-CA; Art. 2437 It-CC.

2. Liquidators' powers and duties

Both in the one-tier and two-tier systems the liquidators are appointed by the shareholders.

The board of liquidators works as a team, but may delegate a single member or an executive committee with powers.

In identifying liquidators with powers of management and representation, the shareholders are also free to set rules on how those powers can be exercised and to introduce limits and conditions. If they are not identified, it is presumed that each liquidator has the separate right to manage and represent the company.

Generally, companies acts stipulate that liquidators have the power to carry out all actions beneficial for the company's liquidation and must discharge their duties with the professionalism and diligence required of the nature of the appointment, with a formulation similar to that which regulates the conduct of directors[12].

Liquidators are prohibited from distributing advances on liquidation profits among shareholders unless the financial statements show that the distribution does not affect the available funds needed for full and prompt settlement to the company's creditors, with consequent personal and joint liability for damages caused to the company's creditors in breach of this prohibition. On the other hand, liquidators can make the distribution conditional on the shareholder providing adequate guarantees. If the available funds should prove insufficient for paying the company's debts, the liquidators can ask the shareholders for outstanding payments on a proportional basis[13].

Revocation of the liquidators is the only cause for termination of office governed by law; it may occur either by the will of the general meeting (normally it is the extraordinary general meeting that decides, with the same majorities as for the appointment) or, if there is just cause, before the court, after each shareholder or the public prosecutor (or the statutory auditors, in the latin model) has submitted a petition.

Failure to present the annual financial statements, the persistent inertia of the liquidation or delays in depositing sums collected from debtors in the company's coffers are normally considered just cause for revocation through court proceedings.

---

12 See i.e. Sect. 268 Ge-PuCA and Sects. 14.13 and 14.17 EMCA (liquidators can also undertake new operations if this serves the purposes of an efficient liquidation).
13 See i.e. Art. 2491 It-CC and Sect. 14.17 EMCA.

3. The liquidation proceedings and the cancellation of the company

After their appointment, the liquidators file it at the companies register together with the definition of their powers and related amendments. With this registration, the office of the directors is terminated and the corporate books, a statement of accounts as at the effective date of winding up and a report on operations for the period since the most recently approved financial statements are handed over (duly recorded) to the liquidators[14].

Normally the liquidators are required to draw up the annual financial statements and submit them for general meeting approval at the end of each year[15]. The principles for drawing up the annual financial statements are applied after a "compatibility" opinion is provided, considering the status of the liquidation proceedings since the accounting information to be disclosed is different from information that is on the financial statements of going-concern companies.

The notes to the financial statements indicate the criteria adopted and the reasons justifying their adoption. On the other hand, the directors' report to the financial statements illustrates the performance of the liquidation, the expected duration of the procedure, and the strategies and objectives pursued[16].

At the end of the procedure, the liquidators draw up the (final) financial statements, a general report on the liquidation and the plan for the distribution of the remaining assets to the shareholders. Usually, pursuant to most national laws, the documents are filed at the companies register and a final general meeting has to take place[17].

In order to simplify the conclusion of the proceeding, some laws set forth that the financial statements are considered to be approved if there are no claims and the liquidators are released by the shareholders after the remaining assets have been distributed. The final statement of accounts is also considered ap-

---

14 Under certain companies acts, instead of placing a company into liquidation, the court may order the immediate cancellation of the company from the companies register without liquidation if the assets of the company are not enough to cover the costs of liquidation or if there is no information about the existence of assets, unless a shareholder, a creditor or a third party undertakes to bear the costs of the liquidation (see Sect. 14.08 EMCA, along the lines, i.e. of Sect. 264 Ge-PuCA and Ch. 20, Sect. 2, Fi-CA).

15 See i.e. Art. 2490 It-CC. This is not, however, always mandatory.

16 According to same laws (and the EMCA), during the liquidation the shareholders periodically have the right to be informed about the progress of the liquidation (for instance, every six months: see Sect. 14.15).

17 Normally shareholders and creditors have a short period of time to challenge the statement of accounts before the court (see also EMCA, Sect. 14.19).

proved if a receipt is issued without reserve when the last distribution amount is paid; if there are shareholders that do not collect the amounts due to them, the liquidators must deposit the corresponding sums with a bank with an indication of the names of the beneficiary shareholders. The liquidators must ask for the company to be cancelled from the companies register after the final liquidation statements have been approved. The company no longer exists from that moment on.

However, any company creditors that have not been paid in full may make claims against the shareholders to the extent of the sums they have collected based on the final liquidation statements and against the liquidators if they are considered to be responsible for the non-payment[18].

Normally the company books must be filed and stored for a period at the companies register, with the option for anyone to examine them after paying the costs.

If a company has been de-registered and new assets are discovered, pursuant to some laws (and the EMCA), the court in the location of the last registered office of the company will have to appoint a substitute at the request of any person having a legitimate interest. The substitute may even re-register the company, to the extent this is necessary for completion of the operations. This shall apply *mutatis mutandis* if new liabilities are discovered, but only to the extent that new assets make it possible to pay them off[19].

---

18 See i.e. Art. 2495 It-CC.
19 See Sect. 235 Da-CA and Ch. 20, Sect. 18 Fi-CA (and Sect. 14.21 EMCA).

12 Listed companies

Summary:
1. The "three legs" of the EU listed companies' legislation
2. Enhanced rights of shareholders in listed companies
3. Rules on takeovers
4. Rules on audit committees

1. The "three legs" of the EU listed companies' legislation

Listed companies present specific features which render them different from common public companies. The main distinctions have to do basically with the fact that the large audience of minority shareholders of listed companies does not have access – and normally is not interested in – active management. Shareholders delegate to a large extent the management powers to the board of directors (the phenomenon is even more accentuated for listed companies adopting the dualistic system).

That requires, on the one hand, greater transparency, and, on the other hand, the possibility – in the few but important cases where shareholders are asked to vote – of adopting measures that may encourage and facilitate their participation in the shareholders' general meeting.

The other fundamental time when the economic position of shareholders is impacted is the change of control stage. The purchase of the company's control by a new acquirer may expose the minority shareholders to risks and therefore requires appropriate procedures and safeguards.

The EU has intervened in these fields – enhanced transparency and control, facilitation of shareholders' votes and takeovers – laying down some specific rules and providing a kind of "three-legged" regulation.

First of all, in 2004, the Council adopted the "Transparency Directive" (Directive 2004/109/EC), requiring companies with shares traded on regulated markets in the EU to make their activities transparent, by regularly publishing certain information. The basic material that has to be disclosed includes yearly and periodic (more analytical) financial reports, information on major changes in the holding of voting rights and "ad hoc" inside information which could affect the price of the shares.

The Transparency Directive was amended in 2013 by Directive 2013/50/EU to reduce the administrative burden on smaller companies, particularly by abolishing the requirement to publish quarterly financial reports, and improve the effi-

https://doi.org/10.1515/9783110725025-014

ciency of the transparency system, mainly regarding disclosing information on voting rights held through derivative financial instruments[1].

The rules contained in those Directives, however, are mainly "capital market" regulations and therefore will not be analyzed in this book.

The second level of intervention by the EU was realized in 2007 with the "Shareholder Rights Directive" (2007/36/EC) (or the "First SRD"), which set out certain new rights – and specified others – for shareholders in listed companies.

That Directive was amended by Directive 2017/828/EU, with the aim of encouraging more long-term engagement of shareholders (the "Second" SRD). Furthermore, in 2018, the Commission implemented Regulation 2018/1212/EU, introducing further requirements as regards shareholder identification, the transmission of information and facilitating the exercise of shareholders' rights.

---

1 Although European public companies – as we have seen above (Chapter 4, § 3) – may deviate from the "one-share/one-vote" paradigm for various reasons, corporate governance in Europe is essentially based on the fundamental principle that shareholders' voting rights should be proportional to economic ownership in the company. In recent years, however, financial derivative instruments have increasingly enabled investors to separate the economic risk of owning shares of a public company from the ability to vote those shares.

Often an investor enters into a contract that obliges him to purchase a certain quantity of shares some weeks (or months) later at a fixed price; the risk involves the possibility that the price of the shares will become lower than the one set in these weeks/months (so called "long" position). To balance the risk, the investor usually takes a parallel "short" position by committing to sell, to another investor who in turn commits to buy, that same quantity of shares at a price slightly higher than that set in the first contract. In this way, the first investor gives up the higher earnings that could have been obtained from a sharp rise in the price of the shares, but protects himself from the risk of its decrease. These commitments to sell and buy "forward" are derivative instruments in the sense that they have their own market, but any gains and losses arise from changes in the price of the underlying (the price of the share), not their own. However, both transactions (buy/sell) may be carried separately (involving more speculation): the investor may simply decide to buy the shares today and agree with another investor to sell them some time ahead. In that case, even if the investor gains voting power, he does not bear the risk of a negative return on the investment (voting power is higher than the economic risk; we may term this "negative decoupling"). Often it is said that this vote is "empty", because, even if the investor may actually vote, he has no real interest in the outcome of the resolution.

On the other hand, an investor can agree to buy the shares but have them delivered a later stage, giving up the voting power today but with the expectation of gaining a return on the investment at a later stage (economic risk is higher than the voting power: "positive decoupling"). This situation becomes particularly interesting during takeover situations because domestic laws often only require the disclosure of voting positions (but not economic exposure). This situation may also misrepresent the company's shareholder base. For the description of the phenomenon in company law see for all Ridge, *Hedge funds and risk-decoupling – The empty voting problem in the European Union*, 2012, at ssrn; Clottens, *Empty voting: a European perspective*, in *ECFR*, 2012, 446; Houben/Straetmans, *Shareholder*, 632.

The third level of EU intervention involved the adoption in 2004 of the Directive 2004/25/EC on takeover bids, laying down minimum standards for the acquisition of shares involving a change of control of traded EU companies.

The rule set forth by Directive 2013/34/EU on annual and consolidated accounts (that we have seen above in Chapter 8) are in a separate position. In the area of corporate governance rules, they require listed company to set up – within the management board – a mandatory "audit committee", comprising non-executive directors, with the task of working together with the executive directors and strengthening the financial control on the company. We shall come back on this committee in the last paragraph of this Chapter.

2. Enhanced rights of shareholders in listed companies

The main function of the First SRD of 2007 was to define minimum rights for shareholders in listed companies across the EU. This Directive was an important measure in the follow-up to the Commission Action Plan of 2003 on modernising company law and enhancing corporate governance in the EU.

The Directive included a number of specific requirements: (i) timely access of shareholders to all information relevant to general meetings; (ii) a right to ask questions at the general meeting; (iii) facilitating the cross-border exercise of voting rights by correspondence and by proxy; (iv) the abolition of practices that constitute major obstacles to voting, in particular for institutional investors.

The first main change from the First to the Second SRD of 2017 had to do with the amendment to Art. 3 which now gives companies the right to identify their shareholders. This creates an obligation on financial intermediaries (which manage the relationship between investors and the company) to send the necessary information to determine shareholders' identity in advance. Intermediaries also have to communicate relevant information from the company to the shareholders to facilitate the exercise of their rights (the Directive ensures that the shareholders can receive confirmation that the vote expressed at the general meeting has been registered and counted by the company)[2].

---

2 On the two SRDs see among others Mamarous, *Is the EU taking shareholders right seriously? An essay on the impotence of shareholdership in corporate Europe,* in *ECL,* 2010, 195; Cools, *The dividing line between shareholder democracy and board autonomy,* in *ECFR,* 2014, 258; Reynisson, *Related party transactions: analysis of proposed article 9c of Shareholders' Rights Directive,* in *ECL,* 2016, 175; Houben/Straetmans, *Shareholders,* 615; Vos, *The AkzoNobel case: an activist shareholder's battle against the backdrop of the shareholder rights directive,* in *ECL,* 2017, 238; Kyriakou, *Harmonizing corporate actions for the achievement of a capital markets union: an analysis*

Secondly, shareholders have been given the right to vote on the remuneration policy of the members of the administrative, management and control bodies (see Art. 9-bis).

Thirdly, the new Directive introduced certain guarantees to protect shareholders, the company and all its stakeholders, subjecting relevant transactions with related parties to the approval of the shareholders or the management or the supervisory body to avoid the risk that these transactions give the opportunity to these parties to appropriate value belonging to the company (see Recital 42). The Member States therefore have been asked to define adequate procedures for approving transactions with related parties.

The aim of both SR Directives – on a general level – is to establish specific requirements in order to encourage shareholder engagement in the company, in particular in the long term. That is particularly clear in the second and third Recitals of the Second SRD, where the EU legislator affirms that "the financial crisis [of 2007–2008] has revealed that shareholders in many cases supported managers' excessive short-term risk taking", that "there is clear evidence that the current level of 'monitoring' of investee companies and engagement by institutional investors and asset managers is often inadequate and focuses too much on short-term returns, which may lead to suboptimal corporate governance and performance" and that, on the contrary, it is the intention of the EU Commission to tackle "a number of actions in the area of corporate governance, in particular to encourage long-term shareholder engagement and to enhance transparency between companies and investors".

This perspective has however been criticized by some scholars, especially where long-term value governance is considered to be superior to short-terminism, on the grounds that, "although promoting long-termism in the asset management industry makes sense for the purpose of financial stability, this may undermine the efficiency of corporate governance. The latter is arguably more

---

of the shareholders' rights directive, the green paper 'building a capital markets union' and TAR-GET2-Securities, in *ECL,* 2017, 121; Van del Elst, *Shareholders holding the reins on remuneration: the European say on pay,* in *ECL,* 2017, 114; Sørensen/Neville, *Suspension of the exercise of voting rights: a step towards deterrent and consistent sanctioning of EU transparency requirements?,* in *ECL,* 2017, 150; Hallemeesch, *Self-dealing by controlling shareholders: improving minority protection in light of article 9c SRD,* in *ECFR,* 2018, 197; Groenland, *Related party transactions in the revised shareholders' rights directive: the EU perspective and implementation in national law,* in *ECL,* 2019, 44.

important than capital market regulation to support innovation and economic growth"[3] (see on this theme also above Chapter 9, § 1).

3. Rules on takeovers

The Directive 2004/25/EC on takeover bids (usually called the "Takeover Directive") determines the "rules of the game" before and after a bid for "control" over a listed company has been made[4].

---

3 See Pacces, *Hedge fund activism and the revision of the Shareholder Rights Directive*, 2017, at *ecgi.org*.

4 The literature is very broad (and many articles are provision-specific). See especially Maul/ Kouloridas, *The takeover bids directive*, in *GLJ*, 2004, 355; Bartman, *Analysis and consequences of the EC Directive on takeover bids*, in *ECL*, 2004, 5; Siems, *The rules on conflict of laws in the European takeover directive*, in *ECFR*, 2004, 458; Enriques, *The mandatory bid rule in the takeover directive: harmonization without foundation*, in *ECFR*, 2004, 440; Edwards, *The Directive on takeover bids – not worth the paper it's written on*, in *ECFR*, 2004, 416; Maul/Kouloridas, *The takeover bids directive*, in *GLJ*, 2004, 355; Werlauff, *The impact of the takeover directive on minority shareholders in companies listed in Denmark*, in *ECL*, 2005, 100; Mucciarelli, *White knights and black knights – Does the search for competitive bids always benefit the shareholders of target companies*, in *ECFR*, 2006, 408; Menjucq, *The European regime on takeovers*, in *ECFR*, 2006, 222; Rygaert, *Cross-border takeover regulation: a transatlantic perspective*, in *ECFR*, 2007, 434; Clarke, *Takeover regulation through the regulatory looking glass*, in *GLJ*, 2007, 381; Lackum/Meyer/Witt, *The offering of shares in a cross-border takeover*, in *ECFR*, 2008, 101; Lamandini, *Takeover bids and 'Italian' reciprocity*, in *ECL*, 2008, 56; Papadopoulos, *The mandatory provisions of the EU Takeover bid directive and their deficiencies*, 2008, at *ssrn.com*; Id., *Infringements of fundamental freedoms within the EU market for corporate control*, in *ECFR*, 2012, 221; Simon, *Adoption of the European Directive on takeover bids: an on-again, off-again story*, in Tison et al. (eds.), *Perspectives*, 345; Davies/Schuster/van der Welle de Ghelcke, *The takeover directive as a protectionist tool?*, 2010, at *ecgi.org*; Psaroudakis, *The mandatory bid and company law in Europe*, in *ECFR*, 2010, 550; Szlachetka/Kluziak, *The hostile takeover in Poland: recent developments*, in *ECL*, 2011, 152; McCahery/Vermeulen, *The case against reform of the takeover bids directive*, in *EBLR*, 201, 541; Gerner-Beuerle/Kershaw/Solinas, *Is the board neutrality rule trivial? Amnesia about corporate law in European takeover regulation*, in *EBLR*, 2011, 561; Mukwiri, *Takeovers and incidental protection of minority shareholders*, in *ECFR*, 2013, 432; Id., *The end of history for the board neutrality rule in the EU*, in *EBOR*, 2020, 253; Skog/Sjöman, *No rule, just exemptions? Mandatory bids in Sweden and the EU*, in *ECFR*, 2014, 393; Hopt, *European takeover reform 2012/2013 – Time to re-examine the mandatory bid*, in *EBOR*, 2014, 143; Oplustil, *The takeover of public companies as a mode of exercising EU treaty freedoms*, in *EBOR*, 2018, 923; Taleska, *Shareholder proponents as control acquirers: a British, German and Italian perspective on the regulation of collective shareholder activism via takeover rules*, in *EBOR*, 2018, 797; Habersack, *Non-frustration rule and mandatory bid rule – Cornerstones of European takeover law?*, in *ECFR*, 2018, 1.

The main rules that have been introduced are: the rules on the "mandatory bid", the rules on the "defensive measures" and the "break-through" rules. These three sets of law reflect the basic economic principles of takeover regulation and the mobility of corporate control in Europe.

In order to properly understand the economic and legislative rationale of the rules on takeover, it is important to recall the situation that the EU had to face before the Directive and the objective that regulators wanted to achieve.

(I) During the 1980s and the 1990s, a considerable number of acquisitions was pursued in Europe through "hostile takeovers", that is to say unsolicited bids by third parties offering to purchase enough shares to control the company on the market. Even when transactions were negotiated, the "hostile bid potential" played an important role.

That happened especially in the UK, but also – even if on a minor scale – in continental Europe (consider, for instance, that Sweden had a total of about 250 takeovers during the period 1990 – 2001, which corresponds to 9 % of the number of listed firms on the Stockholm Stock Exchange)[5].

The wave of takeovers had actually begun in the 1970s in the US, where many spectacular and heavily fought transactions took place.

In the context of these corporate fights, the boards of directors – trying to resist the change of control (and defend their jobs) – often invented unconventional and innovative legal tactics, with the help of top law firms, which frequently resulted however in harming shareholders.

Some of the defensive measures were adopted on the spot to react to a single hostile bid. Others were prepared in advance and entered into the articles of association to be triggered once the company came under siege. These defences are still employed nowadays even though the economic and legal framework has changed.

Let us make some examples. Suppose that the company Flamingo PLC is attacked by the company Mirage PLC, which launches a hostile bid to acquire control and change the management team. What will the Flamingo directors normally do (just seconds after the chairman of Mirage has made a courtesy call to Flamingo's chairman giving advance warning of the unfriendly offer on the market ...)? They will try, for instance, to sell the company's assets to other firms to make the acquisition less interesting (imagine that Mirage – operating for instance in the leisure industry – looks forward to putting its hands on a chain of resorts that Flamingo owns is a certain region; Flamingo's board could try to take Mirage by surprise and sell that business to Bellagio, a competitor, just

---

5 See Berglöf/Burkart, *European takeover regulation*, 2003, 6 f., at http://eprints.lse.ac.uk/69550.

to try to decrease the raider's appetite and drive it away). However, the deal may not be in the interest of Flamingo's shareholders.

Common anti-takeover defences are thus the "sale of assets" to third parties (or giving "options to buy": these are the tactics known as the "sales of crown jewels") or the repurchase of own-shares to increase the market price of the shares and make the purchase more expensive for the bidder, or the search for a "white knight", i.e. the pursuit of a strategic merger with another company that is welcomed by the directors, etc.

As noted above, defences may also be put in place in advance at a time when an attack is still not envisaged. It is common to put "poison pills" into the articles of association (or "shark repellent" clauses), aimed at rendering the acquisition less digestible for the bidder.

It is also common to add a provision that triggers the massive issue of new shares in the event that a new investor reaches a certain threshold of the company's share capital in order to dilute its shareholding; provisions can also be added requiring a supermajority vote in the case of a merger of the target with its major shareholder; or the "staggered board" clause, establishing that only a certain number of directors, usually one third, may be re-elected annually (this is actually a very powerful defence since it inhibits the bidder, once it has obtained control, from immediately removing the board of directors).

US regulators have never felt a strong need to limit these anti-takeover tactics: on the one hand, they have always considered them acceptable – if not desirable – in the context of the market for corporate control (on which see § 1 above); on the other hand, American courts that have been required to take position on the measures adopted have exhibited an increasing management-friendly attitude (a series of rulings have endorsed a broad interpretation of the business judgment rule and given management discretion over key strategic decisions)[6].

The approach of EU regulators towards takeovers and takeovers defences has been, however, much different.

From the beginning they have considered that these types of acquisitions should not be left in the hands of the bidder and directors respectively (and, then, of the judges called to evaluate whether the conduct by the directors had been diligent and fair). The decision on the bid should be assigned to the

---

[6] See Berglöf/Burkart, *European*, 7. The US principal federal legislation (the Williams Act of 1968) is aimed only at procedural disclosure rules in the tender offer process. This Act does not interfere with the power of a firm to resist a takeover bid under its corporate charter. On the business judgment rule, see generally above Chapter 9, § 1.

"owners" of the company, i.e. the shareholders, for whose shares the bid is intended.

That implies, on the one hand, that the bid has to be launched upon all the shareholders (and not only the ones holding the majority stake) and, on the other hand, that the directors have to remain neutral – "passive" – and avoid adopting defensive tactics unless they are specifically agreed to by the shareholders. Regarding the possibility of introducing poison pills and other clauses into the articles of association, it should be basically sterilized.

That is the rationale behind the main rules contained in the Takeover Directive.

(II) Let us begin with the mandatory bid rule (contained in Art. 5 of the Directive). It aims to give all shareholders the right to participate in the sale of the company and gain the corresponding economic benefits, sharing the "control premium"; as for the price, the rule requires the bidder to offer minority shareholders the identical per-share price as has been paid to the majority shareholder in the block trade.

At the same time, the mandatory bid rule provides small shareholders with an exit option, allowing them to sell out their shares to the bidder. The Directive explicitly cites the protection of minority shareholders as the actual aim of the mandatory bid rule (the bidder "is required to make a bid as a means of protecting the minority shareholders of that company": see Art. 5).

Of course, that rule renders the acquisition more expensive for the bidder, who has to tender for the entire share capital (100 % of the outstanding shares) instead of the controlling stake only (which often corresponds to less than 51 % of the share capital since the company is listed and shares are widespread).

As a matter of fact, the mandatory bid rule therefore conflicts with the goal of favoring the market for corporate control and has therefore been criticized by many scholars.

Some of them propose, as a sub-optimal solution, a rule permitting the mandatory bid to be waived if the shareholders' general meeting approves the acquisition, with the exclusion of the bidder's vote (in the case it has already acquired the shares in the company). If shareholders – that have to be "protected" from the acquisition – agree on it, there should be no reason to force the bidder to buy them out[7].

---

7 See e.g. Enriques, *The mandatory*, 448, 451.

Some national rules provide for this kind of exception, granting an exemption to the mandatory 100 % bid rule that is triggered by a majority vote of the minority shareholders (that is the "majority of the minority"'s approval)[8].

Another criticism of the Directive points to the "wide discretion" it leaves to Member States (both at the time of implementation and in the practical administration of the rule as implemented) to set the mandatory bid price and, more importantly, to decide whether a bid must be made once the relevant threshold is crossed (the regime of the "exceptions" is particularly vague)[9].

In any case, sufficient time and information concerning the bid has to be given to the solicited shareholders.

It is interesting to note that the CJEU has refused to acknowledge – in the "Audiolux" decision of 2009 (case C-101/08) – that an "immanent principle" of equal treatment results from the EU legislation that could force the acquirer of a controlling stake to launch a takeover bid on all the shares, and that this type of bid is mandatory for listed companies only as a consequence of the application of the rules laid down in the Takeover Directive[10]. If the Directive were not in force, no bid would be mandatory.

---

8 See for instance, Art. 107 of the Italian Legislative Decree n. 58/1998. That provision states that "the provisions regarding mandatory takeover bids [...] shall not apply where the shareholding is owned as a result of a takeover bid or exchange tender offering on at least sixty per cent of the securities in each category and all the following conditions are satisfied: a) the bidder and persons acting in concert with the bidder, have not acquired shareholdings exceeding one per cent, including shares acquired under forward contracts maturing at a later date, in the twelve months preceding the notice to [the supervisory Authority] [of the launch of the offer] nor during the bid period; b) the validity of the bid is subject to approval of a number of shareholders which together possess the majority of the securities concerned [...] excluding securities held by the bidder, the major shareholder, also in relative terms, if that shareholding exceeds ten per cent, and by persons acting in concert with the bidder; c) [the supervisory Authority] shall grant the exemption after verifying satisfaction of the conditions specified in paragraphs a) and b)".

9 See Enriques, *The mandatory*, 442 ff.; Papadopoulos, *The mandatory*.

10 In 2001, at that time the Luxembourg securities regulation did not provide for a mandatory bid rule and the Takeover Directive was not yet in force, the control of the listed RTL public company changed. Audiolux, a minority shareholder of RTL, in order to obtain a portion of the control premium, argued that the mandatory bid rule derives from a general principle of EU law that existed even before the enactment of the Directive. The District Court and the Court of Appeal of Luxembourg rejected the claim. The ruling of the Court of Appeal was then brought before the Court de Cassation of Luxemburg, which suspended its judgement and referred the questions to the CJEU for a preliminary ruling. The decision of the Court was, however, negative. See Van Bekkum, *Commentary on the EU Courts' decision in Audiolux*, in *ECL*, 2010, 161; Mucciarelli, *Equal treatment of shareholders and European Union law. Case note on the Decision "Audiolux" of the European Court of Justice*, in *EFCR*, 2010, 158.

(III) The other two key provisions of the Directive are the board neutrality rule (also called the "passivity rule", on the defensive measures) (Art. 9) and the "breakthrough rule" (Art. 11).

They are however, "optional" both at the Member State and individual company level (and have been therefore fiercely criticized, since they are considered to miss the goal of protecting minority shareholders which should be one of the legal bases of the Directive[11]).

Indeed, according to the Directive's reciprocity principle (Art. 12), a company, which applies the board neutrality and/or breakthrough rule, is able to opt-out if the bidder company (or the Member State it belongs to) does not apply the same board neutrality and breakthrough provisions.

As far as the "passivity rule" is concerned, Art. 9 of the Directive states that when a bid has been made public, from that moment on the directors must avoid "taking any action [...] which may result in the frustration of the bid". From then on, directors may only carry out transactions with no defensive implications and shift any decision-making power to the shareholders. The defensive activities are therefore not ruled out entirely, but are subject to the condition that any such actions or operations proposed by the directors must first be approved by the shareholders. Art. 9 does not present a list of the operations which the directors are forbidden to perform; they must assess which actions and operations require specific authorization by the general meeting on a case-by-case basis.

Let us come back for a moment to our example, in order to further clarify how the passivity rules works under the reciproprocity principle. Pursuant to the rules of the Directive, Flamingo's directors could not sell the company resorts to Bellagio and would have to ask the shareholders for permission. However, if the raider (the company Mirage) came from a Member State that had not implemented the Directive in that regard or had not inserted the passivity rule into its articles of association, Flamingo's directors would be free to execute the deal, under their own responsibility[12].

---

11 See i.e. Papadopoulos, *The mandatory*, 525.

12 Moreover, even if the board "must act 'in the interests of the company as a whole'" (Art. 3), it is often argued that the interests that have to be considered are much wider: pursuant to Arts. 3 and 9 the board must give its views "on the effects of implementation of the bid on employment, conditions of employment and the locations of the company's places of business" and the "likely repercussions on employment". These provisions however do not conflict with the possibility of interpreting the passivity rule according to a pure "shareholders' primacy" model: cf. i.e. Clarke, *Takeover regulation – through the regulatory looking glass*, in *GLJ*, 2007, 381 (for an opposite view see i.e. Sjåfjell, *The core of corporate governance: implications of the Takeover Directive for corporate governance in Europe*, in *EBLR*, 2011, 641).

Art. 11 of the Directive sets forth the "breakthrough rule", according to which measures such as special rights provided in the articles of association or in shareholders' agreements (like, for instance, voting rights concerning the appointment and removal of board members) lose their anti-takeover effects as soon as the bidder makes its offer, while they are lawful outside the offer period (if they normally are under the national laws). The breakthrough rule makes it easier to accept the bid since it removes any penalties imposed on shareholders by the statutory and contractual agreements entered into by them[13].

(IV) Finally, the Directive introduces, under certain conditions, a right for the bidder to squeeze-out the minorities and the right for minorities to sell out their shares.

The squeeze-out right is governed in Art. 15 of the Directive. Paragraph 2 reads as follows: "Member States shall ensure that an offeror is able to require all the holders of the remaining securities to sell him/her those securities at a fair price." The rule is aimed at allowing a bidder to gain 100 % of the equity. However, the squeeze-out right must only be exercised in the class in which the relevant threshold has been reached (see further on the takeover squeeze out right above Chapter 10, § 7[14]).

The Directive requires also Member States to establish sell-out rights, based on fair pricing provisions similar to Art. 15 on squeeze-out. Art. 16 stipulates that "Member States shall ensure that a holder of remaining securities is able to re-

---

13 According to Papadopoulos, *Infringements*, however, since the fundamental freedoms constitute the cornerstone of EU company law, in any case compliance with these freedoms entails compliance by the Member States with certain common rules governing the internal market, since these common rules are interpreted by the CJEU. Therefore, also in the case of optional harmonizing measures (i.e. different regimes as a consequence of the opt out by the Member States), the fundamental freedoms regulated by the EU Treaties "will prevent widely divergent or even conflicting implementing measures from frustrating the smooth functioning of the internal market"; these (divergent/conflicting) measures could not de facto allow private parties to breach the principles (the reasoning relies on the CJEU jurisprudence developed in particular in the case C-438/05, "*Viking*"). The end of the argument – referred for instance to the passivity rule – is the following: "the hostile behaviour of the board (especially its expression through defensive measures) or the stance of certain activist shareholders of the target company towards the takeover bid, could both be characterised as a restriction of the freedom of establishment, because they inhibit the bidder from exercising this fundamental freedom through the acquisition of shares (and potentially the control of the company)".

14 For a summary see Vos, '*Baby*', 169, noting that squeeze-outs are "not fully harmonised in the European Union and that Member States enjoy some discretion. Indeed, the thresholds for squeeze-outs and the determination of the fair price still leave some room for differences between member states".

quire the offeror to buy his securities at a fair price, under the same circumstances as provided for in Art. 15".

The aim of this rule is to provide an exit to the remaining shareholders (owning a reduced shareholdings) and as a consequence to protect them. Otherwise, the remaining shareholders could very easily be abused by the new controller and the only exit would be to sell their depreciated shares at a low price on the market[15].

4. Rules on audit committees

In EU publicly traded companies, an operating committee of directors charged with oversight of financial reporting and disclosure has to be set up: the "audit committee" (see Art. 39 Directive 2014/56/EU) (we have already discussed of this committee on general terms above in Chapter 3, § 3).

Committee members are drawn from members of the board of directors, with a chairperson selected from among the committee members (or appointed by the supervisory board of the audited company in companies adopting the two-tier system; however if the national law so requires, the chairperson of the audit committee shall be elected annually by the general meeting of the company).

A majority of the members of the audit committee has to be independent. Moreover, it is required that at least one member of the audit committee shall have competence in accounting and/or auditing and the committee members as a whole shall have competence relevant to the sector in which the audited entity is operating. This allows the committee to have a better understanding of the company's operations and to have a fruitful dialogue with the firm's controlling bodies and internal operating units (without being subjected to excessive pressure from executive directors, given the presence of independent directors on the committee).

The chairman of the audit committee shall be appointed by its members or by the supervisory body of the audited entity, and shall be independent. Member States may require the chairman of the audit committee to be elected annually by the general meeting of shareholders of the audited entity.

The audit committee must, *inter alia:* (a) monitor the financial reporting process and submit recommendations or proposals to assure its integrity; (b) monitor the effectiveness of the company's internal control and risk manage-

---

15 See also above Chapter 10, § 8, and Chapter 6, § 5, for squeeze out and sell out rights in unlisted companies.

ment systems; (c) monitor the audit of the annual and consolidated financial statements (by the auditors); (d) review and monitor the independence of the auditors and, in particular, the appropriateness of the provision of non-audit services to the audited company by the auditors; (e) be responsible for the procedure for the selection of auditors.

National laws on auditing must include detailed rules on the audit committee, including provisions on its composition and functions.

In general, the purpose of an audit committee is to reduce the financial, operational and compliance risks and enhance the quality of financial reporting.

In line with other provisions contained in the Model, the EMCA Group affirms that companies with shares listed on "alternative" trading venues should have the burden minimized. Sect. 6 – consistent with Art. 39 of the Auditing Directive – states that the functions of the audit committee may in those companies be performed by the management or supervisory board as a whole.

It is assumed that small and medium-sized companies in the Member States will make use of this solution.

13 Private companies

Summary:
1. Harmonization of the national laws on private companies? A "disproportionate" effort, according to the EU. Despite this, the attempt by the EMCA
2. The "private company" in the Member States and the EMCA: (a) formation and legal capital
3. (b) management and control
4. (c) shares
5. (d) financing
6. (e) protection of minorities
7. (f) directors and shareholders' liabilities

1. Harmonization of the national laws on private companies? A "disproportionate" effort, according to the EU. Despite this, the attempt by the EMCA

The EU directives – as already seen above (Chapter 1, § 5) – apply almost exclusively to public companies (the exceptions are Directive 1132/2017/EU, in the part devoted to extraordinary transactions, and Directive 2013/34/EU on annual accounts, which concern both public and private companies; on the other hand, the Twelfth Directive on single-member companies regards only private companies).

The basic regulation of private companies is therefore left to the Member States.

The idea of trying to harmonize the rules on these companies has been considered over the years by the EU Commission. An impact assessment carried out in 2007 found however that seeking to standardize the company laws of the Member States in that area would entail a "disproportionate" and unmanageable amount of changes.

The distances between the national laws regulating private companies are still considered to be too significant to be covered by an external legislative intervention. Time will tell if these distances will be reduced or not.

The less ambitious effort to provide Member States companies with a statute for a "European Private Company" (the so called "Societas Privata Europea" or "SPE") has also recently failed, as we shall see in Chapter 14.

https://doi.org/10.1515/9783110725025-015

In any case, it is worthwhile to devote a chapter of this book to the models of private companies in the Member States, considering – for obvious limits of spaces – some selected provisions and the EMCA.

The EMCA is actually a very important tool since it provides an overview of the state of the art in the various laws (in its descriptive parts) and a possible legal model for those types of companies.

The EMCA sets forth the goal to "achieve European convergence" in the area of all limited liability companies (public and private: see the Introduction to the Model, Sect. 7). The rules of the Model should therefore be applied to both types of entities ("unless otherwise stated, an [EMCA] provision applies to both private and public companies": Sect. 1.03[1]).

As clearly explained by the EMCA Group, "private companies are typically small or medium companies that require limited liability and legal personality, but do not require access to public funding through the general capital markets, although they can sometimes sell bonds by private placement. Usually, financing comes from contributions by the members themselves or alternatively by bank finance. Therefore, the disclosure requirements for these companies are less onerous and the regulation is generally more flexible" (see comment to Sect. 1.02).

The main feature of the private company model is actually the fact that the personal and fiduciary relationships among the owners and between the owners and management are particularly strong; therefore they are meant to remain "closely held" entities.

They still are, however, "limited liability" companies, targeting profits by employing third parties' money and utilizing a "corporate" legal structure.

The laws governing them therefore include both traits that are characteristic of the rules on partnerships and others that are closer to the laws on public companies.

For instance, in several Member States a private company may be managed by directors acting separately (i.e., without constituting a board of directors, which entails a higher degree of flexibility but also the risk of mismanagement), and sell bonds to professional or even retail investors.

---

1 See also the comment: "the EMCA regulates both public and private companies within one Act but within its Chapters it distinguishes, where appropriate, between provisions dealing only with public companies or only with private companies. In the latter case, where justifiable, the EMCA relaxes the regulatory requirements and looks to formulate rules that take special consideration of the typical ownership structure of private companies".

Pursuant to some (actually few) national legislations it is even possible to solicit third parties to subscribe for shares and even list them on a stock exchange[2].

2. The "private company" in the Member States and the EMCA: (a) formation and legal capital

Beginning with the rules on the formation, publication and nullity of the private company, the national laws of the Member States are normally similar to the ones laid down for public companies (see above Chapter 2, § 2), since the rules of that part of Directive 1132/2017/EU apply to both forms[3].

The differences are more significant – on the contrary – at the level of the rules on share capital (which apply only to public companies).

As far as the minimum amount of capital is concerned, while some Member States allow all private companies to operate with a capital equal to zero (Belgium, Finland, France, Greece, Ireland, the Netherlands, Portugal, etc.), others require a minimum (€ 3.000 in Spain, € 10.000 in Italy, € 25.000 in Germany, € 35.000 in Austria[4]), although they often permit certain kinds of private companies to operate without it. Examples include the "entrepreneurial company" in

---

2 Very liberal is the approach taken by Dutch law, "which does not include a prohibition on listing BV [i. e. private company] shares and the Securities Giro Act ("Wet giraal effectenverkeer") and does not seem to provide for rules or regulations that prevent BV-shares from being included in the securities custody and transfer system. As a result, BV-shares can be listed when the rules of the relevant stock exchange allow this. This is however not customary": see on that Wolf, in *Company laws*, 1359. See also explicitly Art. 5.2 B-CA allowing the listing, and Arts. 5.18 ff. B-CA, permitting the dematerialization of the shares.

On the contrary, pursuant to Art. 223-3 Fr-CC, the number of shareholders may not exceed 100; if that number is trespassed the company must be dissolved after a one-year period (unless the number has decreased below 100 or the company has been transformed). Under other laws the maximum number of members is even lower: 50 according to Art. 12 R-CA. Some Member States have set forth some peculiar restrictions: e. g., according to Art. 223-5 Fr-CC, a private company cannot have a single-member private company as its sole shareholder.

3 Usually the company will be bound by obligations arising from acts performed in its name prior to incorporation only if, after its incorporation, it explicitly or implicitly ratifies them. Otherwise the persons that have acted shall be jointly and severally liable.

4 The minimum is 200 RON under Art. 11 R-CA (approximately € 40); Cărămidariu/Bercea, in *Company laws*, 976, clearly explain that "the rationale behind this very low minimum legal capital requirement is the purpose of encouraging commercial activities".

Germany, the "simplified" private company in Italy and the "new business" private company in Spain[5].

The German "Unternehmergesellschaft" ("UG") is a private limited liability company with a capital requirement of 1 euro, but with strict rules to build up reserves up to € 25,000 (see Sect. 5a Ge-PrCA). The Italian "società a responsabilità limitata semplificata" may operate with a capital of 1 euro, but does not have great flexibility since the articles of association have to follow a model established by the law which cannot be changed (see Art. 2463-bis It-CC). The "sociedad nueva impresa" in Spain is similar, its articles of association must replicate a standardized model, while the company cannot establish a board of directors (see Arts. 434 ff. Sp-CA)[6].

However, the importance of the rules on the share capital relies principally – more than on the rules on the minimum amount and composition[7] – on the ap-

---

5 For some years (2014-2019), Danish law introduced a company with no mandatory capital; the law was however later suppressed: see Hensen, *Companies without legal capital and the strange case of Denmark*, in *ECFR*, 2020, 677. Also Austrian private companies called "privileged at foundation" is an interesting model. They may be established with a minimum share capital of € 10.000, with at least € 5.000 paid up in cash (contributions in kind are however not allowed); the foundation privilege shall however end at the latest 10 years after registration: at that date, an amount of € 17.500 must have been paid in in cash; see Sect. 9a A-PrCA. As for Poland, see the "prosta spółka akcyjna", whose regulation will enter in force in 2021 (see Mazgaj/Mucha, *The new kid on the block on the European Market for corporate legal forms: A Polish laboratory for a modern close corporation*, in *ECL*, 2020, 45).

6 The success of these companies is controversial. In Germany "since its introduction more than ten years ago, the UG has gained a significant practical importance. Today, there are more than 140.000 UGs" (see Stöber, in *Company laws*, 336); on the other hand in Spain "this type of company is hardly used in the current traffic: according to the latest statistics of the central mercantile registry, during 2016 only 48 [...] were created, out of a total of 100.371" private companies (see Martinez, *ibidem*, 1176).

7 Which differ slightly, above all regarding the need to have contributions in kind assessed by an expert or not. Under some laws, for instance, this assessment is not mandatory; both the contributing shareholders and the acquirers of the shares paid with non-cash contributions are however liable to the company and the creditors, jointly and severally for five years, if the contributions in kind do not reflect the real value of the assets (see Art. 74 Sp-CA); if the shareholders want to avoid this kind of responsibility, they may require an expert's assessment (Art. 76). German law lays down a liability rule only too: if the value of the assets transferred to the company as a contribution in kind does not equal at least the nominal value of the shares subscribed to against the contribution in kind, the shareholder must pay the company a contribution in cash in the amount of the shortfall, i.e. the amount of the difference between the nominal value of the shares and the true value of the assets transferred to the company as a contribution in kind (see Sect. 9 Ge-PrCA); a similar solution is provided for, i.e., by Art. 175 Pol-CA, which extends the liability also to the directors. Under Art. 223-9 Fr-CC an expert has to be appointed as a general rule (see also the following footnote); however, the shareholders may either refuse

plication (or exclusion) of the provisions on its maintenance: i.e. the rules on distributions, purchase of own shares, financial assistance and capital mandatory reduction in the case of losses.

On the one hand, a number of States (among which the Nordic countries, Germany, Italy, Poland) also apply most of the rules contained in Directive 1132/2017/EU to private companies, even though some of them are simplified in order to ease the burdens for these firms[8]). Some laws, like the French one, are particularly concerned with cross-shareholdings, along the lines established for public companies[9].

On the other hand, other jurisdictions (Belgium, Ireland, the Netherlands, etc.) have simply moved away from the Directive; as a consequence, contributions may be provided rather freely, controls are relaxed or absent, the subscription and acquisition of own shares is admitted, etc.[10]. These States have however

---

to appoint the expert or give a value that is different than the one established by the expert to the assets in kind: in both cases they remain jointly and severally liable for five years towards third parties for the value established for the assets.

8 For instance, for contributions in kind, the Italian civil code requires a mandatory assessment, but allows the expert to be appointed by the company instead of by a court (see Art. 2465 It-CC). Pursuant to French law, the expert has to appointed by all shareholders or by a court (shareholders may make a unanimous decision to avoid appointing an expert if the contributions in kind do not exceed € 30.000 and the total value of all the contributions in kind which has not been assessed by an expert does not exceed half of the share capital: see Art. 223-9 Fr-CC and Art. D 223-6 introduced by Decree no. 1669/2010). Contributions in kind in the form of the performance of work or the supply of services are allowed (they do not however form part of the share capital: shares issued in contemplation of such contributions entitle holders to share in the profits, subject to their liability for losses: see Art. 223-7 Fr-CC; see extensively Tenenbaum, in *Company laws*, 114). In Belgium, Denmark, Finland, Germany and Greece, private companies may purchase own shares, but with different restrictions attached to these purchases (a common restriction is that the purchase may not exceed distributable profits: see paradigmatically Sect. 197 Da-CA). In Spain, financial assistance (of any kind) may be provided by the private company: the general meeting must authorize the concession of loans or warranties to shareholders (or directors) unless they are a company of the same group (Art. 162 Sp-CA). The shareholders who are to be given this type of financial assistance cannot vote on the authorization at the general meeting (Art. 190). See also i.e. Art. 5.152 B-CA.

9 Art. 233-30 Fr-CC stipulates that whenever a private company holds more than 10% of another company's share capital and the latter company is a public company, this public company cannot hold shares in the capital of the private company.

10 Under Art. 2.175 Du-CC, for instance, at least one share with voting rights in the general meeting must be held by someone other than, and not for the benefit of, the private company or any of its subsidiaries. The possibility of subscribing to own shares (also by means of affiliated companies) is thus very broad. See also, on the acquisition of own shares allowed by Art. 2.207, Wolf, in *Company laws*, 1363.

introduced a regime of solvency tests and other instruments to protect the company and its creditors which substitutes the framework of rules prohibiting distributions and transactions which are deemed potentially harmful for the company's net assets or rely in any case on the rules on directors' duties and liabilities[11].

Sometimes the scenario turns out to be odd. Provisions for private companies may even be more stringent than the ones provided for the public ones: for instance, in France, Italy, Poland and Sweden, companies acts prohibit the acquisition of own shares by private companies, while they allow it upon certain conditions for public ones[12] (the same is true also for the rules on financial assistance). That has evidently to do with long-established traditions. From this viewpoint, an effort of (at least) minimal harmonization – like the one pursued by the EMCA – really makes sense.

The EMCA recommends that private companies have a share capital. On the one hand, it affirms that the requisite minimum level should apply only to public companies; on the other hand, it establishes that the provisions on contributions in kind should also be extended to private entities (the Group "assumes that there is a need to ensure that the consideration is not overvalued": see the comment to Sect. 2.11).

Regarding the provisions on capital maintenance, the EMCA follows an original direction. According to the Model, while the acquisition of own shares and the reduction of capital in the case of losses should be governed in accordance with the same procedures and limits set forth for public companies (see the comments to Sections 7.08 and 8.30 respectively), financial assistance on the other hand should be basically left unregulated for private companies ("the Group does not recommend that Member States include such rules in their legislation for private companies": see the comment to Sect. 7.18).

---

11 Paradigmatically see Art. 5.3 B-CA ("the founders shall ensure that the limited liability company, when it is formed, has equity capital which, taking into account other sources of financing, is sufficient in the light of the planned activity"); Art. 5.4 stipulates that a two years business plan must be prepared; Art. 5.143 regulates a solvency test; Art. 5.144 introduces a special libility regime "if it is established that, when taking the decision referred to in Art. 5.143, the members of the administrative body knew or, in view of the circumstances, should have known that, as a result of the distribution, the company would manifestly no longer be able to pay its debts as specified in article 5.143, they shall be jointly and severally liable to the company and third parties for all resulting damages". The same law contains however a provision obliging the directors to convene the general meeting whenever the net assets "have become negative" (Art. 5.153). On the Dutch system, see Lennarts, *Directors' and shareholders' liability as a means of protecting creditors of the BV*, in *EBOR*, 2007, 131.
12 See i.e. Art. 2474 and 2358 It-CC and Ch. 19, Sect. 4 ff. Sw-CA.

The argument has to do with the fundamental scepticism towards the regulation on financial assistance in general: "it is not clear" – the Group affirms – "if the rules in reality provide any protection for the company's creditors and shareholders. [Moreover] they add complexity to the law, at an additional and substantial transaction cost" (see the comment to Sect. 7.18)[13].

3. (b) Management and control

(I) The rules on management vary considerably in the Member States. The most widely-adopted model for the management of private companies is the one-tier (monistic) system. As an exception, Dutch company law requires the adoption of the two-tier system when the company crosses the threshold imposed also for public companies (turnover above € 16 million, etc.: see Chapter 3, § 2).

Some companies acts allow firms to choose between a one-tier and a two-tier system; others, even when they permit a public company to choose among different management systems, do not provide the private companies with the same opportunity[14]. The EMCA also confirms that private companies should be free to choose the management structure they prefer (one-tier/two-tier).

As far as the one-tier system is concerned, in addition to the model of the "sole director" or the model where a number of directors act as a "board", under some laws there is also the structure where various directors may act simultaneously, either jointly, or sometimes even separately. If directors can act separately, the extent of autonomy is thus significant (normally, other directors

---

13 As far as the regulation of the "single member" private company is concerned, reference should be made to Chapter 2, § 4, where the argument has been extensively addressed with reference to both public and private firms.

14 The former case is for example the one in Austria, the Czech Republic, Denmark, Finland, Germany, the Netherlands and Poland; the latter the one in Italy. In Germany, private companies with more than 500 employees, as required by Sect. 1 of the "Drittelbeteiligungsgesetz", must adopt the dualistic system and have a supervisory board with at least 1/3 of the board members serving as representatives of the employees. Those with more than 1000 employees in the coal mining or steel industries, according to Sect. 1 of the "Montanmitbestimmungsgesetz", require co-determination on a basis of parity. This co-determination requirement also applies to all companies, regardless of industry, with more than 2000 employees, under Sect. 1 of the "Mitbestimmungsgesetz": see on these special provisions Schall, in *Company laws*, 202, note 12. Also pursuant to Sect. 29 A-PuCA, i.e., the company must adopt a dual board if certain thresholds are reached.

can only impede their colleague's actions if they succeed in calling a general meeting and require a vote on the action proposed by the director[15]).

Turning to the rules on the appointment of the management board, alongside the case where directors are chosen by the supervisory board in the dualistic system, they are normally elected by the shareholders in accordance with the appointment system laid down in the articles of association (majority rule, slate voting, etc.)[16].

However, that does not always mean that the directors have to be appointed at the shareholders' general meeting or that they have to follow the majority rule (or a different conventional system, like slate voting). A different result may be obtained by issuing different classes of shares and assigning the right to appoint one or more directors to a class (this option is recognized by some domestic laws: we shall come back on this issue below in § 4)[17].

Usually the companies acts stipulate that it is up to the articles of association to govern the formation and functioning of the board of directors (with some specific notions like the option to have directors voting by proxy[18]). The EMCA takes a similarly permissive approach and states that the "appointment of the board in private companies should be decided by the shareholders in accordance with the articles of association" (see the comment to Sect. 8.02).

The term of office is also regulated in a very flexible way according to the single domestic rules: normally the duration is fixed in the articles of association and can even be indefinite (see also the EMCA Sect. 8.14[19]).

A legal person may be a director under some laws, not in others[20]; occasionally the number of directors may not exceed a minimum and a maximum[21].

---

15 See Art. 2475 It-CC, but also Art. 210 Sp-CA.

16 Slate voting (on which see above Chapter 3, § 3) is permitted in some domestic laws for public companies only: see for instance Art. 243 Sp-CA; the Spanish Supreme Court has, however, allowed the articles of association of a private company to establish a similar mechanism for appointing the directors: see Supreme Court, 6 March 2009.

17 A particular solution is provided for under Italian and Polish law where the decision to appoint the director(s) may be reserved by the company's articles of association – as a "particular individual right" – also to a sole shareholder owning a percentage of share capital below 51% (and even a minority stake, say, for instance, even 1%); see below § 4.

18 Allowed i.e. by Art. 247 Sp-CA.

19 According to Art. 221 Sp-CA the directors are appointed for an indefinite period of time, except when the articles of association provide otherwise. If the articles of association are silent on the matter, an appointment without a set term is then presumed and the general meeting cannot set one (see Pérez Millán, in *Company laws*, 1219).

20 See i.e. Sect. 6 Ge-PrCA.

21 Pursuant to Art. 242 Sp-CA, the board of a private company must have a minimum of three and maximum of twelve members.

Regarding the distribution of powers between the management body and the shareholders (an issue that – as we have seen above – is very intricate for public companies: see Chapter 3, § 4), private companies are accorded great flexibility. As recognized by the EMCA, "generally, there is a freedom to organise the competence between the general meeting and the board. The competence of the general meeting is unrestricted and the general meeting may take business decisions" (see the general comment to Ch. 11). A favorable position towards shareholders is anyway endorsed: Sect. 11.01 states that "in private companies the general meeting has competence in all company matters, except where the articles of association otherwise provide. The general meeting may give direct instructions to the managing director/the board of directors"[22].

Normally, unless otherwise prescribed in the articles of association, shareholders owning a certain stake of the share capital (or a lower percentage as set forth in the articles of association), may always require that a decision has to be made at the general meeting level[23].

As far as the functioning of the general meeting is concerned, there is usually great space for autonomy. Shareholders may be allowed to vote by other means besides voting in presence, that may be governed by the articles of association (for instance, by referendum or written consultation[24]; also the EMCA, at Sect. 2 of Ch. 11, admits the option to circulate written resolutions).

As it has been noted, in private companies "where the shareholders are engaged in running the company, the general meeting (shareholders) is much more involved in the company's business than shareholders typically are" in large companies; "there is a need for private companies [...] for shareholders to be able to act in the daily business, and also to be able to take decisions without

---

22 Thus, for example, Sect. 46 Ge-PrCA includes a catalogue of decisions which should be passed by the general meeting unless the articles decide otherwise. However, the catalogue is deemed not to be exhaustive. The general meeting has a fundamental competence to decide on all company matters.
23 See Arts. 2479 and 2475 It-CC (unless the decision has to do with setting up the organizational structure of the company, which remain within the exclusive competence of the directors). Art. 2.107a Du-CC (that establishes that even if the articles of association attribute responsibility to the board of directors, any resolution passed that causes major changes in the identity or character of the company must be approved by the general meeting) does not refer to private companies. However, according to case law, it is possible to invoke this rule in order to force the board of directors to seek approval of the general meeting in the case of a (nearly full) transfer of the company (see Enterprise Court of Amsterdam, 9 October 2006). In addition, legal scholars argue that Art. 2.107a Du-CC should be applied by analogy to the extent possible (see Roos, in *Company laws*, 1382).
24 See i.e. Art. 2479 It-CC; Art. 5.85 B-CA (requiring unanimity).

a large formal and bureaucratic system" (see EMCA, general comments to Ch. 11). Therefore, Sect. 11.02 EMCA affirms that, especially in private companies, "shareholders may decide matters, without complying with the rules governing the conduct of general meetings, provided all shareholders agree".

(II) Finally, as far as the external controls are concerned, directors in private companies are normally not subject to monitoring by any other corporate body besides the shareholders (and the auditors, who are in charge of the auditing of the financial statements in major ones). If the company, however, adopts the dual system, the usual controlling powers of the supervisory board shall apply.

Under the traditional governance model, the statutory auditors must also be appointed if the company surpasses certain thresholds (turnover, number of employees, etc.) or on a voluntary basis[25].

Some companies acts allow minority shareholders to ask for the appointment by the court of special examiners with the task to conduct special inquiries[26].

(III) Shareholders' agreements are normally admitted to a large extent[27].

4. (c) Shares

As far as the shares – often also called "quotas" – are concerned, the main elements of distinction of private companies regard the option to issue, on the one hand, shares with rights that are "disproportionate" to the stake of owned capital and, on the other hand, specific "classes" of shares.

Beginning with the rule on "disproportionality", certain companies acts permit, on the one hand, multiple voting and, on the other hand, that the number of votes (or share of profits) attributed to certain shareholders does not correspond to the percentage of their contribution to the company's share capital, but is higher or lower.

The former option – multiple voting – is expressly regulated, for instance, by Belgian Companies Act (Art. 5.42). The articles of association may thus state that certain shareholders are given a number of votes that exceeds the share-

---

25 The appointment is mandatory if for two consecutive years the company has exceeded at least one of the following limits: total assets in the balance sheet: € 4.400.000; revenues from sales: € 8.800.000; employees employed on average during the year: 50 units (see Art. 2477 It-CC).
26 See i.e. Art. 5.106 B-CA.
27 For an explicit regulation see i.e. Art. 5.46 B-CA.

holder's participation in the company's share capital (see for public companies above Chapter 4, § 3).

The latter possibility is provided for under German and Italian law, respectively in Sect. 29 Ge-PrCA (with the consent of the shareholders concerned, the articles of association may even state that certain shares do not confer any right to share in the company's profit[28]) and in Art. 2468 It-CC.

Regarding the classes of shares, they can normally be issued with even greater flexibility in private companies (special rights may provide administrative or economic privileges)[29]. The basic rules on special shares recall the ones laid down for public companies (see again Chapter 4, § 3).

A peculiar provision – typical of "closely held" companies – has been implemented in Polish and Italian laws for example. Pursuant to Art. 159 Pol-CC and Art. 2468 It-CC, individual shareholders can be given "particular rights", which, once entered into the articles of association, can only be modified with the consent of all the shareholders (unless otherwise specified in the articles of association). These rights may relate to the administration of the company (i.e. the right to appoint directors – even all of them, including for an indefinite time; the right to adopt or veto certain managerial decisions) or to decisions on the structure of the company (consider i.e. the right of consent to the entrance of other members into the company or the right of first refusal, which – instead of being attributed to all shareholders – may only be attributed to the shareholders owning these "particular" rights)[30].

Hybrid instruments – linked to equity – may be issued (like warrants).

In the case of capital increases, shareholders are usually granted pre-emptive rights[31].

---

28 See Stöber, in *Company laws*, 333; this is not allowed in other jurisdictions as it conflicts with the rule prohibiting the so called "leonine pact".

29 See, to name one provision only, Art. 2.178 Du-CC. Consider also, to provide another example, that Polish law, which is particularly strict with reference to special shares in public companies (see above Ch. 4, § 3), becomes particularly permissive for private ones (see Art. 174 Pol-CC).

30 See Dybiňsky and Manzoni, in *Company laws*, 781 and 572.

31 An exception is provided for by Sect. 69 Ir-CA, which sets forth that "to the extent that the constitution of the company provides otherwise, (a) shares of a company may only be allotted by the directors of the company; (b) the directors of a company may allot, grant options over or otherwise dispose of shares to such persons, on such terms and conditions and at such times as they may consider to be in the best interests of the company and its shareholders". Any director of a company who knowingly contravenes (or knowingly permits or authorises a contravention of) a preceding provision of this section shall be guilty of an offence.

As far as the circulation of the shares is concerned, normally in private companies the transfer can be constrained to a greater extent than in public ones (for instance, the articles of association may stipulate that shares cannot circulate at all, or that they can only be transferred with the simple, and even unmotivated, consent of the company[32]). Sect. 95 Ir-CA even establishes that "save where the constitution of the company provides otherwise, (a) the directors of a company may in their absolute discretion and without assigning any reason for doing so, decline to register the transfer of any share; (b) the directors' power to decline to register a transfer of shares [...] shall cease to be exercisable on the expiry of two months after the date of delivery to the company of the instrument of transfer of the share"[33].

5. (d) Financing

Given their characteristics, private companies rely heavily on bank and/or shareholders' loans.

Normally these forms of financing are not regulated by company law apart the case of shareholders' loans, which are subject to – pursuant to some companies acts – the rules of "postergation" and "restriction on repayment of shareholders' loans" (see above Chapter 2, § 5, and Chapter 5, § 5)[34].

Certain domestic laws on bonds are quite detailed. The legal framework adopted by some States is permissive. In Belgium, Germany, the Netherlands

---

32 See i.e. Art. 5.67 B-CA, Sect. 15 Ge-PrCA and Art. 108 Sp-CA. In the event of the introduction of these traffic limits, the shareholder may – under certain laws – withdraw (but the articles of association may provide that the withdrawal may not take place before a number of years: see Art. 2469 It-CC). For a comparison see Kalss, *The transfer of shares of private companies*, in *ECFR*, 2004, 340; Sund/Andersson/Humphreys, *A European private company and share restrictions*, in *EBLR*, 2012, 483.

33 This rule is explained in the following terms by Thuiller, *Company*, 157: "most companies in Ireland are very small. Many are run by families or by friends. If something happens – a death or a departure – and shares suddenly become available, directors feel happier when they can either refuse to register the transfer of shares or where there is a provision which means that the existing shareholders must be offered the chance of buying the newly available shares before anyone else. Both of these options are possible" (the latter, however, only if a clause on the right of first refusal is in place in the articles of association). In any case, directors cannot simply refuse a transfer in their absolute discretion since case law holds that they may do so only as long as they are acting bona fide and in the interest of the company.

34 A rule of the latter type is in place – for private companies – also under Art. 632 Fr-CC, Art. 342 of the Polish bankruptcy law of 28 February 2003 and Art. 161 of the Romanian Act 85/2014 regarding insolvency proceedings.

and Poland, for instance, bonds can basically be issued by private companies without limits as long as their issue does not trigger application of the securities laws regulating market solicitation, adopted for the protection of investors[35].

The power to decide on the issue of bonds lies normally with the board of directors unless the bond is "convertible" into shares: in that case the resolution has to be made by the shareholders' general meeting.

According to this model, the private company can issue bonds either in a public offering process in compliance with the securities laws or privately (which does not exclude the subsequent admission to trading on the regulated market or one of the alternative trading systems)[36].

The approach of other companies acts is, on the other hand, more prudent. Some laws only admit the issue of simpler kinds of bonds and in any case lay down strict quantitative limits. This is the case of Spanish law: private companies cannot issue convertible bonds. The competence to decide lies with the management body; however, the shareholders' general meeting has to vote on whether to issue bonds where the remuneration is variable. Above all, the law sets forth a stringent quantitative limit on the amount issued, which cannot exceed twice the company's net assets (unless the issue is guaranteed by a real or personal security). It is therefore rather rare for the bonds issued by private companies to be placed outside a small circle of subscribers and significant in volume[37].

---

35 The situation in the latter Member State is actually more restricted. The case of the Polish Act on Bonds is interesting: private companies may issue (i) "participative bonds" (with the right to participate in the issuer's profit), (ii) "subordinated bonds" (with the right to be satisfied after all other debts in case of bankruptcy or liquidation) and even (iii) "perpetual bonds" (which do not have a maturity date and in principle are not redeemable and entitle the holder to receive the interest for an indefinite period of time). As noted by Dybińsky, in *Company laws*, 769, "all three aforementioned types of bonds could be considered hybrid debt securities which although not exchangeable for the company's shares might serve various functions of mezzanine finance". On the other hand, "the limited liability company does not, however, have the capacity to issue two classic types of hybrid securities, i. e. the convertible bonds authorising to take up shares issued by the company in exchange for these bonds nor the bonds with a priority warrant that entitle the bond holders, apart from other benefits, to subscribe for shares of the company with the right of priority over its shareholders. *De lege lata* these types of bonds can be issued only by joint-stock companies and limited joint-stock companies, since the provisions regulating these types of bonds (accordingly Art. 19 and Art. 20 of the Act on Bonds) refer to the share (*akcja*) as a normative type of security present only in these two types of companies".
36 See Art. 2.206 Du-CC; Sect. 35 Ge-PrCA.
37 See Art. 401 and 406 Sp-CA. The requirements of French law are also rather stringent, even if they are not quantitative and basically require the company to be in good financial shape (see Art. 223-11 Fr-CC). The company must have its accounts audited and the last three financial statements duly approved by the shareholders. Since under Art. 223-35 F-CC private companies are

The third approach permits private companies to issue any kind of bonds, but only to "professional investors" (i.e. banks or financial companies). This solution has been implemented, for instance, by the Italian civil code. The company's articles of association have to indicate the power to issue bonds (board/ shareholders) and the possible limits; if the articles of association are silent, bonds can be issued without restrictions and the sole exception is that they cannot be placed directly with retail investors (once they have been subscribed to by professional investors, the latter may sell the securities to retail investors, but remain liable for the firm's solvency[38]).

Regarding their characteristics, bonds may be different, but – according to most laws – they may not be linked only to the performance of the company (in that case they would resemble equity contributions and are thus not allowed): the yield has to be, at least in part, fixed[39].

6. (e) Protection of minorities

The area where the features of private companies (personal relationship among shareholders, shares closely held, etc.) comes mostly to the fore is the one relating to the remedies for the protection of the minorities.

(I) First of all, while investors in public companies have (at least in some jurisdictions) limited access to the company books (see Chapter 6, § 3), shareholders of private companies are recognized basically "full access" to corporate documents. They may – upon certain conditions – inspect company books and ask

---

required to appoint an auditor whenever precise criteria are met (the balance sheet total exceeds € 1.500.000, the turnover is over € 3.100.000 and the average number of employees is above 50), the companies that are allowed to issue debt securities are those of a significant size in terms of balance sheet, turnover or average number of employees. The bonds cannot be offered to the public: they have to be offered directly to potential subscribers, without any public communication or placement through a professional intermediary. However, an information document must be drafted. The bonds have to be registered (bearer bonds are not allowed, pursuant to Art. 223-11 Fr-CC).

38 See Art. 2483 It-CC.

39 There seems to be an exception in Polish law ("notwithstanding some previous doubts expressed in the literature, nowadays there seem to be no doubts that the company may issue participative bonds, which grant the bondholder the right to participate in the issuer's profit (Art. 18 of the Act on Bonds). Depending on the case, the benefit resulting from the right to participate in the profit may be of primary or only incidental nature in relation to the traditional predefined cash payment" (see Dybiński, in *Company laws*, 769).

the directors to provide them with any answers or relevant information they deem necessary.

Let us take the example of Art. 272 Sp-CA: shareholders holding at least 5% of the share capital are entitled to examine (also with the help of an accounting expert) the documents supporting the annual accounts unless the articles of association provide otherwise. Moreover, shareholders holding the same percentage of share capital may request the companies register to appoint an auditor to verify the annual accounts even if the company is legally exempt from this type of audit control (Art. 265)[40].

The EMCA also follows a similar route and states that "each shareholder in a private company shall be afforded an opportunity to review accounts and company documents and ask questions to the extent necessary for the shareholder to be able to assess the company's financial position or a particular matter. The shareholder may act through a proxy or an assistant" (Sect. 11.24).

(II) Frequently the general meeting of a private company can be called by single shareholders or by members owning a certain shareholding. Also, according to the EMCA, any shareholder can request an extraordinary general meeting, which must be called within two weeks of receipt of a request to such effect (Sect. 11.12).

The articles of association generally provide the timeframes for sending out the notice calling the meetings and the mode of notification[41]. Normally shareholders may obtain a court decision on the validity of a resolution passed by the general meeting.

(III) Shareholders' resolutions may require supermajorities (in order to vest minority shareholders with "veto powers"). This autonomy cannot reach the point where unanimity is required for all decisions. Unanimous consent may be however established to a great extent. Under Art. 200 Sp-CA, unanimous consent of all the shareholders is even "legally" necessary – if not otherwise stated in the articles of association – in important cases, like limitations on the transfer

---

40 Art. 2476 It-CC and Art. 199(5) R-CA are even more favorable: shareholders (as long as they do not participate in the company administration) have the right to obtain information from the directors on the management of corporate affairs and to consult, also through accounting experts, the company books and documents relating to the administration. No minimum shareholding is required. For a different approach see instead i.e. Sect. 45 A-PrCA (if a shareholders' resolution requiring the appointment of auditors to examine the most recent financial statements has been rejected, the court may – upon application by shareholders holding at least 1/10 of the share capital – appoint one or more auditors).

41 At least two weeks before the meeting date according to Scandinavian States' rules and the EMCA: see Sect. 11.16; other countries provide for more limited terms.

of shares, the establishment or the modification of causes for withdrawal or exclusion, the payment of dividends in a form other than cash, etc.[42].

(IV) The right of withdrawal is attributed basically more generously than in public companies. For instance, pursuant to Art. 2473 It-CC, shareholders who do not vote in favor of a merger have the right to withdraw from the company and to be paid a fair value for their shares if the company is private (while they do not have the same right if the company is public[43]).

The articles of association may regulate also the exclusion of the shareholders[44], while this possibility is not normally permitted by the laws on public companies.

7. (f) Directors and shareholders' liabilities

The duties of care and loyalty by the directors of private companies are commonly governed in the same way they are for public companies (see above Chapter 9).

A simple majority in the general shareholders' meeting is sufficient to bring an action for liability against the directors, with the automatic consequence of their removal from office[45]. According to many companies acts, however, any shareholder can also bring a derivative action against the directors in the company's name[46].

---

42 Arts. 108, 330, 347, 351, 393 Sp-CA. A similar rule is contained in Art. 192 R-CA: extraordinary resolutions that involve changes in the company's articles of association must be passed by the votes of all the members unless the articles otherwise provide; on the problems raised by this rule, see Stârc/Meclejan/Tec, in *Company laws*, 1009.

43 The right to withdraw is largely recognized also by Arts. 15, 62 and 99 Sp-LSC.

44 Cf. i.e. Art. 351 Sp-CA, Art. 2473-*bis* It-CC, Art. 222-225 R-CA. See i.e. Schmolke, *Expulsion and valuation clauses – Freedom of contract vs. legal paternalism in German partnership and close corporatin act*, in *ECFR*, 2012, 380; and, with reference to particular clauses aimed at resolving deadlocks, Fleischer/Schneider, *Shoot-out clauses in partnerships and close corporations*, in *ECFR*, 2012, 35.

45 See Art. 238 Sp-CA.

46 See i.e. Sect. 109 Da-CA and Ch. 7, Sect. 50-52, Sw-CA. Under Spanish law, a suit can be filed by shareholders holding, individually or jointly, at least 5% of the share capital if the directors have not called a general meeting for this purpose; the company has not filed a suit within one month from the adoption of the resolution; or the resolution voted against the suit. In any case, if the action is based on the directors' breach of their duty of loyalty, shareholders also holding at least 5% of the share capital can bring this action directly regardless of any resolution by the general meeting (Art. 239 Sp-CA). Under Art. 5.104 B-CA the threshold of capital needed is fixed at 10%.

Usually, the general meeting can dismiss the directors at any time (often even if the dismissal was not included in the meeting agenda[47]).

The duties and liabilities of the statutory auditors (when appointed, pursuant to the specific laws) are basically governed by the same rules as provided for public companies.

Many States have also introduced forms of shareholders' liabilities[48]. German case law is interesting. According to the Supreme Court[49], a shareholder may be held liable to the creditors if his private assets are mixed with those of the company, with the consequence that the former and the latter cannot be distinguished and the identification of the assets subject to enforcement by the company's creditors is difficult or impossible. In these cases, the judges have endorsed a "piercing of the corporate veil" approach, and have confirmed the direct liability of the shareholders responsible for the asset mixing.

The jurisprudence that has sanctioned shareholders for the "destruction of the economic basis" of the company is even more important. In its fundamental "Trihotel" ruling of 2007[50], the German Supreme Court decided that a shareholder may incur liability with respect to his company for intentional damage contrary to public policy under Sect. 826 of the civil code if he deprives the company of assets that are required to satisfy its creditors, and if this leads to insolvency or worsens it[51].

Finally, under Belgian law, in case the private company goes bankrupt within three years after its incorporation due to insufficient funding, the founders can be held liable for any loss that third parties may incur.

---

47 See Art. 223 Sp-CA. It is less easy to dismiss directors under Romanian law since the rule of double majority of the members and the capital apply, according to Art. 192 R-CA (unless a different provision is laid down in the company's articles of association).

48 Pursuant to Art. 2476 It-CC, for example, shareholders who have intentionally decided or authorized the performance of acts harmful to the company (and also to other shareholders or third parties) are jointly liable with the directors who have breached their duties of care or of loyalty.

49 Starting from the ruling of 16 September 1985 ("Autokran" case).

50 Ruling of 16 July 2007 ("Trihotel" case).

51 Confirmed by the Supreme Court, 28 April 2008 ("Gamma" case); 9 February 2009 ("Sanitary" case); 21 February 2013 ("Spritzgussmaschinen" case). According to the judges, liability for intervention destroying the economic basis of the company is an exclusively "internal" liability in relation to the company, i. e. not an "external" liability in relation to its creditors. See Stöber, in *Company laws*, 327.

14 Societas Europea and other forms

Summary:
1. The regulation on the "European Company" ("Societas Europea", "SE")
2. The establishment of the SE
3. The corporate governance of the SE
4. Accounts and dissolution of the SE
5. The (aborted) projects on the "Societas Privata Europea" ("SPE") and the Societas Unius Personae ("SUP")
6. Branches of foreign companies

1. The regulation on the "European Company" ("Societas Europea", "SE")

The "European Company" – designated by its Latin name "Societas Europea", or "SE" – is a type of company governed by identical rules in each of the Member States as laid down in Regulation 2157/2001/EC and only on a secondary basis by the laws of the State where it has its seat[1]. The project actually dates back to the early 1970s and took several years to come to fruition[2].

---

[1] The literature in English language on the SE is very broad: see for instance Teichmann, *The European Company – A challenge to academics, legislatures and practitioners*, in *GLJ*, 2003, 309; Ebert, *The European Company on the level playing field of the community*, in *EBLR*, 2003, 182; Edwards, *The European Company. Essential tool or eviscerated dream?*, in *CMLR*, 2003, 445; Edbury, *The European Company statute: a practical working model for the future of European Company law making?*, in *EBLR*, 2004, 1283; Lenoir, *The Societas Europaea (SE) in Europe. A promising start and an option with good prospects*, 2008, at *utrechtlawreview.org*; Gold/Nikolopoulos/ Kluge, *The European Company statute – A new approach to corporate governance*, Lang, 2009; Eidenmüller/Engert/Hornuf, *Incorporating under European Law: the Societas Europaea as a vehicle for legal arbitrage*, in *EBOR*, 2009, 1; Ead., *How does the market react to the Societas Europaea?*, in *EBOR*, 2010, 35; Fleischer, *Supranational corporate forms in the European Union: prolegomena to a theory on supranational forms of association*, in *CMLR*, 2010, 1675; Koster, *The Societas Europaea (SE) revisited*, 2017, at *ssrn.com*; Meiselles/Graute, *The Societas Europaea (SE) – Time to start over? Capturing the Zeitgeist of the 21st century*, in *EBLR*, 2017, 667; Ghetti, *Unification, harmonisation and competition in European company forms*, in *EBLR*, 2018, 814.
[2] For a description of the legislative process see in particular Storm, *Statute of a Societas Europea*, in *CMLR*, 1968, 265; Sanders, *The European Company on its way*, in *CMLR*, 1971, 29; Wehlau, *The Societas Europea: a critique of the commission's 1991 amended proposal*, in *CMLR*, 1992, 473.

https://doi.org/10.1515/9783110725025-016

Under normal circumstances, if an entrepreneur of a Member State sets up a company governed by the national law of that State and afterwards decides to relocate to another Member State, the laws applicable to the company will change completely (for instance, a French "société anonime" moving its seat to Germany will become an "Aktiengesellschaft", subject to the German public companies act).

This implies that any entrepreneur willing to relocate has to be confident and understand how the laws in that other Member State actually work. This gives raise – as explicitly stated in Recital no. 3 of Regulation 2157/2001/EC – to "legal and psychological difficulties", which may prevent companies from executing cross border transactions[3].

On the other hand, the establishment of an SE may allow the company to move its legal seat to any other Member State since it is governed by the same rules, overcoming these legal and psychological obstacles.

Of course if an SE aims to relocate from one State to another, it must ask first shareholders for permission and take some procedural steps (as provided for by the Regulation); in any case, once the shareholders have voted at the general meeting on the transfer and the procedure has been followed, the company will not change the applicable law, which will remain the "supranational" one set forth by the Regulation. The law of the "new" State will only apply to the issues that have not been addressed by the Regulation.

The motives for setting up an SE are thus primarily operational.

As has been noted, however, it is also possible to identify "political" motives that often induce companies to adopt the form of the SE, like the need to emphasize the "European" character of the company (for instance, the CEO of Allianz AktG – when presenting the transformation of the insurance giant into an SE in March 2006 in Münich – announced that the company was European "at heart") or to overcome differences between national cultures which may be a source of tension among shareholders of different Member States (that was why the Airbus Group, former EDS, chose to adopt the SE form in 2015)[4].

---

3 Recital no. 3 of the Regulation explains that "operations involving companies from different Member States give rise to legal and psychological difficulties and tax problems. The approximation of Member States' company law by means of directives based on Art. 44 of the Treaty can overcome some of those difficulties. Such approximation does not, however, release companies governed by different legal systems from the obligation to choose a form of company governed by a particular national law".

4 See Lenoir, *The Societas*, 15. Airbus is registered in the Netherlands and its main shareholders are the German, French and Spanish States. See also Fleischer, *Supranational*, 1689: "one psychological effect of corporate forms, particularly for manufacturing or sales companies operat-

There have been around 3.300 SEs established as of Autumn 2020.

The States that make most use of this corporate form are Germany and the Czech Republic (followed by Slovakia). As for Germany, it is conceivable that the reason for its success could mainly be related to the greater elasticity of the model, which can also be structured according to the monistic system, especially if compared to the regime of the "Aktiengesellschaft" (the public company) which continues to employ the dualistic system only.

In Eastern European countries, the motivation behind the choice may be linked more to the advantages guaranteed by the "European" label and the fact that western European operators may find it easier to identify the operating methods of an SE compared to the uncertainties that could envelop the corporate structures available in countries that have more recently entered the EU.

However, SEs have been adopted in many other States: the Netherlands, France, the Nordic countries, etc. (for further numbers and examples see also Chapter 1, § 1).

The SE legislation represented a milestone in both the field of EU company law and in the European regulations on employee involvement, above all as a consequence of the related Directive on the participation of workers in companies: Directive 2001/86/EC.

2. The establishment of the SE

The Regulation sets forth the provisions on the establishment of the SE, the governance, the accounts and the winding up.

The SE has a minimum capital of € 120.000 and its registered office must correspond to its real seat.

Pursuant to Art. 9 of the Regulation, the SE is "governed (a) by this Regulation, (b) where expressly authorized by this Regulation, by the provisions of its statutes, (c) in the case of matters not regulated by this Regulation or, where matters are partly regulated by it, of those aspects not covered by it, by (i) the provisions of laws adopted by Member States in implementation of Community measures relating specifically to SEs; (ii) the provisions of Member States' laws which would apply to a public limited-liability company formed in accordance with the law of the Member State in which the SE has its registered office; (iii) the provisions of its statutes, in the same way as for a public limited-liability

---

ing abroad, is that a single European brand helps dispel the mistrust of local authorities or business partners".

company formed in accordance with the law of the Member State in which the SE has its registered office" (that is to say: first Regulation, second SE's statutes, third provisions of the state of incorporation relating to SE, fourth provisions of the state of incorporation relating to public companies; fifth provisions of the state of incorporation relating to statutes of public companies). The domestic provisions of the Member States shall thus only be applied on a subsidiary basis.

Although the SE is governed by the law of the Member State in which it has its registered office, SEs can be registered in the Member State of their choice: companies can therefore decide for themselves which laws apply, while locating their business management and central administration in another country.

The Regulation lays down the four ways in which an SE may be formed: by merger (between public companies), by the creation of a holding SE (by public or private companies), by the creation of a subsidiary SE (by any public or private company or another SE) and finally by conversion.

Formations by merger and conversion represent the usual methods of formation of an SE.

An example of the creation of an SE by merger was Allianz SE (to which we have already made reference above). The German insurance company first acquired all of the share capital and voting rights of its subsidiaries in the other Member States and then merged them into a sole SE, while transforming the previous subsidiaries into branches. Having a network of branches rather than subsidiaries was an economic and strategic choice (which allowed savings on structural costs) and helped simplify the overall control of the entities, related to both the need to comply with prudential requirements (imposed by the specific insurance and financial regulations) and the opportunity to respond to a sole national supervisory authority instead of many[5].

However, some factors limit the options to set up an SE. Firstly, it is not possible to create an SE directly by individuals; in the event of the formation of an SE by merger, at least two of the companies taking part in the operation must be based in at least one of the Member States; in the case of conversion into an SE, the company involved must have held a subsidiary for at least two years that was subject to the laws of another Member State (see Art. 2).

As far as capital and shares, while the 1989 draft Regulation contained detailed provision on capital, shares, bonds, etc., the 2001 Regulation decided to leave those matters to the laws of the State of incorporation.

---

5 See Lenoir, *The Societas*, 18.

3. The corporate governance of the SE

(I) The Regulation allows for both one-tier and two-tier structures.

Arts. 43 – 45 of the Regulation contain a description of the one-tier board system and Arts. 39 – 42 provide a description of the two-tier board system.

Art. 38 only allows for these two systems although both systems can be accommodated to suit corporate structures that do not fit this dichotomy.

Common rules that apply to both systems are stated in Arts. 46 – 51 of the Regulation. The dualistic structure is still chosen by the large majority of SEs.

(II) As regards the two-tier model, the law provides that the management board must be appointed by the supervisory board and that the supervisory board must be elected by the general meeting. The management board is responsible for the administration of the company. The supervisory board controls the conduct of the management board. Additionally, the supervisory board may delegate one of its members to act as director if there is no one on the management board, in which case the functions of this person as a member of the supervisory board are suspended (in this hyphotesis, the Member State may provide that the period in question is limited in time).

The provisions relating to the number of members of the governing body and how to determine it are left to the articles of association. However, the legislation of a Member State may set a minimum and/or a maximum number of components.

The management board is in charge of providing adequate information, including the duty to submit a report to the supervisory board on the progress and foreseeable developments of the SE's business at least once every three months and the duty to promptly inform the supervisory board in relation to events that may affect the SE; the supervisory board may also request any information necessary to exercise the control function from the directors. In this regard, based on Art. 41 of the Regulation, a Member State may provide that each member of the supervisory board is entitled to examine all information submitted to it and may carry out any investigations aimed at performing its duties.

(III) With regard to the one-tier system, the provisions of the Regulation provide for what was set out under the dualistic model, but adapt it to the different structure. Since the administration of the company is attributed to a management board, a Member State can require that the directors who are responsible for the day-to-day management must comply with the same conditions as a public company which has its registered office in the Member State. In this case, the number of directors and the rules for determining said number are also left to the articles of association of the SE, while the Member States have the right to set a minimum number and, where necessary, a maximum number of components.

(IV) Regardless of the system chosen, some provisions apply concerning the shareholders' general meeting, which is also subject to a general downsizing of its powers. In particular, the general meeting may only be called to decide on matters which are entrusted to its competence by the articles of association or the legislation of the Member State in which the SE has its legal seat.

A general meeting can be called by the management board or by any other competent body or authority in accordance with the law applicable to public companies of the Member State in which the SE has its registered office.

In addition, one or more shareholders, owning at least 10 % of the subscribed capital of the company, may request a meeting to be called and establish the agenda or request that certain items be added to the agenda.

Except as provided by the articles of association and the law governing public companies in the State in which the SE has its seat, decisions are made at the general meetings with a majority of votes. A two-thirds majority is required for amendments to the articles of association of the SE unless the law applicable to public companies of the State in which the SE's legal seat is located requires a higher majority.

If the articles of association of the SE provide for different classes of shares, each decision of the meeting will be subject to separate voting by the class whose shares are affected by the resolution.

4. Accounts and dissolution of the SE

As far as the annual and consolidated accounts of the SE are concerned, the company is governed by the rules applicable to public companies under the law of the Member State in which its registered office is situated (this concerns the preparation of the financial statements, including the accompanying directors report, the auditing and the publication).

Winding up, liquidation (and insolvency and cessation of payments and similar procedures) are also governed by the legal provisions that would apply to a public company formed in accordance with the law of the Member State in which the SE registered office is situated.

One final remark: even though the laws governing SEs are still incomplete with regard to corporate group law (since the Regulation does not include any provisions relating to groups), this choice still has regulatory effects. The SE may serve – and is often chosen in order to – to establish a holding company of a supranational group and this aspect is very important in business practice.

As far as the rules that apply when an SE is controlled by – or controls – another company, Recital 17 reads as follows: "reference should be made to the law governing public limited-liability companies in the Member State in which the SE has its registered office". In the case of an SE with its seat in Germany, i. e., the applicable law governing the group is thus German law.

5. The (aborted) projects on the "Societas Privata Europea" ("SPE") and the "Societas Unius Personae" ("SUP")

(I) In 2008 the EU decided to take action, starting from the consideration that small and medium-sized enterprises ("SMEs") represent 99% of the companies in the EU, whereas only 8% of them carry out cross-border business activities and only 5% have subsidiaries or joint companies abroad.

Despite efforts to make company formation quicker and easier throughout the EU, SMEs established in the form of private companies still have to face 27 different company law regimes.

Therefore, the EU Commission – with the aim of tackling this problem – considered four policy options in the area of private companies, as follows: (1) taking no action and relying on existing legislation and case law; (2) seeking to harmonize the company laws of the Member States; (3) improving the European SE statute and adapting it to the needs of SMEs; (4) proposing a brand new statute for SMEs.

The latter was the preferred solution. According to the Commission, it could have unravelled "the problems presented above by offering a company form featuring uniform rules on formation throughout the EU, flexibility as regards the internal organisation, thus saving costs. It would also offer SMEs a European label and thus make cross-border business easier"[6].

Therefore, the Council presented a proposal for a Regulation of the Statute for a "European Private Company" (the "Societas Privata Europea", or "SPE")[7].

---

6 See the "Explanatory memorandum" to the "proposal for a Council Regulation on the Statute for a European private company (presented by the Commission), on https://eur-lex.europa.eu/legal-content/EN/TXT/?uri=celex:52008PC0396.

7 See Braun, *The European private company: a supranational company form for small and medium-sized enterprises?*, in *GLJ*, 2004, 1393; Schunk, *On the European Private Company*, in *ECL*, 2006, 275; Hommelhof, *The European Private Company before its pending legislative birth*, in *ECL*, 2008, 799; Drury, *The European Private Company*, in *EBOR*, 2008, 125; Kornack, *The European Private Company – Entering the scene or lost in discussion?*, in *EBOR*, 2009, 1321; Raaijmakers, *The* Societas Privata Europea: *a basic reform of EU law on business organizations*, in Tison et al. (eds.), *Perspectives*, 18; Davies, *The European Private Company (SPE): uniformity, flexibility, competition and the persistence of national laws*, 2010, at *ssrn.com*; Guidotti, *The European Private Company: the current situation*, in *GLJ*, 2012, 313; Ghetti, *Unification*, 826.

(II) The main features of this new supranational company type were the following.

The SPE could have had a statute governed by EU and national laws, such as those recorded as being an SE.

The SPE could have been formed by one or several natural persons and/or legal entities, or also by transforming, merging or dividing existing companies.

The company would have been registered in the Member State of location of the statutory registered office. Subsidiaries would have been governed by the national law where they would have been established.

In any case, the SPE would not have been bound to establish its central administration or main establishment in the Member State of location of the registered office. Administrative formalities and registration costs would have been reduced to the greatest extent possible.

As far as the organization, the shareholders could have determined the articles of association of the SPE (according to the matters listed in Annex I of the Proposal). Matters not covered by the articles of association would have been subject to the national law of the Member State of location of the registered office.

The management body would have been responsible for the management of the SPE, exercising all prerogatives not held by the shareholders. The shareholders would have been responsible for the organization of the SPE. They could have adopted resolutions that were binding upon shareholders, the management body and the supervisory body of the SPE and on third parties.

Accounts management and the preparation, filing, auditing and publication of accounts would have been subject to national law.

As far as restructuring, dissolution and nullity were concerned, the Regulation also referred to national company laws.

The minimum capital of an SPE could have be set at 1 euro; it would have been divided into shares, but not offered to the public or traded on a regulated market.

The management body would have established a list of shareholders, which would have constituted proof of ownership of the shares. All shareholdings would be notified to the management body in order to have them registered on the list of shareholders.

The procedure to exclude a shareholder would have been subject to a resolution of the shareholders, leading then to a request by the SPE to the court having jurisdiction. Similarly, shareholders could have withdrawn from the SPE in order to protect their interests.

(III) The proposal for the SPE faced however severe challenges from the Member States[8]. The possibility of having a company with only a single euro as minimum capital proved to be controversial with many of the States that did not have such a system at the time.

There was also intense discussion on the rights of minority shareholders, which could not be agreed on. The separation between the real seat and the statutory seat proved very divisive too.

Furthermore, at a general level, some Member States did not support the idea of the further implementation of supranational law regimes, where company forms are created by EU law and constitute a distinct type from the ones already in force in the Member States.

As a matter of fact, since the SPE model would have been introduced by a regulation and not a directive and a unanimous vote in the Council was required, the opposition in place between Member States stopped the proposal and it was finally aborted in 2015.

(IV) However, the idea to help SMEs establish cross-border companies was forsaken and the Council decided – on the basis of the report drafted by the "Reflection Group on the future of EU company law" of 2010 and 2011 – to push forward with the model of the single shareholder private company, already harmonized by means of the Twelfth Directive[9].

The report proposed to implement "a new EU directive or an amended Twelfth company law Directive" and "require EU Member States to provide for a simplified company template, which would allow single-member companies, both individual entrepreneurs and holding companies, to save on transaction costs and unnecessary formalities". The directive would have governed the model of a new "Societas Unius Personae" or "SUP".

As has been noted, "there were several advantages to this alternative approach. First, there would be no need to harmonize rules on minority shareholder protection since the proposed form would be a single-member private limited company. The rules that would need harmonization would be limited to key elements, reducing the risk of having to find a compromise among Member States. Second, it would not be an EU company form, which should remove the opposition of some Member States to a [then] '29th company law regime'. As an

---

8 See on that especially Conac, *The Societas Unius Personae (SUP): A "passport" for job creation and growth*, in *ECFR*, 2015, 141 s.

9 See Kravets, *Discussion report: the proposal for a directive on the single-member private limited liability company*, *ECFR*, 2015, 125; Conac, *The Societas*, 139; Malberti, *The relationship between the* societas unius personae *proposal and the* acquis: *creeping toward an abrogation of EU company law?*, in *ECFR*, 2015, 238; Ghetti, *Unification*, 828.

added benefit, since it would be a directive, a qualified majority would be required in the Council instead of unanimity. Finally, the proposal should be easier to adopt since the Twelfth company law Directive of 1989 already provided some rules for single member private limited liability companies, and, therefore, Member States had already accepted the idea that the European legislator could intervene in this area since they already had accepted some degree of harmonization"[10].

The proposal for a directive on the SUP was thus presented in 2014.

The most innovative issues included the profit distribution regime, responsibility for which would have been delegated to the directors (who would have been responsible along with the sole shareholder who had approved the distribution), and which could have been carried out after drawing up a balance sheet and performing liquidity tests[11]. The proposal also would have allowed the private company to acquire its own shares (once again, after performing a balance-sheet test and, if permitted in the articles of association, a solvency test). In any case, shareholders would have decided on the acquisition.

However, that proposal was also subject to considerable resistance by national legislators. The SUP would not only have had (like the SPE) the symbolic amount of 1 euro as the minimum share capital, but it would not have been subject to rules protecting real capital either, with risks of abuse of its provisons by management (and, ultimately, the sole controlling shareholder) to the detriment of creditors.

The proposal for the directive on the SUP was finally withdrawn in 2018, following the criticisms received.

6. Branches of foreign companies

Pursuant to the principle of free establishment for persons and companies in all EU jurisdictions public and private companies can establish branches in other Member States.

---

10 See Conac, *The Societas*, 143 s.

11 The system was inspired by the UK and the Netherlands and was based on a balance sheet and a solvency test. The proposal also defined distributions very broadly to include, for example, dividends, "hidden distributions" and even capital reduction. The directive provided for the liability of the director and of the single-member for the amount of the distribution if they knew, or, in view of the circumstances, ought to have known, that either the balance sheet test and/or the solvency test failed.

In 1989 the Eleventh Directive on branches was enacted (Directive 89/666/ EEC). Later Directive 2012/17/EU and Directive 2017/1132/EU sought to increase legal certainty and improve the performance of the public administration by promoting cooperation between companies registers in Europe, setting out clearer procedures for the registration of branches.

The latter Directive, in particular, has increased the number of documents that must be disclosed and extended the details that have to be revealed (see in particular Art. 37).

The Member States have implemented the Directives differently. Some have entered the Regulation of foreign branches into their companies acts; others in separate bodies of laws. The domestic laws govern various aspects of branches, including the duty to register, the documents and items subject to disclosure, branch managers and their duties, branch names, registration and de-registration on the companies register, etc.

The aim of the Directives is to reduce "the differences in the laws of the Member States [that] may interfere with the exercise of the right of establishment [and] eliminate such differences in order to safeguard, *inter alia*, the exercise of that right" (see the Recitals of the Eleventh Directive).

The EMCA also devotes a chapter to branches (Ch. 16), with the explicit intention to minimize costs and hurdles in the areas covered by the Directives, and more generally. The provisions of the Directives and EMCA are rather detailed and reference only may be made to them here.

However, it has to be underlined that the branch office is not a separate legal entity from the "home-company" (we use this name instead of "parent company" which is often employed in practice, but should actually only be used to describe the relationship between holding and subsidiary companies in groups).

The home-company is directly responsible for all the liabilities of the branch. Therefore, the branch must file the (translated) financial statements of its home-company with the domestic companies register.

The figure of the "branch manager" is relevant, and must be appointed by the home-company (see Sect. 16.05 EMCA: "1. The company must list a branch manager. The branch manager should have the power to represent the company to some extent and as a minimum should be able to represent the company in legal proceedings. 2. The branch manager must fulfil the same requirements as persons who are appointed as directors of domestic companies"). The branch manager also has to be appointed to represent the home-company it in its dealings with the tax authorities.

The branch manager's status is not equivalent to the status of a company director since the responsibility for management of the branch lies in any case with the directors of the home-company. The responsibility of the branch manager will depend on the facts, and essentially on the powers that have been delegated to him and his degree of independence. The more his role resembles that of a mere employee implementing the home-company's instructions, the lower his liability will be except in the event of gross negligence or recklessness in the performance of his employment contract. On the other hand, a branch director who has extensive powers will be exposed to greater potential liability.

Table of cases

ABN AMRO, (NL) Amsterdam Court of Appeal, Enterprise Chamber, 3 May 2007, 91, 99
Akzo Nobel, (NL) Amsterdam Court of Appeal, Enterprise Chamber, 10 August 2017, 91
Audiolux, CJEU, C-101/08, 287
Autokran, (GE) Supreme Court, 16 September 1985, 309
Axel Springer, CJEU, C-435/02, 199
Axel Springer, CJEU, C-103/03, 199

Banca Sella, (IT) Supreme Court, 22 May 2019, 163
BPAV, (IT) Supreme Court, 20 April 2020, 121
Barings, (UK) Court of Appeal, [2000] 1 BCLC 523, 95
British Airport Authority, CJEU, C-98/01, 123
Bruil, (NL) Supreme Court, 29 June 2007, 179

Cadbury-Schweppes, CJEU, C-196/04, 26
Cancun, (NL) Supreme Court, 4 April 2014, 179
Capinordik Bank, (DE) Supreme Court, 15 January 2019, 216
Cartesio, CJEU, C-201/06, 24
Centros, CJEU, C-208/00, 22
Commission vs. France, CJEU, C-89/09, 32
Commission vs. Italy, CJEU, C-174/04, 125
Commission vs. Italy, CJEU, C-326/07, 125
Commission vs. Italy, CJEU, C-531/06, 32

Daily Mail, CJEU, C-81/87, 22
DB vs. A. s.p.a. & IL s.r.l., (IT) sole arbitrator, 10 January 2008, 244
Design Factory, (IT) Court of Milan, 31 March 2008, 131
De Seizoenen, (NL) Amsterdam Court of Appeal, Enterprise Chamber, 30 April 2018, 179
Defrenna, CJEU, C-43/75, 34
Dowling, CJEU, C-41/15, 66
DSM, (NL) Supreme Court, 14 December 2007, 117

E. AG, (GE) Supreme Court, 15 November 2011, 147
Edison, (IT) Court of Milan, 9 October 2002, 121
E.ON Czech Holding, CJEU, C-566/16, 166
Erzberger, CJEU, C-566/15, 78

Gamma, (GE) Supreme Court, 28 April 2008, 309
Gelatine, (GE) Supreme Court, 26 April 2004, 90
Group PCM, (NL) Amsterdam Court of Appeal, Enterprise Chamber, 27 May 2010, 258
Grimaldi, CJEU, C-322/88, 12
Gucci Group, (NL) Amsterdam Enterprise Chamber, 27 April 1999, 99
Gucci Group, (NL) Supreme Court, 27 September 2000, 99

https://doi.org/10.1515/9783110725025-017

Holzmüller, (GE) Supreme Court, 25 February 1982, 90
HVB vs. Unicredit, (GE) Supreme Court, 26 June 2012, 176

IGI, CJEU, C-394/18, 11
Impacto Azul, CJEU, C-186/12, 193
Inspire Art, CJEU, C-167/01, 23

Kali und Salz, (GE) Supreme Court, 10 March 1978, 137
Karella/Karellas, CJEU, C-19 and C-20/90, 136
Kornhaas, CJEU, C-594/14, 232
Kotnik, CJEU, C-526/14, 66
KPN NV/TPG NV, CJEU, C-202/04, 125

Luxembourg v. PPL-Co, (LU) Administrative Court, 26 July 2017, 142

Marleasing, CJEU, C-106/89, 12
Melon, CJEU, C-381/92, 136
MPS, (GE) Supreme Court, 1 December 2008, 177

Ope Intermarché, (FR) Supreme Court, 7 January 2004, 104

Pafitis, CJEU, C-441/93, 136
Pencil, (IT) Court of Turin, 19 April 2017, 213
Polbud, CJEU, C-106/16, 24
Portugal Telecom, CJEU, C-367/98, 125
Portugal Telecom, CJEU, C-171/08, 126

Ravenna Beach, (IT) Supreme Court, 23 March 2017, 148
Rozenblum, (FR) Supreme Court, criminal chamber, 4 February 1985, 171, 181

Sanitary, (GE) Supreme Court, 9 February 2009, 309
Sevic, CJEU, C-411/03, 24
Shell, (NL) Amsterdam Commercial Chamber, 20 December 2007, 261
Société Harpax, (FR) Supreme Court, 29 October 2003, 117
Société Nationale Elf-Aquitaine, CJEU, C-483/99, 123
Société Nationale De Trasport Par Canalisations, CJEU, C-503/99, 125
Spritzgunsmaschinen, (GE) Supreme Court, 21 February 2013, 309

Tipou/Tipou, CJEU, C-81/09, 32
Trihotel, (GE) Supreme Court, 16 July 2007, 309
Thyssen Krupp, (GE) Supreme Court, 8 June 2009, 133

U. GmbH, (GE) Supreme Court, 21 February 2013, 147
Überseering, CJEU, C-212/97, 23

Vale, CJEU, C-378/10, 24
Versatel, (NL) Supreme Court, 14 September 2007, 261

Viking, CJEU, C-438/05, 34, 289
Vivendi, CJEU, C-719/18, 31, 32, 33,
Volkswagen, CJEU, C-112/05, 31, 124
Volkswagen, CJEU, C-95/12, 31, 127
Von Colson, CJEU, C-14/83, 12

Index

Audit (of financial statements)   205
Audit committee
– duties   215
– liabilities   227
– powers   77, 92
  – in listed companies   288
Auditors
– duties   225
– liabilities   230
– powers   77, 96

Benefit companies   39
Board of directors (management board)
– appointment   81
– duties   213
– liabilities   227
– powers   84
– resolutions   98
Bonds
– convertible   136
– exchangeable   142
– ordinary   141
– others   142
– protection of bondholders   142
Business judgment rule   214

Cancellation of the company   275
Capital increase   133
– bonus shares   136
– right of pre-emption   134
– share premium   134
Capital reduction
– capital in excess   66
– losses   62
Carve-outs   252
Challenge of resolutions
– board of directors   99
– other bodies   99
– shareholders' meeting   150
Change of control (clause of)   129
Class of shares
– protection of shareholders   117
– representative   117

– types of special shares   111
Companies register   43
Consent (clause of)   127
Conversions   263
Corporate governance
– models of (monistic, dualistic and
    traditional)   71
  – in private companies   297
Corporate opportunities   219
Council of the EU   5
Court of Justice of the EU   6
Cross-border transactions   266
Cross-shareholdings   60

Decisions   7
Directives   6
– horizontal effect   31
– vertical effect   31
Directives (main in company law)   13
Directors
– competition with the company   219
– duty in the vicinity of insolvency   221
– duty of care   213
– duty of loyalty   215
– duty towards creditors   220
– executive / non executive / independent
    77
– in private companies   306
– removal   82
– remuneration   83
Disclosure in the company register   43
Dissolution of the company   271
Distributions   53
Divisions
– asymmetric   250
– non-proportional   250
– proceedings   248
Drag along (clause of)   129
Dualistic system (two-tier)   80

European Commission   6
European Council   5

https://doi.org/10.1515/9783110725025-018

European Model Company Act (definition)
30
European Parliament   6
Exclusion (of shareholders) in private companies   306

Financial assistance   57
– in private companies   296
Financial statements
– approval and publication   207
– audit   205
– consolidated   205
– layouts   198
– principles of financial reporting   203
 – in listed companies (IAS/IFRS)   208
– profits (and dividends)   210
Financing in private companies   302
First refusal (clause of)   128
Formation of the company   42
Freeze-outs   260

Golden shares   31, 120
Groups
– „contractual"   172
– cross-border   191
– cross-shareholdings   188
– „de facto"
 – disclosure   182
 – right of minorities of the parent   187
 – right of minorities of the subsidiary   184
 – unitary direction and liability   173, 175
– definition   169
– history of legislation   165
– intercompany loans   188
– interest of the group (debate)   165

Harmonization
– history of   13
– of private companies' provisions   291
– soft   27
– vs. competition (debate)   17
– weak   28
Hybrid instruments
– dividend-linked participating loans   140
– participative financial instruments   139
– principal-linked participating loans   140
– profit-sharing debt instruments   139

Information of directors (right and duty to)
70, 215
Information of shareholders (right to)   155
– in groups   182, 187
Instrument of incorporation (definition)   42
Interest (of the company)   38, 217
Internal control system   78, 220

Leveraged buyouts (LBOs)   253
Liability of directors and supervisors
– derivative action   228
– in company and insolvency law   230
– proceedings   227
 – in private companies   306
Liability of shareholders   232
– in private companies   306
Liquidation of the company   274
Liquidators (powers and duties)   274
Listed company
– concept   2
– enhanced rights of shareholders   27
– regulation   277
Litigation (shareholders' suits) and jurisdiction   163
Loans
– intercompany   188
– postergation   47, 143
– shareholders'   143
Loyalty shares   111

Mergers
– cash adjustment   237
– cash payment   241
– compensation for damages   243
– invalidity   242
– merger LBOs   257
– proceedings   237
– protection of creditors   245
– protection of special share- and hybrid instrument holders   247
– special (simplified) mergers   239
Monistic system (one-tier)   76
Multiple voting shares   112

Non-proportional shares
– in private companies   300
– in public companies   120

Nullity (and voidability) of
– board of directors' resolutions   99
– shareholders' resolutions   151
Nullity of the company   44

Options   138

Private company (concept)   1
Profit   39
Proportionality principle   10
Public company (concept)   1

Recapitalization (compulsory in case of los-
   ses)   62
– in private companies   295
Recommendation   7
Redeemable shares   114
Reduction of capital in excess   66
Regulations   6
Representation (power of)   84
Rules
– mandatory and default (debate)   39

Sales of company's assets   258
Sell out (right to)
– in contractual groups (parent's shareholders)   173
– in listed companies   287
– in public companies   161
Shares
– basic and secondary rights of   109
– bearer   105
– classes of   111
– definition   105
– dematerialized   106
– „golden"   31, 120
– in private companies   300
– name   105
– no-par   106
– paper   106
Share capital
– assessment of contributions in kind   51
– definition   47
– in private companies   293
Share buy-backs   56
– in private companies   294
Shares purchases   260

Shareholders' agreements   100
Shareholders' contributions to reserves   143
Shareholders' loans   143
Shareholders' meeting   59, 76, 84, 149
– full quorum meeting   150
– proceedings   150
– special shareholders' meeting   117
Shareholders' primacy vs. stakeholderism
   (debate)   38
Shareholderism vs. managerialism (debate)
   84
Slate voting   82
Single member company   46
Squeeze-outs
– in listed companies   287
– in public companies   260
Societas Europea (SE)   35
– accounts   314
– corporate governance   313
– dissolution   314
– formation   311
Societas Privata Europea (SPE)   35, 315
Societas Unius Personae (SUP)   36, 317
Special examiners   96
Special investigations (in groups)   185
Special shares   see classes of shares
Spin-offs   251
Statutes (definition)   42
Statutory auditors
– duties   223
– liabilities   227
– powers   93
– resolutions   98
Subsidiarity principle   9
Supermajority clauses   126, 151
– in private companies   306
Supervisory board
– duties   223
– liabilities   227
– powers   95
– resolutions   99

Tag along (clause of)   129
Takeovers
– breakthrough rule   286
– mandatory bid rule   284
– passivity rule   286

– regulation   281
– sell-out   287
– squeeze out   287
Traditional (latin) system   78
Tracking stocks   114
Treaty
– on the establishment of the EC (Rome Treaty)   5
– on the EU (Maasticht Treaty)   5
– on the functioning of the EU (Lisbon Treaty)   5

Vote (shareholders' right to)
– in groups (parent's shareholders)   189
– on business decisions   84

Warrants   137
Winding up (of the company)   271
Winding up (shareholders' right to)   162
Withdrawal (shareholders' right to)
– in de facto groups (parent's sharehol-
      ders)   187
   – in de facto groups (subsidiary's sharehol-
      ders)   184
   – in private companies   306
   – in public companies   158
   – of special shares   119